☑ S0-CDB-750

3 0050 01241 6441

CAL STATE HAYWARD LIBRARY

LAST DATE STAMPED BEL

CT 25 .W75 1990

Wu, Pei-yi, 1927-

The Confucian's progress

CALIFORNIA STATE UNIVERSITY, HAYWARD
LIBRARY

THE CONFUCIAN'S PROGRESS

THE
CONFUCIAN'S
PROGRESS

AUTOBIOGRAPHICAL
WRITINGS
IN TRADITIONAL
CHINA

PEI-YI WU

PRINCETON UNIVERSITY
PRESS

CT
25
.W75
1990

Copyright © 1990 by Princeton University Press
Published by Princeton University Press, 41 William Street,
Princeton, New Jersey 08540
In the United Kingdom: Princeton University Press, Oxford

All Rights Reserved

Library of Congress Cataloging-in-Publication Data

Wu, Pei-yi, 1927–
The Confucian's progress : autobiographical writings
in traditional China / Pei-yi Wu.
p.   cm.
Bibliography: p.
Includes index.
ISBN 0-691-06788-0 (alk. paper)
1. Autobiography. 2. China—Biography. I. Title.
CT25.W75 1989
920'.051—dc20   89-32284

This book has been composed in Linotron Bembo

Clothbound editions of Princeton University Press books
are printed on acid-free paper, and binding materials are
chosen for strength and durability. Paperbacks,
although satisfactory for personal collections,
are not usually suitable for library rebinding

Printed in the United States of America by
Princeton University Press
Princeton, New Jersey

CALIFORNIA STATE UNIVERSITY, HAYWARD
LIBRARY

For Mary Jo

CONTENTS

IT IS perhaps not inappropriate to begin with an autobiographical note. In 1969 I chanced upon two seventeenth-century Chinese autobiographies—they appeared unmistakably so even to my untrained eyes—which I found immensely interesting. I decided to look for more. There was—and still is—very little sinological interest in the topic, although a rudimentary Chinese anthology was first published in 1936. My search became almost endless, with every trip to various libraries in this country and Asia resulting in tantalizing, and only occasionally rewarding, leads. It took me longer than I had expected to assemble a collection of useful material, but even more difficult than the search was the effort to make sense of the unwieldy mass of diverse and obscure writings.

One of the difficulties concerned the lack of a Chinese critical tradition with regard to autobiography. The problem can be illustrated by a comparison. Students of Chinese poetry have at their disposal not only elaborately annotated collected works and anthologies of all types and lengths, but also a long and rich native tradition of criticism, which is both highly technical and sensitive to broader issues such as the interplay between poetry and painting or the impact of Ch'an Buddhism. Students of Chinese autobiography, however, are not blessed with anything even remotely comparable. They have nothing to draw upon when grappling with problems of definition, selection, or evaluation. Their temptation, then, is to lean heavily on current theories of autobiography that, claims to universality notwithstanding, have been formulated without having taken into consideration anything Chinese.

Autobiography itself may not be, but autobiography as an academic discipline decidedly is, a unique product of the modern West. Perhaps reflecting the modern origins of the discipline and its explosive growth during the last two decades, recent writers on autobiography tend to concentrate on post-Renaissance developments, except for an occasional bow to Saint Augustine or Cellini.[1] This emphasis may pose a problem to students of Chinese autobiography who seek guidance in recent scholarship: what is often described as the dawning of modern self-consciousness, the beginnings of modern autobiography, coincided more or less with the sunset of what I shall call the golden age of Chinese autobiography. The problem is, then, how one should apply the findings of the discipline,

---

[1] Even Randolph D. Pope Costa, whose avowed purpose in his Ph.D. dissertation, "La autobiografia española hasta Torres Villarroel" (Columbia University, 1973) was to redress the neglect that Spanish autobiography had suffered, did not find anything at all written before 1500.

which mainly concern Western autobiographies written after 1700, to a collection of Chinese works written before that date.

I do not pretend to have solved the problem. While I cannot deny that I have accepted some of the assumptions and absorbed some of the biases of the modern discipline, I have not been able to construct an explanatory apparatus from the dazzling array of poststructuralist theories, a monolithic system that can account for what I take to be the essential facts of Chinese autobiography. My approach, then, is eclectic. I am guided, at least initially, by what I take to be the unique set of circumstances in which Chinese autobiography came into being. Most would-be autobiographers deliberately and avowedly cast their life stories in the form of one or another subgenre of biography. One reason for this was the power of precedents and examples in a uniform and durable literary culture such as the Chinese, the continuity of which remained unbroken for more than two millennia, changes of dynasties and foreign invasions notwithstanding. Authors with an autobiographical urge could unabashedly follow a precedent for their act and choose an example for their narrative.[2] As if anticipating the modern unease about the fundamental instabilities of autobiography, they found security in a well-established, respectable, and easily recognizable genre. Their practice suggests to me a convenient way to identify Chinese autobiographies and thus develop a procedure for constructing a taxonomy and attempting a general survey.

By accepting any biography written by the subject himself as autobiography the reader can bypass the problem of definition. A solution for that problem does not seem possible when the field itself has been so torn by fierce polemics; not only could no two critics agree on one definition but the very existence of the genre itself has been doubted.[3]

Circumvention of the first problem, however, leads to the next. Should autobiography be different from biography? Such a question was never asked in China before this century. When a few self-written biographies found their way into anthologies of literature, they were invariably and indiscriminately housed together with, shall we say, bona fide biographies, demonstrating that no distinction was made between the two forms. This of course goes against the grain of the modern discipline, which stresses subjectivity. If we agree with contemporary critics that the

---

[2] This is the main reason why I occasionally depart from chronology in tracing a theme or developing a topic.

[3] See, for instance, Paul de Man, "Autobiography as De-facement," *MLN* 94 (December 1979): 919–30. "Attempts at generic definition [of autobiography] seem to founder in questions that are both pointless and unanswerable" (p. 919); autobiography "is not a genre or a mode, but a figure of reading or of understanding that occurs, to some degree, in all texts" (p. 921). There are even more negative pronouncements scattered in James Olney, ed., *Autobiography: Essays Theoretical and Critical*, (Princeton: Princeton University Press, 1980).

twain should be different, we cannot fail to notice the heavy price the author of a self-written biography in China often had to pay in return for a sense of security and a ready-made format. He surrendered his privileged position and adopted instead the convention of the impartial, invisible, and unobtrusive narrator. He recorded external events, usually public and official, but seldom tried to probe inner stirrings or disclose complex motives. Each subgenre of biography imposed its own constraints, and other factors, such as the austere economy of classical Chinese prose, reinforced the bondage of early Chinese autobiography. This is why the first section of this book is entitled "The Self Constrained."

Had Chinese autobiography remained a captive, a subsidiary of biography, its long neglect by scholars would have been justified. But by the end of the thirteenth century the hold of biography began to loosen. Among the forces that contributed to this change was a new spiritual fervor to which Confucians, hitherto sober and mannerly, became susceptible. The autobiographers we encounter in Part II each has a compelling story to tell. Their narratives—the long and arduous search for fundamental changes in their individual lives—were so new and their eagerness to recite them so intense that they no longer could or would abide by any of the models provided by biography. Nor need we concern ourselves here with the problem of definition when self-transformation is unmistakably the dominant—and sometimes the only—theme of their narratives. When their individual lives were figuratively, and in many cases literally, journeys, they naturally turned to travel literature for cues in selecting a suitable style or format for their life stories. Although this section begins and ends with a chapter on Buddhist autobiography, the middle, and also the longest, chapter, "The Confucian's Progress," is the heart of our story. Hence the title of this book.

In recent years critics have become less interested in ascertaining the referential truth of individual autobiographies. There is a "widespread critical shift from canons of historical statement to those of self-imagining, rhetorical persuasion, and narrative technique."[4] Autobiography is now seen as a problematic hybrid, forever unstable. On the one side is history: verisimilitude, chronology, truthfulness; on the other, imaginative literature: fiction, myth. The Chinese writers we meet in the first two sections all lean very much to one side: they seldom stray from plausibility even when they report their spiritual ecstasies. The seventeenth century, however, saw a few autobiographers who, benefiting from the dissolution of the old order and responding to the contemporary fascination with the fantastic and the occult, borrowed from fiction both devices and

[4] Avrom Fleishman, *Figures of Autobiography: The Language of Self-Writing* (Berkeley and Los Angeles: University of California Press, 1983), p. 9.

episodes. The fanciful style of self-celebration was also shared by a few painters, who repeatedly depicted themselves in imaginative guises. Two autobiographers and one self-portraitist are examined in detail in Part III, "The Self Invented."

Nearly all the autobiographies discussed in the two preceding sections were written between 1565 and 1680, a period that I shall call the golden age of Chinese autobiography, and one that was also pivotal in Chinese history. Even more interesting is the fact that China and the West, in spite of their fundamental differences, were more alike during this period than ever before or after. European autobiography had its first efflorescence since Saint Augustine during roughly the same time, with Cellini at one end and Bunyan at the other. Similarities between China and the West also extend to the emergence of a new emphasis on sin and redemption, a moral scrupulousness manifested in personal testimonies. Puritans had their counterparts in certain Neo-Confucians, who examined their consciences and confessed their misdeeds with a depth of anguish and remorse unthinkable in classical Confucianism. I have assembled a diverse set of texts documenting their moods and activities. These are described and analyzed in Part IV, "The Self Examined."

At the end of the present study is a short explanation as to why I do not go beyond the year 1680, even though Chinese autobiographical activities went on unabated in the next two centuries and reached, as in the rest of the world, torrential proportions in the present age.

The first full-length study of a topic in foreign literature perhaps should be preceded, or at least accompanied, by an anthology in English. This is especially true with Chinese autobiography since so little has previously been translated. The problem is further complicated by the fact that a large number of the Chinese texts discussed in this book are not easily accessible. To ameliorate the situation, I have translated the entire texts of several shorter autobiographies as well as long excerpts from other works and have juxtaposed them with the discursive portions of this study.[5] In addition, translations of two longer autobiographies and an autobiographical letter are included in the appendixes.

[5] Whenever possible, I base my translations on the texts included in the two standard and accessible Chinese anthologies: Kuo Teng-feng, ed., *Li-tai tzu-hsü-chuan wen-ch'ao* (Anthology of autobiographies) 2 vols. (Taipei: Shang-wu yin-shu-kuan, 1965), hereafter abbreviated as *LTW*; Tu Lien-che, ed., *Ming-jen tzu-chuan wen-ch'ao* (Anthology of Ming autobiographies) (Taipei: I-wen yin-shu-kuan, 1977), hereafter abbreviated as *MTW*.

ACKNOWLEDGMENTS

DURING an early stage of the research for this book I was helped by a fellowship from the National Endowment for the Humanities. A travel grant from the CUNY-PSC Research Award Program enabled me to use the libraries in Taiwan and Japan.

Early versions of several chapters were read before the University Seminar on Traditional China, Columbia University, 1970 and 1976; the Conference on Seventeenth-Century Chinese Thought, Bellagio, 1970; the Regional Seminar in Neo-Confucian Studies, 1977; the International Society for the Comparative Study of Civilizations, Haverhill, Mass., 1977; and the Summer Workshop on Ming History, Princeton University, 1980. Participants at these gatherings as well as other colleagues, who are too numerous to be listed here, are gratefully remembered for their comments and questions.

In addition, I wish to acknowledge my indebtedness to those individuals who read parts of the manuscript at various stages and offered valuable suggestions: Wm. Theodore de Bary, Maude S. Davis, C. T. Hsia, David Johnson, Jean Johnson, Vytaus Kavolis, Edmund Leites, Joel Lidov, Conrad Schirokauer, and Mary White. Irene Bloom, Michael Kowal, and Nathan Sivin, exceeding the obligations of friendship, read the penultimate draft in its entirety and contributed immensely to the final form of this study. None of my benefactors can be blamed for the remaining deficiencies. Finally I wish to express my appreciation to Robert E. Brown of Princeton University Press and his colleagues Margaret Case, Jenna Dolan, Harriet Hitch, Deborah Del Gais Muller, Beth Gianfagna, and others for their patient and cordial assistance.

Some earlier drafts have appeared in a journal and a book: chapter 6 appeared in *The Unfolding of Neo-Confucianism*, edited by Wm. Theodore de Bary, copyright ©. 1975, Columbia University Press. Used by permission. Chapters 11 and 12 in the *Harvard Journal of Asiatic Studies* 39, no. 1 (June 1979): 5–38; permissions to reprint these two articles are much appreciated.

ABBREVIATIONS

CKTC	*Ch'an-kuan ts'e-chin* 禪關策進
DMB	*Dictionary of Ming Biography*
HTC	*Hsü tsang-ching* 續藏經
LTW	*Li-tai tzu-hsü-chuan wen-ch'ao* 歷代自叙傳文鈔
MJHA	*Ming-ju hsüeh-an* 明儒學案
MTW	*Ming-jen tzu-chuan wen-ch'ao* 明人自傳文鈔
SKCSCP	Ssu-k'u ch'üan-shu chen-pen 四庫全書珍本
SPPY	Ssu-pu pei-yao 四部備要
SPTK	Ssu-pu ts'ung-k'an 四部叢刊
T	*Taishō Shinshū Dai-zōkyō* 大正新脩大藏經
TSCC	Ts'ung-shu chi-ch'eng 叢書集成
WHCMIW	*Wu-hsia chung-mu i-wen* 吳下冢墓遺文

PART I
THE SELF CONSTRAINED

ONE

THE ECOLOGY OF CHINESE
AUTOBIOGRAPHY

THE SINGLE most important fact about Chinese autobiography is its close and long association with Chinese biography. This may not be surprising at first glance, for there are obvious affinities between the two genres. In China, as well as in the West, biography antedates autobiography—in fact, the word for the latter, in both Chinese and English, is derived etymologically from that for the former. Both biography and autobiography in general purport to be factual accounts of human lives; as such, they share certain common traits: a single and ostensibly serious narrator and a more or less orderly chronology. Chinese autobiography, however, imitated Chinese biography almost slavishly. Nearly every subgenre of the former can be traced back to a counterpart in the latter; the derivative and its model are often indistinguishable in tone, style, and narrative stance. Chinese autobiographers, for their part, take this as a matter of course. The imitation is often openly and specifically acknowledged; they, and sometimes their editors, tend to include within the titles of their works the name of the relevant biographical subgenre prefixed with the wording *tzu* (auto) or *tzu-hsü* (self-written).

Chinese autobiographers' choice of labels for their works may give us one hint of why Chinese autobiography, at least during its early stage, relied so much on its older sister. There were good reasons for such dependence. Today, when almost every infamous convict and every famous entertainer is ready to tell, and the public eager to hear, his or her life story, the problems that confronted every premodern would-be autobiographer, East or West, are difficult to imagine. Two such problems, I believe, hindered the development of self-literature in the ancient world. One was the lack of a suitable literary form; the other the inhibition, probably universally strong until some four centuries ago, against self-disclosure and self-presentation without a religious context. Chinese biography offered Chinese autobiographers the means to overcome these problems. It offered a ready-made format for telling a life; and by using it, the autobiographer could always protest that he was following a time-honored and respectable precedent: his association with a legitimate enterprise, which he avowed in assigning the title to his piece, might afford him some protection from the censure of egomania, of doing something unconventional.

Chinese autobiography's subservience to biography may have been unavoidable, anyway, in view of the preeminence of the latter in China.
Biography had always been the most voluminous of all forms of prose
writing; its close association with historiography had given it an author-
itative aura, and the didactic uses to which it had been put had made it
widely popular. No wonder it was imitated in other literary forms,
among which were early Chinese ethnological treatises, described as "biographies" of tribes and nations, and fiction, which passed as biographies
of heros or heroines. In its early stages the dependence of Chinese autobiography on biography was made even greater by the absence of alternative models: first-person narratives such as travel literature, eyewitness
accounts of campaigns or missions, or autobiographical fiction did not
exist in ancient China.

Given the importance of biography in the development of Chinese autobiography, we should take a good look at that well-established genre
before we proceed any further. What we would recognize as biography
today went under a variety of names in traditional China. The subgenre
that enjoyed the widest vogue and resembled the modern form most is
the *chuan*. The term was first used in this sense by Ssu-ma Ch'ien (145?–
90? B.C.) to denote the biographies that constituted the bulk of his *Shih
chi* (*Records of the Historian*), the first comprehensive history of China from
the beginning of time to his own day. The style and format of this massive
work have been followed by subsequent historians, especially those who
were commissioned in successive dynasties to compile the so-called dynastic, or standard, histories. Thus, in each of the twenty-five dynastic
histories—the *Shih chi* being the first—biography or the *chuan* dwarfs the
other sections in its bulk. As the main vehicle of historiography, the *chuan*
could not help but acquire certain definite traits, but even in its earliest
days the didactic function of the word had already been foreshadowed. In
its verbal form the word means "to transmit," and it was used in its nominal form before Ssu-ma Ch'ien's time to denote a commentary or exegesis of a canonical text. On etymological grounds historians were then
justified in pressing the *chuan* into service: as biography, it should contain
what was worthy of transmission to posterity, and its contents should
illustrate or demonstrate general principles. Consequently biography in
China was not primarily a "representation of a life," as it was in ancient
Greece, but mainly a way of transmitting to posterity certain aspects of a
life. The didactic role of history therefore contributed to the highly selective processing of the type and quantity of incidents considered appropriate to biography. Most of the multitudinous secondary figures are accorded no more than a few lines in the dynastic histories: theirs are not
even miniature portraits in a side gallery of history but merely entries in

a vast ledger, each owing his place in the book to some meritorious deed or infamous act.[1]

Long and diligent service to historiography left indelible marks on biography. Even biographers in later ages who did not write as compilers of dynastic histories or who employed subgenres other than the *chuan* could not escape this bondage. To satisfy the dictates of historiography biographers tended to maintain what may be called the convention of the impartial, invisible, and unobtrusive narrator. Even when the biographer wrote about subjects he knew personally, the canon of objectivity demanded that he shun his own observation and rely on archival materials or reports made by others. Any information based on his personal knowledge could be mentioned only in a section clearly set apart from the biography proper. This section, appended to the biography and usually marked by a heading such as "the Grand Historian says" or "in appraisal we say" is the only place where the biographer might depart from complete anonymity, use the first-person pronoun, or offer personal comments.

Chinese biography's subservience to historiography was further reinforced by the fact that its most important subgenre, the *chuan*, was not considered literature. Early Chinese literary critics—who in actual practice were genre theorists or anthologists—excluded the *chuan* from their consideration while historiographers always concerned themselves with it. Lu Chi (261–303), in his pioneer treatise the *Wen-fu* (Rhyme prose on literature), made no reference to the *chuan*; nor did Hsiao T'ung (501–531), the compiler of the *Wen hsüan* (Anthology of literature), the earliest extant anthology of Chinese literature with a comprehensive scope, include the *chuan* among his thirty-seven genres. Obviously he considered the *chuan* a branch of history, for he excluded history from his anthology. In the preface he explained: "As for histories and annals, they praise and blame right and wrong and discriminate between like and unlike. Clearly they are not the same as belles lettres."[2] Although Sung and subsequent anthologists of literature were less exclusive and did include *chuan* in their collections, their practice did not discourage the historiographers, who always had a chapter on the *chuan* and sometimes on other subgenres of biography as well in their treatises. The last great historiographer Chang

---

[1] An example of this selective principle at work is the treatment of T'ang Hsien-tsu (1550–1616) in one dynastic history. To many modern critics the greatest of Chinese playwrights, T'ang even in his own day was widely recognized for his literary talent. The short biography in the *Ming shih* concentrates only on his political career. More than half of the page-long piece is devoted to a lengthy quotation from his critical memorial to the emperor. Not a word is said about his plays.

[2] Quoted in James R. Hightower, "The *Wen Hsüan* and Genre Theory," *Harvard Journal of Asiatic Studies* 20 (1957): 530.

Hsüeh-ch'eng (1738–1801) maintains that "there are histories of the realm, the locality, the family, the individual. Biography in its variety of types is the history of the individual; genealogical charts and clan records are the history of the family; prefectural and county gazetteers are the history of the locality; the comprehensive record of a reign is the history of the realm."[3]

Biography being what it was, we may then ask, what were the constraints that were forced upon Chinese autobiographers, who were, wittingly or not, guided by biography? First of all, if an autobiographer was conscious of his role as a historian, he could not move away from the style and content dictated by the very narrow view of what history should be. He could only record facts of a life that were ostensibly documentable from archival materials or secondhand sources, facts that were public and exemplary or cautionary. His inner world, the privileged domain known only to himself and largely inaccessible to biographers, must be excluded because it was patently unverifiable. The subjective and personal would only find an outlet in lyrical poetry—the reason why every educated Chinese prior to this century indulged in versification, many to excess.[4] Indeed the demarcation between *shih* (history), public and objective, and *wen* (belles lettres), private and subjective, was consistently maintained in China. Anthologists and literary critics often referred to such a fundamental distinction, but the case was best presented by the great historiographer Chang Hsüeh-ch'eng:

> When the man of letters writes, he strives for originality, while the historian's greatest concern is to avoid having himself as the authority for anything he writes. The two proceed from entirely different principles. The proper thing for the historian to do is to recount, not to originate. If he himself is the authority for any statement, then that statement is without evidence. A statement without evidence will not be credible to posterity.[5]

Most of the characteristics of Chinese autobiographies can be understood in the light of Chang's cogent statement. The disinclination to use the first person, perhaps a virtue in a historian, has rendered many an autobiography indistinguishable from biography: they share the same impersonality of tone, the same suppression of an individual voice with its own whims or quirks, the same opacity as to the yearnings of a heart

---

[3] *Wen-shih t'ung-i* (General principles of literature and history) (Taipei: Shih-chieh shu-chü, 1968), p. 133.

[4] One of the reasons why so many dreams have been recorded in China is that the authority of the dreamer is seldom assailable.

[5] *Chang-shih i-shu* (Written legacy of Mr. Chang) 2 vols. (Shanghai: Shang-wu yin-shu-kuan, 1930), 2:20.

or the inward workings of a mind, whether they be the slow and gradual acquisition of an outlook or a sudden breakthrough in the course of a quest. Only the subject himself could be the authority for how he lived through a crisis, for the complex way his motives were balanced in making a momentous decision, for the poignancy of his sufferings or the flavor of his joys; thus none of these things could find a place in a proper autobiography. Even adventures that were palpable and hence presumably documentable could not be easily accommodated because often the only eyewitness was the autobiographer himself. The same problem was faced by ancient travelers who wrote about their wanderings. Those who contented themselves with short trips to scenic spots could stay completely within the realm of *wen* (belles lettres) and write short pieces on the beauty of mountains and rivers; they were not subject to the exigencies of historiography. Those who traveled to foreign lands and had much to report had no choice but to adopt the stance of the historian and write rather like nineteenth-century ethnographers or folklorists. They described the states they had visited and quoted the local lore and myths rather than reporting their own experiences. They behaved as they did because their main concern was credibility, not entertainment or self-expression.

The truth of Chang Hsüeh-ch'eng's observation is nowhere more clearly demonstrated than in the contrast between the travel account dictated by the monk Hsüan-tsang (596–664), the most famous Chinese pilgrim to India, and the biography of him compiled by his disciples Hui-li and Yen-ts'ung.[6] The biography, running to nearly eighty-thousand characters—the longest up to that time—recounts a most unusual life in a plain and straightforward manner. The great pilgrim braved severe dangers and suffered great hardships in the crossing of deserts and high mountain ranges, and almost lost his life during several encounters with murderous bands in various regions. During his sixteen years of peregrinations throughout Central Asia and India he mastered several tongues, studied with various venerable teachers of indisputable lineage and, as his fame spread, received homage from kings and potentates. His greatest triumph came near the end of his pilgrimage when he presided over a grand assembly convened by Harsha, emperor of India, and attended by more than six thousand kings, monks, Brahmans, and clergy of other cults. Hsüan-tsang challenged the participants to a debate on his interpretation of Buddhist doctrines and offered his head to anyone who could defeat him over even one point. After eighteen days he was proclaimed the victor by Emperor Harsha. The biography, probably the best ever

[6] The travel account, entitled *Ta-T'ang hsi-yü chi* (T'ang records of the western regions), is in *T*, 51:868c–947c. For the biography of Hsüan-tsang see *T*, 50:221b–80a.

written in premodern China, says very little about the master's fears or joys, his spiritual growth, or sense of triumph. In line with the format of traditional Chinese biography, the great pilgrim's inner life, unverifiable and undocumentable, is hardly touched upon. But Hsüan-tsang's own account of his sixteen years abroad is even more reticent in this regard. Some twenty thousand characters longer than the biography, the *Ta-T'ang hsi-yü chi* (T'ang records of the western regions) gives the barest outline of the traveler's own activities but dwells on the description of the some one hundred and thirty states that he visited. The description is based on secondary sources—local lore and legends—and almost never on his own observations. The stance of the historian prevails over that of the traveler; the narrative gains credibility to the extent that the individual voice is suppressed. His two disciple-biographers enjoyed greater freedom in reporting his activities in distant places than he did because everything they wrote had a putative source—the teacher—other than themselves, while he himself was the only authority for anything he narrated about the journey.

The dilemma that confronted Hsüan-tsang is indeed a dilemma shared by all autobiographers in the ancient world. The impersonality, the suppression of the personal voice, was probably a universal narrative convention in all cultures like traditional China and classical Europe, where history enjoyed supreme prestige. Prior to 1560 very few Chinese autobiographers could bring themselves to abandon the posture of the historian and thus to depart from third-person narration. Commenting on the rarity of first-person narration in pre-Roman prose, Scholes and Kellogg almost echo the words of Chang Hsüeh-ch'eng:

> The reason for this employment of third-person narrative in historical works may be that the reliability of the *histor* seemed to the ancients clearly greater than that of the eye-witness. A document aspiring to achieve truth of fact had a better chance of being appreciated as factual if it did not seem too personal. This is another way of saying that history rather than mimesis dominated ancient empirical narrative.[7]

Indeed the development of autobiography both in China and the West lies precisely in its movement away from *shih* (history) in the direction of *wen* (belles lettres). It is the tension between the two contrary pulls that gives autobiography a unique position among all literary genres; and the dilemma, in spite of the gradual and seemingly inexorable movement, will never be resolved. Autobiography can never make a total break with his-

---

[7] Robert Scholes and Robert Kellogg, *The Nature of Narrative* (New York: Oxford University Press, 1966), p. 243.

tory, notwithstanding the stunning insight in Ernest Renan's remark that "ce qu'on dit de soi est toujours poésie."[8] Although modern autobiography certainly has come a long way in the direction of *wen*, the speed of the movement has not satisfied everyone. We still hear autobiographers being exhorted to "liberate themselves from technical constraints better suited to biography." Furthermore,

> the formal subordination of autobiography to biography is both obsolete and damaging; it has saddled autobiography with rules of composition that should long ago have been revised in order to make more intelligent use of the autobiographer's remarkable privilege, of remaining an autobiographer no matter what he writes about himself. From any formal point of view, autobiography is a parasitical mode of writing, too timid or inert to shake off the convention of biograpy.[9]

If modern autobiography, whose innovation and daring know no bounds, is still too timid, how much less able was traditional Chinese autobiography to escape from the tyranny of historiography and break the chains of biography? It is not surprising then that the reticence of Hsüan-tsang was repeated again and again.[10] Although none of the subsequent autobiographers could match the great pilgrim in distance traveled or in scale of adventures, some of them did have their share of hazards—shipwrecks, captivity, etc.—that they chose to tell. Yet in almost every case the canon of objectivity and impersonality obtains; what in the modern age would have been the stuff of long novels or grist to the autobiographical mills is narrated only with the severest economy. In 1281 the Mongol conquerors of China launched a huge armada against Japan. The combined fleets from Korea and southern China were hit by a typhoon and very few of the 4,500 ships survived the natural disaster and the avenging Japanese. Our autobiographer Sung Wu, then an army clerk

[8] Quoted in Philippe Lejune, *L'autobiographie en France* (Paris: Librairie Armand Colin, 1971), p. 188.

[9] John Sturrock, "The New Model Autobiographer," *New Literary History* 9, no. 1 (Autumn 1977): 52–53.

[10] The preference for sources rather than one's own personal knowlege as displayed by Hsüan-tsang as well as by countless Chinese travelers and biographers is also shared by medieval Russian chroniclers, and the reason given for the Russian case is another echo of Chang Hsüeh-ch'eng's astute observation. See J. M. Lotman, "Point of View in a Text," *New Literary History* 6, no. 2 (Winter 1975): 342: "And here again the unity of point of view was achieved by the chronicler not expounding his own position but identifying himself totally with a tradition, a truth, and a morality. He could not speak except in their name. And truth was considered to be whatever did not appertain to his personal viewpoint, so he chose to make use of legend, popular tales, the accounts of others. The chronicler treated all these as given and established, and hence true."

of twenty-one, was probably the only eyewitness who wrote about the expedition. But what a succinct and impersonal account!

> In the fifth month the army assembled at Ssu-ming and then boarded the ships going in the northeasterly direction. The staff and commanders were scattered in different ships; as a result orders and commands could not be heard. Those who had a late start caught up in south Korea with the vanguard, which had not proceeded any further on account of the typhoon and the loss of a guide. In the seventh month all ships reached the Chu Island [Cheju Do]. Assaulted by hail, rainstorms, and a strong gale, the ships could not moor. Most were dashed to pieces by the raging waves. Fortunately my ship survived, but it drifted for some time among Korean coastal islands. I was taken ill: having lost all the hair on my head, I came home just a bag of bones.[11]

Sung Wu recovered from these calamities and lived in peaceful obscurity as a scholar and schoolteacher. When he wrote his autobiography at the age of eighty,[12] he must have realized that the ill-fated sea campaign was one of the most momentous events in Chinese history and easily the most unusual incident in his own life. Yet in his telling there is so little sense of his participation that a reader would not know until almost the end of the narration that the autobiographer was on one of the ships.[13] One could argue that Sung Wu, a callow youth and a lowly clerk, could see himself as no more than a passive victim of events beyond his control or comprehension. But the same impersonality and reticence in reporting crucial incidents in their lives obtain even with autobiographers who were commanders or ministers, for whom the crises they experienced or witnessed at first hand obviously had much greater meaning. Take, for in-

---

[11] *Wu I-shih Sung Wu tzu-chih* (Self-Notice of Sung Wu, a hermit of Wu), in *WHCMIW*, p. 35.

[12] Throughout the book I follow the traditional Chinese way of reckoning age. A person is one year old at birth, and another year (*sui*) is added with the passing of each lunar year.

[13] That Sung Wu, like most other Chinese autobiographers who traveled to distant foreign lands or bore witness to the making of history, does not make more of this kind of experience—the word itself bears a very modern stamp—is a very good indication of the fundamental difference in sensibilities and perceptions between the traditional and the modern worlds. To begin with, the craving for experience and the rumination over it are very much a part of the modern temper. Modern autobiographers tend to classify certain incidents as experience and value them as such. By definition experience is completely personal and subjective, hence the reportage of experience needs no corroboration from other sources. The consciousness of experience is heightened to the extent that the self is perceived as a protagonist against the forces of nature, a participant in the dramatic enactment of history. On the other hand, a Chinese autobiographer is preoccupied with historiography, but not history: the writing of history, but not the living of history.

stance, another great sea battle that took place in the South China Sea just two years before Sung Wu embarked on his disastrous voyage. This time the Mongols scored a total victory, destroying the entire Chinese navy, which numbered more than a thousand ships. A helpless eyewitness to the battle of Yai-shan was the great Sung loyalist Wen T'ien-hsiang (1236–1283), whose autobiography will be discussed in detail in the next chapter. Taken prisoner earlier by the Mongols and held captive on one of their ships, Wen saw with his own eyes the fiery destruction of the Sung fleet, the last hope of his forlorn cause. How does the heart-stricken prime minister report that fateful event in his autobiography? "On the thirteenth day [of the first month the ship on which I was held] arrived off Yai-shan. On the sixth of the second month the provisional court at Yai-shan collapsed. On the thirteenth of the third month the enemy ships returned to Kuang-chou."[14]

The brevity of the report belies the intensity of Wen T'ien-hsiang's feelings. From the numerous references to that battle which Wen made elsewhere in his writings we can gauge his unbearable grief. For instance, he writes, "As I saw our defeat with my own eyes my agony was worse than any torture imaginable. I tried day and night to jump into the ocean, but the guards never gave me an opportunity" (*Wen-shan hsien-sheng ch'üan-chi*, 16:23b). And, "a lone loyal minister sitting in a northern ship, I looked southward and wept bitterly" (14:1b). The battle is lamented and graphically represented in several of his poems, and in the prose preface to one of the poems Wen even goes into a detailed analysis of the tactical errors made by the Chinese side (16:10a–b).

The total suppression of the personal in Wen's autobiographical account is of course attributable to his awareness of his role as a historian and not a man of letters, a distinction we have seen again and again. But the paucity of detail in Wen's narration as well as in that of countless others is also a characteristic of classical Chinese prose style. What I shall call narrative economy is the result of many conditions. The Chinese writing system, consisting of characters rather than phonetic notations, had determined from the very beginning that in its written form the language was to be used to record facts or communicate information rather than to transcribe speech verbatim. This divorce of the writing system from actual speech had several consequences. The written language, shared by many diverse dialectal groups, tended to become their common language: a standard language, concise and clear, devoid of regional peculiarities. As it was not identified with any particular dialect, it did not grow

[14] *Wen-shan hsien-sheng ch'üan-chi* (Complete works of Master Wen T'ien-hsiang) SPTK, 17:33a; hereafter cited as *Wen-shan hsien-sheng ch'üan-chi*.

or change with the vernacular, nor could it absorb a rich colloquial vocabulary or accommodate the prolixity of the oral style. The laborious
task of inscribing characters on stone or bronze or bamboo further encouraged the telescoping tendency. The result is a prose style succinct,
compact, terse, highly selective in what it could represent or express. Reality may be represented evocatively or allusively; a close-up and detailed
view is seldom possible.[15] Narrative economy is nowhere more severe
than in the earliest historical writings such as the *Ch'un ch'iu* (*Spring and
Autumn Annals*) and the *Shang shu* (*Book of Documents*). Later historians
were often held in rein by the prestige of these two early models, which
were recognized as Confucian canonical classics. Events are summarized
rather than reenacted, people are given names and often nothing else, di-
alogues are condensed for their pithiness, and connecting tissues are to be
filled in by the reader. Particularity is what classical Chinese is least capable of providing.

In discussing particularity in narrative style F. W. Bateson and B. Shak-
evitch set up two opposite poles, the proverb and modern prose fiction:
"The concrete details in a proverb are all functional. Nobody wants to
know what kind of stone it is that gathers no moss, or that is thrown by
the inhabitants of glass houses. The exact size, colour, weight and shape
of the respective stones are irrelevant, because a proverb demands immediate implicit conceptualization."[16] Katherine Mansfield's *The Fly* represents the other pole: "But in a realistic short story the particularity is a
large part of the meaning. Suppress Mr Woodifield's name, the colour of
the armchair, the day of the week allotted to his City visits, and the convention collapses. They are indispensable signals from author to reader;
they also assume a common interest and confidence in the concrete detail
of a phenomenal world."[17] Now Chinese historical narrative is closer to
the proverb than to the realistic short story in the above formulation because its main concern is the demonstration of general truth. In every
county and prefecture gazetteer, in nearly every dynastic history, there is
always a section on virtuous maidens and chaste widows. Numbering in
the tens of thousands, these good women for two millennia performed
more or less the same deeds, each earning one or two lines of encomium
in written history. They remain faceless and in most cases nameless, only
identifiable by the surnames of their fathers or husbands. Their lives approach a proverb in that their roles are practically interchangeable and the

---

[15] For a detailed and illuminating comparison between the vernacular and classic Chinese
styles see Patrick Hanan, *The Chinese Vernacular Story* (Cambridge: Harvard University
Press, 1981), pp. 1–19.

[16] Quoted in David Lodge, *Language of Fiction: Essays in Criticism and Verbal Analysis of the
English Novel* (New York: Columbia University Press, 1966), p. 43.

[17] Ibid.

outcome of their brief stories is completely predictable. What saves these biographical sketches—they were as necessary as ritual—from total inanity is classical Chinese which, with its elegant set phrases and its own steadfastness—the language hardly changed at all from the first dynastic history to the last, the twenty-fifth—is well suited to handle the recurrent and the typical. Above all it is the perfect instrument for stating and restating the exemplary. One might even say that classical Chinese was the perfect handmaiden of Chinese historiography, or rather, that they continued to reinforce each other. The reticence and impersonality of Chinese historical discourse are fully in accord with the terseness, selectivity, and uniformity of classical Chinese. Narrative economy unites the two.[18]

Modern autobiography is of course much closer to the other pole, and even Chinese autobiography began to move in that direction by the late thirteenth century. How some autobiographers succeeded in overcoming the combined forces of the historiographical model and classical prose, how they freed themselves from these constraints, gaining a personal voice and asserting their individuality—that is the story of this book from chapter 4 onward. In the meantime, to see the dilemma of early Chinese autobiographers in a different light, we may turn for comparison to Japanese writings during the Heian period.

The Japanese autobiographies in diary form surviving from that period are marvels of world literature, and scholars today are still puzzling over the suddenness of their efflorescence. Nowhere else in the world at that time or even in the next five or six centuries was there such a vivid and varied description of daily life, a free and easy avowal of feeling and thought, or a leisurely, unhurried pace of narration. In her sharpness of observation and fine scale of representation Sei Shōnagon was a true sister of Katherine Mansfield. Behind the Japanese triumph are a few indisputable facts that may throw some light on the obstacles confronting early Chinese autobiographers. The Heian diarists and novelists were almost all women, and as women they were not encouraged to learn or to write in classical Chinese, which was reserved exclusively for the use of men. While the men labored with classical Chinese in the preparation of government papers, legal documents, chronicles, and histories, the women writers used a largely phonetic script and a language which, although not completely colloquial, was close to what was spoken in the elegant circles of the capital. The Heian men, writing exclusively in classical Chinese,

[18] It would take us too far afield to delineate in any greater detail the context in which early Chinese autobiography evolved. For many of the broad issues in the relationship between various Chinese literary genres and historiography that bear on our study see Andrew Plaks, ed., *Chinese Narrative: Critical and Theoretical Essays* (Princeton: Princeton University Press, 1977), especially his elucidating article in that collection, "A Critical Theory," pp. 309–52.

left hardly anything of literary value,[19] while the Heian women, supposedly innocent of Chinese historiography and using a prose unburdened
by overpowering models, speak to us with a freshness and immediacy not
dimmed by the passage of a millennium. They were free from the kind of
constraints that we have discussed.

[19] There were a few exceptions, the most notable of whom was Ki no Tsurayuki, author
of the *Tosa Diary*. But he pretended to be a woman writer.

TWO

SELF-WRITTEN
BIOGRAPHIES

IF autobiography is defined as a biography written by the subject himself, then T'ao Ch'ien (365–427) is the first Chinese autobiographer. Ostensibly he only wrote a biography, not an avowed autobiography. But that the subject of the *chuan*, a certain "Master Five Willows," was none other than T'ao himself has never been doubted by critics or literary historians. The work, entitled *Biography of Master Five Willows* (*Wu-liu hsien-sheng chuan*), is as follows:

The origins of the Master are not known, nor are his family and given names. There were five willow trees by his house, hence he acquired this appellation. Quiet and reticent, he did not covet glory or profit. He liked to read, but never sought a thorough comprehension; every time he found coincidence of his ideas with those in the books, he was so pleased that he would forget food. He was addicted to wine, but being poor he was not always able to obtain it. His relatives and old friends, knowing his desires, often acquired wine and invited him. Every time he went he always drank to the last drop, hoping for inebriation. After he became inebriated he left without lingering. His house was empty: the bare four walls could hardly shield him from the wind and the sun. His short and rough clothes were full of holes and patches; his food basket and drinking ladle were frequently empty. But such things never bothered him. He often found amusement in writing, in which he fully expressed himself. He was indifferent to losses and gains, and wished to end his days in this way.

Eulogy: [The wife of] Ch'ien Lou said [of her husband]: "He did not lament his poverty or low station, nor did he crave wealth and high position." Do these words not fit the likes of the Master? Finding self-satisfaction in drinking and composing poetry, was he not a citizen of the reigns of Wu Huai Shih and Ko T'ien Shih?[1]

---

[1] *LTW*, 2:247–48. After the death of the hermit Ch'ien Lou his wife, in an exchange with Tseng Tzu, a disciple of Confucius, made the above comment. The quotation is from Liu Hsiang, *Lieh nü chuan* (Biographies of women) SPPY, 2:8a. Wu Huai Shih and Ko T'ien Shih, legendary rulers of high antiquity, were believed to have governed the world with a minimum of laws and institutions.

Notwithstanding the novelty of being a self-written biography, "Master Five Willows" breaks no new ground as a narrative in the *chuan* style. The piece owes much in tone, content, and format to the *Kao-shih chuan* (Biographies of lofty recluses), a work attributed to Huang-fu Mi of the third century. By the fourth century eremitism was already such a well established alternative to the life of government service that literature and history abounded in exemplary stories of resistance to worldly gains and glories. It is, then, almost inevitable that every detail of Master Five Willows's portrait can be traced to a precedent and that most phrasings in the short piece appear to be echoes of earlier writings. At this point a modern reader might wonder if this paragon of all lofty virtues was not an ironical portrait, mocking an ideal that was already too acceptable. This interpretation, however, finds no support in other works in T'ao's corpus, nor was an irreverent attitude toward lofty recluses possible so early in Chinese history. Yet we cannot ignore the potential here for more irony than is inherent in every autobiography. There is always an unavoidable disparity of knowledge or divergence in point of view between the author who is writing and the subject that he was. In T'ao's case the injection of a Master Five Willows further complicates things. An ironical touch can be detected in T'ao's feigned ignorance of the details regarding the master's background: during no other period in Chinese history was birth so much a prerequisite to membership in the elite, and T'ao's own pedigree sharply contrasts with the alleged obscurity of the master. The master's poverty is less patently false, but it must be seen in the social context of a China probably at its least egalitarian. Given the prominence of T'ao's family—for many generations his forebears held high positions in the government—his own straitened circumstances cannot have been as stark as the master's. Indisputable irony nevertheless can be found in the fact that some time after the autobiography was written T'ao was, according to his biographers, driven into governmental service by poverty, a fate Master Five Willows would have done anything to avoid.

Why T'ao, to many one of the greatest poets of China, chose to write a biography of himself in the *chuan* format is a question that cannot be answered, but that he should have done so is not surprising in the light of his other writings. Much of Chinese poetry is autobiographical, and T'ao's is more so than any up to his time. His self-preoccupation was such that he made innovations in two other established genres of Chinese writings, the *chi-wen* (requiem) and *wan-ko-shih* (mourning song). The former was usually composed on the occasion of a sacrifice: the piece, addressing the dead in laudatory and affectionate terms, would be read aloud before the libation was poured. The latter is believed to have originated from the singing of ancient hearse-drawers; later it was taken up by the friends and relatives of the dead who marched in the funeral procession. T'ao's innovation consists in writing the pieces for an imaginary occasion, his own death. Thus he is at once the mourner and the mourned. T'ao departs further from the convention by making himself the persona of the deceased—the dead speaking in the first person lamenting his own death. As an example of his style the following is the third of his "Three Mourning Songs":

> The poplars were shivering amid endless withered grass
> When I was sent, in the frost-laden autumn, far away from
>   the town.
> Where I was laid down by my friends and relatives, I saw no
>   houses, only lofty mounds.
> In the desolate wind the horses, with their faces turned up,
>   were neighing.
> Once the dark chamber was closed, it would not dawn even
>   in a thousand years.
> If it would not dawn in a thousand years, even the sage or
>   worthy would not know what to do.
> People who had seen me off now each returned to his home.
> My relatives may grieve a little longer; the others are finished
>   with their mourning song.
> What can be said about death?
> It is no more than that the buried body had become a part of
>   the hillside.[2]

T'ao's self-preoccupation not only endows his dead self with both an awareness and a voice but also, in other writings, extends such privileges to what may be called the components of the living self. He wrote a set of three poems, each purporting to be the respective utterances of Form (*hsing*), Shadow/Reflection (*ying*), and Spirit (*shen*). Form addresses a complaint to Shadow/Reflection, the latter tries to justify its own behavior, while the concluding poem represents the mediating words of Spirit, meant to soothe his two companions.[3] In these poems T'ao's greatest innovation perhaps lies not in the use of personification and dramatization—both rare in Chinese poetry—but in entertaining, even if only just as a literary device, what may be called a divided view of the self and allowing the trio to speak each in the first person. That T'ao the poet was even more inventive than T'ao the autobiographer and that the poetic self, even when dead or fragmented, may speak in his own voice, whereas the living Master Five Willows must always remain mute, is another testi-

---

[2] *Ching-chieh hsien-sheng chi* (Works of Master T'ao Ch'ien) SPPY, 2:8a.
[3] For a translation of these poems see *The Poetry of T'ao Ch'ien*, trans. James Robert Hightower (New York: Oxford University Press, 1970), pp. 42–44.

mony to the power of historiography. The biographer, writing *shih* (history), can only report observable or documentable facts—hence the possibly mocking assertion of the historian's ignorance as to the master's origins—while the poet, writing *wen* (belles lettres), can freely explore the boundaries of the self.

T'ao's fame grew in subsequent centuries, first as a recluse of unbending principle and integrity, then as a man of letters, until he became one of what may be called the cultural heroes of China, every trait of his character and every innovation in his writings widely admired and imitated. T'ao's prominence, in the formation of which "Master Five Willows" was a centerpiece, insured that writers with an autobiographical urge would have a precedent and a ready-made format. If they could not unabashedly and boldly write about themselves in good earnest, they could at least create an alter ego, a persona like the Master Five Willows, behind whom a version of their selves could emerge.

Yet T'ao's prominence, initially helpful in overcoming the inhibition that troubled every premodern would-be autobiographer, in the end proved almost as constraining as the long arm of historiography. His example has been followed only too slavishly: every stock device or every prop that T'ao employed in constructing the self-disguise was borrowed by his imitators. Without exception each feigned to write the biography of a person with a blatantly fictitious name, such as "Master Five Gallons" (*LTW*, 2:252), a man obviously with an even greater capacity for wine than T'ao's alter ego, or "Mr. Nameless," the double of the Sung Neo-Confucian philosopher Shao Yung (1011–1077) (*LTW*, 2:283). The ironic assertion of obscurity is almost always echoed. Sometimes T'ao's phrase, "the origins of the Master are not known," is repeated verbatim, as by Lu Yü (?–805) (*LTW*, 2:253) and Lu Kuei-meng (?–881) (*LTW*, 2:264). Nowhere is the disparity between the biographer's avowed ignorance and the enormous renown of the subject greater than in the opening sentence of the poet Po Chü-i's (772–864) biography of himself: "As for Master Singing When Intoxicated [*Tsui-yin hsien-sheng*], he forgot his family name, given name, place of origin, official title. In a state of inattention he did not know who he was" (*LTW*, 2:256). Of all the autobiographers who wrote in this fashion none held higher office in the government or commanded a larger army than Yüan Ts'an (?–477), but in his eagerness to emulate his mentor in writing of poverty and withdrawal from worldly affairs—he was T'ao's earliest imitator—he totally dispensed with truth. He asserts that his double, Master Subtle Virtue (*Miao-te hsien-sheng*), "went into government service against his own wish because his family was poor. He covered his tracks and concealed his intentions. Consequently, even some among his closest friends did not understand him, let alone the ordinary people. Where he lived the rush doors were always closed and the pathways to his house barely passable" (*LTW*, 2:249).

In summary we might say that T'ao Ch'ien as well as his followers paid a heavy price for disguising autobiography as biography, for adopting for the self a guise too narrowly designed. What they achieved is not a portrait but a pose; they conceal more of themselves than they reveal. Their posturings of course serve useful purposes: self-amusement, self-defense, self-justification, or even self-advertisement. But preoccupied with cultivating, perhaps half in jest, a self-image more or less at variance with reality, they fail to perceive the possibilities that are inherent in T'ao's device. To play the game to the hilt, they could have exercised the privileges of a biographer and written a full account of themselves, using mock documentation or citing imaginary eyewitnesses as they went along. To do so of course presupposes an irreverence toward the conventions of historiography, an adroitness in exploiting the narrative stances that were available, and a willingness to defy certain contemporary taboos—all the qualities it would be anachronistic to ask of a premodern writer. All these preconditions, however, happened to manifest themselves in an extraordinary sixteenth-century individual who, while ostensibly towing the line within an established literary form, subverted historiography from the inside and stood the narrative conventions of biography on their head.

Li Chih (1527–1602)

A rebel and iconoclast all his life, Li Chih (better known by his *hao* or alternate name Cho-wu) in his early fifties wrote what is in reality a fairly substantial autobiography, recounting his life up to 1577.[4] The work, however, purports to be something else written by another person—if one naively accepts the face value of its title, format, narrative stance, and the opening and closing remarks that frame the narration. The title, *Cho-wu lun-lüeh* (A brief comment on Cho-wu), gives the first suggestion that the piece is modeled on the *lun* section sometimes appended to the biographies in the dynastic histories, where the historian gives his personal opinion on the subject. This suggestion is reinforced by the opening sentence, "K'ung Jo-ku remarks, I was old enough to have met the Retired Gentleman Cho-wu, so I am able to make a general comment on him," for it is this way that a *lun* usually begins, going back to Ssu-ma Ch'ien,

---

[4] One of the representative and most fascinating figures of the late Ming, Li Chih will recur in the present study. For a cogent discussion of his place in intellectual history see Wm. Theodore de Bary, "Individualism and Humanitarianism in Ming Thought," in *Self and Society in Ming Thought*, ed. Wm. Theodore de Bary (New York: Columbia University Press, 1970), pp. 188–225.

the first dynastic historian. The biographer-historian always carefully sets aside his own comment from the text proper of each biography and marks the boundary by a phrase like "the Grand Historian remarks." In this section the first person singular is sometimes used, especially when the historian discusses his own personal knowledge of the subject. Enjoying the freedom and personal voice that is allowed the biographer only when he is writing a *lun*, the putative historian and narrator K'ung Jo-ku goes on to recount the life of the Retired Gentleman, quoting him at length and even on occasion reporting K'ung's own participation in the unfolding story. The fascinating narrative soon far exceeds the usual length for a *lun* and threatens to become a biography longer than most *chuan*. To justify what he is doing, our commentator-narrator explains why he is undertaking to write about the subject—a bow to the convention that obtains when the biographer is not an official historian—and then, modest and correct, insists that he is not writing a biography.

> One day the Retired Gentleman said to me: "As you have known me long, I ought to ask you to write my tomb inscription after my death. However, if I die in the company of other friends, I shall let them handle all the affairs. If I die somewhere on the road, my body shall be cremated or thrown into water. The locals should never be burdened with a burial. So I shall not ask you for a tomb inscription. But how about a biography [*chuan*]?" I replied: "How can I claim to have known you well? In the future there will be someone who will capture your essence as expertly as the portraitist Ku K'ai-chih." Thereupon I wrote a commentary [*lun*], summarizing his life. [5]

At the end of the *Cho-wu lun-lüeh*, K'ung, ever scrupulous in his documentation and completely impartial in choosing evidence, lets two conflicting reports on the subject speak for themselves: "Later I traveled to distant places and for a long time did not see him. For that reason I have not included the events of his life after the Nanking period. I have heard from one source that he died in Nanking. Others said, 'He is still alive and residing in southern Yünnan' " (*MTW*, p. 121).

The *Cho-wu lun-lüeh*, with its pro forma compliance with all rules of historiography and the plausibility of its narrative structure, appears so genuine that a few twentieth-century scholars have been led to believe that K'ung Jo-ku was a real person distinct from Li Chih. To Li's contemporaries the ruse must have been quite transparent, for the very name of the biographer-commentator, whom Li Chih is supposed to have known long and trusted deeply, would have signified to them that K'ung was made of nothing more than thin air. Taken literally, the phrase *k'ung jo ku*

[5] *MTW*, p. 121.

would mean "an aperture as large as a valley." It suggests something completely hollow. That the combination is an appropriate name for a non-existent person is supported by other considerations. The character *k'ung* in archaic Chinese is an exact homophone—same sound and tone—of *k'ung* (empty) and can be used in that sense. In the *Lao Tzu*, the Taoist text for which Li Chih wrote a commentary, the compound *jo-ku* is sometimes glossed to mean "vacuous" rather than "like a valley" in its literal sense. Thus to a seventeenth-century Chinese "K'ung Jo-ku" represented a real person no more than "Utopia" signified a real place to a sixteenth-century Englishman.

If the narrator-biographer in the piece is fictitious, how about the subject, the Retired Gentleman Cho-wu? In this case the disguise is totally transparent, for by the sixteenth century the use of the appellation *chü-shih* (retired gentleman) and the adoption of a *hao* (alternate name) were a common practice not just limited to autobiographers who followed the example of T'ao Ch'ien. The title *chü-shih* was used almost indiscriminately: one did not have to be either a lay associate of a particular religion or have retired from office, as was the case when the term was first used, to confer it on oneself or be addressed as such. While the practice of adopting one or more *hao*—there is no limit to how many one can have—besides a *ming* (official name) and *tzu* (courtesy name) probably goes back to the beginning of history, the combination of a *hao* with a title to establish an alternate identity may have begun only with T'ao Ch'ien. A more immediate exemplar for Li Chih may have been the statesman and writer Ou-yang Hsiu (1007–1072) who wrote, one year before he left a most distinguished official career, a very short autobiography entitled *Liu-i chü-shih chuan* (The biography of the Retired Gentleman Six-One).[6]

One might wonder why Li Chih took the trouble to create a web of fabrications while bowing, mockingly no doubt, to all conventions. On one level we may interpret his actions as a deliberate attempt to parody what were by now hackneyed rules and constraints, slavishly observed by most but not inviolate to a rebellious spirit like him. On another level he may have used all the subterfuge simply to circumvent the obstacles that had hitherto prevented Chinese autobiographers from telling their true life stories.

The whole truth Li did not attempt to tell. What he did tell affords us a glimpse of what had hitherto been forbidden ground in Chinese biographical literature, the domestic scene not screened by pious generalities nor adorned by exemplary acts. As reported by the fictitious K'ung Jo-ku, one day in 1564 when Li Chih was serving in the capital as an erudite in the National University, news came from his hometown that his

[6] See *LTW*, 2:279–82.

grandfather had just passed away. On that very day Li Chih's second son also died. "I [K'ung] went over to offer my condolences. When I entered his house, I found the Retired Gentleman no different from usual. He said to me: 'There is something I want to discuss with you' " (*MTW*, p. 120). At this point Li went into a scheme that continues to puzzle his biographers to this day. As he told K'ung, he was going home to arrange for the formal burials of his great-grandparents, grandparents, and parents. But instead of bringing his family back with him, he wanted to leave his wife and three daughters at Kung-ch'eng, a city almost halfway between Peking and Fukien, where he had lived for five years as an educational official in the local government. He would spend half of his savings to buy land and property for his family to live on and the other half for the expenses of the burials. Neither K'ung nor Li comment on this obviously absurd and, as it turned out, disastrous scheme, but apparently Li was somewhat uneasy about it, from what we are told by K'ung:

> The Retired Gentleman said to me: "I am afraid my wife will not agree to it. I am going in to talk to her. If she does not listen to me, perhaps you can give her a try." He went in and had a protracted discussion. His wife said: "It is not that your idea is wrong; it is simply that my mother, an old widow, lives only for me. Even though she knows that I am alive and well, she still misses me so much that she weeps day and night, and now she is blind in both eyes as a result of weeping. When she sees you without me, she will surely die. . . ." Before she could finish she burst into a torrent of tears. The Retired Gentleman remained calm and paid her no heed. After a while his wife, realizing the hopelessness of her cause, dried her tears and tried to look more cheerful. "All right, all right," she said. "When you see my mother, tell her that I am well as usual. Tell her not to feel sad and that she will see me soon enough. Go and do the best you can. Even though I am not going with you, I don't dare to feel resentful." Thereupon the Retired Gentleman prepared to leave. He bought land and set up his family as he had wished. (*MTW*, p. 120)

True to his role as an impartial historian, K'ung Jo-ku—or shall we say Li Chih?—does not take sides in the domestic dispute or favor either party in his narration. Certainly Madame Li comes out far better in the episode, judging from the facts as presented. Earlier we had been told that their older boy died a few years back, and now the husband is leaving right after they lost their second and only surviving son. More blows are to follow. "After the Retired Scholar left for his hometown, there was a bad drought. The land he had bought yielded only a few bushels of tares. The oldest daughter, long used to hardship, ate tares as if it had been grain. The two young daughters could not swallow what was given them, fell sick, and died" (*MTW*, p. 120). We are not told why it took Li Chih almost three years to complete his affairs in his hometown, nor why he failed during the entire time to get in touch with his wife. We are nevertheless told that thanks to the generosity of an old friend and the fortitude and industry of the wife she and their only surviving child eked out a living until his return.

> The Retired Gentleman said: "After I buried my parents, grandparents, and great-grandparents and discharged my duties to them, I no longer had any interest in an official career. But looking back, I was overwhelmed by my longing for my wife and children, who were thousands of miles away. I then returned to Kung-ch'eng. Arriving at home, I was very happy to see my wife. But when I asked about my two young daughters I found out that they had died within a few months after my departure." His wife was then on the verge of tears but, noticing her husband's expression of disapproval, apologized. She then asked about the family funerals and inquired after her mother's welfare. The Retired Gentleman told me: "That night when I faced my wife under the light of candles, it was just like a dream. I knew that the woman's memory was vivid and her sadness genuine, but I purposely concealed my true feelings in order to calm her. Only later did I realize how completely shattered I myself was!"[7]

The story told above epitomizes the woes of women in the premodern world—the death of almost all her children in infancy, long separation from her own mother, an unfeeling and unsympathetic husband with whom she could not share grief and whose long absence from home exposed her and her children to hunger and disease, and the resulting necessity to strive for survival—could not be told better by feminist historians. That the story could be told with such immediacy and candor owes much to Li Chih's artful manipulation of all the narrative conventions. The key to his success is the invention of the narrator-commentator K'ung, whose supposed closeness to Li made him privy to the domestic life of the biographical subject and afforded him an omnipresence seldom enjoyed by biographers. K'ung's professed insistence on writing a *lun* rather than a *chuan* relieved him of the necessity of relying on secondary sources and gave legitimacy to his narrative stance—reporting as an eyewitness and quoting at length from his subject. Li Chih himself, or rather the Retired Gentleman, could then unabashedly employ the "I" as long as he remained in the sanctuary of direct quotations. This device, together with

---

[7] *MTW*, p. 121. For an interpretation of the last line of the text see my review of *Li Zhi, philosophe maudit (1527–1602): Contribution à une sociologie du mandarinat chinois de la fin des Ming*, by Jean-François Billeter in *Harvard Journal of Asiatic Studies* 41, no. 1 (June 1981): 315.

the persona of the Retired Gentleman Cho-wu, provides the autobiographer with sufficient distance that such a painful and personal story could be told without any effort to spare the protagonists, especially Li himself.

SELF-WRITTEN NECROLOGIES

The Chinese practice of commemorating the dead with a short biographical sketch goes back at least two thousand years. The prose piece is frequently followed by a short eulogy in verse, but sometimes the verse by itself suffices. Alone or in combination, the composition is inscribed on a tablet made of wood or, more commonly, stone; the tablet is either erected in front of or buried a short distance from the tomb. Sometimes inscriptions are made on bricks or bronzes. Commemorative texts, inscribed or hand-written, may be placed on or in the coffin. These diverse practices and the various ways of naming such compositions afforded a field day to traditional Chinese genre theorists, who never tired of classifying these writings and labeling them, disputing classifications made by others, or taking to task writers who ignored fine but often imaginary distinctions. Since all such compositions are quite similar in function, we shall refer to them simply as necrologies, be they called *chih* (notice), *ming* (inscription), *mu chih ming* (tomb notice and inscription), *k'uang-chih* (grave notice), *lei* (dirge), *shou-ts'ang-chih* (sepulchre notice), *pei* (epitaph), *chuang* (obituary), or any other name.

If the Chinese did not mourn their dead as lavishly in architecture or ritual as some other civilizations, they certainly excelled in the attempt to perpetuate the memories of the deceased by the power of the written word. The filial children would spare no expense to seek a prominent writer for a necrology, then a skillful calligrapher to insure that the text would be as memorable in its visual form as for its content. Only then would a stone carver be employed to trace the calligraphy. The practice was so widespread that from the seventh century on in the collected works of every author, however minor, there is always a section of necrologies, written either as a favor to the survivors or for money. Appreciation of calligraphy and antiquarian interests, which grew rapidly from the tenth century on, converged in the preservation of thousands of inscribed necrologies in the form of rubbings, even though in most cases the stone had long since crumbled away.

Given the prominent place of necrology in Chinese life, it was inevitable that sooner or later some writer, having written so many necrologies for others, would be tempted to write one for himself. The temptation could only be abetted by the widespread practice of selecting a burial site for oneself and even beginning the construction of the crypt when one was still alive. Furthermore, of all subgenres of biography, necrology probably incited the autobiographical impulse the most. In a sense all autobiographies are self-written necrologies: a glance at the great void that lies in the not too distant future would very likely compel a backward look, and the contemplation of death cannot fail to prompt an examination of what one has done in life, a final accounting that can no longer be postponed. Indeed the consciousness of mortality must have been one of the powerful forces that enabled a premodern writer to overcome the taboo against writing about oneself.[8] The charge of vanity, so often hurled against early autobiographers, could be met by Chinese autonecrologists by asserting that they were motivated simply by humility, that their sense of scrupulousness was so strict that they would not entrust their necrologies to others who would only be too laudatory.

The first autonecrologist to avail himself of this sort of justification was Ch'eng Hsiang (1006–1090), the father of the Neo-Confucian philosophers Ch'eng Hao and Ch'eng I. His self-written tomb notice (mu-chih), brief and free from eulogistic phrases, is no more than a list of the offices held by his great-grandfather, grandfather, and father; the titles posthumously granted to his great-grandparents, grandparents, and parents; all the offices he himself ever held; as well as the names of his sons, grandsons, great-grandsons, daughters, sons-in-law, granddaughters, and grandsons-in-law. To the piece he appended a note to his descendants: "When I am buried you must not seek a necrology from a worthy. Since there are no great deeds to record, empty expressions and excessive praise would only add burdens to my deficiency in virtue. Just inscribe my own composition on a stone and place it against the wall [of the tomb]. You would only display your ignorance if you should depart even slightly from my instructions" (LTW, 2:345).

Before Ch'eng Hsiang there had been only a handful of necrologies written by the subjects themselves, but beginning in the fourteenth century the practice of writing one's own necrology became increasingly popular. When Chu Yüan-chang (1327–1398), the first Ming emperor, wrote his, he too expressed his distrust of the pens of others.

> In the fourth month of the eleventh year of Hung-wu [1378] I ordered Wu Liang, the marquis of Chiang-yin, to supervise the construction of a new imperial sacrificial hall. When I looked at myself in a mirror and saw only a pallid face and hoary hair, the hardship and difficulties of former times came to mind. Aware that inscriptions on the stelae before imperial mounds have always been written by embellishing literary officials and have thus not been sufficiently cautionary to descendants in later generations, I take this occasion to

---

[8] The same conciousness may also have contributed to the autobiographical act in the West, but I can think of only one halfhearted autonecrologist—Stendhal.

narrate my own hardships and difficulties and clarify the imperial
fortunes so that successive generations can see for themselves.
(*MTW*, p. 68)

The emperor then bursts into a versified account of his early sufferings
and later victories in a mixture of inane clichés and dubious allusions,
occasionally descending to the level of doggerel. To his credit, he claims
no auspicious birth signs or any prefiguration of his imperial future.
During his first twenty-three years he was no different from any other
peasant youth, perhaps only more downtrodden, hapless, shiftless, and
mawkish: "Listening to the gibbons' cries under the moonlight, I felt forlorn" (ibid.). There was none of the youthful resolve or exuberant heroics
that abound in the early life of almost every founder of a dynasty. Nor is
the emperor helpful to modern historians who are interested, above all,
in how Chu, with his unprepossessing beginnings and limited outlook,
rose above all other contenders for the empire, attracted a large pool of
able lieutenants, went on to vanquish the Mongols, and ascended the
throne, the first truly plebeian sovereign in Chinese history. The autobiographical sketch simply glosses over the transition from timorous and
anxious youth to brilliant leader of men, giving no evidence of what today is called charisma.

What is important to us is the question of why Chu Yüan-chang should
have decided to write his own necrology. His distrust of fawning officials
aside, what are the other forces that led the emperor to a literary activity
that had seldom been undertaken by other rulers in Chinese history? The
construction of the imperial mausoleum was ordered around the same
time as the death, at the edge of the Gobi Desert, of Chu's archrival Ayu-
sividara (1338/39–1378), son of the last Mongol emperor and pretender
to the Chinese throne, whose enmity Chu had tried in vain to propitiate.
Whatever the sequence of the two events, their combination could not
but appear to Chu as a strong reminder of his own mortality. The most
catalytic event, however, must have been the emperor's seeing his own
reflection in the mirror. Recent literature on Western autobiography has
made much of the powerful effects of mirrors on the premodern psyche,
especially one's fragile sense of identity, and attempts have been made to
link the rise of the new autobiography in Europe to the perfection of the
Venetian mirror.[9] That the mirror incident is mentioned at the beginning
of Chu's autonecrology suggests its possible impact on his decision to
undertake an autobiographical sketch.[10]

[9] See, for example, Paul Delany, *British Autobiography in the Seventeenth Century* (New
York: Columbia University Press, 1969), pp. 12–13.

[10] To my knowledge Chu's is the only instance in Chinese history prior to 1700 in which
peering into a mirror immediately preceded the autobiographical act.

Humbler autonecrologists than the Ming emperor often also express the same distrust of others' pens and cite it as the justification for writing their own biographical sketches. Thus Liu Ta-hsia (1437-1516) asserts near the end of his autonecrology:

Alas, I have often seen that members of prominent families at the death of their beloved fathers or elder brothers seek out celebrated writers to write tomb notices in which the accomplishments of the deceased are much embellished. Those who compile the official history of the reign often rely on such writings and incorporate them into their compilations. I wish to be different. Relying on the accumulated virtues of my ancestor, for forty years I have undeservedly enjoyed successes in examinations and government offices. Nothing that I have done, whether in my hometown or in court, is worth notice in a biography. I am afraid that my descendants might be so partial as to mislead a celebrated pen with untruth. Even if this act should succeed in deceiving others, would my bones not rattle with shame in my grave? Therefore I have narrated the events of my career to be inscribed on the stone. (*MTW*, p. 332)

His sense of unworthiness notwithstanding, Liu gives an account in the piece of his varied and distinguished official career up to the autumn of 1498 when he petitioned the throne for permission to retire on account of illness. The necrology was written just before he left for his hometown, where he "would prepare a grave on the south side of the East Mountain and wait for the end" (ibid). He soon recovered his health, however, and returned to government service. For several years he was minister of war and the closest confidant of the emperor, and when he finally died his heirs apparently disregarded his early admonitions and had a much more elaborate necrology written by Lin Chün (1452–1527), the minister of justice.

If Liu Ta-hsia was one of the most eminent among the autonecrologists, Sun Ai (b. 1452) was probably the most obscure. Although both his father and one of his sons succeeded in obtaining the *chin-shih* degree, he never passed the examinations. Apparently still in good health in 1526, he wrote a very short necrology for himself—in fact most of the piece is devoted to an enumeration of the achievements of his ancestors and his children as well as a listing of his grandchildren. As for writing the piece, he gives the same justification as Liu Ta-hsia.

Alas, etiquette requires that a burial always be accompanied by a tomb notice. It often happens, however, that after one's death the children and grandchildren in their eagerness seek out a prominent writer for a tomb notice that deceives posterity by its exaggerations.

I in my humble way despise such a practice. As for me, my life has not been known or beneficial to the world. No one knows the facts of my life as well as I. Therefore, not depending on the pen of others for the inscription on my tombstone, I myself have written the above. (*MTW*, p. 179)

Other justifications were sometimes offered. When the bibliophile and poet Yang Hsün-chi (1458–1546) decided, at the advanced age of eighty-five and in failing health, to prepare for his own burial, he knew, as he hinted in the autonecrology, that he could not depend on his children to seek a necrology from others. "Afraid that once I disappear like the morning dew there may be none to record my life, I have written this notice to be inscribed on the tombstone" (*MTW*, p. 306). The same sentiment was expressed by Ku Te-hui (1310–1369), a wealthy art collector who wrote his own grave notice in 1358 when his region was ravaged by war and famine. "I fear that once I die I may sink forever into oblivion" (*WHCMIW*, p. 72). Ku's fears were unnecessary, for he survived all the upheavals and lived to see the establishment of a new dynasty. When he finally died, his son had a more laudatory and much longer necrology written for him by a member of the local literati.

Modesty, or restrained self-praise, is an unavoidable characteristic of self-written necrology. Another feature that distinguishes autonecrology from necrology is the expression of resignation, frequently found in the former but hardly in the latter. Acceptance and equanimity are the themes that run through the earliest extant autonecrology dating from the late sixth century. Its subject-author, Li Hsing-chih (d. 581?), had held a number of high government offices. When he became ill he refused medical attention and dictated the following necrology on his deathbed:

Li Hsing-chih of Lung-hsi died on a certain day of a certain year at a certain place. Having served as an official during four reigns, he lived to almost seven decades. As the Way could neither be seen nor heard, he forgot all the rights and wrongs of affairs. Although he did not live up to his original goals of great virtue and lofty exemplification, he was not ashamed of anything that he had done. He thought that life came through the transformations of material forces and that death was but life transformed. For life was only the function of things and death the end of every man. Why should there be any joy or sorrow regarding life or death? He composed the following *ming*:

> As life is only a temporary lodge,
> Death should be taken as returning home.
> In the vast, boundless night
> What is wrong and what is right?
>
> (*LTW*, 2:335)

In contrast to the worldly successes that Li Hsing-chih enjoyed, a humble life of retirement and obscurity was the lot of Liu Hsün (1240–1319), who after the fall of the Sung refused to seek his fortune among the conquerors. Like most of the loyalists in Chinese history, Liu Hsün died without regrets. Near the end of his necrology he expresses his sense of resignation and even satisfaction: "It is fate that determines whether one is successful or obscure. In accordance with Principle [*li*] one lives or dies. To be content with fate and to submit to Principle is to be in the right. What more can be said if one dies while one is in the right, and this being so, what is the cause for grief?"[11]

No one should face death with greater equanimity or care less about their physical remains than Buddhist monks. Neither should they be concerned with posthumous fame. Nevertheless, no sooner did Buddhism take root in China than it began to acquire almost all Chinese concerns and preoccupations, sometimes with only slight modifications. In the matter of death the stark and simple Indian ways were replaced by more elaborate Chinese practices, and quite a few monks even wrote their own necrologies to be put in or inscribed on the stupas where their ashes were deposited. Perhaps because he was somewhat defensive over such secular concerns, the monk Ching-lung (1393–1466?) begins his autonecrology with a justification: "To serve the living and to bury the dead with proper sacrifices are what is taught in the school of Confucius. To cremate the dead and to bury the remains in a stupa are what is taught in the school of Śākyamuni. These teachings have been followed by everyone, in ancient times as nowadays" (*MTW*, p. 392). Others simply take the writing as a matter of course: if they feel any need for justification, their reasoning is no different from what is usually to be found in secular autonecrologies. When the monk Ch'ao-hung (b. 1605) wrote his own *T'a-ming* (stupa inscription), he closed the prose portion with the following words:

> In the year *wu-wu* [1678] the master reached the age of seventy-four. He realized that his days were numbered: he would not last much longer than the morning dew or spring frost. His disciples Ming-yün and others had a stupa built for him to the west of the Hsüeh-feng Temple. He knew that during his lifetime he was slightly blessed and poorly endowed. When he was alive he hardly benefited the world; after his death he would not be known to posterity. No pen of others should be allowed to falsify or exaggerate his achievements in enlightenment, thus incurring ridicule from the knowledgeable. Consequently he himself narrated the events that had led him to the Way. When this statement is, on his death, deposited to-

---

[11] *Shui-yun-ts'un kao* (Manuscript from the Shui-yun Village) SKCSCP, fourth series, 8:12a–b.

gether with his remains in the stupa, all the affairs of his life will have been completed.[12]

Although Ch'ao-hung used the by-then standard reason—distrust of the pens of others—to justify his autonecrological act, his real motivation may have been his need to explain how he came to join the Buddhist priesthood rather late in life. Born into a scholarly family and educated to follow the usual Confucian path, his career was shattered by the fall of the Ming when he was barely forty. Many of his class submitted to the new dynasty but quite a few, in different ways and to varying degrees, persisted in resistance to the ends of their lives. One form of drastic, if passive, resistance was the taking of Buddhist orders. Although the Manchus—in contrast to modern totalitarian governments—tolerated passive dissidence with few exceptions, the lot of those loyalists who embraced monasticism late in life was not an easy one. Lack of total Buddhist conviction, shame at not having taken a firmer stand, anguish over the turn of events—any of these could further burden a lonely life of austerity and self-denial. In Ch'ao-hung's case loyalism—a theme we shall meet again in other autobiographies—is balanced with a profession of genuine Buddhist faith:

> When he was twenty-seven he became gravely ill. He realized that the physical elements were not durable, and life and death were a great matter. Thereupon he read the *Vimalakīrti Sūtra* and became even more convinced that in the Ch'an Buddhist school there was the possibility of going upward. The idea of leaving this world was inspired. From that time on he befriended Buddhist monks. . . . Detained by mundane concerns he tarried for many years, although his worldly ambitions gradually subsided. When a new dynasty was established and the order to change one's hairstyle was issued, he said to himself with resolution, "Alas, the time is come!" He then bade adieu to his parents, took leave of his wife and children, and took Buddhist orders. (*Sou-sung chi*, p. 440)

What looms large in the consciousness of almost every autonecrologist is death, and in the face of it there is the natural need for a last attempt at self-vindication, at rescuing a life not so much from oblivion as from insignificance. Occasionally the writer succeeds, whenever there is a respite from the need for justification or the profession of equanimity, in presenting a self-portrait, as if to insure that a version of the self, something unique and memorable, would survive the dissolution of the flesh. Perhaps Buddhist monks, supposedly unconcerned with transitory mat-

---

[12] *Sou-sung chi* (Works collected under a lean pine) (Taipei: Hsin-wen-feng ch'u-pan kung-ssu, 1975), p. 441; hereafter referred to as *Sou-sung chi*.

ters and not the least deluded by egotism, should not have had a hand in such an enterprise, yet one of the best of the self-portraits embedded in a Chinese autobiography is made by the seventeenth-century Buddhist monk Chen-i. In fact, his short autonecrology deals with hardly anything else:

I lived in an area without scenic beauty, but I have always been fond of picturesque landscape. Having heard so much about the fame of the West Lake, I decided to visit it. Just before I reached the lake I took ill. On the seventh day, near death, I said: "Could someone help me to get to the lake? I would rather die in the water, so a coffin will not be needed." As soon as I saw the lake, almost half of my illness had gone. When I got to a few yards from the shore, I suddenly forgot my illness and my body. It was like a feverish patient eating the pears of Hsüan-chou—a great relief for both mind and body. Since that trip I have been back and forth for more than thirty years, without once getting tired of the lake. Born into an impoverished family, I never had any formal schooling, but in listening to the chanting of prose I can tell the good from the bad, like a slumbering man waking to loud sound. I often walk out on public lectures, but I usually enjoy reading Ch'an books. Born in a backward region, I have made no attempt to befriend members of the gentry. When I chance upon them, I neither slight them nor act bashfully or obsequiously. When I converse with them, I am without words of flattery. Yet they often think highly of me. I treat money lightly and like to start good work. As I am not very competent in practical matters, I often make mistakes, but I do not blame others or become resentful. In the end I am often forced to abandon the good work that I began. I am especially fond of installing statues of Buddhas and printing Buddhist texts. In doing so I am never hindered by toils or setbacks. By nature impatient and short-tempered, I often curse people. The only one in my life who understands me is Cho Tso-chü, whose friendship I always regain after an altercation. The rest do not have such understanding. By nature arrogant, I have become gradually estranged from nearly all the local personages I once knew well. Only Huang Ju-heng [1558–1626] swore eternal friendship with me for he, being arrogant himself, appreciated my arrogance. When I encounter monks who are the rages of the day, I refuse to greet them as a disciple, not even those who are much older than I. Many of their followers would take offense and slander me, but I have not been fazed. When I meet an itinerant monk in rags I treat him like a brother, talking with him without getting bored, giving him the clothes off my back, and sharing my meal with him. I cannot refuse a poor and sick man anything he asks, for I always have compassion for a man in such a plight. I love to plant bamboo and plum trees, and I do not mind menial work. In my old age I make a living by selling bamboo shoots, plums, tea leaves, firewood, and sutras. In the early autumn of the *chi-ssu* year [1629] of the Ch'ung-chen reign I came down with chills and fever. Knowing that my mortal body will not last much longer, I am preparing my own stupa inscription by writing down my life story. (*MTW*, pp. 386–87)

Chen-i's piece is no less than a complete breakaway from the usual format of autonecrology. The irrepressible monk unabashedly pours forth all his idiosyncrasies, likes and dislikes. The celebration of a robust and self-assured life, which was after a fashion lived to the full, overcomes all inhibitions and almost succeeds in banishing the idea of death, the very occasion for the composition of the piece. That an obscure monk could have depicted himself unapologetically and in a prose style at once simple and familiar owes much to the late Ming climate, the rise of individualism and egalitarianism—to which we shall try to do full justice in later chapters.

Annalistic Autobiography
(*Tzu-hsü nien-p'u*)

The *nien-p'u* form of biography first appeared during the Sung dynasty. The term *nien* (year) suggests that the life of the subject is arranged in annalistic sequence while *p'u* hints at the affinity of this type of biography with a large category of writings very popular from the tenth century on. Used as a suffix, *p'u* stands for any kind of catalogue, list, or chart, for example, *chia-p'u* (genealogy), *chu-p'u* (catalogue of bamboo plants). The purpose of the earliest *nien-p'u* writers was to supply a chronology juxtaposing the literary compositions of prominent men of letters with their other activities, thus facilitating the dating of individual works, providing contexts for exegesis, and in turn confirming or reconstructing biographical facts. Given the original meaning of the term *p'u* and the earliest uses to which the *nien-p'u* were put, this type of biography may be said to be no more than a diachronic catalogue of events and works. As such, the *nien-p'u* was limited in narrative format and choice of possible subjects. This may have been the reason that throughout the Sung there were comparatively few biographies written in the annalistic form.

The first annalistic autobiography was written shortly after the dynasty came to an end by the celebrated Sung loyalist Wen T'ien-hsiang (1236–1283). Although in his collected works, assembled and first published by his grandson, the autobiography is labeled *Chi-nien lu* (Record of the years) rather than *nien-p'u*, it does not differ in style or structure from works under the usual rubric. In fact the term *nien-p'u* was not always used as part of the title of many subsequent annalistic biographies and autobiographies. Like all annalistic biographies, Wen's account leaves large gaps: the yearly entries for most of his childhood and early youth are completely empty. The narration is brief and succinct even for the most eventful years, 1276 to 1279, when in quick succession he was sent to the Mongols as an envoy suing for peace when the Southern Sung capital was about to fall and then kept by them against his will; escaped despite great hazards and returned to the new Sung court in the deep south; reorganized the remnants of the Sung forces as prime minister and commander in chief; led the hastily assembled and poorly trained army from defeat to defeat and fell into the hands of the conquerors shortly before the final collapse of all resistance. We have seen in the preceding chapter how little he says in his autobiography about the disastrous sea battle of Yai-shan, to which he, a prisoner on a Mongolian ship, was an anguished and reluctant eyewitness. His account, however, becomes much more detailed when he turns to his first year of imprisonment in the Yüan capital: he gives a thorough report of his interrogation by the Mongol prime minister Po-lo, and the spirited exchange is sometimes quoted almost verbatim. His conduct bears out his resolution, stated earlier in the autobiography, that as the last loyal minister of a fallen dynasty his only choice is martyrdom.

> When I entered into the hall I greeted my interrogators with my arms. The interpreter shouted, "Kneel!" I replied: "A southern greeting with the arms is equivalent to the kneeling in the North. As I am a man of the South, I have already fulfilled my part of the protocol. How can I do the unnecessary by kneeling?" Po-lo then ordered his men to force me down. I sat on the ground and refused to do anything. Some of his men pulled my neck, others pulled my arms, and one pushed my back with his knee, all trying to force me to kneel. As I was thus rendered totally immobile the interpreter asked me, "What do you have to say?" I said: "Dynasties rise and fall, and every generation has seen emperors, kings, generals, and ministers destroyed or executed. I have been consistently loyal to the Sung to this day. My only wish now is to be executed without delay." The interpreter asked, "Is that all you have to say?" I said: "As I was the prime minister of the Sung, when my country fell it was my duty to die. Now I am in your hands, by your law I should die. What more can I say?"[13]

[13] *Wen-shan hsien-sheng ch'üan-chi*, SPTK, 17:33b–34a; hereafter referred to as *Wen-shan hsien-sheng ch'üan-chi*.

The purpose of Po-lo and other interrogators, as described by Wen, was to break down his resistance. This they first tried to do by treating him like a common criminal. Next they tried to challenge the legitimacy of the last two Sung princes successively enthroned by Sung loyalists as their cause became more and more desperate. Having failed in overwhelming Wen by their argument, they then denigrated Wen's effectiveness in the cause and his wisdom in embracing it.

> Po-lo asked, "If you knew it was hopeless, why did you persist?" I replied: "A minister serves his sovereign as a son serves his father. If the father is unfortunately ill and the son knows that it is hopeless, still there is no reason that he would not try every medicine. I have done my best. That our cause was lost was because of the will of Heaven. Today I, Wen T'ien-hsiang, having come to this pass, there is nothing more for me except death. Why must you keep on talking?" At this point Po-lo became noticeably enraged. He shouted at me: "You want to die but I won't let you die yet. I am going to imprison you!" I replied, "As I am going to die for my principle, what harm would imprisonment do to me?" Po-lo became even more angry but the interpreter stopped translating his words. (*Wen-shan hsien-sheng ch'üan-chi*, 17:35b)

Wen's autobiography, probably more than any other, is meant for posterity. He died a martyr's death, but before he died he apparently wanted a full airing of his cause and the role he played in it. Like so many "political" trials of the twentieth century, his interrogation, or the quasi-judicial processes conducted by his Mongol tormentors, was a welcome occasion for the defendant to proclaim his side of the story. But unlike the modern trials in more civilized countries, there was no press to report every word of eloquent defiance, so Wen had to be his own press. Furthermore, he could not have failed to realize that he himself was the only reliable witness to his own conduct in captivity: only his own testimony could save the final manifestation of his valor from oblivion or distortion. That this was probably what prompted him to write his autobiography—something still quite unusual in thirteenth-century China—and that he began the composition around that time can be seen from his note near the end of the entry on 1279, the year of the interrogation: "I am now writing down what has happened since I entered the jail. I shall die soon. I hope there will be some who will know my heart and soul" (ibid., 17:36a). Elsewhere in his voluminous writings he expressed similar wishes. In 1280 when his brother came to the prison to see him he entrusted to his kin for safekeeping a two-*chüan* manuscript containing the poems he had written since capture. In a note nestled between the two *chüan* Wen says: "I hope that my brother will see to it that my poems will not be lost to the world. I would die without regret if even a fragment or two survive to make my conduct known to the world. How much more would I be gratified if the full text of my writings could be preserved!" (14:16a).

Given the autobiographical urge that Wen apparently felt in the shadow of death, could he have chosen a form other than the *nien-p'u*? His choices were limited. The pseudobiography, invented by T'ao Ch'ien and employed by a few in the intervening centuries, was too playful in its narrative stance and too frivolous in its tone for the last prime minister of a fallen dynasty who wished to state his case in good earnest. The adoption of a fanciful alias, the feigned disdain for mundane enterprises—all the posturings would have obscured his determination and detracted from the rightfulness of his cause. Irony is always inimical to martyrdom.

As for the self-written necrology, the other autobiographical form available to Wen, it would not have done much better. Its format—a brief summary of the autobiographer's career in a mixture of apparent self-effacement and subtle self-praise—and its tone of elegiac resignation would not easily have accommodated the unequivocal and righteous testimony of a martyr or the detailed record of Wen's confrontation with his enemies. Even if he had thought of dispensing with the usual restraints of the genre and greatly enlarging its scope—something not attempted until four centuries later—the uncertain circumstances of his prospective burial, completely at the disposal of the Mongols, would have prevented him from entrusting his posthumous vindication to such a composition.

The *nien-p'u*, on the other hand, was much more amenable to his purposes. Judging from the extant specimens written during the Sung, their serious and formal style is matched by the prominence of their subjects. It was the proper form in which to recount an exemplary life. In the words of the scholar Hang Shih-chün (1696–1773),

> the *nien-p'u* follows the style of the biographies of noble houses in the dynastic histories, hence it must be written in a way more exacting than any other type of unofficial biography. Only those whose virtue and achievements are lofty and illustrious, those who have distinguished themselves in literature, deserve to be the subjects of this genre. For a man who lives and perishes as obscurely as plants or weeds, no life of his should be accounted in a year-to-year and month-to-month fashion.[14]

Even during the darkest hour of his imprisonment Wen could not have entertained any fears of having led an obscure life. Having written so much on loyalty and compared himself so often to loyal ministers and

[14] Quoted in Hsieh Kuo-chen, *Ming-Ch'ing pi-chi t'an-ts'un* (Studies of Ming-Ch'ing miscellaneous notes) (Shanghai: Chung-hua shu-chü, 1962), p. 326.

heroic figures in history, he was very aware of having a place in history—it is this awareness that guided his entire career and sustained him through all his ordeals. Now with his country completely overrun, official historians killed or dispersed and government archives abandoned, he must have realized that he had to act as his own historian, the biographer of the last pillar of the dynasty. It was, then, fitting for him to choose the stately form of the *nien-p'u*; to close the last entry in the third person—the only exception in an otherwise first-person narrative—with the phrase "Sung prime minister Wen T'ien-hsiang hereby wrote his last word"; and, following the practice of all dynastic historians in pronouncing a judgment on the subject at the end of the official biography, to include in the last entry of his annalistic autobiography a self-written *tsan*:

> Confucius said, "Complete your humaneness."
> Mencius said, "Choose the righteous."
> Only when the righteous has been completely done
> Is humaneness attained.
> Studying the books of the sages,
> What else is there to be learned?
> Now and hereafter
> I shall be ashamed of nothing.[15]

Traditional China no less than Christian Europe abounded in martyrs, yet hardly any before Wen had ever attempted to write their own testimonies. That Wen should have done so was apparently owing to a number of factors, some of which we have discussed already. His long imprisonment is another circumstance not shared by many martyrs. Living in the shadow of death must have led him to reflect on his fate and recollect his past. Most decisive, however, may be the fact that he was, in prose and in poetry, one of the most autobiographical of all Chinese writers. During his first captivity and subsequent escape in 1276 he wrote a series of poems on all the travails, the pains and humiliations inflicted by his captors, as well as the perils and privations he encountered during his long and arduous search for a way to return from behind enemy lines to the ever-diminishing territory still controlled by the Sung. In the poems,

---

[15] 17:40a. *Analects*, 15:8. "The Master said: 'The determined scholar and the man of humaneness will not seek to live at the expense of injuring their humaneness. They will even sacrifice their lives to complete their humaneness'" (Legge translation modified). *Mencius*, 4A:10: "So, I like life, and I also like righteousness. If I cannot keep the two together, I will let life go, and choose righteousness" (Legge translation). These two lines underscore Wen's determination to die in accordance with the teachings of the Confucian masters, after having done his utmost in the futile struggle against the Mongols. The last line alludes to the deathbed utterance of Master Tseng, a disciple of Confucius, in *Analects*, 8:3. Tseng assured his students that throughout his life he had done nothing unworthy.

in the prose prefaces to individual poems, and in the preface and the post-face to the collection, he wrote voluminously about himself: his fears, hopes, and bitter disappointments; his family, his friends and associates. During his second captivity he wrote again in the same fashion. Having written so readily and so abundantly about himself, it would be only one step further to write an autobiography. That step, however, was an un-bridgeable chasm for nearly all premodern writers.

There are quite a few reasons why Wen should have been the first an-nalistic autobiographer. One additional reason emerges in light of the vast amount of poetry that he composed under all circumstances. Of all the earlier poets he admired Tu Fu (712–770) the most: not only did he una-bashedly adopt Tu's prosodic forms and imitate Tu's style, he even pro-duced—to while away the long days during his second year in jail—two hundred poems by recombining individual lines selected from Tu's cor-pus. These two writers were much alike in their sufferings from the rav-ages of war and in their ardent loyalty to their dynasties. That Tu Fu, with whom Wen identified almost completely, was the subject of two of the earliest specimens of the *nien-p'u* must have contributed to his decision to write one for himself.

In the preceding chapter we have discussed the constraints that Chinese autobiography had to contend with from its nascence. The power of these constraints is nowhere more conspicuous than in the case of Wen, who was, paradoxically, at once the most autobiographical of writers and al-most the least revealing as an autobiographer when he wrote about any-thing not germane to his role as a loyal minister. A comparison between Wen's self-written *nien-p'u* and his other autobiographical writings will show the clearly drawn division between *shih* (history) and *wen* (belles lettres), between what is official and public and what is personal and pri-vate, a division that, as we have seen and shall see again and again, very few Chinese autobiographers could overcome before the sixteenth cen-tury. As for Wen, one instance of the contrast—in addition to what we have seen above—will suffice. His family was decimated after each calam-ity that was visited on the crumbling Sung forces on its retreat to the south. The only time in his autobiography that he ever mentions the loss of those most dear to him he does so in the most succinct and matter-of-fact fashion. "We were overtaken by the pursuing cavalry at K'ung-k'eng. I lost my wife, my son, and two daughters. The field command collected the remnants of our troops and we entered T'ing-chou in the tenth month" (ibid., 17:24a).

The *nien-p'u* has four more yearly entries but never does he mention his family again, as if his private grief were crowded out by the events, by his heroic stance amidst the most extreme adversities. During these four years—three of them in prison—he wrote copiously, and it is in the writings other than his autobiography that he expresses his affection for his family, describes its decimation, and pours out his sorrows. I shall just quote two of the instances in which he mourns the loss of his daughters. In the prose preface to one of the recombinations of Tu Fu's poetry Wen states:

> I had six daughters: Calm, Willow, Jade, Prudence, Reverence, and Longevity [Ting-niang, Liu-niang, Huan-niang, Chien-niang, Feng-niang, and Shou-niang]. In *ping-tzu* [1276] Calm and Longevity died of illness in San-chiao of Ho-yüan. In *ting-ch'ou* [1277] Willow and Jade were lost. That left me only Prudence and Reverence. But how sad it was that the two survived only to perish a year later in the chaos following our defeat at Ch'ao-yang. (16:44b)

During his last imprisonment, following Tu Fu's style and format Wen wrote a suite of six laments over the destruction of his family, one of which touches on the fate of Willow and Jade, the two daughters who were captured along with their mother by Mongolian horse soldiers:

> Daughters I have two, both bright and sweet.
> The older one loved to practice calligraphy
> while the younger recited lessons sonorously.
> When a sudden blast of the north wind darkened the noonday
>   sun
> The pair of white jades were abandoned by the roadside.
> The nest lost, young swallows pecked in vain in the autumn chill.
> Who will protect the girls, taken north with their mother?
> Alas, I have become even sadder when I sing the third lament.
> But my tears flow not just for my children.
>
> (14:23b)

In his poetry Wen mourns the death of his two sons and four daughters, but even harder to bear was the fate of the two live daughters, held captive nearby. In his numerous references to them a sense of guilt is hinted, for he must have realized that the two young girls repeatedly suffered the consequences of his unflinching loyalty to the fallen dynasty. He had to abandon them at K'ung-k'eng because as commander in chief he could not risk capture by the enemy. Now a small gesture of accommodation to the new regime could win his release so that he could resume the responsibilities of a father, but his refusal to compromise his integrity remained unswayed. Although in his poetry he could confess that "as a father I feel ashamed" (16:43a) when he thought about his two captive daughters, in his autobiography no conflict of contrary claims, no complexity of motives, could be acknowledged. In fact it is this singleness of view, the presentation of no more than one aspect—the public and official—of a life that we shall see again and again in subsequent autobiographies written in this form.

The annalistic autobiography gained great popularity during the late Ming period. While there were only three practitioners of this craft born between the death of Wen T'ien-hsiang in 1283 and 1499, there were nine born between 1500 and 1549, twelve between 1550 and 1599, and twenty-five between 1600 and 1649.[16] Its popularity during the Ming may owe something to the veneration of Wen T'ien-hsiang that grew as the dynasty declined. With the northern frontiers frequently breached by nomadic hordes and southern and eastern coastal cities ravaged by Japanese pirates, the heroic figure of Wen, the symbol of loyalty to the dynasty and resistance to foreign invaders, loomed larger and larger. He must have been a source of encouragement especially to those imprisoned Confucian officials who had fought hopeless battles against eunuchs and other favorites of emperors. If he was an exemplar in his defiance and bravery, his autobiographical innovation was a most suitable model for those such as Yang Chi-sheng (1516–1555), Wei Ta-chung (1575–1625), Fang Chen-ju (1585–1645), or Cheng Man (1594–1639), who wrote their annalistic autobiographies in the shadow of death. Like Wen, they wanted to make one last defense of themselves, narrate their confrontations with their persecutors, describe the tortures inflicted on them by their interrogators and jailers, and express their hope of eventual vindication by history.

The appeal of annalistic autobiography was not limited to prisoners who were dying for a lost cause. But almost all autobiographers writing in this form followed the model of Wen T'ien-hsiang with little deviation. They tend to be public, official, and reticent. Prominent Neo-Confucian philosophers such as Lo Ch'in-shun (1465–1547) and Keng Ting-hsiang (1524–1596) give us no inkling of their intellectual or spiritual development, while men of letters such as Hsü Wei (1521–1593) and Wang Ssu-jen (also known as Wang Chi-chung; 1575–1646), known otherwise for their eccentricity and irreverence, appear no different from their more conventional confreres.[17]

[16] This information is culled from Wang Te-i, Chung-kuo li-tai ming-jen nien-p'u tsung-mu (A comprehensive catalogue of annalistic biographies of eminent Chinese) (Taipei: Hua-shih ch'u-pan-she, 1979). The acceleration flattened somewhat as the Ch'ing dynasty consolidated, but during the nineteenth century the vogue for this subgenre reached torrential proportions. More autobiographies were written in this form than in all other subgenres added together. It went into a decline only in this century, after the introduction of the Western autobiography and the ascendancy of the modern vernacular as the literary language.

[17] A manuscript copy of Wang's work, entitled "Wang Chi-chung tzu-hsü nien-p'u" (The annalistic autobiography of Wang Ssu-jen) is preserved in the Peking University Library. In 1971 when I passed through Kyoto Professor Yoshikata Iriya gave me a photocopy of it. I should like to acknowledge my indebtedness to him for this and other acts of kindness.

There was, however, one work that rises somewhat above the convention. The autobiography of Hsü Jih-chiu (1574–1631) looks very much like a curriculum vitae upon first glance, for the narrative begins exactly with *keng-hsü* (1610), the year in which Hsü passed the metropolitan examination and obtained his first office. Nothing is said at all about his life before then. On the other hand, the title that Hsü chose for the work, *hsüeh-p'u* (record of education) suggests that his year-by-year account of his life will be different from the usual *nien-p'u*. The pursuit of *hsüeh*, as we shall see in chapter 5 of the present study, led a group of Neo-Confucians to write autobiographies in the mode of *Bildungsroman*, but with Hsü his official career is the main staple of the narration. The idea of education, however, frequently informs the presentation of his fortunes in the bureaucracy: he always inquires into the background of the corrupt practices that he battles against, and each defeat leads to a new understanding of officialdom or the way of the world. His concern with education sometimes leads to introspection, a trait seldom found in annalistic autobiography. The following entry is a good example of the sort of self-examination he occasionally exercises:

> The fifteenth day of the tenth month. I dreamt in the night that I was somewhere when suddenly a report came that tough robbers were approaching. I noticed that a man went to block the door and the situation looked critical. I hurried to a room on the lower level, unsettled and not knowing what to do next. From the window I saw men and women running in great confusion, all beset with fear. Later news came that the robbers were gone. I went out and found a sedan chair, but I noticed that the carriers were old women, strong and fierce-looking. Startled, I woke up. Thereupon I sighed over the fact that all the study I had done was no help at all. I had thought that I was gaining competence through each concrete affair I had to cope with and that my courage grew with each crisis. Now I know differently. Although nobody will know this, I still must not pamper my weakness. Therefore I am writing down the episode as if I were making a judicial record of my acts in order to see if I am going to improve in the future.[18]

Elsewhere he is just as unsparing of himself: "As I see myself, during all my life lust (*ai-se*) has not been as strong as avarice (*ai-ts'ai*); avarice has not been as strong as my love of fame (*ai-ming*); my love of fame has not

[18] *Chen-shuai hsien-sheng hsüeh-p'u* (Master Hsü Jih-chiu's record of education) (National Library of Peiping microfilm reel 491), *jen-hsü*: 11b–12a; hereafter referred to as *Chen-shuai hsien-sheng hsüeh-p'u*.

been as strong as my concern for personal well-being (*ai-shen*)" (*Chen-shuai hsien-sheng hsüch-p'u, kuei-hai:* 3a).[19]

Later in life he was even more contrite. In 1625 he was expelled from the government and demoted to the rank of commoner as a result of his bold remonstration with the emperor. On his way home from the capital he still hoped that his exile would only be temporary, but now he realized that in a few years there would be other things more important than a government career.

> I decided that on the first day of my fifty-eighth year I would make a statement before my parents' graves and the ancestral temple, swearing that I would henceforth break away from all worldly pursuits. From that time on I would firmly devote whatever years Heaven should choose to grant to me to the search for my original self. Every hour that I live I would devote to such a purpose. I said to myself: "Do not stumble into old age and miss the great opportunity. If you do so, no amount of regret can bring you back." I said these words on the afternoon of the twelfth while riding in a donkey cart on the route to En-hsien. I wrote them down when I reached the next post station. I believe that ghosts and spirits were present when I made my decision and that when the time comes they will see to it that I will not go back on my word. (*i-ch'ou:* 44a)

The great search was not to take place. In 1628 he was, just as he had hoped, recalled to serve as a military supervisor in coastal Fukien. But three years later, when the time came for him to leave office and embark on the quest as he had promised, he died. Had he made a serious attempt early in life at what he hoped to do near the end of his life, he might have written a different autobiography. He would then have found a place in our chapters on Buddhist and Confucian spiritual autobiographies and joined the ranks of those whose life stories are dominated by but one theme—the tortuous search for enlightenment, for the ultimate meaning of life.

[19] Hsü's unprecedented illusionless self-observation can be seen as one instance of the late Ming and early Ch'ing confessional literature to be explored in chapter 12. The entry may also reflect the vogue of the maxim or aphorism in seventeenth-century China when men of letters circulated their collected gems among friends for their comments and then published the collections with the comments. Although no attempt can be made here even to outline this interesting and hitherto neglected genre, it must be said that Hsü's stark self-stricture contrasts with the usually playful and sunny tone of other writers. In his unadorned severity Hsü approaches La Rochefoucauld more than any Chinese aphorist, although the Frenchman is only unsparing of humanity, not of himself. The two are alike in placing amour-propre above everything else, but that trait is represented in Hsü's formulation by the last two proclivities, *ai-ming* and *ai-shen*.

THREE

AUTHORIAL
SELF-ACCOUNTS

IT OFTEN happens that the author of a book includes a section, usually set aside from the text proper, in which he explains the organization and purpose of the book and the circumstances under which it was written. In ancient China, as well as in the classical West,[1] a few authors would add to this section a brief account of their lives. This section is variously labeled *tzu-hsü* (self-written preface or postface), *tzu-hsü* (self-account),[2] *hsü-chuan* ([self-written] preface-biography) or *tzu-chi* (self-record). This type of writing, henceforth referred to as the authorial self-account, is of course not autobiography in the strict sense of the word, yet it is often more self-revealing than the subgenres that we have dealt with above.

The earliest recognizable specimen of this type is the postface appended by Ssu-ma Ch'ien to his *Shih chi* (*Records of the Historian*), the first Chinese dynastic history. Presumably aware of the canon of objectivity and impersonality that we have discussed in the previous chapter, Ssu-ma Ch'ien throughout the *tzu-hsü* refers to himself as the Grand Historian, without ever using the first person. The postface begins with a lengthy genealogy, tracing his ancestry all the way back to a royal sacrificer who lived in the time of the legendary kings. Everything he says about himself has to do with either the preparation or execution of his great work. The most traumatic event in his life, the controversy over Li Ling (d. 74 B.C.), he treats only as an additional incentive to write his masterpiece. When his friend General Li was defeated and captured by the Hsiung-nu the historian took a great risk in praising Li's bravery and loyalty before the emperor. When it turned out that Li had not died a hero's death but had instead shifted his allegiance to the side of China's mortal enemies, Ssu-ma Ch'ien was charged with the crime of deceiving the emperor and punished by castration. For the circumstances that led to this grave injury and humiliation and the punishment itself he has only the following to say: "For the next seven years The Grand Historian devoted himself to writing and arranging his books. Then he encountered the misfortune of the Li Ling affair and was plunged into the dark, in bonds. He sighed bitterly and said,

[1] See Georg Misch, *A History of Autobiography in Antiquity*, trans. E. W. Dickes, 2 vols. (Cambridge: Harvard University Press, 1951), 1:307–25.

[2] Here the character *hsü* (account, narrative) is sometimes used as a synonym for its homophone, the *hsü* (preface or postface) in the preceding compound.

'Such is my fault, such is my fault, that I have brought mutilation to my body and may never again serve my lord!' "[3] He then goes on to cite numerous examples in Chinese history in which adversity paved the way for great literary accomplishments, as if his own calamity was almost a blessing in disguise. His equanimity, however, is no more than posturing: it is in keeping with the lofty and formal tone of the rest of the writing but cannot be taken to represent how he really feels about the event. A better measure of his true feeling is to be found in his letter to a friend written in 93 B.C., six years after the calamity. Speaking in his own voice and very likely with posterity not far from his mind, he makes a full account of the Li Ling affair as he sees it, justifying his own conduct in every way. Most of the letter is an outpouring of his sense of grievance, and the anguish reaches rhetorical heights near the end.

> It is not easy to dwell in poverty and lowliness while base men multiply their slanderous counsels. I met this misfortune because of the words I spoke. I have brought upon myself the scorn and mockery even of my native village and I have soiled and shamed my father's name. With what face can I again ascend and stand before the grave mound of my father and mother? Though a hundred generations pass, my defilement will only become greater. This is the thought that wrenched my bowels nine times each day. Sitting at home, I am befuddled as though I had lost something. I go out, and then realize that I do not know where I am going. Each time I think of this shame, the sweat pours from my back and soaks my robe. I am now no more than a servant in the harem. How could I leave of my own accord and hide far away in some mountain cave? (Watson, *Ssu-ma Ch'ien*, p. 66)

With his literary fame and great prestige as the Grand Historian and the author of the first dynastic history, Ssu-ma Ch'ien has been emulated in every way, including the practice of appending an authorial self-account to his work. Three compilers of subsequent dynastic histories followed suit, but they are even less autobiographical than the Grand Historian, although they are just as boastful of their long genealogies. They, as well as Ssu-ma Ch'ien, lend weight to the supposition that Chinese historiography posed probably the most formidable obstacle to what is nowadays valued in an autobiography—a personal voice, a private point of view, or any self-revelation.

Writers other than historians, less susceptible to the disabilities mentioned above, could make better use of authorial self-account as a vehicle

---

[3] Translated by Burton Watson in his *Ssu-ma Ch'ien: Grand Historian of China* (New York: Columbia University Press, 1958), p. 42; hereafter referred to as Watson, *Ssu-ma Ch'ien*.

for their autobiographical act, and quite a few, with varying degrees of
success, reveal a little of themselves in the prefaces or postfaces to their
books. The first and the most revealing author to do so was the philosopher Wang Ch'ung (A.D. 27–97?). He does not include a preface or postface in his *Lun heng*, but the last chapter, entitled *Tzu-chi* (Self-Record)
does not differ in format or style from the *tzu-hsü* written by Ssu-ma
Ch'ien or subsequent authors. Consistent with the iconoclastic content of
the book and in contrast to historians who often boast an illustrious and
lengthy genealogy going back to mythic antiquity, Wang Ch'ung seems
to take a perverse pleasure in denigrating his ancestors.

> For several generations the Wangs were engaged in farming and ser-
> iculture. Ch'ung's great-grandfather, daring and impetuous, was not
> well liked by others. During a year of bad harvest he wilfully injured
> and killed people. Thus he incurred much hatred. When the country
> plunged into chaos, Ch'ung's grandfather Fan, fearing the retaliation
> of ancestral enemies, moved the family away from K'uai-chi and set-
> tled in Ch'ien-t'ang. He earned a living as a merchant and had two
> sons, Meng and Sung, the latter being the father of Ch'ung. For sev-
> eral generations the Wangs were impetuous people, and this trait
> reached its extreme with Meng and Sung. Arrogant and rude, they
> treated the local people in a high-handed manner. Finally, after hav-
> ing made enemies in such powerful families as the Ting Pos, they
> moved the family to Shang-yü. (*LTW*, 1:136–37)

He is as generous to himself as he is unsparing to his ancestors.

> Ch'ung was born in the third year of Chien-wu [A.D. 27]. As a child
> he was never aggressive or improper with his playmates. They loved
> to catch birds or cicadas, flip coins or climb trees, but Ch'ung would
> not join them in such activities. His father Sung marveled at his be-
> havior. When he was five he began his education. Willing and pliant,
> he was extremely respectful to all adults. Always proper and going
> about quietly, he had already set his mind on great things. His father
> never flogged him, nor did his mother ever scold him. Not a word
> of censure was ever uttered by his neighbors. At eight he entered the
> academy. There were more than a hundred boys there, and every one
> of them was at one time or another punished for misbehavior or
> whipped for bad handwriting. Ch'ung, advancing daily in his callig-
> raphy, was never guilty of any offense. After he perfected his hand-
> writing he received instructions on the *Analects* and the *Book of Doc-
> uments* from a teacher, memorizing one thousand characters each
> day. When the classics were understood clearly and his virtues were
> formed, he took leave of his teachers and went into specialized stud-

ies. Everytime he wielded a pen the mass of readers marveled. His reading became more and more extensive. He was highly talented, but he did not write lightly; eloquent, but he was not talkative—he would remain silent all day long if he was not in suitable company. When he began to talk people reacted unfavorably; but if they heard him out, they became fully convinced in the end. His writings tended to be received in the same way. And so were his conduct and his way of serving his superiors. (*LTW*, 1:137)

The glorification of the self continues unabated. He was discriminating in the choice of friends, "Although his friends might be humble in station and young in age, as long as they transcended the common he would associate with them" (1:138). Those whom he shunned became resentful and "fabricated stories on the basis of his minor faults, thus trying to undermine him. He never attempted any self-defense, nor did he hate the rumor mongers" (ibid.). He was upright in office, uncorrupted by luxury, unbowed in poverty, contented in retirement. He even takes pride in his self-effacement: "He often examined himself, but never stooped to self-display. He strove to construct a foundation on integrity, but considered shameful any attempt to gain fame through talents. In any assembly he would talk only when asked; and during audiences with governors and generals he would not speak out of turn" (ibid.).

As an autobiographer, Wang Ch'ung's greatest advantage over Ssu-ma Ch'ien and T'ao Ch'ien—each a pioneer in a subgenre, is his freedom from historiography. Ssu-ma was too much a historian to adopt a personal voice while T'ao's choice of form and narrative stance imposed severe limitations on the presentation of the self. Wang, on the other hand, never took any interest in the writing of history. Living in a time before the second dynastic history was written, he could still write about his own life without having to contend with the model of the *chuan*, which had not yet achieved its dominance over autobiography, documented in the preceding chapter. Furthermore, as a philosopher in the mold of the ancient schools, when a hundred flowers were truly blooming, he wrote with few inhibitions. To him, personal observation and reasoning were more important than precedents, conventions, or secondhand reports. He took his contemporaries to task for their failure to rely on their own knowledge. "Those who narrate events love antiquity and despise the contemporary, value what they hear but slight what they see. The debaters talk about the past and the men of letters write about the distant: the wonders of the contemporary world are never cited and the unusual events that are occurring today are not recorded."[4] It was this kind of

---

[4] *Lun-heng chi-chieh* (*Balanced Discussions* with collected commentaries), ed. Liu P'an-sui, 2 vols. (Taipei: Shih-chieh shu-chü, 1962), 1:384.

independence of mind, reinforced by a contentious iconoclasm, that led to the first untrammeled autobiographical expression in China.

The next author who wrote a substantially autobiographical preface was Ts'ao P'ei (187–226), Emperor Wen of the Wei. In contrast to Wang Ch'ung's failures, Ts'ao inherited his father's hegemony and ruled as the first emperor of the Wei. Like his father and younger brother, Ts'ao P'ei also distinguished himself as a man of letters. His main prose work, the *Tien-lun*, is no longer extant except for two sections, one of which is the *tzu-hsü*. Curiously, the preface says nothing about his book. Nor does it include a genealogy, which is understandable because his father rose from very plebeian beginnings. It concentrates on his own excellence in a variety of things: horsemanship, archery, swordsmanship, and other martial arts. His self-applause, which even exceeded that of Wang Ch'ung, led him to record episodes with almost fictional details, an innovation that did not reappear in Chinese autobiography for another fourteen centuries. The episode that he seemed to be most proud of is his victory in a fencing match. One day in his youth he was drinking with his cronies, and among them was the great swordsman of the time, General Teng Chan.

> I discussed swordsmanship with them for a while and said to Teng Chan: "You, my general, are not correct in your method. I have been fond of the sword for a long time and, furthermore, I have mastered the use of it." Thereupon the general requested that we have a match. At that time, intoxicated and flustered, we were just in the middle of chewing sugarcanes. We each took hold of a cane and went down to the yard. In just a few moves I hit him thrice on the arm. The spectators all burst out in laughter. Chan was unconvinced and asked for another round. I said: "My method emphasizes speed. Therefore it is easier to hit the arm than the face." "Let us have another round," Chan said. I knew he would wait for an opportunity to take me by surprise, so I feigned a deep thrust. Responding, he moved forward. I turned around on my heel and hit him right in the forehead. Everybody was amazed. (*LTW*, 1:155–56)

Another innovation, the use of the first person throughout the piece, is a departure from historical narrative. In the end the self-assured emperor does pay his respects to historiography when he closes his autobiographical account by saying that, "as for whether I have been able to convert the ignorant with my intelligence, rouse the timid with my bravery, treat people with kindness, and show generosity to those below me, I leave to the good historians of posterity" (1:157). The statement, coming at the end of the portrait of a private individual with all his innocent complacencies and successes—even his mastery of a parlor game is mentioned—can be read as a tacit recognition of the boundary between *wen* and *shih*: when writing about himself a man of letters should concentrate on the personal, leaving the public man to the biographers.

Next to the piece by Ssu-ma Ch'ien, by far the longest autobiographical *tzu-hsü* was written by Ko Hung (250?–330?), the Taoist philosopher and occultist. Running to roughly forty-five hundred characters, it constitutes the fiftieth and last chapter of the second or Confucian section of his *Pao-p'u tzu*—the first section is a compendium of Taoist theories and practices. It is clear that when he wrote the piece he had in mind the precedents set by Wang Ch'ung and Ts'ao P'ei, for he made references to his predecessors in describing his own life. They, however, were definitely not his models when he elaborated on his illustrious lineage; his pride and piety were more akin to those of the dynastic historians. Several of his forebears were great warriors, and a few gained noble titles and fiefdoms on account of their military exploits. The family, however, declined with the death of Ko Hung's father, and the orphan at the age of thirteen had to support himself as a farmhand. But long before then Ko Hung had already displayed commendable precociousness—a topos he shared not only with Wang Ch'ung and Ts'ao P'ei but many subjects of Chinese biographies. "Inert and slow-witted, Hung has few hobbies. In his childhood he did not throw tiles or engage in wrestling—he never played with other boys. Nor did he ever take an interest in cockfights, dog or horse races, or boxing" (*LTW*, 1:170).

Poverty and independence, so characteristic of his youth, are the two themes that run through the rest of his life. "As a man Hung was rustic and obtuse. Inarticulate and ugly, he never tried to justify himself in words or embellish his appearance. His hats and shoes were worn and dirty, and sometimes he was in rags, but he did not feel ashamed" (1:161). "His clothes were not equal to the cold, the roof of his house leaked, he could not eat to satiation, and his name did not travel beyond his gate—all these nevertheless did not trouble him" (1:162). Anticipating T'ao Ch'ien and the followers of Master Five Willows, Ko goes on to elaborate the life of lofty reclusion. "As he was too poor to have servants, the fences and walls surrounding his house were unmended, thorns and brambles filled the yard and weeds blocked the steps. He could not go out the door without pushing aside tree branches; on entering the house he always brushed against grass" (ibid.). As a self-made and self-reliant man he named the books he read but not his teachers; he rose to high official positions, but there was no mention of an apprenticeship. Much of his claim to poverty and independence is a necessary element of the other-worldliness that he, as a Taoist adept, had to cultivate. At the same time he stresses his ability in his official career for, as the structure of his book indicates, he is at once a Taoist and a Confucian.

Following the precedent of Ts'ao P'ei our Taoist warrior takes pride in his acquisition of martial abilities. "As archery is one of the six Confucian arts and can be used for self-defense or to capture birds and beasts, Hung studied it. When he was once pursued by enemy cavalry he shot his arrows without a miss, killing two men and one horse, thus escaping with his life" (1:171). An emperor may not need to record his full-dress military campaigns himself—historians presumably would record such public and official facts—but the mundane successes of a Taoist adept might quickly be forgotten. Mindful of his own military heritage, Ko Hung had one more reason to record his own daring feats, especially the kind of achievement in organized warfare that had brought glory to his ancestors.

> There was once a victory over a detachment of the enemy forces, who left behind mountains of coins, silk, and other valuables. Soldiers under other commanders all lay down their arms and collected the spoils. Carts followed one another and carrying poles almost joined. Hung ordered his troops not to leave their positions without permission. A few of them disobeyed and came back with loot. Hung had them executed immediately as a warning to the rest. As a result none under his command dared to repeat the offense. Just as Hung expected, all of a sudden several hundred enemy soldiers who had concealed themselves burst out and launched a fierce attack. Since most of the troops were absent from their positions, there was no resistance. Furthermore, as the horses and men were heavily laden, there was no longer the will to fight. Consequently the army panicked and scattered, with many dead or prostrate with injuries. The day was almost lost. Only the troops under Hung's command remained intact, their equipment undamaged. That they were able to rescue the rest of the army from a complete rout was largely Hung's doing. (*LTW*, 1:166–67)

The contradiction between the otherworldliness of a Taoist recluse and the vanity of a brilliant man of affairs was not resolved or even acknowledged. In a sense his life is reflected in his book, whose two disparate parts—the inner section and the outer section, as he labeled them—are without a unifying theme or integrated framework. But it was, as the autobiography shows, a most varied and full life, even though the inner man is never revealed. Unlike the self-accounts that many Buddhists and Neo-Confucians were to make from the late thirteenth century on, his is not at all a *Bildungsroman* or spiritual autobiography. It is too early to expect, even from someone who asserts a mastery of the secrets of longevity and alchemy, a perception of change or development, a willingness to report on internal transformations.

AUTHORIAL SELF-ACCOUNTS
INDEPENDENT OF BOOKS

All the authorial self-accounts we have discussed so far are organic parts of books: each of them exists as a preface, postface, or chapter of a book. Writers who were not authors of books soon began to make use of this form and wrote about themselves. Feng Yen, a first-century man of great military and literary talents, is known to have written an independent *tzu-hsü*, which has not survived. The earliest extant specimen was written by Ts'ao Mao (241–260), the grandson of Ts'ao P'ei. His brief self-account is no more than a record of his auspicious birth. The next author, Chiang Yen (444–505), wrote a longer piece, but even though his text is labeled *tzu-hsü*, it differs very little in style or content from a typical *chuan* in a dynastic history. In fact his autobiographical piece has been absorbed without much change into his biography in the *Nan-shih* (History of the Southern Dynasties).

Another near-contemporary composition written by Liu Chün (463–522) is very short: except for a brief sketch of his life at the beginning, his *tzu-hsü* is no more than a detailed comparison between himself and Feng Yen, also known as Feng Ching-t'ung.

> I have compared myself to Feng Ching-t'ung: we are alike on three points and differ on four. What are they? Ching-t'ung's heroic talent was unexcelled by his contemporaries, and his resolution was as strong as metal or stone. Although I am not up to his greatness, we are alike in integrity and bravery. This is our first similarity. Ching-t'ung lived under a brilliant monarch who restored the dynasty but never employed him; I myself was also rejected by a great emperor. This is our second similarity. Ching-t'ung had a wife so jealous of other women that she would not admit any into the household to do the chores, while I am married to a shrew who has also brought great difficulties to the family. This is our third similarity. (*LTW*, 1:7)

He goes on to list their dissimilarities and ends his short *tzu-hsü* with the last one of them. "Ching-t'ung has aways been admired by the notable worthies. The redolence of his fame becomes stronger with time. I am, on the other hand, quiet and invisible, not known to my contemporaries. Once I am gone, my name shall perish just like autumn weeds. This is our fourth difference. Therefore I have striven to write my own account for those among posterity who might be interested" (*LTW*, 1:8).

One may wonder why Liu Chün sought self-definition almost entirely through comparing himself with another person, a relatively minor fig-ure in the vast gallery of history who, separated from him by five centu-ries, was hardly an object for emulation. The most likely reason is that in the sixth century it was still too early for a would-be autobiographer to venture into the enterprise unabashed and unapologetic. Pretexts or excuses were needed. Liu Chün could defend his autobiographical act by the fact that he was not taking a liberty but merely following a strict precedent. If Feng Ching-t'ung was justified in writing about his life, then Liu, having lived a life so similar, was also justified in writing, if not a full-dress autobiography, at least about their similarities. His fear of oblivion, a sentiment frequently uttered by Chinese autobiographers before and after, was one more justification for doing something unusual.

LIU CHIH-CHI (661–721)

If Liu Chün's practice was no more than imitative, he had his own imitator two centuries later in Liu Chih-chi, the foremost Chinese historiographer. Near the end of the *tzu-hsü* chapter in his *Shih-t'ung* (Universals in history) Liu Chih-chi, citing Liu Chün's comparison of himself to Feng Yen as a precedent, launches into a detailed comparison of himself with Yang Hsiung (53 B.C.–A.D.18), a Han scholar whose authorial self-account was, like Feng Yen's, already lost by the seventh century. The comparison, like its predecessor, ends with a self-effacing somber note: Liu Chih-chi, while noting that both he and Yang Hsiung failed to impress their respective contemporaries with their writings, fears that his book, unlike Yang Hsiung's, will be rejected by posterity and thus sink into oblivion.[5]

As befits a historiographer, the remainder of his self-account is modeled more on the postface to the Grand Historian's *Shih chi* in that Liu Chih-chi discusses how he came to write his masterpiece. But unlike Ssu-ma Ch'ien and the three other dynastic historians who wrote *tzu-hsü*, Liu dispenses with genealogy and begins with his childhood.

> As a child I received instruction from my father and had an early exposure to the classics. When I was a little older I was taught the *Book of Documents* in the ancient-script version. As I was troubled by the text, which I found difficult and vexatious, I was unable to chant or memorize. I could not master it even though I was frequently beaten. In the meantime my father was explaining to my older brothers the *Tso chuan* version of the *Spring and Autumn Annals*. When I heard him I dropped the book I was supposed to study and listened. Every time he finished his session I would take over and expound the lesson for my older brothers. I sighed and said to myself, "If all the books were like this, I would not be as slow as I have

---

[5] *Shih-t'ung t'ung-shih* (*Universals in History* with collected annotations), ed. P'u Ch'i-lung (Taipei: Shih-chieh shu-chü, 1962), pp. 140–41; hereafter referred to as *Shih-t'ung*.

been." Impressed, my father began to teach me the *Tso chuan* and in a year's time I finished reading and memorizing it. I was then just twelve years of age. Although my comprehension of my father's explanations was by no means profound, I understood the general idea of the book. My father and older brothers wanted me to read all the commentaries on the book so as to achieve a thorough mastery of this Classic. I declined on the ground that this book did not cover the events that had occurred since the death of Confucius. Instead I begged that I might be allowed to read other books of history, thus broadening my knowledge of the field. (*Shih-t'ung*, p. 138)

In contrast to his model, Ssu-ma Ch'ien, and all other writers of authorial self-accounts, Liu Chih-chi takes an interest in describing his own intellectual development as a historiographer. No other Chinese autobiographer up to this time had a sense of continuous growth, moving gradually to maturity. Liu does not conceal his inauspicious beginnings as a student, nor does he ignore the intermediate steps that led from a boy's stumbling upon his future calling to his becoming a great historiographer. He gives a systematic and coherent account of how his natural affinity for history brought him to a thorough and far-ranging reading of all types of writings, extending even to books of anecdotes and fiction. His keen interest in reasoning and consistency, which he had displayed since his early youth, sharpened his critical faculties and made him aware of the errors of this or that historical work. He tried his hand at history writing as an offical in the National Bureau of History, but the jealousy of his colleagues and ignorance of his superiors prevented him from putting into practice his ideas as to how history should be written. It is disappointment that led him to the writing of the *Shih-t'ung*. Following the critical tradition that had obtained in other fields during the previous five centuries, his own book was a response to "the historians among my contemporaries who have been errant. I intend to clarify the goals and purposes of historical writings and examine exhaustively their styles and forms. Although my book is mainly concerned with historiography, its ramifications will reach all directions and include everything from the Way of the kings down to fundamental principles of ethics" (ibid., p. 140).

    With the scope of his book so broad, it is only natural that he should, as he did, devote a chapter to a critical examination of authorial self-accounts. The inclusion was all the more understandable in the light of several additional but related facts. Four authors of dynastic histories written up to his time had each included an authorial self-account in their works, thus making it a fitting topic for historiographical scrutiny. Its affinity with biography, the very staple of Chinese history writing, further insured its place in Liu's book. That Liu himself also wrote an authorial self-account as a chapter of his book is the final indication that he could not possibly have excluded the topic from his masterpiece.

What is strange is that no other Chinese historiographer or literary critic ever broached this subject again until the present century, as if Liu's judgment were final, allowing not even a slight modification. This fact coupled with the great prestige of his book insured the continued impact of his ideas on Chinese autobiography for the next several centuries. A close reading of the chapter is then in order.

Although the chapter is entitled *Hsü-chuan*, the same term that the dynastic historian Pan Ku used to label the postface to his *Han shu*, the topic is broadly conceived, for included in the discussion are practically all the authorial self-accounts we have seen so far.[6] Liu Chih-chi makes no distinction between the pieces on the basis of their different names. Nor does he separate self-accounts as parts of books from those independent of books. In view of the inclusiveness of the topic, what he had in mind was not much different from what we would call autobiography, although it must be said that Liu made no reference, in this chapter or elsewhere in the book, to the two still-fledging subgenres, autonecrology and pseudobiography in the style of T'ao Ch'ien's *Biography of Master Five Willows* (*Wu-liu hsien-sheng chuan*). That it was Liu and not a literary critic who wrote the first and, until this century, the only discourse on autobiography is another indication of the power that historiography exercised in traditional China. The chapter begins with what may be called the prototype. "As for the self-account made by an author, did it not originate during middle antiquity? When Ch'ü Yüan in the beginning section of his *Li sao* described his clan and genealogy, his birth and his naming, and then his early life, it was the beginning of self-account" (ibid., p. 122).

Technically Liu Chih-chi is correct in claiming Ch'ü Yüan (340?–278? B.C.) as the originator of the self-account. If an author in subsequent centuries wanted to say anything at all about himself in the preface or postface to his book, he would most likely, *at the outset*, follow the procedure initiated by Ch'ü Yüan. But upon closer examination the rest of the *Li sao* resembles very little the other *tzu-hsü* cited by Liu. Written in verse, narrated throughout in the first person, and couched in a highly allegorical and ornate language, the piece purports to tell of the journey of the narrator-protagonist through mythic lands in search of the ideal woman or goddess, he himself having been rejected by his lord who, weak and

---

[6] The self-account by Liu Chün, which Liu Chih-chi cites as his own precedent when he compares himself to Yang Hsiung in his own *tzu-hsü*, is not mentioned in this chapter. The piece is, however, named in another chapter when he deprecates various writers as unfit for the serious task of writing history. Here the stern historiographer does not even spare his precedent but pronounces Liu Chün's *tzu-hsü* to be "excessively loose and petty," *Shih-t'ung*, p. 119.

faithless, had listened to evil slanderers. As our hero, clad in exotic flowers and fragrant leaves, roamed far and wide, riding in a chariot pulled by
a team of dragons and attended by the Thunder God and other divinities,
he only encountered more bitter disappointments. The piece ends with
the hero's longing for home and a hint of his intention to end his sufferings by drowning himself.

It may seem puzzling that Liu, so stern in his criticism of historians
who gave credence to the fanciful or supernatural, should have counte-
nanced Ch'ü Yüan's piece. Perhaps the great historiographer's uncharacteristic tolerance for the fantast was motivated by the emerging evaluation
of Ch'ü Yüan, beginning in early Han and culminating during the
Southern Sung, not as an imaginative poet but as a paragon of Confucian
virtues, a loyal and righteous minister who was exiled as a result of his
brave remonstrances to a misguided king. A more subtle reason may have
been the fact, nowhere mentioned in the *Shih-t'ung* or discussed by the
commentators on the book, that Liu, having traced his family line to the
royal house of Ch'u in a pursuit separate from his historiographical activities, discovered that he himself was no other than a collateral descendant
of the great poet-loyalist.[7] What greater claim could he have had to be the
authority on self-account than the fact that a collateral ancestor of his was
the very progenitor of the genre?

Liu's uncharacteristic critical tolerance in this case could also be explained by his placing the account of the mythic journey beyond the pale
of history, for he hastens to add that "Ssu-ma Hsiang-ju [179–117 B.C.],
however, was the first one to write a self-account as biography (*chuan*)"
(ibid.). The keyword here, I think, is *chuan*. As we have seen again and
again, once a Chinese author attempted to write a biography or anything
similar, or even a travel account, he would have to answer to historiography. Living in an age prior to the ascendance of historiography and
drawing on the folk traditions of Ch'u, Ch'ü Yüan the poet was free from
most of the constraints enumerated above.

Although Ch'ü Yüan's use of first-person narration in an account of
adventures was almost never followed in Chinese prose fiction,[8] many of

---

[7] *Hsin T'ang shu* (New dynastic history of the T'ang) (Po-na ed.), 132:1b.

[8] The only premodern Chinese prose fiction that I know of in which the narrator and the
protagonist coincide is the T'ang tale *Yu-hsien k'u* (The grotto of playful goddesses), probably written by the popular author Chang Wen-ch'eng (657?–730). That this type of fictional narration is otherwise unknown in traditional China and that the tale quickly went
into total oblivion in China but survived in Japan should give us another view of the severe
circumscription imposed on all Chinese first-person narratives. Some of the constrains discussed above seem to obtain in other fields as well and persist even to this day. The *Ichroman*
has flourished in modern Japan but failed to take root in China, in spite of the efforts of
Japanese-educated writers such as Yü Ta-fu. To current Chinese dissident literature the lack
of a suitable narrative tradition poses an obstacle perhaps as great as the lack of privacy.

the themes of his life and his writing have been echoed in subsequent *tzu-hsü* and other types of autobiography. He was mentioned by Ssu-ma Ch'ien—who included a sympathetic biography of him in the *Shih chi*—in both the *tzu-hsü* and the autobiographical letter to Jen An, where the Grand Historian described his own grievances and drew parallels between the two lives, both unjustly ravaged by their sovereigns. Ch'ü Yüan's flight from an unsympathetic officialdom and his complaints of being misunderstood by the world anticipate autobiographers like T'ao Ch'ien who professed a contempt for the mundane and found solace in nature. His wanderlust as well as his endless quest anticipate two of the major themes we shall see in late Ming autobiographies. Perhaps after all Liu Chih-chi was right in placing his own collateral forebear at the head of the chapter.

Ch'ü Yüan is the only author who escapes censure from Liu: all the others are taken to task for various offenses. Genealogy seems to be the most common failing that Liu found among the autobiographers. For historians who include an authorial self-account in their books, Liu does not think they should trace back their line beyond the time frame covered in their works. Some are criticized for exaggerating the accomplishments of their forebears, others for falsely claiming descent from illustrious clans or legendary kings. On this point Liu displays the full measure of indignation of a truth-seeking historian, for his list of culprits includes names not associated with autobiographical writing. He advises authors to leave the genealogy section blank if they have nothing worthwhile to say. That in his own *tzu-hsü* he says not a word about his ancestry does not at all mean that he was not interested in genealogy or that he could not boast of royal descent. According to his biography in the *Hsin T'ang shu* (New dynastic history of the T'ang), he wrote a history of the Liu clan as well as a revision of his family genealogy. His research not only established his descent from the royal house of Ch'u, as we have mentioned above, but traced his line as well as the line of the Han imperial house all the way to a legendary figure in high antiquity, Lu Chung, who was worshipped in later generations as the God of Fire. His own great interest in genealogy may have contributed to his harsh judgment of other practitioners of the pious craft, less scrupulous or more amateurish than he, but it is still puzzling that none of his research went into his own authorial self-account. Perhaps he draws a line between genealogy and historiography. At any rate his strong feeling on this issue is sustained to the very end of the chapter, when he states that "no spirits or ghosts would want to enjoy the sacrifices if the offering is not addressed to their true names, and it is a perversion of virtue to worship the ancestors of others. Those who write autobiographies should clearly understand this truth. If one leaves a blank space because of lack of information, what harm is there?" (*Shih-t'ung*, p. 123).

Liu Chih-chi is equally stern in his criticism of autobiographers who boast of themselves. A modest form of self-expression he will tolerate, for he quotes with approval a few instances from the *Analects* where Confucius speaks of himself or encourages his disciples to express their wishes. But he finds faults in almost all autobiographers. "Writers of self-accounts, beginning with Yang Hsiung, all indulged in exaggeration. When it came to writers such as Emperor Wen of the Wei, Fu Hsüan (217–278), T'ao Mei, and Ko Hung, they went even beyond that. Whatever good deeds or talents they had, however minor or trivial, they insisted on recording in detail and with great verbosity" (ibid.). The worst offender was Wang Ch'ung, who committed the double sin of boasting of himself at the expense of his ancestors.

> Wang Ch'ung in the self-account section of his *Lun heng* tells about how his forebears were despised by the local people on account of their wrongdoings. He then compares himself to the two sage kings who had evil fathers. Now when one talks about his ancestors in a self-account he should be mainly concerned with enhancing the family's fame and distinguishing his ancestors. If there were none worthy of mention, he may simply leave this section blank. As for lavishing praises on oneself while heaping insults on one's ancestors, how is such behavior any different from a son's testifying against his father for stealing a sheep[9] or a student calling his mother by her name?[10] We must censure such behavior in the name of Confucianism and consider it as an act of unfiliality, the worst of all felonies. (*Shih-t'ung*, pp. 122–23)

In the Confucian canon truth is never absolute and the whole truth can or should be withheld under certain circumstances. Next to filial piety, propriety sometimes takes precedence over candor. Or rather discretion and reticence must be, in the view of Liu Chih-chi, exercised by autobiographers.

> What should a self-account be? If the author conceals his shortcomings and presents his good deeds without falsification, then what he writes is a veritable record. Yet Ssu-ma Hsiang-ju in his self-account mentions his unlawful acquisition of his wife Cho while traveling in

[9] Alludes to *Analects* 13:18:2 where Confucius said that fathers and sons should conceal each other's misdeeds.

[10] Alludes to a story in the *Chan-kuo ts'e* (Intrigues of the Warring States) SPTK, 7:48a. The student, led astray by his long study abroad, was rebuked by his mother for his disrespectful way of addressing her. For a translation of the episode see *Chan-kuo ts'e*, trans. J. I. Crump, Jr. (Oxford: Oxford University Press, 1970), p. 431.

Lin-ch'iung. What the *Spring and Autumn Annals* would have treated with reticence he boasts about. Although the episode may well have been true, there is nothing commendable about it. Is it not shameful to include such an episode in a self-account? (Ibid., p. 122)

Strong opinions expressed by powerful arbiters such as Liu Chih-chi cannot fail to exercise their influence on the course of subsequent events. One cannot, however, always point with certainty to this or that specific effect of Liu's work on such an amorphous and elusive—one might almost say furtive, at least until the sixteenth century—genre as autobiography. The impact of Liu's criticism of Wang Ch'ung and Ssu-ma Hsiang-ju for their indiscretions may have been an important factor in discouraging subsequent autobiographers from revealing either their own misconduct or that of their forebears. There were hardly any written confessions during the next eight centuries, and until the seventeenth century no writer ever admitted, with any specificity, to a serious wrongdoing. The gradual consolidation of Confucian norms during the Sung was probably a greater factor in enforcing autobiographical reticence, but Liu's voice may have been decisive during the transition. Similarly, autobiographers also tended to be more modest about their virtues in subsequent centuries, but the seventeenth century again saw radical departures from the Confucian norm.

Liu's greatest impact may have been in contributing to the decline of the subgenre itself. He finds fault with virtually every specimen that he cites, and his verdicts are delivered with destructive forcefulness. Elsewhere in his book, when he mentions autobiographies in passing while holding forth on other topics, he never has a good word to say but expresses his disapproval in four instances (pp. 119 and 229). His own austere example is equally forbidding. A perfect model of probity and organization, confident but not boastful, it does not invite wide following, for very few subsequent writers had a life story like his to tell: a clearly defined path, even though sometimes twisting or turning in response to fortuities, leading to a glorious destination.

If Liu's formalization of the rules seems to have signified the beginning of the end of the game, it is because authorial self-account had better fortune earlier and thrived much more than we have shown. The extant works represent only a portion of what once must have been a sizable corpus. Several of the specimens mentioned by Liu are among the lost autobiographies; these include the one by Yang Hsiung, to whom Liu compares himself in his own *tzu-hsü*, and the confession of Ssu-ma Hsiang-ju, the progenitor of the subgenre (if we do not count the mythologue Ch'ü Yüan). When Liu Hsüan (544?–611?) wrote a short autobiography—cited disparagingly by our bilious historiographer in the chapter on historical talent (p. 119)—in the hope that his name would not perish with his flesh, he mentioned four illustrious predecessors.[11] Two of them were the same people just mentioned; the other two, Ma Jung (79–166) and Cheng Hsüan (127–200), were both great masters of the emerging Confucian school. The autobiographies of the four probably perished during the decline of the T'ang when the capital was repeatedly ravaged. Tung-fang Shuo (b. 161 B.C.), the celebrated court jester, is believed by Liu Chih-chi (p. 229) to have also made a contribution, albeit inferior, to the genre. Had these works, known to have been lost, actually been preserved, we would not only have a truer measure of the extent of autobiographical activities during Han times but a much greater sense of the variety in the background of the autobiographers. That these works written by prominent men should have vanished is an enigma of the first order, and an attempt at solving it may throw new light on the nature of the genre.

A useful hint for the solution can be found in Liu Chih-chi's book. In discussing the sources of the dynastic histories of the Former and the Later Han, Liu asserts that several biographies in the official history were nothing but copies of autobiographies written by the subjects (p. 229). Apparently at the time when Liu wrote he still had access to several of the works—in their original form—that are no longer extant. As for the biography of the court jester Tung-fang Shuo in the *Han shu*, Liu also believed it to be adopted verbatim from an autobiography, not on the basis of comparison of the two texts, because the putative autobiography did not exist—nor was there any record that it ever existed—but on the basis of the biography's style and content. From Liu's comments we may draw the inference that if autobiographies disappeared from sight, both prior to and since Liu, at least some of them did so because they were absorbed into official histories as biographies. We may even go further and suggest that the number of "lost" autobiographies, autobiographies that went by the above route, is much greater than Liu and other sources indicate. The suggestion is based largely on an analogy with the fate of the vast majority of Chinese biographies.

Biography was more popular than all other types of prose, but it was also the most perishable. We have a clue as to the huge number of biographies that have not survived from records of them in various bibliographies, references to and quotations from them in commentaries to dynastic histories and other extant books, and proliferation of the subgenres that had once existed. Before the invention of printing the fate of any book was of course precarious, but biography in China was more vulnerable because it was often treated as no more than raw material for offical

---

[11] *LTW*, 2:532.

historiography. Once a piece was made use of—frequently adopted al-most verbatim—by the compilers of dynastic histories or local gazetteers, there was no longer any need for the preservation of the original texts. The lack of respect for the textual integrity of biography was further ag-gravated by the widespread and humble service performed by biography as part of the ritual for honoring the dead, as we discussed in the section on necrology. In this connection thousands of draft biographies were written each year by the children or friends of the dead subjects, to be used as sources for the finished products penned by eminent writers of the day. After the processes were completed the drafts were discarded.[12]

If biography was so often treated as provisional and dispensable, wor-thy of no more than a temporary existence, to be consigned to the dustbin of history once its service was no longer needed, how would its close kin autobiography fare in such an environment? If anything, autobiography was even more vulnerable. Biography at least had legitimacy, with its every subgenre recognized by critics or at least anthology makers, while autobiography remained shadowy and unclaimed, largely ignored by an-thologists. Occasionally one or two specimens did stray into an anthol-ogy, but they did so always in the guise of biography and were housed indiscriminately with their kin. If for any reason they were discarded, as were many of them, we believe, they would be even less lamented. An autobiography that appeared as a preface or postface or chapter of a book would live or die with the book, but autobiographies independent of books did not fare better than biographies in terms of survival.

Whatever the actual number of lost autobiographies may be, that so few survived could not but have detrimental consequences for the devel-opment of the genre. A greater survival rate would have provided more models for later generations. The importance of precedence being what it was—we have seen quite a few autobiographers citing predecessors to fortify their resolve in an enterprise they were not completely comfort-able with—the *Bildungsroman* might have had a much earlier genesis in China if the self-accounts of Ma Jung and Cheng Hsüan, the two great masters of the Confucian school that was emerging during the Later Han, had not vanished. Similarly, the example of the great court jester might have broadened the range and variety of the genre, encouraging the less conventional to try their hands at a craft largely reserved for a small elite. Conversely, some would-be autobiographers may have been discouraged from the activity when they realized, judging from the fate of ealier spec-imens, that what they might write would probably not survive.

We cannot leave this topic without mentioning one autobiographical innovation in Liu Chih-chi's own *tzu-hsü*. Fairly early in the narrative,

---

[12] For a lament over the fate of the drafts see Chang Hsüeh-ch'eng, *Chang-shih i-shu*, 2:23.

after the section on his apprenticeship and right before he cites the example of Confucius as the great founding father of historiography and
wonders, with the required modesty, whether a "petty person" like himself could dare to continue the pratice, he mentions his youthful need for
camaraderie, for congenial souls with whom he could discuss things.
Only rather late in life he met Hsü Chien (659–729) of Tung-hai, and the
affinity that developed between the two he describes as comparable to the
great friendships celebrated in ancient history. He goes on to name six
more friends. "Similarly, we approved and admired each other's words
and ideas, and our friendship was based on our sharing of principles. We
always felt free to unburden ourselves to one another" (ibid., p. 139). Liu
does not further characterize them but it is significant that all seven, well
known for their courage and competence, had impeccable records in government service. Like him, each enjoys a niche in the biographical section
of the dynastic history, an award they very well deserve for, again like
Liu, all but one of them labored at one time or another in the National
Bureau of History.

If the naming of friends had no precedent in the earlier autobiographies
that now survive, it is an innovation with no shortage of imitators. As we
have seen above, even a misanthrope like the monk Chen-i mentions in
his autonecrology one bosom friend. Several obscure autobiographers
cite the most illustrious names of the time, basking in reflected glory.
Others, such as Ch'ien Shih-yang (1554–1610), divide their friends in categories. The father of the well-known writer Ch'ien Ch'ien-i (1582–
1664), he compares himself in his autobiography to Liu Chün and Feng
Yen as fellow sufferers on three accounts. As for friends, he chooses carefully: one he fears, four are literary friends, and two are drinking companions.[13] Other autobiographers, less discriminating, boast of long lists.
Wang Yü (1204–1234) during his short life acquired fifty friends. After he
enumerates them in his autobiography he hastens to add that "their names
were written down at random: no order of any kind was intended."[14] For
good measure he amends the list with two "mind acqaintances," people
he never met but knew indirectly.

The most touching testimony to the profound need for friendship is
found in the deathbed autobiography of Huang Hsing-tseng (1490–1540),
narrated almost entirely in terms of how Huang went through life being
admired or befriended. Even at the age of eight he on several occasions
impressed prominent scholars of the day and formed friendships with
them in spite of great differences in age. At the end of the enumerations
of his associations with the high and mighty and the repeated listings of

[13] *MTW*, p. 351.
[14] *LTW*, 2:292.

friends, he leaves the world with only one regret, that on account of illness he was not able to reply to or adequately receive all the correspondents and visitors numbering more than two thousand.[15] When Liu Chih-chi the innovator quoted Confucius on friendship, saying that "the man of virtue is never solitary: he will always have friends,"[16] he struck a chord that has resonated down through the centuries.

OTHER SELF-ACCOUNTS

If Liu as an autobiographer has made some contribution to the development of the genre, as a critic he must bear some responsibility for the decline of the authorial self-account. In any case, authors of books did not talk about themselves during the next eight centuries as much as in the preceding eight, even though they continued to write prefaces or postfaces. On the other hand, self-account independent of a book, seemingly the most promising of all subgenres of autobiography, was also the most fragile. Its lack of formal rules or limitations and the freedom that it afforded every practitioner were, paradoxically, its undoing. In the premodern world a would-be autobiographer could seldom do without precedents, pretexts, or even subterfuge. He could hardly set out to write about himself blatantly or unabashedly. This is why self-account, in spite of its early beginnings and its anticipation of the modern genre, did not flourish. Those whose autobiographical urge was irrepressible seem to have felt more comfortable with other, newer and more restrictive, forms. They increasingly turned to pseudobiography, which allows the autobiographer to hide behind both a mock generic form and an elusive persona; or to autonecrology—the excuse for writing one was easy to establish; or to annalistic autobiography, with its glorious beginnings and simple, unambiguous format. All the upstarts shared one advantage over self-account in their close associations with biography. If each suffered from the particular limitations inherent in the subgenre of biography from which it was derived, they all, precisely because of such derivation, afforded the autobiographer a ready-made format, a large pool of possible models, and a sense of legitimacy that in premodern China usually sustained imitators.

After Liu Chih-chi, self-accounts were fewer and farther between, and we shall mention just three of them in this chapter. Feng Tao (882–954), living in a period of dynastic instability and great chaos, managed to survive and even prosper by shifting his allegiances from one short-lived dynasty to another. Near the end of his long and successful life he wrote an

[15] *MTW*, pp. 290–93.
[16] *Analects* 4:25.

autobiography entitled *Ch'ang-lo Lao tzu-hsü* (Self-Account of the Old Man of Perpetual Happiness). Although the title—with its use of an alternate name—recalls Master Five Willows and thus suggests an affinity with the subgenre of pseudobiography, in the narrative there is no attempt to create a persona at an ironic distance from the autobiographer. The piece is not much more than a straightforward list of all the sovereigns that he has served and all the high offices and honors that he has been awarded. There is a sense of complacency in enumerating the glories that he has brought to his ancestors and the sinecures that he obtained for his sons but, in contrast to earlier writers of *tzu-hsü*, he hardly boasts of any specific personal triumphs or achievements. Whether or not he was aware of the great offense of disloyalty of which subsequent historians frequently accused him, his autobiography lacks the exuberance of its forerunners and betrays almost unease. The first-person singular is used three times in the first half of the piece while he is making lists; its total absence thereafter is consistent with the increasingly somber tone. As a high official he may have been guilty as charged, but as an autobiographer he does not display impudence or blatancy to the extent that was frequently attributed to him. At any rate his numerous and severe critics during the Sung contributed to the elevation of loyalty as a central issue in autobiography. As we have seen above, it was the sense of loyalty that gave Wen T'ien-hsiang and his imitators the impetus to assume the historian's role and write about their own exemplary lives. None of the survivors of the fall of the Ming could avoid soul searching on this score when they wrote about themselves.

In light of the role of loyalty in the writing of Chinese autobiographies, the circumstances under which the *tzu-hsü* of the grand eunuch Liu Jo-yü (1584–1642?) was written are not without their ironies. Educated and facile with the written word, Liu possessed abilities not often found among inner-court attendants. Therefore he was useful to Wei Chung-hsien, the illiterate but powerful chief eunuch who, enjoying the confidence of a weak sovereign, for several years ruled the country with a ruthlessness unmatched until modern times. He and his cabal were not able to silence the opposition of Confucian officials, many of whom fought and died in the name of loyalty to an uncomprehending emperor.

One of the martyrs was Wei Ta-chung (1575–1625), who in jail wrote an autobiography using the annalistic format favored by loyalists. After the emperor died in 1627, the eunuchs of the Wei Chung-hsien faction, having lost their patron, were brought to justice. Initially Liu was only exiled to work on a state farm, but in 1636 he was sentenced to die for his role in the persecution of Confucian literati. While he was waiting for execution in his cell, could he escape from reminders of the fate of his old enemies who had been tortured to death only a few yards from where he now was? Did he realize that in writing an apology in the shadow of death he was repeating exactly the act that brought posthumous glory to one of his victims?

Liu's apology, entiled *Lei-ch'en tzu-hsü* (Self-Account of an incarcerated vassal), constitutes the last section of his book on life in the palace.[17] The section begins with a very brief mention of his early life: "Jo-yü, the incarcerated vassal, disobeying the instructions of his father and older brother, had himself castrated as the result of a strange dream. He then abandoned Confucian studies and began to read medical books and practiced the teachings on health and longevity. In the *hsin-ch'ou* year [1601] of the Wan-li reign he was admitted into palace service" (*Ming-kung shih,* 8:1a).

Tantalizingly brief as it is, Liu's account of the circumstances that led to the point of no return is the only one that we have from a eunuch's mouth. Liu's humiliations were probably more poignant than those suffered by other members of this powerful but despised group for he, lettered scion of a good family, could easily have had a normal life and a respectable career. If his emphasis on his education and literary functions in the palace betrays a wistfulness for a different career, he clearly identifies himself with the loyal eunuchs he lists early in his self-account, those who remonstrated with impulsive emperors, acted in concert with Confucian ministers during time of crisis, contributed to imperial education, and even shielded innocent officials from the wrathful vengeance of evil prime ministers. Following such illustrious examples, he himself can boast of several occasions when he managed to outmaneuver chief eunuch Wei Chung-hsien or his most trusted lieutenant and thus spare the life or lessen the punishment of a prominent official. For such activities he risked his own life and received many penalties.

Having established a good character reference for himself, he launches into a spirited defense against the most serious charge that brought him the death sentence, the charge that his handwriting was found in an altered document instrumental in the persecution and death of several prominent victims of the reign of terror. His defense apparently failed to sway the judges, for we have no record of his ever leaving prison, even though the death sentence is not known to have been carried out.[18]

When Liu wrote his apologia he probably only hoped, like his predecessors from the Confucian world, for the vindication of history. His reason for writing the book is that, "his family having received great favors from the state for many generations," he must present his views on the

---

[17] *Ming-kung shih* (History of the Ming palace) (Kuo-hsüeh fu-lun she, 1910); hereafter referred to as *Ming-kung shih.* For a bibliographical history of this book see Liu's biography in *DMB,* 1:950–54. The edition I use is inferior but accessible.

[18] See his biography in *DMB.*

present dangers that the country is facing as well as report on "what he heard with his own ears and saw with his own eyes during the last four years of the late emperor, making a clean breast of the total truth without any embellishment" (ibid., 98:4a). His hope is that his writing will insure that "the grievances of the dead will not be forgotten while the living will not be free from the judgment of public opinion. Will those in future generations who take an interest in history, when they realize that all the entanglements described herein are true, not sigh deeply upon closing this book?" (ibid.).

Unlike most Chinese autobiographers, Liu gives his genealogy at the end of his work. Until he wrote the book he had managed to conceal his background, apparently to avoid bringing dishonor to his family. That he should now proceed to tell all is consistent with his earlier protestation of utter truthfulness. Besides, with all his near relatives already dead and the family line coming to an end, the disclosures would embarrass no one. For several generations his family held on to a hereditary military rank in a northern military garrison, and both his father and elder brother Liu Mao-fang rose to be generals on account of their distinguished service. The father, outspoken and upright, fell victim to the machinations of a jealous and cowardly rival. During the first purge of the eunuchs in 1628 Liu Mao-fang was wrongly taken to be the younger brother of another eunuch with the same surname and as a result lost his military post. All the major themes of Liu's autobiography—the example of good eunuchs who have been all but forgotten, loyalty to the throne undiminished by unjust treatment, bravery in the face of overwhelming adversity—seem to manifest themselves in the circumstances surrounding his brother's death. Our author could not have invented a more fitting story. When the Manchu invaders attacked Ch'ang-p'ing in the fall of 1636—just a few months after the autobiographer had received the death sentence—General Liu Mao-fang, responding to the call of a eunuch who was entrusted by the new emperor with the supervision of the military, joined the defenders. The locale of the brother's last action is all the more significant in light of two additional circumstances: it was the site of the Ming imperial tombs and General Liu had commanded the garrison forces there until he was wrongly dismissed. When Ch'ang-p'ing fell both the eunuch and the general perished (*Ming-kung shih*, 8:5a).

Liu Jo-yü the apologist is at his best in the way he concludes what, as he himself admitted earlier, must appear to be a tangled tale in the eyes of future readers. If the blood shed by the brother in the service of the throne was not sufficient to wash away the stain on the honor of the family, the death of the grieving mother within the year should win sympathy for Liu from his readers, if not from his judges. The apology ends with his admission, not of the crimes as charged, but of the unnamed sins against his mother and brother. "Would Heaven ever forgive, ever forgive the sins of the incarcerated vassal's unfiliality and unfraternity?" (ibid., 8:5b).

The age in which Liu lived was one of the worst in Chinese history. His own life story exemplifies much of what was wrong with the times— weak and wrongheaded emperors, reigns of terror imposed by those who had the ear of nominal rulers, defeated and demoralized Confucian ministers, and the resultant increasingly precarious security of the northern borders, where the Liu family held a hereditary garrison post for several generations. Eight years after the battle of Ch'ang-p'ing the Manchus entered Peking and began their conquest of China. Yet Liu lived right in the middle of an age when autobiography flourished more than ever before. Moral and political anarchy may have contributed to the loosening of all conventions and restraints, thus giving self-expression a freer rein. Indeed the fact that a man of Liu's station should have decided to engage in an activity that had hitherto been almost exclusively reserved for the members of the literati is a measure of how much the late Ming differed from earlier times.

In contrast to Liu's times, the Sung dynasty (960–1279) had been in many ways the golden age of China. It was, curiously, also an age in which very few autobiographies were written. Perhaps the climate of the Sung—civility, moderation, tolerance—did not foster either great need for self-justification or license for self-adulation among the mannerly Confucians. Apologies written by prisoners, a type of autobiography of which we have just seen an unusual specimen, began only after the fall of the Sung for the simple reason that no prominent Sung man of letters ever languished in jail. During the first three hundred years of the dynasty, for that matter, no civilian official was ever executed for offending the emperor, nor did any lose his life in the competition for power or in the contention over differences in policy—a record unmatched in world history.

The invention of printing during the Sung led to the wide circulation of books, but bibliomania and prolixity among Sung writers emerged even before printing became readily available. Yet writers, in spite of the great increase in their numbers, left almost no autobiographical prefaces or postfaces. Nor did they tell their life stories elsewhere.[19] The only notable exception is the poetess Li Ch'ing-chao, whose autobiographical postface deserves a close look not so much because it is the only autobiography written by a Chinese woman until fairly recently but because it succeeded, as no other *tzu-hsü* did up to that time, in portraying vividly

[19] For two Sung reminiscences of childhood see my article, "Education of Children during the Sung," *Neo-Confucian Education: The Formative Stage*, eds. Wm. Theodore de Bary and John Chaffee (Berkeley: University of California Press, 1988), pp. 307–24.

a most unusual life, a life exemplifying the most civilized in an era renowned for its civility and refinement.

In the postface to the *Chin shih lu* (A record of stone and metal inscriptions), Li Ch'ing-chao (1084–1151?) tells us, in a language at once vigorous and wistful, of the life that she shared with her husband Chao Ming-
ch'eng (1081–1129). Ardent collectors of books, paintings, and antiques,
the couple enjoyed above all copying or making rubbings of as many of
the inscriptions on stones or bronzes of previous dynasties that they could
obtain. Their idyllic life was rudely interrupted when the Jurchen invaders attacked the Sung capital in 1126. As they fled south they were repeatedly compelled to abandon parts of their vast collection, and after the
death of the husband in 1129 the remnants of their precious belongings
suffered further depletions. Some were left behind by the widow, who
was often barely ahead of the Jurchen marauders, others were lost to loot-
ings, vandalism, and appropriation. Among the very few things that survived was the manuscript of the *Chin shih lu*, the authorship of which she
attributes to her husband, but elsewhere in the postface she makes it clear
that in this enterprise, as in all other undertakings of theirs, she was an
equal partner. The manuscript consisted of two thousand entries, long
sections of commentaries as well as colophons to individual items. Now
with peace reestablished, for the first time enjoying a respite from the
constant search for refuge, Li reexamined the manuscript, recalled the
lost happy days, and wrote the postface.

The occasion afforded Li a perfect opportunity for autobiographical
discourse, for the anthology was not only the result of their collaboration
but the most tangible memento of the perfect union of two kindred spirits
who shared the same antiquarian passion and bookish tastes. This fact,
made clear throughout the postface, could justify the inclusion of her detailed remembrances of their conjugal bliss from the very beginning.

> I was married into the Chao family in the *hsin-ssu* year [1101] of the
> Chien-chung reign. At that time my late father was a vice-director
> in the Ministry of Rites, my father-in-law, who later served as prime
> minister, was the vice-minister of personnel, while my husband,
> then twenty-one, was a student in the National University. Both the
> Chao and Li clans were poor and accustomed to frugality. On the
> first and the fifteenth of each month my husband, after having ob-
> tained leave from the university authorities, would pawn some of his
> clothing to obtain five hundred cash. With the money in hand he
> would walk into the market in the back of the Hsiang-kuo Temple
> and buy stone rubbings and fruit. After he came home we would sit
> next to each other perusing and admiring the texts while slowly

munching the fruit. Contented, we likened ourselves to citizens of an ancient utopia.[20]

The telling of the young couple's halcyon days, deceptively simple and spontaneous, belies its radical departure from a narrative style that hitherto had been dominated by historiography. Here for the first time in Chinese autobiographical discourse we have a representation of a life that may be called entirely private and personal, bordering almost on the whimsical. The key to Li's effectiveness lies in her use of random and seemingly insignificant details, of which the munching of fruit is certainly the most remarkable. With just a few strokes she has succeeded in portraying a young bride—Li was at that time only seventeen by Western reckoning—as a unique individual, at once precocious in her antiquarian interests and childlike in her fondness for fruit. But even then she was not just an echo of her husband, and as their collection of books grew she often held the upper hand in their innocent if pedantic games. Previous *tzu-hsü* writers from time to time emerged triumphant from duels or contests, but Li differs from her predecessors in that her text, whether reflecting the peaceful nature of Sung culture or simply following from her life as a woman in the premodern world, is the first recording of a purely *domestic* or private game, a game without the sting of defeat or cheering spectators.

> I happen to be good in memory. Every evening after dinner we would repair to Kuei-lai Hall for tea. We would play a game by challenging each other to give the answer as to the exact location—at which line, on which page, in which volume, of which book—of a certain allusion. The one who gave the correct answer would drink the first cup of tea. Sometimes the winner laughed so much that the cup held in the hand would be overturned and not a drop of tea drunk. During those days we wished that life would go on forever just like that. (*LTW*, 1:193)

Unmentioned in the text but well-known to her contemporaries is the fact that Li was one of the best writers of *tz'u*-type poetry. The awareness of her own great literary talent, which far exceeded her husband's, must have lain behind the self-confident tone so characteristic of the postface. Some of her poetry—she was capable of a variety of styles—has always been praised by critics for its feminine sensitivity, but unlike her Heian sisters she had no access to a language exclusively reserved for women. When she draws parallels between her life and those of historical figures,

[20] *LTW*, 1:192. The postface is expertly translated and interpreted with sensitivity and depth in Stephen Owen, *Remembrances: The Experience of the Past in Classical Chinese Literature* (Cambridge: Harvard University Press, 1986), pp. 80–98.

the allusions are all to men, not to good wives or virtuous widows. Only when she lists the ways she economized in order to gratify her bibliophilia does she mention one category distinctly associated with her gender. "By nature I am impatient of frills. From the beginning I ate little meat and wore simple clothing. My head is not adorned with bright pearls or green jade, nor my furniture decorated with gilt or embroidery" (ibid., 193–94). But even here her rejection of jewelry sets her apart from most of her sisters.

Since she is the first Chinese woman autobiographer, the question will always remain as to what role her femininity played in the writing of the postface. One could argue that her readiness in reporting her personal life and the circumstantial descriptiveness of the narration owed more to her being a practitioner of *tz'u*-type poetry than to anything else. A *shih* writer often maintains distance and impersonality, while a finer and more direct representation of feelings is expected of the *tz'u*. Being a woman may have paradoxically enabled her to insert so much autobiography into a postface, for ostensibly she writes only about the events in her husband's life that led to the making of the annotated anthology, not about herself. The single most significant fact of her life, her indisputable excellence in *tz'u*-type poetry, is never mentioned. She could, if she must, justify her presence in the narrative because she was a part of the story. We have seen how Li Chih managed to write an unusual autobiography by presenting it as a biography of himself written by a fictitious close friend. Here, similarly, Li Ch'ing-chao is able to afford us such vivid glimpses of herself precisely because ostensibly she is writing only a postface, not an autobiography of herself, nor even a biography of her husband. The two Lis succeeded in telling more about their domestic and private lives than what was normally permitted in biography or autobiography, but the almost surreptitious quality of their success only confirms the far-reaching power of Chinese historiography and the constraints under which all writers had to labor.

PART II
THE SELF TRANSFORMED

FOUR

BUDDHIST TESTIMONIES

CHINESE Ch'an masters seem to have had nearly all the traits successful autobiographers in premodern times needed in order to overcome their inhibitions, traits such as boldness, ebullience, exaltation of the individual, disdain for conventions and rules, and frequent contemplation of the self.[1] We have reason to expect more of Chinese Buddhists if we agree with Starobinski that "one would hardly have sufficient motive to write an autobiography had not some radical change occurred in his life—conversion, entry into a new life, the operation of Grace."[2] It must have been a drastic act for a Chinese youth to leave home and join a religious order. No other change in traditional China was as momentous as the break away from the strong bonds of family and community in which the individual's sense of identity was submerged. To Kenneth D. Barkin and other modern critics, such bonds must have been loosened sufficiently to allow some men to live in partial independence of the community; only then could autobiography have its genesis.[3]

A revered Buddhist master, secure in his station and independent of the Confucian world, certainly had the psychological strength and freedom to reflect on the distance that he had traveled from his origins. Neither inhibited by the Confucian sense of decorum nor burdened by the weight of secular historiography, he should have been free to set down his self-reflections on paper if he had so chosen. Yet even though a loudly shouting and wildly gesticulating master may not have obeyed any laws, as soon as he laid down his staff and grasped a pen instead, he would become almost as helpless as his Confucian brethen, subject to nearly the same gamut of disabilities. The act of writing, in China even more than in the rest of the premodern world, would deprive the writer of whatever freedom he had in his other roles and impose on him a set of constraints he could seldom defy.

First and foremost, a would-be Buddhist autobiographer could not have found in Buddhist biography any model for what I shall call a conversion narrative. It is not that Chinese Buddhists were, like their Indian predecessors, uninterested in recording the achievements and miracles of

---

[1] For this characterization of Ch'an masters see my article, "Varieties of the Chinese Self," in *Designs of Selfhood*, ed. Vytautas Kavolis (Rutherford, N.J.: Fairleigh Dickinson University Press, 1984), pp. 110 and 116–18.

[2] Jean Starobinski, "The Style of Autobiography," in *Autobiography: Essays Theoretical and Critical*, ed. James Olney (Princeton: Princeton University Press, 1980), p. 78.

[3] Kenneth D. Barkin, "Autobiography and History," *Societas* 6, no. 2 (Spring 1976): 95.

monks in their human pursuits. Hagiography began almost as soon as Buddhism took root in China. It was a rare abbot who did not have his biography or tomb inscription composed by a learned monk or member of the Confucian literati. Collections of the lives of eminent monks were first compiled in the sixth century, and the efforts were repeated during each succeeding dynasty, enjoying a semiofficial status. But none of the writers, whatever his religious persuasion, escaped from the rigid canons of Chinese historiography. Almost all biographies of monks are short, succinct, and sketchy. Next to nothing is ever said about their interior life; where a modern reader is most curious the biographer is usually reticent. We are almost never told if there were any first stirrings of religiosity, any subsequent doubts or backslidings. Nor is there ever any description of the gradual transformation of the inner self or the circumstances that accompanied sudden illumination. In both content and format Chinese religious biography does not differ from secular biography. The same classical language is used by both Buddhist and secular biographers with the same consequences. Whatever their merits, narrative economy, circumspection, and referential indirectness are certainly not conducive to a full depiction of spiritual life.

Perhaps genuine religious experience is truly ineffable, but some religions, such as Christianity, seem to have been blessed from the beginning with articulate believers who would reveal their inner selves. In this regard it might be instructive to compare the personal testimonies of Saint Paul and Hui-neng (638–713), the Sixth Ch'an Patriarch. Both went through extraordinary transformations and became great leaders of their adopted religions. In doing so both had to overcome rather inauspicious beginnings, the one a rabid persecuter of Christians, the other an illiterate and downtrodden hawker of firewood in a remote province far from any Buddhist centers. Each in his own words, transcribed presumably by disciples, spoke of his earlier career and mentioned the events that drastically changed his life. But here the similarity ends. Saint Paul made a plausible case for his conversion: the shattering train of events that occurred on his way to Damascus was narrated with such particularity that an impartial listener could understand why Saint Paul came out of the crisis a totally different man. Hui-neng, however, did not seem to take an interest in reporting the *process* of his transformation. What must have been a momentous turning point in the history of Chinese religion was told in the briefest outline. One day he went to collect payment from a customer. "Having received my money and turning towards the front gate, I happened to see another man who was reciting the Diamond Sutra. Upon hearing it my mind became clear and I was awakened."[4]

---

[4] *The Platform Sutra of the Sixth Patriarch*, trans. Philip B. Yampolsky (New York: Columbia University Press, 1967), p. 127; hereafter referred to as *Platform Sutra*.

Totally innocent of any Buddhist doctrine or diction and having never been exposed to any bookish learning, Hui-neng cannot be said to have had any plausible preparation for the great awakening. Such a preparation, however, does not seem to have been necessary if one accepts the doctrine of sudden enlightenment or subitism, the belief that a sentient being with certain endowment can suddenly leap to total and supreme enlightenment without knowledge or learning, without long years of meditation and cultivation. If Hui-neng's initial awakening exemplifies this doctrine, the rest of the story is no more than a further confirmation.

After the episode of the Diamond Sutra Hui-neng abandoned his trade and joined the Fifth Patriarch in a temple far away from home, but when he arrived he was received very coldly by the abbot and sent to work in the threshing room. For eight months he trod the pestle and did nothing else. Then by accident he heard of a verse contest that would determine the patriarchal succession. Unable to write, he had a monk transcribe his versification, which impressed the abbot so much that Hui-neng was chosen as the successor. A modern student of religion would like to know what took place within Hui-neng during those eight months, but the master is completely silent on this point. He does mention two further instances of illumination, but again he chose to be terse rather than informative. The first instance took place the night after the verse contest. "At midnight the Fifth Patriarch called me into the hall and expounded the Diamond Sutra to me. Hearing it but once, I was immediately awakened, and that night I received the Dharma" (*Platform Sutra*, p. 133). The second and last spiritual experience occurred shortly afterwards. "I set out at midnight with the robe and the Dharma. The Fifth Patriarch saw me off as far as Chiu-chiang Station. I was instantly enlightened" (ibid.).

Given Hui-neng's doctrinal commitment to subitism, he cannot be expected to reveal a gradual, graded progress from ignorance to enlightenment. If the ultimate truth is so complete, infinite, and utterly indivisible, then there can never be stages of partial understanding. Nor is there any higher realm to attempt once one has been enlightened. Hui-neng's nominal discipleship with the Fifth Patriarch fully demonstrates this corollary. During the eight months of physical labor he never once went near the lecture hall; he did not seek education even in its narrowest sense: he remained innocent of reading and writing. His autobiographical account offers a striking contrast to the nineteenth-century *Bildungsroman*. On his arrival at the temple Hui-neng was already a perfect being; he needed no further education nor could he profit from additional experience.

Hui-neng is believed to have died in 713. His teachings continued to dominate Chinese Buddhism so completely that all subsequent Ch'an masters, whatever their sectarian identification or doctrinal emphasis, revered him as the Sixth Patriarch and claimed him as the ultimate spiritual progenitor. If any of them ever felt the stirrings of autobiographical im-

pulse, the example of Hui-neng seems not to have offered much encouragement. For the next five centuries there was not even a repetition of his
meager self-revelation in the numerous sermons delivered throughout
China. Besides the doctrine of subitism, there were other facets of Ch'an
Buddhism that tended to inhibit the autobiographical act. Chief among
them were the characteristic Ch'an distrust of the written word and the
insistence on not telling things too plainly (*pu shuo p'o*). To Ch'an Buddhists truth, being immediate and undifferentiable, could be hinted at or
suggested by gestures and metaphors, but not conveyed by declarative
prose. Another obstacle to self-revelation was the usual mise-en-scène in
which Ch'an monks encountered each other, where performance in verbal combat was dependent on quick thrusts and agile dodging. No duel-
ing master could fail to parry any direct query. His best defense was to
utter paradoxes or epigrams: to talk about himself in earnest or use plain
and denotative language was to expose his flanks and give his antagonists
an opening for attack. Lu Shih-i (1611–1672), a critical Confucian ob-
server, offered the following explanation for what appeared to him to be
the manic but inarticulate behavior of Ch'an monks:

> When a Confucian sage has reached enlightenment, he likes to tell
> others and share it with all people in the world. . . . A Ch'an master
> upon reaching enlightenment, however, does not like to tell others:
> he keeps to himself the secret experience. But his exultation is ex-
> pressed in such wild behavior as leaping up and down, shouting and
> hitting people with his staff, and cursing loudly. There is no limit to
> his unruliness. To the clear-eyed this sort of conduct is nothing but
> willful eccentricity. Even if a Buddhist is thoroughly enlightened,
> there is still no reason for going to such extremes. But we must not
> forget that a Ch'an Buddhist has no alternative. He certainly cannot
> tell people what he has gone through in his enlightenment, for the
> very reason that is expressed in the saying, "I told it to you, but you
> ridiculed me for it."[5]

Lu's observation may have been true with regard to the vast majority
of Ch'an Buddhists, but it fails to apply to a group of thirteenth-century
masters who spoke unabashedly and in great detail about their own enlightenment. A few of them even went beyond this extraordinary innovation: they reported on their long and tortuous quest, dwelling on every
setback and describing every breakthrough. In doing so they not only
broke several fundamental Ch'an tenets but created a new genre in Chinese literature. Their self-accounts are the first Chinese spiritual autobi-

---

[5] *Lu Fu-t'ing Ssu-pien-lu chi-yao* (The essentials of Lu Shih-i's *Records of Deliberations*), ed.
Chang Po-hsing, 2 vols., TSCC, 1:40.

ographies. That such a revolutionary act should have been launched by Ch'an Buddhists and not by any other group testifies to the anarchic tendencies of the Ch'an school: if Buddhas and patriarchs are to be killed and sacred texts discarded—metaphorically, of course—then what is there to prevent one from throwing all the interdicts to the wind and giving free rein to one's autobiographical impulse? That it should have occurred in the thirteenth century and not earlier is a much more complex story. In recent years scholars have characterized the Sung as one of the pivotal periods in world history.[6] To some neo-traditional China or early modern China began with the Southern Sung. It is therefore quite probable that the monks' self-revelations were not merely solipsistic utterances generated in the insularity of Ch'an monasteries but responses to larger forces and movements in the outside world.

Even within the Ch'an school great changes had taken place during the five centuries following the death of Hui-neng. The increasing exchange and even camaraderie between Buddhist monks and Confucian literati had by now brought about a new clerical style that stood in striking contrast to the unabashed illiteracy and rusticity exemplified by the Sixth Patriarch. Many Southern Sung Ch'an masters left voluminous collected works, vying in kind and mass with secular writers. These learned monks not only excelled in exegetical treatises but even penned copious occasional poetry, memorial pieces, tomb inscriptions. The exchange of letters between monks and Confucian officialdom was a commonplace. As Sung China evolved Ch'an masters became increasingly prone to use expository language to expound on the methods and procedures that would help disciples to reach illumination. Learned monks such as Tsung-kao (also known as Ta-hui P'u-chüeh, 1089–1163) would write copiously explaining what once had been believed in Ch'an circles to be beyond language or cognition.[7]

The key term that united Buddhist and Neo-Confucian pedagogies is *hsiu* (cultivation). The word, which recurs in the discourse of both schools, suggests the importance of perseverance, of long years of slow and graded endeavor. The new style in Buddhist education in no way rejected the doctrine of instantaneous enlightenment, but much more emphasis was placed on preparation for such a goal. If the intermediary steps and stages could be understood and studied, then the learning ex-

---

[6] Cf. William H. McNeill, *The Human Condition: An Ecological and Historical View* (Princeton: Princeton University Press, 1979), pp. 48–52.

[7] A measure of this great master's success in bridging the Buddhist and Confucian worlds is the fact that shortly after his death a biography was written for him in the *nien-p'u* format which, as we have noted earlier, had hitherto been reserved only for the most celebrated men of affairs and letters. This fact will be discussed in greater detail in chapter 6 on the Ming Buddhist master Te-ch'ing.

perience of a Ch'an master—his *Bildungsroman*—could be edifying. Students might benefit from his errors and successes. This was precisely the justification that the first Buddhist autobiographer gave for his unprecedented account of the self.

TSU-CH'IN (1216–1287)

Known also as Hsüeh-yen, the first Ch'an autobiographer was a member of the Lin-chi sect, which had by his time overwhelmed all rival denominations and established its paramount place among all Buddhists. During the Southern Sung Ch'an monks involved themselves in court life more than in any period before or after. No other dynasty saw so many prominent masters residing in the strategically important temples in or near the capital, nor was the court ever so directly involved in the appointment and transfer of chief abbots. Consequently a Ch'an master of eminence enjoyed a secular prestige seldom achieved by his T'ang or Northern Sung predecessors. Tsu-ch'in, moreover, had the enviable advantage of being the principal heir to Shih-fan (also known as Wu-chun, 1178–1249), for many years the undisputed leading abbot in the capital region. This line of apostolic succession—to be recognized by a prominent master as his principal heir over many other acknowledged disciples—went back unbroken for at least five generations. All these circumstances in combination suggest that Tsu-ch'in must have been a more than usually self-assured master, fully conscious of his place in the annals of Buddhism and confident that his line would be perpetuated. The apostolic succession indeed continued from his principal heir on down for at least another fourteen generations, undisturbed by two changes in dynasties. Supreme self-confidence and a sense of history, which he may well have had in large measure, probably contributed to his decision to talk unabashedly about himself.

Like the Sixth Patriarch, Tsu-ch'in narrated his life story while ostensibly delivering a sermon. The theme of his preaching on that day was death, a theme apparently prompted by the recent decease and cremation of the assistant abbot and another monk. More than anything else, a renewed sense of mortality may have prompted the master to depart from the usual practice: his is another example of the observation made earlier that all autobiographies are autonecrologies. Halfway through the sermon, after repeatedly admonishing the audience on the urgency of reaching illumination before being overtaken by death, he suddenly mentioned that two disciples had recently come to his office and asked for specific instruction. He turned them down, saying that "there is no Buddhist truth here that can be passed on from mouth to mouth or transmitted from mind to mind." The best thing for them to do, he suggested, was to come to the next general assembly when he would expound on the way of endeavor (*tso kung-fu*) by using himself as an example. Now, to fulfill his promise that he would do so in public, he proceeded to tell his life story.

> When I was five years old I entered into a temple. As a footboy to the abbot, listening to his conversations with visitors, I came to know that there was such a matter and believed that I could achieve it. I studied sitting-in-meditation. But on account of my obtuseness all my life I have suffered repeatedly and bitterly. I became a monk at sixteen and started traveling at eighteen, determined to get to the bottom of this matter.[8]

What he meant by "this matter," which he used twice in the above quotation, becomes quite clear as his life story unfolds, but the remarkable thing is that neither he nor his emulators had a suitable term to denote their long and arduous quest, the theme of their life stories and the ultimate concern of every Buddhist. Perhaps there was still a vestigial reluctance to name things, to engage too blatantly in conceptual and logical thinking. Fortunately this distrust of language was not stronger than the combined forces of autobiographical impulse and pedagogical zeal.

> I then joined Master T'ieh-chüeh-yüan of Shuang-lin in his assembly of sitting-in-meditation. From morning to night I stayed in the monks' hall and never went outside. Even when I was walking in the dormitory or to the washroom I held my hands in my sleeves and crossed them in front of my chest. Walking ever so slowly, I never looked left or right, nor did I see anything more than three feet in front of me. Ts'ao-tung masters usually taught a disciple to concentrate his mind on Ch'an paradoxes [*kung-an*] such as "whether a dog has Buddha nature." When random thoughts and extraneous ideas occurred the disciple was supposed to visualize the character "*wu*" [nothingness] and balance it, ever so gingerly, on the tip of his nose. As soon as the random ideas disappeared, he would discard the character. In this fashion he silently sat, waiting for purification and maturation. After a long time perfect understanding would occur of its own accord. The Ts'ao-tung method was so elaborate and perplexing that a disciple could easily spend ten or twenty years without getting anywhere. This was the reason that not too many stayed with the sect. (*HTC*, 122:512)

By this time the Lin-chi sect had fully established its dominance: the only surviving contender, the Ts'ao-tung sect, was already in a state of

---

[8] *Hsüeh-yen ho-shang yü-lu* (The sayings of Master Tsu-ch'in), in *HTC*, 122:512.

extreme decline. Traditionally the Ts'ao-tung sect relied more on reasoning and verbal instruction than its chief rival. Whether or not this type of
training had anything to do with Tsu-ch'in's willingness to report on his
tortuous spiritual career, his desertion of the declining and difficult
school, and his eventual ascendance in the rival sect must have sharpened
his sense of personal change and perhaps also of his uniqueness. There
may even have been a lingering sense of regret over his abandonment of
a sinking ship and therefore a need for justification.

Tsu-ch'in's sitting-in-meditation seemed promising for a while. He
reached such a state of imperturbability that he no longer noticed the
passage of time. The abbot was moved to praise publicly his achievement. Nevertheless he stayed only a few months before he took a momentous step: he went to the Ling-yin Temple, a major Lin-chi center
just outside of the Southern Sung capital. He does not dwell on the
circumstances under which the change of allegiance took place; his account is very brief: "At nineteen I went to Ling-yin as a temporary resi-
dent. I saw Miao-feng. After his death Shih-t'ien succeeded him" (HTC,
122:513). Miao-feng (also known as Chih-shan, 1152–1235) was one of
the most prominent masters in the capital, sought after constantly by the
rank and fashion. His pedagogical method was diametrically opposed to
that associated with the Ts'ao-tung school: he was famous for his adept
inducement of illumination in his disciples by a few well chosen words or
gestures. As he died soon after Tsu-ch'in's arrival, he apparently did not
benefit the novice. Shih-t'ien (also known as Fa-hsün, d. 1241), another
prominent Lin-chi monk, shared the same master with Shih-fan, who
was to become, at least nominally, Tsu-ch'in's paramount teacher. As
Tsu-ch'in says nothing more about him, we may assume that the new
abbot was no more helpful to the novice than the old one. Help came,
however, from an unexpected source.

> I met a monk-scribe who came from Ch'u-chou. He said to me:
> "Brother Ch'in, your endeavor is like dead water; it won't do you
> any good. You have broken your activity and inactivity phases into
> two separate things." What he said about me was quite true. When I
> sat down, I felt I was in an unusual state, but it would disappear when
> I started to walk, picked up a spoon, or put down chopsticks. He
> said further: "To engage in Ch'an endeavor one must have doubts.
> Great doubts lead to great enlightments; small doubts lead to small
> enlightenments: there is no enlightenment without doubt. One must
> struggle with Ch'an paradoxes and puzzlements." (Ibid.)

While there is no reason to doubt that the encounter with the monk-
scribe did actually take place—indeed nothing in Tsu-ch'in's autobiographical account strains our credulity—the episode contains several stan-

dard topoi of spiritual autobiography. A period of negation or mental housecleaning marks the beginning of progress; help may come fortuitously from the least expected sources; the benefactor may be humble in station and casual in manners. Our monk-scribe, who was not significant enough to rise above anonymity, is a far cry from the early Ch'an masters. His language is plain and matter-of-fact while his gradation of enlightenments would have been branded a heretical act by the subitists. Following his advice, Tsu-ch'in embarked on a regimen of doubt. "I doubted everything and stood every idea on its head. Although I devoted myself to the new endeavor all the time—I sealed my beddings and my back never touched the sleeping mat—I remained confused: everything seemed messy and chaotic from morning to night, whether I was walking or sitting. There was never a minute of peace or clarity" (ibid.). The results did not seem very promising. In his desperation Tsu-ch'in decided to move to another Lin-chi center in the neighborhood. "I heard that Abbot T'ien-mu had waited on Sung-yüan for a long time and was his heir. He must have heard Sung-yüan speak. Therefore I moved to Ching-tz'u Temple" (ibid.).

Why it is that the words of Sung-yüan were so alluring, even once removed, Tsu-ch'in does not explain. The name was invoked once before when Tsu-ch'in explained why he took to heart the monk-scribe's suggestions. Even though the monk-scribe "was not himself very much engaged in a Ch'an regimen, he had been to the Ch'an assembly led by Pu-an who, having been an heir of Sung-yüan, must have spoken cogently" (ibid.). This time, even instructions twice removed from the great source were worth listening to. Why this was so needed no explanation to Tsu-ch'in's audience, for Sung-yüan (also known as Ch'ung-yüeh, 1132–1202) was one of the towering figures of his generation. He was more than usually agile, articulate, and sharp-tongued for a Ch'an master. His great prominence made him a suitable role model for Tsu-ch'in the novice; in several important aspects his life prefigures Tsu-ch'in's subsequent career.

A restless wanderer, Sung-yüan in his youth first called on Tsung-kao (also known as Ta-hui P'u-chüeh), the greatest patriarch of his time. He abruptly abandoned this master for another. After his first awakening, he went to visit all famous monks but found none equal to his expectations. When he first met his eventual teacher, he could not make any progress. Following his teacher around, he struggled with the problem so strenuously that he ignored food and sleep. Illumination came much later and entirely fortuitously. During the last six years of his life he presided over the Ling-yin Temple, surrounded by a crowd of admirers and disciples. Among Southern Sung masters his was indeed the paradigmatic life.

His favored disciple T'ien-mu (also known as Wen-li, 1167–1250) was another great monk much sought after by the capital elite. An exponent of the intricacies of the *I ching* (*Book of Changes*), he is reputed to have dispensed instructions to such Neo-Confucian notables as Chu Hsi and Yang Chien. When Tsu-ch'in called on him, the master was at the height of his powers; there was no reason to expect him to accommodate a callow youth barely twenty years of age. After hearing the acolyte out on his past efforts, the great master expressed no approbation but immediately alluded to the humbling and mortifying travails no Lin-chi disciple could avoid in the process of gaining insight and understanding. Tsu-ch'in was annoyed.

> Master T'ien-mu's words were of course meant to be uplifting, but I was not pleased. My illness had me completely befuddled and his medicine had only an adverse effect. I couldn't help addressing him in my mind: "You know nothing about Ch'an endeavors. All you have is clever verbiage." Usually a disciple, after having received his initial instruction from a master, presented one last round of incense and prostrated himself three times before the teacher. This is called "expressing gratitude for good fortune." I left without the obeisances. (Ibid.)

Both the abbot's cool reception and the novice's rebellious response are standard elements in a Ch'an student's journey toward illumination. The abbot was no more discouraging than the Fifth Patriarch, who upon first meeting the future Sixth Patriarch called him a barbarian and made a dire prognosis for the eager but unlettered youth who had traveled a thousand miles in the hope of receiving instruction from the master. Tsu-ch'in's meeting with the abbot exemplifies one of the central paradoxes of the Ch'an school. A young novice must seek out teachers during his peregrinations, but he could only rely on his own mind for enlightenment. A teacher must not encourage dependence, nor could he ever flatter himself that he had anything of value to impart. In real life, however, the doctrinal and institutional aspects of the Ch'an school did not always match. Insistence on self-reliance contrasted sharply with the complexities of teacher-disciple designation: in no other Buddhist school was patriarchal succession so emphasized. No great Ch'an master was without an illustrious sectarian lineage. The acknowledged—one might even say the officially determined—paramount teacher of an eminent monk was almost never the humble cleric who tonsured the future master in his obscure youth. If a Ch'an monk was ambivalent toward his teacher, doctrine and institution were united in breeding such an attitude. For Tsu-ch'in, if his life story is to be an allegorical tale of the Ch'an quest, an exemplar for the edification of his audience, he has every reason to downplay the help, if any, that he received from prominent masters during his years of struggles. His inauspicious first meeting with the abbot, disappointing as it must have been to him, is only a step in his progress. What is surprising to us is the fact that he remained in the Ching-tz'u Temple even after he rudely walked out on the abbot. He went about his own way and resumed his old practice of sitting-in-meditation.

> There were seven brethren from Chang and Ch'üan prefectures, and we formed a sitting-in-meditation group. For two years in the Ching-tz'u Temple we did not open our beddings, nor did our backs ever touch the mats. There was a monk by the name of Hsiu who also came from Chang prefecture, but he did not join our group. He practiced sitting-in-meditation all by himself. Every day he sat on the rush seat with his back straight like an iron pole. When he walked he also kept his back straight, opened his eyes wide, and let his arms hang. Again he was like an iron pole. Every day he was like this. Often I tried to get close to him and talk with him, but as soon as he saw me approaching, he turned around and went in the opposite direction. For two years I got nowhere with him. As I had not made any headway in my Ch'an endeavor for two years, I became very tired and confused. I could no longer distinguish day from night, walking from sitting. Everything seemed to have been blended into one chaotic mess, and this utter disarray was like a lump of dank mud. One day I suddenly realized that I had not made any progress at all with my study of the Way, yet my clothes were now in shreds and my flesh wasted away. Tears began to fall unawares and I became homesick. I asked for leave to go home. (*HTC*, 122:513–14)

Now Tsu-ch'in had apparently reached the nadir of his spiritual career. Undoubtedly before him many Chinese seekers of truth or salvation had undergone hardships equal to or greater than his, but none had made such a candid admission of the despair or described the agonies in such plain and direct language. If Tsu-ch'in's unabashed account owes nothing to an earlier model, it certainly conforms to what may be called the universal pattern of religious life. His desperate plight is akin to what Western mystics denote as the "dark night of the soul," a stage almost unavoidable in the tortuous course of every spiritual quest. It is a foil to the subsequent stage of illumination; its agonies are matched by ensuing ecstasies. Compared with other tormented souls, however, Tsu-ch'in's release was relatively swift and he profited noticeably from his difficulties. "For two months I let go all the discipline. When I returned to the temple and resumed my endeavor, I felt completely reinvigorated as a result of the break, even though I had to start work from the beginning. Now I knew that to forego sleep would not help. To remain vigorous one must have deep and sound sleep in the middle of the night" (*HTC*, 122:514). This change combined with some fortuitous help brought him to his first breakthrough.

One day as I was taking a stroll in the corridor I ran into Brother Hsiu. From a distance he seemed to be completely at ease and even self-satisfied. I walked over to him and as he did not avoid me, I knew he had succeeded in some way. I asked him, "Why is it that when I tried to speak with you last year, you always avoided me?" He replied, "My respected brother, a man who genuinely works on the Way has not even the time to clip his fingernails, much less to chat with you." He asked about my efforts and I told him the story from the beginning. Then I said, "I am now beset by confusion and perplexity, which I cannot handle." He said: "What difficulties are there? It is only because you are not driving yourself hard enough. You must sit on a high rush seat, straighten your spine, keep every disk taut, cover up every one of your 360 bones and eighty-four-thousand pores with the word 'nothingness' [wu]. Then see what confusion and perplexity you still have." Following his advice, I found a thick rush mat and put it on my station. I sat on it and straightened my spine, making every disk taut. From head to bottom I forcibly lifted up all the 360 links of my skeleton, as if fighting alone against ten thousand enemies. When I became completely exhausted I dropped everything. Then with all my strength I made another desperate attempt. All of a sudden I was no longer conscious of either my mind or my body, and I saw in front of my eyes nothing but a huge, solid substance, like a silver mountain or iron wall. This pure and clear state lasted for three days, whether I walked or sat. For three nights I did not close my eyes. In the afternoon of the third day I was walking under the gates, but I felt that I was still sitting. Suddenly I ran into Brother Hsiu again. He asked me what I was doing there. I replied that I was working on the Way. "What is it that you call the 'Way'?" he asked. As I was not able to answer, I became very perplexed. Intending to go back to the hall and resume sitting-in-meditation, I first went to the back gate. Without realizing what I was doing I arrived at the back hall. The head monk there asked me, "Brother Ch'in, how is your work on the Way?" I replied, "I should not have asked so many people about it; now, contrary to what I expected, I am stuck." He said, "You only have to open your eyes wide and see what the matter is." I was quite struck by the last sentence and hastened back to the meditation hall. As soon as I lifted my body up to the rush seat all of a sudden everything burst open in front of me, as if the earth had collapsed. At that time I found myself unable to describe or even suggest what had happened to others, be-

cause I had no way to compare it with anything in this world. I did
not know what to do with my joy so I left the meditation mat and
went to look for Brother Hsiu. He was on the sutra table. As soon
as he saw me he greeted me with folded palms and said: "Congratulations! Congratulations!" Holding each other's hand we took a
stroll on the willow-shaded embankment in front of the temple. I
looked up and down, viewing all the myriad things of the universe.
Suddenly I realized that it was actually from my subtle and bright
true nature that all things flowed out, all the things that in the past
had repelled my eyes and disgusted my ears, all the ignorance, troubles, perplexities, and confusion. What floated closely before my
eyes now was a vast presence, absolutely silent and completely de-
nuded of shape and form. (Ibid.)

In several important ways the above passage represents a landmark in
the history of Chinese narrative. The most obvious innovation is the time
scale that Tsu-ch'in employs in describing his encounter with the monk
Hsiu and the ensuing events that led to his first breakthrough. The episode covers only three days of his life, but his account runs to six hundred
characters, longer than most traditional Chinese biographies that ostensibly represent an entire lifetime. It is this leisurely pace of narrative that
made possible, perhaps for the first time in Chinese history, a baring of
the inner self. Ian Watt, in his discussion of the development of the novel
as a representation of private experience, has stressed the importance of
time scale in fiction, but the same can be applied equally well to autobiography:

> The main problem in portraying the inner life is essentially one of
> the time-scale. The daily experience of the individual is composed of
> a ceaseless flow of thought, feeling and sensation; but most literary
> forms—biography and even autobiography for instance—tend to be
> of too gross a temporal mesh to retain its actuality; and so, for the
> most part, is memory. Yet it is this minute-by-minute content of
> consciousness which constitutes what the individual's personality re-
> ally is, and dictates his relationship to others: it is only by contact
> with this consciousness that a reader can participate fully in the life
> of a fictional character.[9]

That Tsu-ch'in was able to employ such a fine time scale was the result
of a combination of circumstances. The first is the format of the Buddhist
sermon as it was practiced in the thirteenth century. To express the ineffable or perhaps simply to enliven the sermon, many Ch'an monks ex-

[9] *The Rise of the Novel* (Berkeley and Los Angeles: University of California Press, 1967),
pp. 191–92.

perimented with various devices either borrowed or derived from the theater. Judging from extant transcriptions of the sermons, irrepressible masters indulged in elaborate and varied gesticulation, pantomime, clowning, shouting, and dialogue with an imaginary visitor. Even the monk's crosier was frequently pressed into service: sometimes the sermonizer struck the ground with it to punctuate a statement; sometimes it was poised to confront an imaginary opponent; sometimes it even ostensibly acquired a voice of its own and joined the sermonizer in a dialogue or debate, with its lines delivered, ventriloquially I presume, by the monk himself. The ultimate measure of the theatricalization of the sermon is the trancribers's insertion of glosses that are virtually stage directions, not unlike those in the scripts of the popular drama that were to be formally written down toward the end of the century. If the Ch'an sermon was fast approaching theater what, then, is the effect on Tsu-ch'in the autobiographer?

It was probably more than a coincidence that the first self-revealing autobiography should have emerged just when the theater was beginning to capture both popular claim and literary attention.[10] The dramatist's art is predicated on the articulate and energetic egocentrism of the characters in his plays. They must project themselves on stage: they begin with a self-introduction to the audience and in their own voices unveil their inner feelings and narrate events not convenient to enact. Even the most humble and self-effacing have to make their appearances, each baring some of his or her private self. No bashful peasant maiden, however tongue-tied, can be denied a voice and even some eloquence. Thus a performer on the stage is the very opposite of a writing historian: the performer is nothing if he fails to project himself through his words while the latter has to operate under the convention of the selfless compiler, mute and invisible. A sermonizing master is, then, much closer to a performer than to a historian. If he can borrow so many trappings from the theater, why may he not also borrow the declamatory voice, the robust egotism, the expository self-introduction?

As an oral performer Tsu-ch'in shares his narrative fluency with another contemporary group of public entertainers. The Southern Sung

[10] That Tsu-ch'in and his disciples were familiar with the performing arts can be seen from their casual references to the subject. When the disciple Yüan-miao wrote a letter to Tsu-ch'in reporting his progress, he compared his peaceable state resulting from illumination to the denouement of an early thirteenth-century play, the *Water Demon* (*shui-mu*). A translation of that letter is included in appendix A. Tsu-ch'in himself alluded to the puppet theater in a sermon: "Let us talk about going to a puppet show. Whether a puppet has a demon's face and a god's head or a god's face and a demon's head, it is always pulled by strings. Many spectators perhaps see only a beautiful damsel dancing exquisitely with a white silk fan. For their benefit I am going to tear down the curtain [behind which hide the puppeteers]" (*HTC*, 122:505).

capital was renowned for its numerous and highly skillful storytellers, who competed daily in the marketplaces with the acrobats, magicians, actors, puppeteers, and shadow-play operators. The best of them frequently plied their craft in noble houses and imperial palaces. When an ebullient sermonizer gives free rein to his autobiographical urge, his narrative stance is closer to that of the storyteller than of the historian. If he attempted to *write* his life story, even the most uninhibited Ch'an master could not escape the dictates of historiography or classic prose. But the monk-raconteur speaking extemporaneously in the vernacular and spurred on by the excitement generated by the occasion is under very few constraints. A storyteller expands and elaborates where a historian would condense and delete. The entire life of a biographer's subject is summarized in a few pages while a storyteller would dwell for hours just on one heroic exploit in the active career of a legendary figure. Severe narrative economy now gave way to the sheer joy of representing the richness of life in all its randomness and complexity.

The language of Tsu-ch'in's sermon is no less similar to that of contemporary popular entertainers. By the thirteenth century the vernacular, finely-honed by storytellers and nourished by the *ch'ü* and *tz'u* lyricists, had become a flexible and effective vehicle, and Tsu-ch'in made the most of it. The new lyric poetry emphasized a direct and minute description of feelings, while the *shih* genre in earlier times based its evocative powers on indirectness—allusion and suggestion rather than open and insistent avowal. Perhaps one can amend the quoted passage from Ian Watt by adding that the problem of portraying the inner life is equally one of language. The Sixth Patriarch, whom we have met at the beginning of this chapter, could not, even if he had freed himself from the subitist dogma, have described what he experienced immediately prior to and during his illumination. Had he been educated, an eighth-century monk would only have exchanged the timorous inarticulation of the unlettered for the decorous obliquity of the literati. Tsu-ch'in, on the other hand, had at his disposal the descriptive phrases from popular literature to convey his sense of perplexity or his heightened state after the first breakthrough. The ancients may have been content with a meager and succinct representation of reality; our innovative and expansive autobiographer, living in an age when the means for telling and describing were ample and the habit of doing so strong, bemoans his inability to do more. "At that time I found myself unable to describe or even suggest to other people what had happened, because I had no way to compare it with anything in this world" (*HTC*, 122:514).

To tell all or nearly all seems to have been the order of the day, for Tsu-ch'in went on in his sermon from revelation to revelation. Shortly after the marvelous vision on the willow-shaded embankment he lost his self-assurance. His new problem, as he describes it, was his entrapment by his vision, which prevented him from progressing to a higher stage of perception. When he fell into a deep sleep during the middle of the night, in his dreamless and thoughtless state when nothing was seen or heard, whatever unity he had once achieved shattered. The present problem reminded him of the criticism made earlier by the monk-scribe from Ch'u-chou—his inability to unify his waking and somnolent phases. Nothing seemed to offer a solution. Even his great teacher Shih-fan, with all his eloquence and wisdom, was no help to him at all. A less startling revelation is his inability to discover anything useful after a sustained and assiduous search through all the sutras and recorded Ch'an conversations. For ten years he remained in such an impasse. Finally he moved to east Chekiang and alternated his residence between two monasteries. Without any conscious effort he was suddenly delivered from his predicament:

> One day I was walking in front of a temple and my mind was leisurely and aimlessly wandering. I raised my eyes at random and caught sight of an ancient cypress tree. All of a sudden the sight triggered off the understanding I had reached in the past, but in the next instant it vanished. In a great burst all the obstacles also dispersed. I felt like a man who had walked into the bright sun from a dark room. From now on I no longer had doubts about life or death, the Buddha or the patriarchs. (*HTC*, 122:515)

Tsu-ch'in ends his sermon with what amounts to a balancing act between acknowledging the subitist validity for some and recommending the gradualist approach for most. His own tortuous course, he concedes, would never have been necessary to men with great force and great endowment. "There are those who have great powers or seeds from previous lives. As they do not depend on effort it is impossible to talk about their courses and paths. There are also those who have never made any effort, so there is nothing to be said" (ibid.). When he expounds the gradualist position, he reverts to the perennial journey metaphor: "To carry out this undertaking is like going on a journey. Those who stop after having walked one, two, three, four, or five miles can only talk about the first one, two, three, four, or five miles. Those who have traveled a hundred, thousand, or ten thousand miles have seen what the journey of the thousand or the ten thousand miles has been like and can talk about the thousand or ten thousand miles" (ibid.). He then makes a final bow toward subitism, "But you must know that this matter lies beyond millions of miles, outside the universe" (ibid.).

That Tsu-ch'in himself was aware that his autobiographical act was totally unprecedented can be seen from one of his concluding remarks. "Do not remember a word of what I have just said. If you do, your life would be led astray. This is why the great masters have never discussed their own endeavors, their own paths to illumination, their own insights" (ibid.). But once he set an example, there was no shortage of followers in the next generation of Ch'an monks.

Tsu-ch'in's Successors

The oldest among the next generation of Buddhist autobiographers, Meng-shan I (also known as Te-i, 1231–?), was not one of Tsu-ch'in's acknowledged disciples, but he visited the master the year before he finally reached illumination. That he may very well have benefited from Tsu-ch'in's example can be inferred from that fact that his autobiography resembles the master's in both format and content. It was also in the context of a sermon that he gave an account of his spiritual life that, perhaps not surprisingly, parallels Tsu-ch'in's course.

Meng-shan I was, as he tells his audience, first aware of the pursuit of enlightenment when he was nineteen and still a layman. But he took no serious interest in it until twelve years later when he began to visit Ch'an masters for instruction. He tried almost twenty of them to no avail. At last he was told to meditate on the word "nothingness," "All day and all night one must be as alert as a cat trying to catch a mouse, as unceasing as a hen hatching eggs, as persistent as a rat gnawing a coffin."[11] After eighteen days of continuous and diligent endeavor, Meng-shan I, while drinking tea, came to an understanding of the basic Ch'an principle: truth can only be conveyed through hints and gestures, not by words. Overjoyed, he told several masters about his newly gained insight, but they remained unimpressed.

Two years later Meng-shan I was struck down suddenly by a disease which seems to have been cholera. Racked by pain, anxiety, fear, and hallucinations, he found no help in his Ch'an accomplishments. Thereupon he pulled himself together and made preparations for the worst.

> I sat up on a praying mat; with incense burning, I gradually steadied myself. Silently I prayed to the Three Divinities and Dragon Kings. I repented all my past wrongdoings. If my life was coming to an end, I prayed that by the power of Wisdom I be reincarnated again as a man so I would be able to join the Buddhist orders early in life. If I was going to recover, I would abandon all worldly concerns and seek enlightenment as a monk so that I would contribute to the salvation of future seekers. Having made my wish I concentrated on the word "nothingness" while reflecting on myself. Before long my entrails began to turn and twist, but I paid no heed to it. After a while my

[11] CKTC, p. 14.

eyelids stopped moving, and eventually I ceased to be aware of my body. But my concentration on the word "nothingness" never faltered. At evening when I got up from the praying mat, half of my illness was gone. I went back to sitting-in-meditation until the small hours of the next morning, and by then all the ailments had disappeared. I felt light and peaceful in both mind and body. (*CKTC*, p. 14)

Distress, afflictions, and despair—components of what the mystics often refer to as the "dark night of the soul"—are familiar to most seekers of illumination. If Tsu-ch'in was the first Chinese autobiographer to report on this kind of experience, Meng-shan I's plight, seemingly fortuitous, was far more extreme. It also led to more momentous developments. Two months after the miraculous cure he had himself tonsured. During the next year, when he traveled widely as an itinerant monk, he came to the realization that spiritual endeavor had to be brought to completion in one stretch: interruptions were not allowed. So he decided to sit in meditation for as long as he could endure it.

When the first wave of sleepiness came upon me, I defeated it easily by simply bracing myself. The second wave was met the same way. The third time I left the praying mat and distracted sleepiness by going through obeisances on the floor. When I returned to the praying mat I decided on a regimen to cope with the devil of sleepiness. At first I took short naps by placing my head on a pillow. Then I discarded the pillow and used my arm instead. Eventually I was able to endure without bending my torso. (*CKTC*, pp. 14–15)

How to overcome sleepiness while sitting-in-meditation is a problem every Ch'an monk had to resolve—Tsu-ch'in's struggles may have served as a model for the younger monk. Like Tsu-ch'in, Meng-shan I's exertions brought him an important breakthrough.

After two or three nights I became exhausted all the time. My feet seemed to be floating in the air. Suddenly it seemed that a mass of dark clouds burst open right in front of my eyes, and my body felt so much at ease and clean as if I had just come out of a bath. Although the doubts in my mind became greater, they unfolded and departed in front of me without any effort on my part. Now all the sounds, sights, desires, and concerns could not penetrate to my mind, which had become as fresh as snow in a silver basin, as clear as the autumnal sky. (*CKTC*, p. 15)

Again like Tsu-ch'in, after the breakthrough Meng-shan I was not able to follow a linear upward path, to leap to illumination. He was beset by new doubts and backslidings. But he persisted, whether sick or well, traveling or staying in one place. One day when Meng-shan I was concentrating his mind on the word "nothingness" while sitting in the meditation hall, the chief monk came in to burn incense. "As he tried to open the incense box he made a loud noise, and instantly I achieved a thorough understanding of the self" (ibid.). Next spring, apparently without any effort on his part, he reached the final goal. "One day I was returning from a visit outside of the city. As I climbed up the stone steps I suddenly felt that all my doubts were dissolving like melting ice. I was not even aware that I had a body which was walking" (ibid., pp. 15–16).

Although the shape of Meng-shan I's spiritual progress as he tells it during the sermon does not differ from Tsu-ch'in's, his life story is much shorter and adorned with fewer specificities. The practice of oral autobiography was continued by four younger sermonizers, all in one way or another related to the great master. Tsu-ch'in's principal heir, Yüan-miao (also known as Kao-feng)—about whom we shall hear more later—made several brief references to his travails leading to illumination. The brief autobiographical account delivered by T'ieh-shan Ai (also known as T'ieh-shan Ch'iung), another acknowledged disciple of Tsu-ch'in's, consists of only two episodes, each centering on his encounter with one of the first two Ch'an autobiographers we have discussed.[12] T'ieh-shan Ai's own disciple Wu-wen (also known as Ssu-ts'ung) in turn carried on the tradition, but his account of his spiritual quest was also short. By this time the autobiographical impulse among the Ch'an sermonizers seems to have run its course. The last autobiographical sermonizer whom we are going to study in some detail is Wen-pao, who may not have been chronologically the last, but whose account of triumphs may throw some light on the reasons for the genre's demise.

Wen-pao (also known as Fang-shan) was a disciple of Miao-lun (1201–1261, also known as Tuan-ch'iao), who in turn shared a teacher with Tsu-ch'in. Most of Wen-pao's writings are lost, but in one of the extant sermons he mentions the circumstances leading to his illumination. Similar to the accounts of others, his discussion notes that his teacher Miao-lun offered no explicit help and a random event served as the catalyst for his sudden breakthrough.

> Every time I went into my teacher's office and asked for instruction he hit me over the head with his staff. One day I became very perplexed. As I sat straight in my hut I looked outside and saw a hut-mate approaching the door with paper and candles. Suddenly everything in front of me burst open. All that I had hitherto cherished disappeared and my mind and body became as transparent as glass.

[12] For T'ieh-shan Ai's testimony, see *CKTC*, pp. 21–24.

Mountains, rivers, and the entire earth also became like glass; in the all-penetrating transparency there was not the slightest obstacle between within and without.[13]

Again like his predecessors, his breakthrough was not the attainment of the final goal but only the preparation for it. His denouement, however, came about rather swiftly. The very next day he went to his teacher and reported what had happened. The abbot was just as obstreperous as before and the interview ended with Wen-po storming out of the abbot's office and shouting, "Injustice!"

After the meal all the monks were asked to pick vegetables. Soon the teacher arrived. When he noticed that my hands were idle he asked me abruptly, "Is your basket free from weeds?" I replied, "As free as you can get." He reached into my basket and picked a *hsien* root. Throwing it in front of me he asked, "What is this?" Thereupon I reached total freedom. The teacher then beat the drum to summon all the monks to the hall, where he announced to the assembly: "Monk Pao has gone through. Move the wrapper of his begging bowl to the hut for the head monk." From this time on I no longer had any doubts about the Buddha or the patriarchs. Nor did I doubt any of the teachings of the Five Schools or the seven hundred Ch'an paradoxes [*kung-an*]. Only when one has reached this realm can he become a free man who roams leisurely in the world, truly unburdened and truly happy. There is nothing in or outside of this world that is comparable to it. All of you who are diligently studying the Way must not rest until you have reached this realm. (*HTC*, 122:454)

That Wen-pao was instantly rewarded, not only spiritually but also institutionally—he was installed as head monk—may have been in perfect conformity with the reality of the Ch'an monastic world in early Yüan. Besides, one could always look back and point to the precedent of the Sixth Patriarch himself. But his self-satisfaction at both his spiritual and institutional success certainly went against the grain of his religion. Other sermonizers may have been even more complacent. Although the few autobiographical digressions that have been preserved in the extant transcriptions of Ch'an sermons—we have studied three of them in some detail—do not suggest a vogue of blatant self-revelation, the opposite is indicated by the strong reaction of the great master Ming-pen (also known as Chung-feng or Huan-chu, 1263–1323), as reported by Wei-tse (also known as T'ien-ju, b. 1286?), one of his disciples:

I often heard him say that in spite of a lifetime of Ch'an endeavor he never achieved illumination. Even at that time I secretly doubted

[13] *HTC*, 122:454.

what he was saying. Later I realized that the old master was truly a great man. He was never extreme, eccentric, conceited, or boastful. All his life he refused to tell how he himself achieved illumination. His disciples were all under strict orders not to go against his example even when they were not under his eyes. His intention was to shame and intimidate the contemporaries who falsely boasted of attainment of illumination or verification of such attainment, fraudulently claiming great wisdom in order to deceive the common people.[14]

From what is reported above it is clear that in the early fourteenth century there was much flaunting of spiritual attainments among Ch'an clerics. Their excesses must have brought so much dispute to the whole school that Ming-pen, the leading Lin-chi master, had to take a strong stand against self-revelation. His stance is all the more ironical in the light of his lineage, for he was the principal heir of Yüan-miao (1238–1295), who in turn stood in the same relation to Tsu-ch'in. Although Yüan-miao was far less effusive than his teacher in revealing the circumstances of his illumination during a sermon, he did chart his spiritual progress in a long and candid letter to his teacher—which we shall attend to presently.

Ming-pen, then, virtually turned his back on a tradition that had begun gloriously with his direct spiritual forefather, all but once removed, and continued, if in a different medium, with his own teacher. If he of all people should advocate a return to the time-honored Ch'an position that certain things should be left unsaid, who could disagree? Who would openly defy such a prolific writer and eloquent preacher, admired by the imperial family and the literati alike? Lowly members of the cloth may have continued their lucrative imposture in obscure corners of the empire, but the self-respecting masters, those whose sermons were likely to survive in transcriptions, apparently heeded the admonitions of Tsu-ch'in's legitimate heir. My search in the vast collection of Buddhist sermons has not yielded any more digressions on the sermonizer's own spiritual experience beyond Ming-pen's time.

We cannot end this chapter without paying some attention to the above-mentioned autobiographical letter, for it was in its own way a remarkable innovation. The practice of telling parts of one's life story in a letter can be traced back to Ssu-ma Ch'ien, the Grand Historian, as we have seen earlier. Judging by extant letters, this practice apparently did not flourish during the next fifteen centuries. A historian or writer might explain his literary activities, a father might offer his own examples to his children, or an office seeker might try to impress the high and mighty

---

[14] *HTC*, 122:454.

with his accomplishments, but there was no true confiding, no plain narration without rhetorical embellishments.[15]

The only precedent for Yüan-miao was his teacher Tsu-ch'in, who in a letter to a prime minister gave a summary of the quest that he narrated in detail during one of his sermons. But it was the disciple who wrote what may be called the first truly autobiographical letter in China.[16] Yüan-miao's letter has only one subject—his long spiritual journey, which began when he was fifteen. Addressed to Tsu-ch'in, the letter purports to be a disciple's report to the master. As autobiography, the letter broke no new ground, for it does not surpass some of the autobiographical sermons in descriptive detail, self-awareness, or range of reported activities. Absent are the narrative spontaneity and colloquial exuberance of Tsu-ch'in, which could have occurred only in an act of oral performance, but not in writing. Yet Yüan-miao's innovation lies precisely in demonstrating the possibility of a *written* spiritual autobiography.[17] None of the autobiographers in the next chapter ever acknowledged an indebtedness to Yüan-miao, but his example must have been known at least to some of them, given his prominence as a great Lin-chi master and the syncretic climate in which the new autobiographers thrived.[18]

[15] There are twelve autobiographical letters included in *LTW*, but none of them, not even the famous letter of Ssu-ma Ch'ien that we have seen earlier, is very revealing.

[16] *HTC*, 122:678–80.

[17] A complete translation of the letter is included in appendix A.

[18] For an overview of this climate see Wm. Theodore de Bary, "Neo-Confucian Cultivation and the Seventeenth-Century 'Enlightenment,' " in *The Unfolding of Neo-Confucianism*, ed. Wm. Theodore de Bary (New York: Columbia University Press, 1975), pp. 141–216.

FIVE

THE CONFUCIAN'S
PROGRESS

To cultivate the person, to examine the self, to develop each individual to the utmost—these are among the themes most frequently discussed in classical Confucianism. They were the main points of departure when Sung Neo-Confucian philosophers expounded their own theories or doctrines. But, curiously, not until the fifteenth century did any Confucians ever write about such themes as crucial events of their own lives. They seldom shared with readers the genesis of their ideas, their false starts or slow gropings, reversals or sudden discoveries. The great Northern Sung masters seem all to have sprung to full maturity without painful apprenticeship or tortuous search. When they wrote about each other they were equally reticent. Many of their disciples, following the precedent of Ch'an Buddhists, took elaborate notes on the daily sayings of the masters, and a sizable corpus of such notes has been preserved. Most of them seem to be verbatim transcriptions of actual utterance. All circumstances—the informal setting, the small and congenial company, the relaxed and colloquial conversational style, the Confucian emphasis on personal example and the presumably exemplary experience of the masters—were conducive to a measure of self-revelation, but the Neo-Confucian masters, unlike Tsu-ch'in and his Ch'an followers, chose to be reticent in this area of possible discourse.

The diary was another potentially flexible vehicle of self-expression available to Sung Neo-Confucians. Judging by the number of extant works and contemporary references to the practice, we may assume that diary keeping was a widespread habit during the Sung. But surviving Sung diaries seldom afford us even a glimpse of the author's inner world—it is of course unreasonable to expect a Lady Nijō or an Amiel in twelfth-century China. Chinese diaries were nothing more than logbooks of external activities, receptacles of reading notes and anecdotes. For any record of self-examination and self-cultivation we have to wait until early Ming when Wu Yü-pi (1392–1469) wrote what might be described as a subjective diary. He displayed an unabashed interest in his own moods and frequently probed his own deficiencies. Occasionally the autobiographical mode obtains:

In temperament I suffer from stubbornness and quickness to anger. I had not realized this until the year *keng-yin* [1410] of the Yung-lo reign when, at the age of nineteen, I studied with Mr. Yang, chief librarian in the palace of the heir apparent. . . . Since then, although I have from time to time tried to overcome my faults, I have had little success in coping with the rashness and destructiveness to which my faults led. During the last fifteen or sixteen years I frequently indulged my recklessness, but whenever my conscience was awakened, I was overwhelmed with anguish and regret. From last winter to this spring I worked very hard on my problems, yet I found it more difficult to improve in my daily affairs. I became afraid that I would never reach even a slight resemblance to the sages, and that I would inevitably end up a mean person. Since the beginning of the fifth month, having noticed some encouraging signs, I applied myself even more assiduously. As a result, I have been making daily progress. My mind is now more at peace. Although I still react to frustrations, I can get over things without doing harm. On the twentieth of the month there was some unpleasant event that I could not get out of my mind. This made me even more unhappy. Now I realized that in the past I only tried to restrain myself without actually trying to eradicate the causes of my problems. After much self-observation I have come to know that my recent difficulties lie in my insistence on peace of mind and my resentment of any external adversities that might disturb my internal peace. This is wrong. The mind is originally vacuous. It should not be fixed with any of the seven emotions. When one comes into contact with external things, there are bound to be a variety of consequences, some sweet, some bitter. How could I resent those that I find contrary? The only right thing to do is to ascertain carefully the principle of the myriad circumstances and to respond accordingly. When I reached this conclusion I became much at ease.[1]

As the pioneer Neo-Confucian of the Ming, Wu was revered throughout the dynasty. His innovation as a diarist was recognized by Chang Kun, a sixteenth-century critic. "Wu's diary is the history of an individual. Everything in it is about his own affairs, presented in his own words. He is quite unlike other diarists, who either add their voices to or support their own opinions with the established ideas: they speak only in broad generalities."[2] Wu is indeed a *historian* of the self, but only in a limited sense. On a given day he may reminisce or anticipate, as he does in the entry just quoted, but only occasionally does he rise above the concerns of the day and see the pattern of his endeavor—the very essence of history. By writing a subjective diary Wu indeed freed himself from both the

[1] Quoted in *MJHA*, p. 3.
[2] *MJHA*, p. 2.

usual style of Chinese diary and historiography, but the format of the genre does not encourage a sustained vision of life as a process. It is precisely this vision that united the Buddhist autobiographical sermonizers we have met in the preceding chapter and the Ming Neo-Confucian spiritual autobiographers who were in a sense Wu's heirs. If Wu himself stopped short of writing a true history of the self, he nevertheless demonstrated to the succeeding generations of Neo-Confucians the feasibility, hitherto unattempted, of writing about one's own moods and discoveries, struggles with faults and small victories over them. If the pioneering master of the dynasty could unabashedly tell about himself, perhaps others need not remain reticent. For our purpose Wu represents the transition from the sober and mannerly Sung masters to the fervent and restless Neo-Confucians of late Ming. His self-observation and self-revelation anticipate the next century but his emphasis on quiescence and reverence places him solidly in the old camp.

In contrast to the diary, travel literature had a much greater impact on the course of Chinese autobiography. Up to this point the only models that Chinese autobiography had had were biography or the authorial preface, and, as we have seen again and again, inherent in the models was the heavy and far-reaching hand of historiography, which had long held Chinese *written* autobiography in thrall. However, during the sixteenth century a combination of circumstances led to the adoption of travel literature as an alternative model for autobiography, and the result was a totally new subgenre, which we shall term spiritual autobiography. How it came about was a complex story, which we shall begin with a digression.

LIFE AS JOURNEY

There are obvious parallels in form between travel literature and autobiography. In the vast majority of cases both are first-person prose narratives of presumably factual events. The traveler and the autobiographer, as the protagonists of their stories, are both concerned with movement: ostensibly the former is more interested in spatial locomotion, the latter in chronological unfolding. Both must adopt at least an implied temporal scheme, which is usually longer in an autobiography. All the distinctions, however, disappear when the autobiographer chooses to cast his narrative in the form of a travel account, ignoring almost all other aspects of his life. This is especially true if the overriding concern of the narrator is a search for absolute truth, a quest for the understanding that will utterly transform the self. In other words, spiritual autobiography can and has been narrated as a travel account.

Why this is so has much to do with the universal and perennial figure of life as journey. In China from time immemorial both the ultimate truth and the pursuit of it have been represented by the word *tao*, literally a "road." "Way" is a better translation, but the German *Weg* is still better in conveying the metaphysical sense of the word. Similarly, the life with purpose, the life of endeavor, has often been represented with figures of locomotion. The third-century B.C. Confucian Hsün Tzu demonstrated the feasibility of self-cultivation as follows:

> A thoroughbred can travel a thousand *li* in one day, yet even a tired old nag, given ten days to do it in, can cover the same distance. . . . If those who have gone before stop and wait, and those who are be-hind keep going, then whether sooner or later, whether first or last, how can they fail all in time to reach the goal? If he keeps putting one foot in front of the other without stopping, even a lame turtle can go a thousand *li*; . . . if they take one step forward and one step back, pull now to the left and now to the right, even a team of six thor-oughbreds will never reach their destination. Men are certainly not as widely separated in their capacities as a lame turtle and a team of six thoroughbreds; yet the lame turtle reaches the goal where the team of thoroughbreds fails. There is only one reason: one keeps on going, the other does not. Though the road is short, if you do not step along you will never get to the end.[3]

In the *Chen Kao* (True commandments), a collection of Taoist admonish-ments and commandments compiled by T'ao Hung-ching (ca. 500), the journey metaphor is used quite explicitly: "To study the Way is like tak-ing a ten-thousand-mile journey: one notices and experiences the cold, heat, good and bad things, vegetation, water, and soil of all the places that one passes through. The test is in them."[4]

By the sixteenth century the journey metaphor had become a com-monplace in the Neo-Confucian discourse on *hsüeh*, one of the key no-tions of Confucianism. The term is usually translated as "to learn" or "to study," but it has a much broader meaning than either of the English words. It can also mean "to emulate" or "to imitate," as in "imitation of the sages"; in its nominal form it can stand for a school or an academy, the totality of the theories or teachings of a person or a school, or any systematic body of knowledge. In the Neo-Confucian usage it can rep-resent moral, spiritual, or intellectual endeavor; sometimes it encom-passes all three. The goal of such endeavor, theoretically possible for all mankind, is Confucian sagehood. For many Neo-Confucians in the late

[3] Burton Watson, trans., *Basic Writings of Mo Tzu, Hsü Tzu, and Han Fei Tzu* (New York: Columbia University Press, 1967), pp. 28–29.

[4] *Chen kao*, TSCC ed., p. 94.

sixteenth and seventeenth centuries the endeavor or the regimen of striving as denoted by *hsüeh* took on a more subjective turn as it became increasingly strenuous and exigent. Li Chih says in a nutshell what many
contemporary Confucians tried to do all their lives, "Everyone who is
engaged in *hsüeh* does so for the sake of fathoming the ultimate cause of
his own life and death, searching for the destination of his own nature and
endowment."[5] The endeavor of such a person lends itself very readily to
comparison with the travails of a traveler. Ch'en Chia-mo (1521–1603)
observes that "when engaged in *hsüeh* one must keep on pursuing and
searching until one arrives at a spot completely roadless and blocked from
all four directions; only in such a place can one gradually find the true
beginning of the road. This road has to be found by oneself."[6] A similar
thought is expressed by Teng I-tsan (1542–1599): "One must pursue and
search for *hsüeh* in one's own body and mind. Even though one may
make a thousand false starts and ten thousand wrong moves, as long as
one keeps on walking one will eventually find the right road at the end of
the river and the foot of the mountain."[7] The juxtaposition of the two
sentences makes explicit that it is an inner journey that Teng is concerned
with.

Other Confucian writers extend the journey motif to include voyage
over water—a very hazardous undertaking in traditional Chinese perception and fraught with symbolic perils and archetypical meanings. Chou
Ju-teng (1547–1629?) maintains that "those who climb mountains do not
begrudge the toils of walking; those who cross rivers must depend on the
facilities of boats; those who are committed to the Way must exhaust all
the efforts of cultivation and action."[8] The idea was most elaborately expressed by Lo Ju-fang (1515–1588):

> The roads in the world are inevitably rocky and uneven; the rivers
> cannot avoid having rapids and shoals. But rocks cannot obstruct the
> swift wheels of a cart if the carter is skillful; nor can rapids and shoals
> defeat the facile oars and poles of a competent boatman. . . . The
> road to Confucian learning has always been, from ancient times to
> the present, simple, direct, and straight; to embark on it is an easy
> and joyful undertaking. Every day there are in the world thousands
> of carters driving, and I have never heard of one who turns around
> because the road is difficult; every day there are in the world
> thousands of boatmen sailing, and I have never heard of one who
> stops his boat on account of rapids and shoals. Then why is it that

[5] *Hsü Fen shu* (Sequel to *A Book to Be Burned*) (Peking: Chung-hua shu-chü, 1961), p. 1.
[6] *MJHA*, p. 209.
[7] *MJHA*, p. 208.
[8] *MJHA*, p. 376.

some of us who undertake to emulate the sages should anticipate obstacles even before the cart is moving and worry about rapids and shoals even before the anchor is weighed? Is it the road that obstructs us, or is it ourselves that obstruct us?[9]

The proliferation of the journey metaphor was not merely a literary convention, a new rhetorical vogue. It reflected a reality of wanderlust. Many literally took to the road. The allures of nature, always a justification for travel, were even more irresistible in late Ming. Travelers like Yüan Tsung-tao (1560–1600) "craved for mountains and lakes as a hungry and thirsty man would for food and drink."[10] Many were attracted to the southern and western border regions rarely visited for their own sake in the T'ang and Sung. It is true that travel literature touched on such regions before the Ming, but the earlier literary sojourners went invariably as exiles and stayed only as long as necessary. Now countless travelers roamed the breadth and length of their vast country, exploring inaccessible areas for their scenic beauty and admiring the sort of wild grandeur that Europeans did not find appealing until about one century later. Some members of the literati such as Hsü Hung-tsu (also known as Hsü Hsia-k'o, 1586–1641) even forsook their official careers to devote their entire lives to climbing high mountains and tracing river sources in remote areas never explored before. For our purpose, however, the most interesting group of travelers consists of those Neo-Confucians whose inner quest for truth and understanding manifested itself in long peregrinations, whose burning sense of urgency and almost compulsive restlessness distinguished them clearly from the sober and mannerly Sung masters.

Typical of those wandering seekers is Lo Hung-hsien (1504–1564), a prominent member of the Wang Shou-jen (1472–1529) school and the teacher of Hu Chih and Wan T'ing-yen, both of whom wrote spiritual autobiographies. After leaving government service Lo retired to the Stone Lotus Grotto where he practiced quiet-sitting and meditation to the exclusion of all worldly affairs. For three years he never walked out of the gate. But once he went out on a journey,

> he would stay on the road for more than a year. He sought teachers and consulted friends, without discriminating between Buddhists and Confucians. He would humbly solicit instruction from anyone who had something to offer him, like a patient seeking cure from a physician. In his quest he discarded nearly all the decorum and priv-

[9] MJHA, p. 377.
[10] Yüan Hung-tao, Yüan Hung-tao chi ch'ien-chiao (Collected writings of Yüan Hung-tao with bibliographical notes), ed. Ch'ien Po-ch'eng, 3 vols. (Shanghai: Shang-hai ku-chi ch'u-pan-she, 1981), 3:1672.

ileges of a scholar-official. He traveled all alone, braving hunger, cold, and other hardships of long journeys. The hazards of sailing over waters in uncertain weather were nothing to him, nor did he ever mind the insults and abuses encountered in country inns.[11]

Such Confucian seekers were not unlike the itinerant Buddhist monks we met in the preceding chapter. We may recall that for a Ch'an monk Buddhahood was achieved not by scriptural learning or devotional practices but through comprehending his own mind and seeing his own nature. The Sixth Patriarch made this point very clear when he declared, "Since Buddha is made by your own nature, do not look for him outside your body."[12] But paradoxically this inner quest, often necessitated extensive travel, for as Hui-neng admonished, "If you cannot gain enlightenment for yourselves, you must seek a great teacher to show you the way to see into your own self-nature."[13] Our ambulatory Neo-Confucians behaved as if they had taken the patriarch's advice to heart. In many of their biographies and autobiographical fragments the phrase "to look for a teacher and to visit friends" recurs like a refrain. If crucial portions of such lives were not only literally lived on the road but were figuratively no different from the journeys so often cited in Confucian exhortations, then travel literature seemed to be the natural medium for recounting such lives. The autobiographical Ch'an masters in the last chapter had already given us an inkling of this possibility when they reported their progress as a series of double movements—from temple to temple as well as from one spiritual crisis to another. Even their final breakthroughs seldom came about without the catalyst of some physical act, as if illumination had to be preceded by locomotion.

TENG HUO-CH'Ü (1498–1570?)

The first author to make use of this possibility and write a spiritual autobiography in the format of a *yu-chi* (travel account) was a Confucian apostate who was not quite a Buddhist. Teng Huo-ch'ü in many ways represents the culmination of the late Ming temperament—restlessness, fervor, daring, adventurousness. Many of his contemporaries displayed varying degrees of sympathy for and understanding of Buddhism, but Teng was the first notable member of any Neo-Confucian sect who actually took the momentous step of joining a Buddhist monastic order. Even his new faith could not cure him of his waywardness, for he ceased to observe the vows and other niceties five years after his tonsure. His

---

[11] *MJHA*, p. 158.
[12] *Platform Sutra*, p. 158.
[13] Ibid., p. 152.

double identity, however, made him the perfect logical link between the Buddhist autobiographical sermonizers we met in the preceding chapter and the Neo-Confucian spiritual autobiographers, who were in all likelihood exposed to his example.

Born in Nei-chiang, Szechwan, Teng was a perennial student, living on government scholarships as the holder of a preliminary degree and lecturing on Confucian studies. In 1539 Chao Chen-chi (also known as Ta-chou, 1508–1576), a native son who had already begun a brilliant career in government, returned home on leave. For a while Teng and Chao were rivals in the local academy, giving lectures at the same time in opposite halls. It was an unequal contest, for Chao, a prominent member of the T'ai-chou sect of the Wang Shou-jen school, had all the advantages. Gradually Teng came to realize that Chao had a much better understanding of the Way. Consequently Teng, at the age of forty-one, formally acknowledged Chao, a man ten years his junior, as his master. From this time on his zeal for truth made him such a stranger to his family that he left home and lived in a dilapidated Buddhist temple. "One day on his way to a meeting with his newly acknowledged teacher he happened to pass by the door of his own house. When his children saw him they came out to beg him to step in. He refused. The children held on to the lapel of his coat and wailed, but he broke away."[14]

His restlessness and spiritual fervor grew to the point where he could no longer stay within the confines of either his hometown or Confucianism. One day he just took to the road and never returned. In his quest for truth and illumination he went west as far as the region bordering on Burma and east as far as the sea. Many years later when he was staying in Wei-hui, a town in northern China, he heard that Chao Chen-chi, now a high official, was going to pass through Wei-hui on his way to Peking. He went out of the city and waited for Chao by the roadside. Startled to see his long-lost disciple, Chao got down from his carriage and greeted Teng warmly. Talking and weeping, they walked side by side behind the carriage for ten miles. Blaming himself for Teng's vagabondage, Chao deeded over to Teng dozens of acres of high-yield farmland in their native county and urged him to return home. After they parted Teng ignored his teacher's advice, sent back the deed, and resumed his peregrinations.

[14] Keng Ting-hsiang, *Li-chung san i-jen chuan* (Biographies of the three eccentrics who once resided in my neighborhood), *Keng T'ien-t'ai hsien-sheng wen-chi* (Collected works of Master Keng Ting-hsiang), 4 vols. (reprint, Taipei: Wen-hai ch'u-pan-she, 1970), 4:1633. Cf. John Bunyan, *The Pilgrim's Progress*, ed. Roger Sharrock (New York: Penguin Books, 1981), p. 41: "So I saw in my dream that the man began to run. Now he had not run far from his own door, but his wife and children perceiving it began to cry after him to return: but the man put his fingers in his ears, and ran on crying, 'Life, life, eternal life.' So he looked not behind him, but fled towards the middle of the plain."

When Chao was appointed grand secretary in 1569 Teng proceeded to the capital, but Chao refused to see him. Instead Chao entrusted Teng to a subordinate who was about to leave for an administrative post in Szechwan. On the way south Teng fell ill. The official, impatient of any delay, left his charge behind in a deserted temple, where the perpetual wanderer died alone.[15]

There would have been nothing much to distinguish Teng from countless adventurers who roamed the length and breadth of late Ming China, earning at best a controversial and ephemeral fame, had he not written a most unusual autobiography in 1565. Although in format his book loosely follows the travel literature that was then in vogue, the itinerary is less concerned with landscape and human interest—the stuff of most Chinese travel literature—than with the creation of a unique persona who is as free of restraint and as rambling as any traveler. His meandering way of truth seeking is mirrored by the fortuitousness and contingency of journey, and his encounters with specific settings, scenes, and places are but backdrops for his changes of outlook, flashes of insight, or spiritual discoveries. As befits a double journey, the book abounds in figures of travel and locomotion.

The very title of the book, *Nan-hsün lu* (The record of a quest in the south) resonates with allusive force.[16] The phrase *nan-hsün* was frequently used by Sung commentators on the *Hua-yen ching* (*Avataṁsakasūtra*) to represent the journey of the youth Shan-ts'ai (Sudhana) in search of truth and illumination. The most compelling figure of the sutra, Shan-ts'ai, traveled to more than one hundred and ten places in south India and sought instruction from fifty-three benefactors. The journey took him to many wonderlands described in sensuous detail, while the diversity of his teachers—gods and goddesses, divine and semidivine beings, boy and girl acolytes, healers, seafaring pilots, perfume makers, singers, kings and queens, and even a holy man renowned for his silence—is unmatched in any imaginative literature. Shan-ts'ai's story, with its theme of quest and exuberant mythology, was widely popular in China. Even Chu Hsi (1130–1200), the great defender of Confucianism against Buddhist encroachments, cited the Indian youth without disapproval.[17] For Teng, re-

[15] The facts of Teng's life, here and later in the chapter, are from Keng Ting-hsiang, 4:1633–38.

[16] Although the book enjoyed a great vogue in the decades before and after 1600, none of the many editions is known to have survived in China. A copy of the edition published in or shortly after 1599 with a preface by Li Chih, probably the only extant copy of the book, is preserved in the Naikaku Bunko; hereafter it is referred to as *Nan-hsün lu*. I wish to express my gratitude to Professor Yoshitaka Iriya, who kindly helped me to secure a photocopy of this rare volume when I visited Kyoto in 1971.

[17] *Chu-tzu yü-lei* (1473 ed., reprint, Taipei: Cheng-chung shu-chü, 1972), 118:3a–b.

cording his floating life at the age of sixty-seven, identification with Shan-ts'ai gave shape to his meanderings, promised attainment of his goal and justified his Buddhist involvement, however precarious it may have been.

The text proper of *Nan-hsün lu* begins abruptly with Teng's acknowledgment of his teacher: "On the twenty-second day of the first month in the year *chi-hai* [1539] I made my obeisance to the teacher in front of the Sheng-shui Cliff in Nei-chiang" (1a). Nowhere in the text is the teacher explicitly identified by name, nor is the reader informed of the circumstances under which the teacher came into the autobiographer's life. Chao's name is mentioned later in the text, but only as someone who did Teng an injustice. That the teacher was no other than Chao Chen-chi the reader can only discover from sources external to the autobiography. The abruptness of the beginning and the omission of necessary facts, puzzling as they may seem, constitute but the first expression of a lasting ambivalence that Teng felt toward his teacher, who will reappear under different guises at almost every turn of the road. Teng's obscuration—the pangs of defeat and submission perhaps still rankle—is balanced by the implied homage he pays to Chao by placing the anonymous teacher at the very beginning of the journey as if acknowledging, however unwillingly, that it was Chao who had set him in motion. The initial episode is so crucial to him that he specifies the exact date and location—in contrast to his other reticences—very much in the way that a typical autobiographer begins with the announcement of his birth. What Teng's life was like before the rebirth he mentions only briefly, but not in the text proper: "Born obtuse, I have been unreceptive to the popular but eager for self-cultivation ever since childhood. When I grew up, I devoted myself to the study of the Way. Although I am slow and handicapped, I have always resolutely held myself aloof from the crowd" (*Nan-hsün lu*, "Prefaces," 3a).

This persona of a self-directed and unyielding individual, consistently maintained throughout the book, cannot abide a teacher for very long, especially someone who was so high in popular esteem and vanquished him in a public contest. In no time at all he becomes dissatisfied with the teacher's brand of Neo-Confucianism.

> After I received instructions from my master I had no other concern: all day and night I was preoccupied with the endeavor and strove with all my effort. Gradually things began to open up. I now felt that the "innate knowledge" advocated by Wang Yang-ming could not solve the problem of life and death. I also felt that all human life is involved with sentiments and that those scholars who cannot transcend sentiments will not reach liberation. In addition I came to some ineffable intimation of the unsurpassed wondrous Way that is

beyond language and thought but is witnessed by all Buddhas. (*Nan-hsün lu*, 2a)

Even early in his quest Teng seems to have renounced his teacher by implication, for the concept of innate knowledge is the cornerstone of the Wang Shou-jen school. Many of the more radical members of the Wang school flouted convention and experimented with diverse doctrines, but none would go so far as to abandon innate knowledge as the guiding principle. To Teng, however, "innate knowledge, although it is the awakening of spiritual brightness, is still within the cycle of birth and destruction. No matter how penetrating it is, it is still linked to creation and transformation: it cannot go beyond them" (2b).

As Teng went beyond the confines of Confucianism, he also began to travel. First he went to the Ch'ing-ch'eng Mountains, where he read Buddhist texts. In 1545 he traveled to Yünnan. Early in 1547 he ascended the Chi-tsu Mountain, the most prominent Buddhist center in the province, and stayed in the San-t'ai Monastery. Realizing that halfway measures would not lead to the ultimate truth, he received the tonsure and became a monk in the spring of 1548. What is most intriguing is the brevity with which he describes the event. We are not told into which Buddhist sect or order he was received. There is no mention of either the name of the master who presided over the ordination or of the religious name he received on that occasion. If he was indeed given a religious name, it must have been privy only to him and his ordainer, for none of his detractors or critics ever referred to him by that appellation. The book gives no indication that his commitment to Buddhism was ever strong. No reference is made to a Ch'an regimen or any devotional practice. The only insight that he gained during his nominally Buddhist phase came to him fortuitously:

> When I was in Yünnan I heard someone say that to pick flowers and use them as an offering to the Buddha is neither an offense nor a meritorious deed. I was quite struck by the saying. Ever since then I have never plucked a blade of grass or broken a twig without reason. I heard people say that every leaf and every grain are living beings. This brought great awareness to me. Since then I have never wasted any food or water. (3b)

After he took Buddhist vows he traveled even more extensively. Presumably many doors were open to him, now an articulate and charismatic monk. From his account there seems to have been no shortage of admirers and benefactors. Although he called on various prominent Confucians and Buddhist monks, he displayed very little humility or even eagerness to learn from others, his purported emulation of the youth

Shan-ts'ai notwithstanding. In 1553 he let his hair grow back and ceased to wear the clerical habit. The reason he gives was that, when he was traveling in Chekiang, Buddhist monks encountered great inconvenience on the road. As Japanese pirates were rampant in the coastal regions of southern China, Buddhist monks were subject to strict surveillance on account of the generally held belief that Japanese spies operated under the guise of itinerant monks. The real reason may have been his difficulties in observing priestly vows.

> It was in Ching county of the Ning-kuo prefecture that for the first time I broke the dietary laws. The night before I dreamt that someone gave me chicken meat to eat and after I ate all my teeth felt an acid sensation and my stomach felt very uncomfortable. The following day when I arrived at the Ching temple the monk killed a chicken and warmed wine to entertain me. Before I knew it all the teeth in my mouth suffered an intolerable sensation of acidity. The dream suddenly came back to me and I began to feel very uneasy. I tried to bear it but my stomach started to act up. The grumbling and pain lasted several days. This was caused by the typical inhibitions of a Confucian pedant but even to this day my persistent gluttony puts me to shame. (7b)

In some sense the above episode marks the lowest point of his journey. In contrast to the life stories of Tsu-ch'in and his followers, Teng's narrative is almost completely free from expressions of doubt, despair, or resultant agonies. His reaction to his final act of apostasy is lightly passed over: whatever physical symptoms he had he attributes not to a sense of guilt over the violation of Buddhist vows but to his incomplete liberation from Confucianism. To him the implications of his gluttony are not so much the destruction of life—that he is not totally oblivious to committing the worst sin for a Buddhist is suggested by his wording, "the monk killed a chicken"—as the existence of a weakness, a trait inconsistent with his self-image of a totally liberated being. For this he felt shame. But he may have felt much more strongly than he avows. His remembrance of his brief and somewhat unsatisfactory experiment with Buddhist priesthood must have been accompanied by intense feelings, for immediately after the sentence that ends with the word "shame" he invokes, for the first time and quite abruptly, his teacher's name:

> When I had myself tonsured and joined a Buddhist order, people of my hometown blamed it on Chao Ta-chou, saying that it was he who ruined me. Ta-chou, trying to evade the responsibility, said that he had nothing to do with it. Earlier when I was still back home lecturing on the teaching of the Sage (sheng-hsüeh), I was very poor.

Ch'i-yen said, "Teng Huo-ch'ü is dying of starvation." Chao replied to that by saying, "It would be a fine sight on Kuei-hu Street if Teng starves to death there." I now declare, "It would be a fine sight if Chao Ta-chou ruins Teng Huo-ch'ü." (7b–8a)

This jumble of names, hearsay, and reported utterances is as confusing as Teng's intent was complex. That Chao Ta-chou is no other than the unnamed teacher revered at the beginning of the autobiography presumably poses no problem to Teng's contemporary readers, to whom Chao Chen-chi (Ta-chou) was a household name. For us it is possible, however, to attempt a reading of this segment of the narrative in light of the biography of Teng written by Keng Ting-hsiang and Li Chih's laudatory preface to *Nan-hsün lu*. What is immediately palpable is the great bitterness that Teng still felt toward his teacher when he wrote the above years after the humiliating incident. The intensity of his resentment, the need for self-justification, the reluctance to disclose the whole truth even if only from his point of view, and the impossibility of renouncing once and for all the teacher who has been hitherto kept out of view—this powerful combination of motives is responsible for the ellipses and opacity in the text and even for a reversal in the chronology of actual events. To unravel this jumble we shall begin with the penultimate narrative unit.

The comments on starvation signify that after Teng was defeated by Chao at the lecture contest he was no longer able to eke out a living as a struggling and aging candidate for a higher degree. Chao, the most prominent son of their hometown and a rising star both in politics and Confucian academe, is portrayed as a callous victor, unmoved by the plight of the vanquished. He became defensive only when he was criticized by the townsmen for making Teng's position so untenable that Buddhist priesthood was his only possible alternative. Going further back to the last quotation, we see that priesthood was indeed almost a ruination: Teng was tormented by dreams when he kept his vows; when he broke them he suffered even more. His contemplation on his current gluttony touched off a stream of consciousness that brought him to the remembered hunger, and the train of remembrances abruptly ended with his semi-ironical declaration of being indeed ruined by his teacher.

Whatever the poignancy of defeat and exile, however he may regret his sojourn in the Buddhist order, Teng recovers quickly. He will have the last word as far as Chao is concerned, for the name of the teacher never appears again in the text. The world as well as Chao may have seen him as a ruined man but, he goes on to say, it is men of this world, Chao included by implication, who will suffer and perish in the end:

Now that the Three Teachings have declined, the people of the world all drift and float in accordance with their karma. They sink and perish. They live like fish in marshes: they are born there and they die there. How many of them will ever leap over the Dragon Gate [Lung-men]? They commit all sins and suffer the cycles of reincarnation. There is no peace or joy in their lives. This is what the ancients meant when they spoke of "the man who forsook his path and did not follow it or the man who let his mind wander off without seeking to regain it. How lamentable it is!" (8a)

When the art of spiritual autobiography is at its best, even a discursive passage like the one above is alive with kinetic energy. If the pervading image here is that of water, spatial and locomotive figures abound, as befits the recounting of a life in which the quest theme obtains both metaphorically and literally. People without imagination or determination would "drift," "float," "sink," or languish "like fish in the marshes." They are destined to suffer from perpetual "wheel-return [*lun-hui*, the Chinese term for cycles of reincarnation]." The concluding quotation from *Mencius* (6A:11:2) was probably chosen as much for the extension of the locomotive figure as for its ironic effects. Confucians who are incapable of breaking away from either hometown or orthodoxy are not only condemned to stagnate but must also suffer the flaunting of the sacred words of one of their most revered sages. If only Chao Chen-chi could have been present and forced to listen to the sacrilege mouthed by the apostate! The most suggestive element of this rich texture, however, is the allusion to the Dragon Gate whose resonances, both within and beyond the text, demand our attention.

An old Chinese legend had it that fish from all rivers and seas assemble under a certain cascade in the Yellow River. Those who succeeded in leaping above the cascade and thus passing through *Lung-men* (Dragon Gate) would be transformed into dragons while those who failed would have their foreheads branded and their gills exposed. Magic powers and unbounded freedom would be granted to the victors but unerasable shame would mark the less fortunate—the vast majority of the contenders—for life. The legend, the origin of which may have been in the natural phenomenon of fish swimming upstream to spawn, was very popular in China. It reached back to the archetypal motives of test, challenge, or ordeal that abound in any quest story. The great leap upward over a hazardous precipice and the ensuing metamorphosis are the appropriate denouement for a spiritual journey, a physical representation of the Buddhist sudden illumination. To the Confucians, who constantly made references to the legend, it had almost all the exemplary elements of the national examination system. The candidates for the final degree came to the capital from all parts of China and a happy few would, through their own talent and effort, emerge victors from the excruciating competition.

Here our irrepressible iconoclast stands the cliché on its head: the implication is that Chao Chen-chi, who achieved the final degree with high honors in his youth, would languish in the marsh while his former student would, by virtue of his faith and insight, end his quest a totally liberated and transformed being, a being of the higher realm, however the world might judge the pair.

Related to the figure of Lung-men is the *kuan*, literally a "pass" or fortified checkpoint with gates and walls. A *kuan* is usually so strategically located that a traveler cannot easily go around it and an outlaw must approach it with all his wits. The successful negotiation of a *kuan* guarded by hostile forces often occurs as one of the most memorable episodes in the life of a Chinese hero, be he historical or fictional. In the vocabulary of spiritual journey Lung-men and *kuan* are cognates—configurations akin to the biblical strait gate. Both are spatial figures reminiscent of the rites of passage, rituals of initiation, ordeals, or tests of personal worth; the challenge is fraught with perils but also promises great advances. While Lung-men stands for one specific place, *kuan* can be a part of any number of place-names—for instances, the Yü-men-kuan (Jade-Gate Pass). This is one reason why *kuan* has been used frequently in the discourse on cultivation or quest, where the student has to prove himself repeatedly. To the religious Taoists a sequential system of *kuan* is more or less symbolically located in every human body, and to achieve immortality one must follow an elaborate program of penetrating each and all of the internal *kuan* while fighting temptations and fending off demons. This topographical term also abounds in Ch'an Buddhist discourse, with the *wu-men-kuan* (gateless pass) one of the most famous Ch'an paradoxes. It is natural then that Ming Neo-Confucians, who increasingly perceived their endeavors in terms of change and progression, should have introduced into their own metaphorical language this figure from legend, geography, and military strategy. One of the first to do so was Wu Yü-pi, the subjective diarist we encountered earlier in this chapter, who states that "after dinner I sat under the eastern window. My limbs were at ease and my spirit was bright and clear. For several days I was in good spirits and my study progressed steadily. All in all I must have gone through another pass [*kuan*]."[18]

There are other occasions in Wu's diary when the locomotive figure of going through a pass (*kuo-kuan*) is employed to suggest that in his quest he has, so to speak, turned a corner or reached a new stage. Unlike his more theoretically minded confreres, Wu does not number his passes or specify a sequential relation between them. For many writers on spiritual regimen a graded progress through three—a magic number—passes was

[18] *MJHA*, p. 3.

in order. The idea of a triad of passes (*san-kuan*) may have come from the ancient Chinese geopoliticians, who never tired of identifying in such terms sets of topographical barriers that lay on routes of military operations. To reach any worthy goal a marching army almost always had to penetrate a set of *san-kuan*. Religious Taoists and Ch'an Buddhists were the next to adopt this magic set. Of the numerous exponents of the Confucian progress in a three-stage formulation we shall concern ourselves with only two. To Keng Ting-hsiang, an acquaintance and biographer of Teng, "there are Three Passes [*san-kuan*] in our endeavor [*hsüeh*]. To penetrate the Initial Pass one must be able to understand the truth that the mind is the Way. To advance through the Second Pass one must be able to perceive that every event is a matter of the mind. Only when one is able to distinguish the undertaking of a great man from that of a petty person can one achieve the negotiation of the Final Pass."[19] Each of the passes is named and described by Liu Tsung-chou in his essay *Sheng-hsüeh ch'ih-chin san-kuan* (The three crucial passes in the sagely endeavor). They are the Pass Dividing the Others and Self, the Pass Dividing Reverence and Licentiousness, and the Pass Dividing Enlightenment and Straying. The essay begins appropriately with a string of journey metaphors: "The first thing in our undertaking is to inquire about the correct route. . . . Only then can we make strides."[20] It ends with a justification of the use of the word *wu* (enlightenment) for fear that Buddhist connotations might be read into his usage. His apprehension was certainly not unfounded, for one of the most popular books of his time was the *Ch'an-kuan ts'e-chin* (Cantering through Ch'an passes) whose author, the monk Chu-hung (1535–1615), draws parallels between a Ch'an regimen and the negotiation of successive passes. Teng Huo-ch'ü, on the other hand, had no such qualms. In his numerous uses of the pass figure (*Nan-hsün lu,* 11a, 19a, 28a, 28b, 34b, 42b, 44b, 45a) he mixes Confucian formulaic schemes with Buddhist ideas. The following is a typical passage:

> He who wants to surpass the common and reach to the sacred must lay down everything. Yet if he tries to do so deliberately, he will not succeed. If he simply eats when he is hungry, sleeps when he is tired, goes about without concerns, then his mind will be laid down without his endeavoring to do so. If everything is laid down—whether he is concerned with any affairs or not—his person will be peaceful. When his person is peaceful, then his mind will be vacuous yet supremely responsive, solitary yet wondrous. He will then spontaneously surpass the common and reach to the sacred. The secret of

[19] *MJHA*, p. 211.
[20] *MJHA*, P. 712.

surpassing the common and reaching to the sacred lies in the negotiation of several passes [*kuan*]. (Ibid., 28a–b)

Teng goes on to describe three such passes and then poses the question as
to how they are to be negotiated. The two-line verse that passes for an
answer to his own question is as enigmatic as it is rich in journey imagery:

> Alas, the road is far, the night is long, and it is difficult to carry a
> burning torch.
> Let all of us blow out the flame and walk in the dark !²¹

Among the episodes in Teng's own life journey, the one that contains
almost all the elements of the *kuo-kuan* figure occurred three years after
he left the Buddhist priesthood.

> In the year *ping-ch'en* [1556] I crossed the Pa-pa Ridge in Kwangsi. It
> was a precarious route on account of the hostile Yao aborigines. In
> spite of extreme hunger and fatigue I forced myself to climb to the
> foot of the summit. I stumbled several times, and for a while it
> seemed that I could no longer proceed. Thereupon I sat in the lotus
> position on a rock, resting with my eyes closed. All feelings and
> thoughts gone, there was no more anxiety over life and death or
> gains and losses. Suddenly and clearly pure precious light appeared.
> Words cannot describe these intimations and visions, which I had
> never before experienced. Extreme hunger and fatigue compelled
> me to a direct confrontation with what I had been before I was con-
> ceived by my parents. But I did not reach liberation then and there,
> for my endeavor had not been completed, my cultivation had not
> been perfected, and my search and study had not been sufficiently
> penetrating. I was not ready for release from worldly toil. (Ibid.,
> 11b–12a)

Although in the above account Teng makes no explicit reference to a pass,
the highest point at which the road crossed the Pa-pa Ridge was the usual
place where a *kuan* would be located. The strategical point was presumably not guarded or roadblocked to deny him passage, but all the symbolic trappings of the ordeal represented by the *kuo-kuan* were present—
physical danger, extreme hardship, ascent to great heights, and breakthrough. The passage through merely one *kuan* seldom brings the seeker
directly to the promised land, but Teng was afforded his first glimpse of
the journey's destination. Both metaphorically and literally the traverse
of the Pa-pa Ridge represents a high point in his protracted quest.

Teng had left the Buddhist priesthood three years before the above ep-

---

²¹ *Nan-hsün lu*, 28b–29a. This couplet was also quoted by Tsu-ch'in in a sermon (*HTC*,
122:544).

isode took place, but his experience on the ridge is reminiscent of the struggles described in the Ch'an sermons we discussed in the preceding chapter. Hunger and fatigue compelled him to dwell on a *kung-an* (Ch'an paradox) which was the staple for countless Ch'an disciples, and visions of pure and precious light frequently accompanied Buddhist illumination. The wilderness motif is new. It is a telling sign that Teng's ultimate model may have been a Confucian one. Wang Shou-jen, the founder of the Wang school of Neo-Confucianism, had had his great awakening under almost identical circumstances. It happened in 1508 during his exile in a neighboring and even more remote province. There were the same desolate terrain, inhospitable climate, and unpredictable aborigines. Both were suffering from extreme privation and both, just before their deliverance, had first risen above concerns with life and death. Wang Shou-jen had a stone coffin made and meditated next to it, while Teng chose to meditate on a rock.

There is another link between Wang and Teng, although it has little to do with the founder's spiritual experience. The very site of Teng's travails may have even been trodden thirty-eight years earlier by the great master himself, then no longer an exile but the commander of an army, for it was in Kwangsi that Wang Shou-jen fought his last campaign, against the very tribesmen whose descendants still menaced hapless travelers. There is of course no record of Wang Shou-jen's ever facing a lonely death against a wild landscape, but this tableau of Teng's own plight was prefigured in one of Wang's most memorable essays. One evening in the second year of his exile to a godforsaken corner of Kwei-chou, Wang saw from his hut a petty clerk from the capital with a retinue of two seeking to be put up in an aborigine family. During the next two days reports came on the successive deaths of the three travelers at the foot of the Centipede's Hill. Wang, saddened by their lot and mindful of his own uncertain fate, went to the site with two boys and dug holes by the hillside for simple burials. In a very moving lamentation Wang stated his belief that trying to climb steep hills combined with extreme hunger and fatigue contributed to their death.

There is every reason to believe that as Teng was trudging up the forbidding ridge—and at other critical moments of his perpetual wanderings—he was aware of historical and even iconographical precedents in the great drama of the founding father's life. After all it was Wang's teaching, with Chao Chen-chi as its instrument, that first set him in motion. Every one of the prominent scholar-officials he visited, with one possible exception, was a member of the Wang school. The master was mentioned by name on eight pages of the *Nan-hsün lu* (2a, 6a, 8b, 10b, 36a, 39a, 39b, 44b) and alluded to even more frequently, even though there is no explicit reference to him in the telling of the present episode. Whether or not

Teng deliberately arranged or even invented the stage set that he describes in the Pa-pa Ridge story, it is obvious that at the time Wang's image was not far from his mind; only one page earlier he had described his visit to Wang's hometown: "In the spring of *chia-yin* [1554] I passed through Shao-hsing and stayed in the shrine for Yang-ming. In my fathoming of the message of Yang-ming I succeeded in apprehending his main points. Therefore I was able to lay down all concerns and roam at will. There were no more restraints" (10b). Having proclaimed his understanding of Wang's secret teaching and declared his freedom from convention, what could have prevented him from taking the next step—embarking on a truly hazardous pilgrimage and reenacting with all the accoutrements the master's celebrated illumination?

Undoubtedly many Neo-Confucians of the Wang school found Teng's appropriation of the founder's memory highly offensive. To them an even greater outrage was the apostate's constant invocation of Confucius himself. The master is mentioned by name eighteen times (5a, 5b, 12a, 12b, 17b, 19b, 22b, 36a, 36b, 37a, 39a, 43b, 44b, 49a, 49b, 50a, 50b, 51a). The words of the great Sage were cited either to show how far his latter-day followers—to this group Teng relegated almost all his contemporaries—had misunderstood or strayed from true Confucianism; or to justify Teng's reaching out to Buddhism; or simply to parade his knowledge of the canonical classics—almost every page of the *Nan-hsün lu* is replete with quotations from or allusions to the sacred texts. As a full examination of Teng's use or misuse of classical Confucianism would take us too far afield, we shall concern ourselves with only two such instances. In the first one Teng carries the egalitarianism of the T'ai-chou sect one step further, stands on its head what had become almost a refrain in Neo-Confucian discourse—to imitate the Sage—and strikes once again at his enemies:

> To imitate the ordinary people is to imitate Confucius. The ordinary people [as mentioned in the classics] are now the peasants—some would call them bumpkins. They are totally without artifice. . . . The ordinary people will succeed in imitating the Sage, while the worthy and wise will not succeed in imitating the Sage. . . . The ordinary people are innocent, while the worthy and wise are full of artifice. (36a–b)

In the next example Teng tries once more to settle his old score with didactic Confucians in general and in particular with Chao Chen-chi, who dared to be his teacher.

> Scholars of old tried to ferry people from this shore only after they themselves had reached the other shore. Scholars of today try to

ferry people when they themselves are still on this shore and before they have found a boat. Their crazed minds never know rest. One might say that the "trouble with men lies in their liking to be the teachers of others."[22] When the scholars of old had not yet reached the other shore, they felt as if they had been crossing the East Ocean in a small boat, awash amidst huge waves and rocked by gigantic billows. Filled with anxiety and fear for their lives, they could see the other shore but could not reach it. How could they have the leisure and peace of mind to seek people to save? (40b)

Here Teng returns once more to journey metaphors. In an earlier instance the voyage over water represented hope and promised liberation: the fish who stayed behind in stagnant marshes would perish while those who leaped over the Dragon Gate would reach instant immortality. Now our traveler seems to have lost his bearings and the boundless prospects in front of him inspire not more wanderlust but a sense of uncertainty. The sea between the two shores, perilous even for the wiser brand of scholars, is another barrier that only a happy few will ever overcome. Others such as hapless Confucians are consigned to die there: "They are like a man in the sea. Even though he can raise his head above the water, he cannot lift his body. He will never make it to the shore" (34b). For Teng himself, in a happier moment the sea need not be so threatening: "I am no different from others, but there is a governing agent within me that allows me an anchorage during the storm" (17a). The crossing over to the other shore where scented palaces decked with precious stones await the traveler is a locomotive figure often used by Buddhists. Teng makes full use of this figure in a passage where the journey metaphor is joined with the archetypal motif of return.

On the other shore there are palaces and pavilions with precious stones tinkling in every room. A native of that land, I do not know when I strayed to this shore. The family I lodged with here was unbearably filthy and smelly. It happened that an elder pointed to the place on the other shore decorated with precious stones and told me that it was my homeland. I had not seen it before, but now that my eyes have been opened, I am fully determined to return. How can I be detained any longer on this shore, so filthy and smelly? (18b)

The sensuous imagery used to contrast the two shores is a Buddhist staple, reminiscent of the wonderlands visited by Shan-ts'ai during his quest. Whereas the Indian youth, good-natured and eager to learn, received advice and instructions from many, the Chinese seeker almost never expressed gratitude for any assistance. Who the elder was, the one

[22] Alludes to *Mencius*, 4A:23.

who pointed to the other shore, will always remain a mystery. If Teng had been less insistent on hurling veiled attacks in the direction of his only teacher, we might take the helping elder to be Chao Chen-chi, who was after all the one who demolished Teng's old complacency and caused him to abandon his mundane home. Of all the eminent monks and Confucian scholar-officals Teng visited during his peregrinations, none was acknowledged to have offered him useful spiritual guidance, much less to have opened his eyes to his true destiny. There are two episodes in the *Nan-hsün lu* in which he describes how he achieved some sort of spiritual breakthrough and was allowed a glimpse of the final destination of his journey, but in neither case did he owe his visions to a fortuitous helper. The episode of the Pa-pa Ridge we have already discussed. The other breakthrough came to him nine years later:

> One day I was sitting in Ch'u-k'ung's thatch pavilion when I heard a rooster crow. Suddenly I found myself entering into a pure, vacuous clarity, totally unobstructed by worldly troubles, which dispersed like floating clouds in the distant sky. The following morning when I heard the dog bark I reentered into the pure state, clear and translucent without the slightest distraction of this world. This was the intimation of my eventual passage, through illumination, to the Great Bright Storehouse. (31b–32a)

The episode described above took place early in 1565. Ch'u-k'ung, whose formal name is Keng Ting-li (1534–1584), was a younger brother of Keng Ting-hsiang, the biographer of Teng. The two brothers were quite unlike, even though both were considered members of the T'ai-chou sect. While the senior had a distinguished official career and a large following among Neo-Confucians, the junior eschewed the examinations and led a life of independent inquiries and, by sixteenth-century standards, bold experiments. It is that reputation that attracted many free spirits and adventurers to the Keng household in Huang-an. The forbearing elder brother occasionally expressed his displeasure at the motley crowd who depended on Ting-li's generosity.[23] Whether Ting-hsiang hastened his departure or not, shortly after he experienced visions in the thatched pavilion Teng left Huang-an, where for the first time in several trouble-ridden years he had found a comfortable but brief refuge. By now he had become weary of constant roaming and thought about a more permanent sojourn. The quest, he now admitted, had not been successful. He was not specific about his difficulties, but his language betrayed a note of desperation: "Having drifted for half a year, I finally ar-

---

[23] The most notable among the house guests was Li Chih, whose difficulties with Keng Ting-hsiang broke into an open feud shortly after the death of the younger brother.

rived in Huang-an in the ninth month of the year *chia-tzu* [1564]. In the first month of the next year Liu Ming-ch'ing took me into his household so as to spare me the ravages of severe frost" (47a). It was the same kind-hearted Liu who in a joint effort with Keng Ting-li found another refuge for Teng in the neighboring Nan-t'ang Hills, where shortly after his arrival in the fourth month of *i-ch'ou* (1565) Teng wrote the following:

> I am like a traveler far away from home who, although still unable to go back, now knows clearly the return route. Therefore I am entering deep mountains and secluded gorges to nourish myself. I shall close the gate to all chattering visitors and distance myself from all false friends, thus terminating all worldly acquaintances. I shall move or pause of my own accord, sing and chant to myself. Swimming leisurely in my daily existence I shall wait for my worldly feelings to dissolve so as to depart from the sorrows of life and death. I shall then hurry into perfect tranquility and concentration, enter into the Great Bright Storehouse. When all births and extinctions are extinguished, Nirvana will be happiness. End! End! ("Prefaces," 4a)

Even for an inveterate traveler like Teng new people or vistas eventually palled. He still continued the journey metaphor, but now he proceeded, as it were, homeward. The farewell passage contains several ironies, none of them apparent to him then. His optimism and sense of freedom proved to be short-lived. According to his biographer he was then involved in a dubious business deal with a local rogue by the name of Chu who soon turned out to be a false friend and fled with the money that the credulous Teng had raised from his patrons. He himself admits that right after he achieved a state of concentration (*ting*) in the Nan-t'ang Hills he was "hindered by Chu Ying-lung, so a complete illumination was not possible" (48a). Early the next year another debacle in connection with an unreliable patron from a neighboring town made his permanent exile from the haven provided by Keng Ting-li and other patrons inevitable. The text proper of the *Nan-hsün lu* ends with him once more on the road, still hopeful of reaching his destination in the not-distant future:

> Day after day my endeavor is becoming increasingly profound and distant. Now there is no longer the self or the Way. I spend the whole day in the middle of human affairs and situations, but it seems that I have nothing to do with them. I hear voices and laughter without being aware of them. Flowingly I proceed like an empty boat or a flying sail without guide or goal. My mind is vacuous without my knowing it to be so; my mind is quiescent without my knowing it to be so. My worldly sentiments are about to be exhausted; my holy

transformations are nearly completed. Now is the time to shift my flesh and to alter my bones. (48a–b)

The holy transformations were not to take place until some four or five years later, under circumstances unpredicted and most likely unwished for by Teng. During his lifetime he attracted a wide following, and even his apparently inglorious end did not deter his great admirer Li Chih from believing that Teng the perpetual seeker did reach his final destination. In a highly laudatory preface of 1587 for an edition of Teng's book, Li, in many ways no less a rebel than Teng, performed a most deft balancing act, doing his best to redeem Teng while praising Chao Chen-chi for having set Teng forward on his great journey. Once Teng was set in motion, there was no turning back.

> Even if he had not wanted to hear the Way, he would have had no choice. Even if he had not wished to leave home, travel afar, abandon his worldly success and his wife and children in order to seek beneficial friends, he still would have had to do so. I have no doubt that the master in the end did reach the Way. Now the *Nan-hsün lu* exists and students may read it for themselves. They will see how he traveled ten thousand miles, braving all hardships in order to seek what he had to seek. As steadfast as a rock, as unbending as iron, he persevered for thirty years. He was not surpassed even by Confucius, who was so determined in his pursuit that he forgot about food, that he did not realize that old age was about to befall him. I myself am ashamed by the realization that I do not have even one ten-thousandth of Teng's resolution. Therefore I have made a copy of this book and decided to write this preface in order to admonish myself as well as my fellow students.[24]

Li Chih's appreciation for the book notwithstanding, when he tried his own hand at autobiography he wrote something in an entirely different format. There are many striking parallels between the lives of the two celebrated rebels, but Li was too much a sceptic to sustain the consistent vision and coherent stance of a seeker.[25] Li Chih could never have written a spiritual autobiography, however much he stretched, with his subversive wit and mocking inventiveness, the narrative convention of biogra-

[24] *Nan-hsün lu*, "Prefaces," 1b–2a.

[25] Much was written on Li Chih on the Chinese mainland during the last years of the Cultural Revolution. Teng was, however, a nonperson in the avalanche of articles and books on the other rebel, uniformly acclaimed as a "progressive" thinker. Li Chih is also lauded in the first full-length study published in the West: Jean-François Billeter, *Li Zhi, philosophe maudit (1527–1602): Contribution à une sociologie du mandarinat chinois de la fin des Ming* (Geneva: Librairie Droz, 1979). For an account of the affinity between the two rebels see my review of Billeter's book in *Harvard Journal of Asiatic Studies* 41, no. 1 (June 1981): 304–17.

phy to its limits. In other words, earnestness in tone seems to be a necessary quality in a spiritual autobiographer. It is a quality we shall never
fail to see throughout the rest of this chapter.

Hu Chih (1517–1585)

The first bona fide Neo-Confucian to write a spiritual autobiography was
Hu Chih, a native of T'ai-ho county in Kiangsi and a member of the
Wang Shou-jen school. Although in his collected works Hu made no reference to Teng Huo-ch'ü, there is every reason to believe that Hu was
familiar with the *Nan-hsün lu* and its author. Hu knew all the three major
characters—Chao Chen-chi and the Keng brothers—in the supporting
cast of Teng's life story well. There is no record that Hu ever exchanged
letters with Keng Ting-li, but his friendships with the elder Keng and
Chao were renewed from time to time by lengthy correspondence. Another measure of their closeness is that Hu wrote the definitive biography
for Chao at his death, while Keng Ting-hsiang in turn wrote the tomb
inscription for Hu. The clearest evidence that Hu knew about the *Nan-
hsün lu* is contained in one of Chao's letters to Hu, where he denounces
the book for its insolence and extremism and hints at regret over the fact
that Hu may have been impressed by Teng.[26] This letter was mentioned
by Keng Ting-hsiang near the end of his biography of Teng. Then he
pointedly added: "Even his [Teng's] teacher has already completely rejected him. Yet many of our confreres are still deluded by him. Is this not
a mistake?"[27]

Whether Hu was included in the group of the deluded or not, Teng's
power over his contemporaries cannot be doubted. It is true that Hu's
autobiography shows no specific or readily identifiable indebtedness to
Teng, yet the two works are alike in telling a life story entirely in terms
of a quest, a perpetual search for truth and enlightenment almost to the
exclusion of everything else. To perceive life in such a way was not completely novel, for there was enough support in classical Confucianism and
subsequent commentaries for such a life—imitation of the Sage, in short.
But in recording such a life in detail—in committing to paper the tortuous
process of the quest, with all its doubts and setbacks as well as its mo-
mentary triumphs—Hu had absolutely no model in earlier Chinese biography or autobiography. He may or may not have read Tsu-ch'in or
other autobiographical sermonizers, but for *written* spiritual autobiography there was no precedent other than the *Nan-hsün lu.*

---

[26] Chao Chen-chi, *Chao Wen-su kung wen-chi* [Collected writings of Chao Chen-chi] (Fukien, 1586), 22:10a.
[27] Keng Ting-hsiang, *Li-chung san i-jen chuan*, 4:1638.

The last character of the title of Hu's spiritual autobiography, *K'un-hsüeh chi* (A record of learning through difficulties), is crucial to understanding his innovation. The word *chi*, meaning "a record" or "an account," appeared so rarely as a part of the title or label in early Chinese literature that no pre-T'ang genre theorists had ever included a *chi* category in their classifications. With the rise of travel literature from the T'ang onward the term *chi* has often been used in connection with this new and thriving genre. Instead of *chi*, occasionally a travel writer would use its synonym *lu*, the same character that Teng Huo-ch'ü used as a part of his autobiography's title. To form the title of a travel piece the word *chi* is usually suffixed to a place-name, sometimes with the additional word *yu* (traveling) between or as the first character of the title. For example, the T'ang writer Liu Tsung-yüan entitled his account of a visit to Huang-ch'i *Yu-Huang-ch'i chi*. Sometimes the term *yu-chi* (travel account) can be attached to the name of a season to form a title. Hu's teacher Lo Hung-hsien gave the title *Tung yu-chi* (Winter travels) to his account of the trip he took with other leading members of the Wang school in the winter of 1539. He succumbed again to his wanderlust in the summers of 1548 and 1554, and again he wrote about his trips under similar rubrics. Notwithstanding the titles, all three pieces dealt very little with scenery or other staples of travel literature but concentrated on the philosophical discussions between Lo and his friends. His example may have shown Teng and Hu the possibility of broadening the *yu-chi* format to include philosophical issues, even if in his travel accounts there is not much evidence of reflectiveness or autobiographical revelation. For an antecedent of such qualities one can always point to another Neo-Confucian master, the introspective diarist Wu Yü-pi. Thus in labeling their works *chi* or *lu* rather than in using one or another of the subgenres of biography, as most earlier autobiographers had done, Teng and Hu escaped from the sort of historiographical constraints that we described in chapter 1. In all likelihood they were simply driven to record their intense personal experience without concerning themselves with narrative models from previous biography or autobiography, now that a flexible and amorphous format, thanks to the flourishing travel literature, was at their disposal.

K'un-hsüeh, the term that constitutes the first part of the title of Hu's autobiography, aptly summarizes the theme of his life story and underscores his link with the Confucian past. *K'un* (difficulty, beset by difficulties) and *hsüeh* (to learn) are juxtaposed in an often-quoted saying of Confucius: "Those who are born with knowledge are the best. Those who gain knowledge through learning are the next best. Those who strive to learn when they are beset by difficulties (*k'un erh hsüeh chih*) are still below them. Those who are in difficulties yet do not learn are the lowest of the people" (*Analects*, 16:9). The implications of the third category, a mixture of humility, earnestness, and hope, appealed so much to Neo-Confucians that the term *k'un-hsüeh* found its way into the titles of quite a few books, whatever the ease with which some of the authors appear to have gained their knowledge. To many members of the Wang school who pursued knowledge with great strenuousness and a sense of urgency, *k'un* with its rich associations was a keyword in their perception of their own undertakings. For Hu the authority of an appropriate canonical allusion must have given him encouragement to attempt what was unprecedented—to report without inhibition or embellishments a life of endeavor that was literally and amply beset by difficulties.

For a prominent Confucian Hu had an inauspicious beginning, and throughout his youth he suffered from one kind or another of what he must have recognized in retrospect as inner difficulties, hindrances to a Confucian enlightenment:

> As a child I was rather ignorant. From time to time I heard my father discussing Confucian studies with others, but I did not know how to participate. At seventeen I boarded at the county school in town where I led an untrammeled and pleasure-seeking life. In the winter my father died and I became even more self-indulgent. . . .
>
> I was short-tempered, full of desires, constantly agitated, and lacking in self-control. I wrote an essay on the investigation of things to refute the theory of Wang Shou-jen. (*MJHA*, p. 221)

Among Chinese autobiographies the *K'un-hsüeh chi* comes closest to that well-established genre in the West, the conversion narrative. Both Hui-neng, the Sixth Patriarch, and Teng Huo-ch'ü probably had a more interesting story to tell—their changes were more radical, but for one reason or another they chose to be reticent about what would interest the modern reader most. Compared with the personal testimonies of Christian converts, whose lives before conversion were often characterized by boisterousness, abandon, and even exuberant sinfulness, Hu's disclosures may seem tame. There is, however, one misdeed that was serious by contemporary standards—his attempt to refute the cornerstone of Wang's teachings. The act was almost a sacrilege in itself in light of Hu's subsequent discipleship with several of Wang's students; the offense was all the greater on account of the fact, not mentioned in the *K'un-hsüeh chi*, that Hu's father T'ien-feng was himself one of the most devoted of Wang's followers. It took great courage, then, to admit such an unfilial act, committed against the father's memory so soon after his death.

When Hu Chih was nineteen he began to feel uneasy about his wild ways and decided to pursue serious studies. In his new endeavor he was joined by his best friend Ou-yang Wen-ch'ao, but their good intentions did not long prevail over their old habits. Within two months they were backsliding. For seven years Hu made no progress—another admission unusual for prominent Confucians, who had hitherto always been held up as paragons of virtue for lesser souls to emulate. Hu's own exemplar appeared on the scene in 1542 in the person of Ou-yang Te, a revered member of the Wang school and a senior clansman of Wen-ch'ao's.

> It happened that Master Ou-yang Te came to town from his country residence. He met with his old friends and gave public lectures. Every member of the local literati went to the meetings, but I refused to go. A few days later Wen-ch'ao said to me, "Couldn't you at least pay him a courtesy call?" Thereupon I went with Wen-ch'ao to call on him at the P'u-chüeh Temple. As soon as Mr. Ou-yang saw me he addressed me by my old name, I-chü, and said, "Why did it take you so long to come?" Then he asked my age. When I answered, he said, "On the basis of your age you should take your seat next to Mr. So-and-so." Impressed by his simplicity in word and manner, as well as his freedom from the current fashion, I was completely won over by him. (Ibid.)

At the time of the meeting Ou-yang Te (1496–1554) was approaching the height of success both in his brilliant official career and as a popular Neo-Confucian lecturer. Yet he did not take offense at Hu's initial rudeness but took the trouble to find out and remember the familiar form of the obscure young man's name. No wonder Hu's rebelliousness melted away in the benign presence of the most illustrious landsman of the older generation, almost exactly the same age as Hu T'ien-feng (1495–1534), the father who was mentioned but twice in the *K'un-hsüeh chi*, and only in terms of his absences—his death was referred to in the opening paragraph, and his delayed burial was cited (*MJHA* p. 222) as one of the new distractions for the son, who had just emerged from a spiritual breakthrough.

Both Ou-yang and the senior Hu were natives of T'ai-ho and followers of Wang Shou-jen, but the similarity ends there. A child prodigy and the youngest of Wang's disciples, Ou-yang won the approbation and even affection of the master. He was such a moving public lecturer that at one time half of the adherents of the Wang school claimed him as their teacher. Equally admired by the public for his courage and outspokenness at court, where he angered the emperor on several occasions by his contrary interpretation of protocol and precedents, he had achieved the *chin-shih* degree at an early age and rose eventually to the lofty position of minister of rites. Such victories and glories were totally denied Hu Chih's father. Unsuccessful as a candidate for higher degrees, Hu T'ien-feng remained poor and obscure to the end of his short life. To eke out a simple living he had to leave his hometown and hire himself out in distant cities as a family tutor during almost all his adult years, a fate much lamented in Sung-Ming literature. The stark contrast between the two holds the key to many of Hu Chih's early difficulties as well as his subsequent devotion to Master Ou-yang. An absent and fumbling father was hardly the role model for a headstrong youth, while the distinguished and benevolent elder would provide guidance and support at crucial points in the maturing man's long struggle.

For more than a month after the initial meeting Hu followed his new master around every day, listening to his exegesis of Confucian principles. "One day I heard him chanting a line from Chu Hsi's poetry, 'In the boatman's song there is the mind that has come down from an eternity.'[28] Suddenly everything became clear to me, and I felt that my bad habits could be eradicated. For the first time my mind was truly set on higher goals" (*MJHA*, p. 221). However, in spite of his determination and the frequent encouragement of his exemplar, Hu's progress was far from consistent. During the next five years there were unavoidable interruptions, occasional relapses, new temptations. "I realized that my efforts in learning were ineffective and regretted the passage of time. My main defects were love of florid composition, anger, and desires. All three were deeply entrenched within me. From time to time I succeeded in overcoming them, but the victory never lasted. I was already over thirty, yet I remained unsettled in my aim. What more could I say about my sins?" (p. 221).

In the depth of his depair Hu toyed with the idea of abandoning everything and embarking on a journey to faraway places, a temptation many found irresistible and one from which Teng Huo-ch'ü never recovered. A friend of his, trying to dissuade him, took him to see Lo Hung-hsien who, as we have noted earlier in the chapter, frequently succumbed to wanderlust himself. Presumably the meeting went well for Hu reports, somewhat precipitously, "After I had stayed at Stone Lotus Grotto and listened daily to Mr. Lo's words for a month, I was moved to acknowledge him formally as my teacher" (Ibid.). The succinct and matter-of-fact announcement contrasts with the memory—specific and tinged with feeling—he has of his first meeting with Mr. Ou-yang. Nor did Lo's instructions seem crucial in his progress toward enlightenment. The following is the entirety of his education under Lo's tutelage:

> At first he did not care too much for the theory of innate knowledge; yet he did not turn his back completely on the teachings of Wang

---

[28] The poem can be found in Chu Hsi, *Hui-an hsien-sheng Chu Wen-kung wen-chi* (Collected writings of Master Chu Hsi) SPTK, 9:6b: "Above Wu-ch'ü the mountains are high and clouds deep. / Lingering mist and rain darken the forest below. / In the forest there is a visitor nobody knows; / In the boatman's song there is the mind that has come down from an eternity."

Shou-jen. He instructed us students solely on quietude and desire-lessness. Although I was not in full accord with his teachings, as I listened daily to his exhortations on desirelessness, I became more accustomed to his method and practiced it each day with greater earnestness. In the end I came to understand the meaning of scrupulousness in personal conduct. (Ibid.)

In contrast to the ever-approachable Mr. Ou-yang, who seems to have been always ready to offer encouragement or assistance, Lo Hung-hsien made no more appearances in the *K'un-hsüeh chi* until near the end of the narrative, when Hu had already overcome all his demons and negotiated all the passes without having once avowed any benefit from his formally acknowledged teacher. It is perhaps in the allegorical nature of spiritual autobiography that real help seldom comes from the obvious source.

Hu's first concrete and lasting progress came the following year, and his benefactor was not even a practicing Neo-Confucian. For many years he suffered a lung disease, and now he was in such an agitated state that he could hardly sleep at night. In desperation he sought relief first from Taoism and then from Buddhism. A fellow teacher in the school by the name of Teng Lu, who had once been a student of Ou-yang Te but now devoted himself solely to Ch'an Buddhism, offered help.

He told me, "Your disease is a form of inflammation and should be treated by Ch'an." Henceforth every day after class he and I got together and practiced quiet-sitting, sometimes on the bed, sometimes on a mat on the floor. We often sat until late in the night. After a brief sleep we would resume sitting when the cock crowed. The endeavor was directed chiefly at the calming of the mind and the ceasing of random thoughts. The goal was the perceiving of one's true nature.

Accustomed to a life of galloping activities, I could not but begin to see strange apparitions day and night after having practiced sitting for a month or two. Mr. Teng said: "This is the realm of Mara as described by Buddhists and Taoists. The anger, desires, greed, vanity, and various thoughts and anxieties of your past have transformed themselves into these sights. This is what is meant in the *Book of Changes* when it speaks of 'the wandering souls bringing about change.'[29] Do not be startled by them. They will disappear of their own accord when your endeavor has reached a certain stage." Just as he said, in four or five months, the strange sights gradually went away. At the end of the sixth month they disappeared altogether. (*MJHA*, p. 222)

[29] *Chou I cheng-i* (Correct meaning of the *Book of Changes*) SPPY, 7:6a.

Quiet-sitting, as we have seen in the preceding chapter, was an important means for Ch'an Buddhists to gain health and a clear understanding of the self. A number of prominent Neo-Confucians had since the Sung adopted this regimen for more or less the same purpose, even though very few would go so far as to dwell on a Ch'an paradox while sitting. As promised by his guide, Hu Chih was completely cured of his disease after six months of the Ch'an regimen. Just before that, however, he had what may be called his first important insight. "One day my mind was suddenly opened and illuminated. It was completely free of extraneous thoughts. I saw into heaven, earth, and the myriad things: they are all the substance of my mind. With a deep sigh I said, 'Now I know that heaven, earth, and the myriad things are not external to me!' From that time on I could confront all circumstances without anxiety as if I could cope with everything." (ibid.).

The notion that the external world is only an extension of one's mind was always a basic tenet of Buddhism. To go beyond a mere metaphysical position, however, and realize its true meaning and implications would take, at least in Hu's case, months of concentration and meditation. Only when a by then hackneyed notion was transformed into a fresh and for-tuitous insight could Hu be free from worldly preoccupations and anxi-eties—the causes of his disease. The arrival at the insight, paradoxically, also signified his return to Confucianism, even though both the regimen and the resultant insight were thoroughly Buddhist. That his insight was also a Confucian one became obvious to him a few months later.

> One day I went sight-seeing to Chiu-ch'eng Terrace with several members of the literati. Just as I stood up and stretched myself after having sat down for some time, the insight suddenly came back to me that heaven, earth, and the myriad things are truly not external to me. I verified this insight against what various Confucian masters had gone through—Tzu Ssu seeing the Way above and below,[30] Mencius finding all things already complete in the self,[31] Ch'eng Hao forming one body with all things,[32] Lu Chiu-yüan believing the uni-verse to be his mind[33]—and they were in perfect accord. I examined my previous understanding and everything became clear and coher-ent once more. (Ibid.)

The belief in a boundless, undifferentiated continuum of the self, running through all the human and nonhuman world and even coextensive with

[30] Alludes to *Mean*, 12:3. Tzu Ssu, the grandson of Confucius, is traditionally believed to be the author of this Confucian classic.

[31] Alludes to *Mencius*, 7A:4.

[32] Alludes to *Erh-Ch'eng i-shu* (Written legacy of the two Chengs), 2A:3a, in *Erh-Ch'eng ch'üan-shu* (Complete works of the two Ch'engs) SPPY.

[33] Alludes to *Hsiang-shan ch'üan-chi* (Complete works of Lu Chiu-yüan) SPPY, 22:5a.

the entire universe, has often been held by mystics of all persuasions. As Hu explained above, such a belief, or at least elements of such a belief, could be found in Confucianism.

The first serious test of his mettle, the first measure of his achievement as a reconverted Confucian, came in the winter when he was on his way to the capital to try his hand once again at the metropolitan examination.

> As we were sailing in the P'eng-li Lake a tempest raged during the night. Unable to reach a harbor, the ship was rocked several times to the verge of capsizing. Most people on the boat wailed until dawn, while I alone ordered wine and proceeded to drink to my heart's content. After singing a few tunes loudly I fell into a deep slumber. I did not awake until daybreak when the wind abated. Some of my companions criticized me for having no feelings, but it did not matter to me. (*MJHA*, p. 222)

His bravery in the face of grave danger may have owed more to his residual swagger—in his rebellious youth he was given to bravado in his emulation of heroic figures in history—than to the Buddhist unconcern with life and death that he gained as a result of following the sitting regimen. The boat episode itself, however, has a much larger meaning in that it represents one of the archetypal situations that recur in the lives of Neo-Confucians. Tests and ordeals of course abound in fairy tales and the *Bildungsroman*. In China the challenge of sailing over a body of water, especially amidst a tempest, seems to have a greater allegorical meaning than other trials. As we have seen earlier in the chapter, for Teng Huo-ch'ü the sea and other aquatic images are the most powerful cluster of figures in the account of his spiritual journey. If life was indeed a journey to those who strove with a purpose or progressed toward a goal, passage over stormy waters would evoke primordial fears and demand appropriate responses. To insure a safe passage under any circumstances was precisely the power that Wang Shou-jen attributed to *liang-chih* (innate knowledge), the cornerstone of his doctrine. "Formerly I had some doubts. Now that I have gone through so much, I know that with innate knowledge [*liang-chih*] I need nothing else. It is just like having a good rudder when one is in a boat: with it one sails as one pleases through calm or swelling waters, shallows or rapids. Even if one encounters powerful wind and billows, with such a helm in hand one can escape sinking or drowning."[34]

Powerful as *liang-chih* may have been, not every Confucian helmsman acquitted himself well in the face of mortal dangers. A lesser member of the Wang school confessed to his teacher Chou Ju-teng (1547–1629) that

[34] *Wang Yang-ming ch'üan-shu* (Complete works of Wang Shou-jen) 4 vols. (Taipei: Cheng-chung shu-chü, 1955), 4:125.

when the supreme test came, he actually failed. "Since last year I have been engaged in this matter [Confucian studies]. I verified its effectiveness in real situations and it seemed to be good. But a few days ago I was overtaken by a storm while in a boat. I was very anxious. Only then did I realize that I was no match at all when confronted with matters of life and death."[35] Such a failure or the admission of such a failure was unthinkable for prominent Confucians. For them imperturbability under stress was de rigueur. One of the early exemplars was Lü Tuan (935–1000), who was once dispatched to Korea as an imperial emissary. When a windstorm hit his ship and broke the mast, people on the ship panicked. "The master remained calm as if he had been in his library or office."[36] For Ming Neo-Confucians the tone was first set by Wu Yü-pi. In 1411, when he was a mere youth of twenty, he encountered a storm while sailing on the Yangtze River. "When the boat was about to capsize, the master straightened his robe and sat erect. Afterwards he was asked how he could do so. He replied, 'I did no more than hold on to what was proper while waiting for the inevitable.' "[37]

If Lü's story is no more than what may be called the kernel of the archetypal situation, Wu's story contains an interesting elaboration, the discourse subsequent to the event.[38] In Hu Chih's recounting of his experience, the discourse element was further elaborated to the point that the event itself was almost rendered insignificant.

> One day I reported the tempest incident to him and asked for his comment. Mr. Ou-yang remarked: "What you did was of course not ordinary. But to accord with the substance of humaneness it was not." I asked him what one should have done to accord with the substance of humaneness. He replied, "If one's mind remains undisturbed when confronted with a crisis, yet one is able to devise plans for succoring others—then and only then is one in accord with humaneness." Although I acceded to him, I was unable to search deeply into his meaning. (MJHA, p. 222)

Imperturbability in the face of danger, so valued by earlier Confucians, was no longer sufficient to the members of the Wang school such as Ou-yang Te, whose commitment to this world would demand a more active and altruistic response to the situation. What Ou-yang Te would have had

[35] Chou Ju-teng, Tung-Yüeh cheng-hsüeh lu (Testimonials to learning in East Yüeh) 2 vols. (1595 ed., reprint, Taipei: Wen-hai ch'u-pan-she, 1970), 1:394–95.

[36] Ibid., 1:320–21.

[37] MJHA, p. 1.

[38] The elaboration may have begun with Ch'eng I (1033–1107) who also proved his mettle under similar circumstances. See Erh-Ch'eng yü-lu (The sayings of the two Ch'engs) TSCC, 17:270–71.

the young man do represents a return to the robust and activist standard of classical Confucianism, transcending the mere transcendence of Buddhism or Taoism. The storm episode then took on, as it often did, an allegorical significance that nevertheless escaped Hu at the time when the exchange took place, much as he admired and respected his mentor. The irony that is found in the persistent ignorance of the complacent hero is of course the staple of *Bildungsroman*, but we have seen few instances of it in Chinese autobiography up to this time. Teng Huo-ch'ü was too engrossed in self-vindication to see beyond the main theme of his own life story, the quest for truth as implied by the very title of his account.

What Hu wrote can be called a reconversion narrative. In such a narrative the movement from ignorance and confusion to enlightenment can best be charted by episodes precisely like the storm and the subsequent exchange. True to the title of his story, the progress is painfully slow and lessons are hard to learn. His admission in the above passage that "although I acceded to him, I was unable to search deeply into his meaning" foreshadows the repetition of his behaving as less than a true Confucian. Indeed, next year there was another nautical crisis and again Hu failed to respond as a compassionate man more concerned with helping others than with retaining his own equilibrium. "Toward the end of the winter I embarked on my homeward journey from I-chen. For three days we saw pirates, but fortunately each time a favorable wind took our ship out of their reach. Some of my shipmates wept. I alone remained undisturbed because I calculated that if worse came to worse I would simply give the boarding pirates all my money—I saw no other reason for worry" (ibid.).[39] Hu did not fare any better during the next four years. As in the past, there were relapses and altercations. Once again he failed the metropolitan examination. Just when he was at his lowest—he began to have fundamental doubts—the news came that his beloved mentor, Ou-yang Te, had died. "I set up a memorial tablet for him and wept bitterly before it. When I thought that my teacher was now far away and I had not accomplished anything in learning, I began to reproach myself for the wasted years. I felt a bitter remorse over having failed both my teacher and myself" (ibid.). As we have noted before, Ou-yang Te was more a father to Hu than his own father, and more a teacher than Hu's nominal teacher Lo Hung-hsien. Hu's intense grief over the death of his mentor may have been compounded by the sense of guilt underlying his estrangement from his father. But the intense grief and remorse brought about a fundamental change in the course of Hu's life, the first change that en-

---

[39] For a different interpretation of this passage see Rodney L. Taylor, "Journey into Self: The Autobiographical Reflections of Hu Chih," *History of Religions* 21, no. 4 (May 1982): 334.

dured. Shortly afterwards, perhaps as a homage to Ou-yang, Hu wrote
an essay on a passage from the *Analects* in which Confucius said, "The
superior man, extensively studying all learning, and keeping himself under the restraint of the rules of propriety, may thus likewise not overstep
what is right."[40] In doing so he settled his long-held differences with various ideas contained in the classics as well as clarified his position toward
a number of controversies raging between different sects of Neo-Confucians. The composition of the essay seems to mark a real turning point in
the long tortuous course of his struggles. "From that time on none of my
endeavors seemed to be in vain. My handling of daily affairs also seemed
to have improved, and my relations with the above and the below looked
somewhat better. Only now did I understand completely the idea of the
substance of humaneness expounded by Mr. Ou-yang Te" (*MJHA*, p.
224).

Everything took a turn for the better from that time on. He finally
passed the metropolitan examination and began, if somewhat belatedly,
his official career. With new confidence and successes, he met all the leading Confucian scholars of his day. In discussing issues with them, Hu
never departed from the philosophical position that he formulated in the
essay. If there were any more reversals or backslidings, they are not mentioned in the remainder of the *K'un-hsüeh chi*. As his fortune improved,
his interest in recounting his life seemed to decline. The autobiography
goes on to cover nineteen more years of his life, but in space this portion
takes up less than one tenth of the total narrative. Perhaps his intention,
as clearly demonstrated by the title he gave to the narrative, was to describe the long painful process of his quest, not the unfolding of his triumphs.

His confidence and maturity notwithstanding, he remained vigilant
and humble, for he continued to seek confirmation from Lo Hung-hsien,
his formal teacher. Lo, characteristic of Confucian teachers, was ever cautionary. "He said, 'The important thing is to have both eyes and feet.' He
was afraid that I might set my sights too high for my weak feet" (ibid.).
The double figure of the eye and foot, often found in the discourse on
spiritual journeying, was especially apt to the Buddhist debate on illumination between the subitists and the gradualists. For instance, the fifth-
century monk Hui-kuan argued for the gradualist position by likening
the process leading to final illumination to the progress of a pilgrim
climbing a sacred mountain. Long before the pilgrim reaches the destination his eyes will now and then see the peak above the clouds, but the
implication is that the feet are just as necessary for the endeavor.[41] Long

[40] 6:25 (Legge translation).
[41] T'ang Yung-t'ung, *Han Wei Liang-Chin Nan-pei ch'ao fo-chiao shih* (A history of Bud-

engrossed in the study of Buddhism, Lo may well have had in mind Hui-kuan's analogy. At any rate his admonition was quite to the point, for the recurring pattern of Hu's difficulties as it emerges from the pages of the *K'un-hsüeh chi* shows that Hu, while not lacking in visions or insights, too often stumbled over obstacles and thus failed to carry out his resolve.

Although in the last nineteen years of his life story there is not one specific instance of adversity, near the very end of the narrative Hu reverts to the mood, if not the substance, of his earlier years. The ominous word *k'un* reappears. "Now I am more apprehensive and perplexed than ever before, for I think there has been none, from ancient times to this day, who is as much beset by difficulties [*k'un*] as I am" (*MJHA*, p. 224). But he ends his autobiography on a more optimistic note by alluding, in the very next sentence, to a passage in the *Chung-yung* (*Doctrine of the Mean*), which is an elaboration of the *Analects* quotation that gives his narrative its title. The passage reads: "Some are born with the knowledge; some gain it by study; and some acquire the knowledge after undergoing difficulties. But once the knowledge is acquired, it comes to the same thing. Some practice it under easy circumstances; some with quickness; and some by strenuous effort. But once the achievement is made, it comes to the same thing."[42] The allusion not only echoes once more the theme of his life story but offers, as a fitting conclusion, a vindication of the protracted course of his progress.

Secondary Spiritual Autobiographies

Hu Chih's extraordinary act was not repeated until a generation later when Kao P'ang-lung, using exactly the same title, made a detailed account of his own arduous pilgrimage. In between there were several other Neo-Confucians who wrote what may be called fragments of spiritual autobiography. Although their efforts were dwarfed by the two major works, they deserve our attention for several reasons. Their existence makes it possible to speak of a subgenre rather than just two or three isolated expressions of Confucian spiritual fervor. Their adherence to the basic format employed by both Hu and Kao confirms the reality of a

dhism during the Han, Wei, two Chins, Northern and Southern Dynasties) 2 vols. (Peking: Chung-hua shu-chü, 1963), 2:672.

[42] *Mean*, 20:9. The two key words in this passage, *k'un* and *chih*, "knowledge," were combined by Lo Ch'in-shun (1465–1547) to form the title of his book, *K'un-chih chi*. Although they belonged to different schools of Neo-Confucianism, Hu must have been aware of Lo, the most prominent man of his county. In choosing the title for his book Hu may have even been inspired by his senior. For an elucidating exposition of Lo's book see Irene Bloom, *Knowledge Painfully Acquired: "The K'un-chih chi" by Lo Ch'in-shun* (New York: Columbia University Press, 1987).

subgenre. Finally, knowledge of their various links as well as similarities to the major figures of this chapter will lend further support to one of the themes stated earlier—that late Ming Confucians were essentially different from their predecessors in their spiritual wanderlust, their earnest and protracted quest.

Wan T'ing-yen had a great deal in common with Hu Chih. Both were natives of Kiangsi, sons of members of the Wang Shou-jen school, and disciples of Lo Hung-hsien at the Stone Lotus Grotto. They also resembled each other in the early stages of their endeavors. "Even in my early youth I knew I should order my mind. But I was distressed by the difficulties I encountered in trying to calm my thoughts. I concentrated on quiet-sitting, and after a while I felt that in doing so there could be found a place for the mind to rest."[43] Like Hu, Wan gained a measure of success through what was originally a Buddhist regimen, "Gradually my mind became pliable and tamable, like a monkey that had settled" (*MJHA*, p. 212). Again, like Hu, he soon lost his footing and entered into a long trough.

> After I began government service I had a wide range of acquaintances. The opinions and discussions I heard were confusingly varied. As my capacity was shallow and my mind fluttering, I gradually began to waver and felt giddy. For nearly twenty years I oscillated in my attempts to strike a balance between activity and tranquility, nonaction and receptivity, or to mediate between emptiness and consciousness, substance and vacuity. From time to time I achieved a breakthrough and took my understanding to be broad and profound. But when I examined my mind I found extraneous thoughts now rising and now disappearing, never allowing any calm or peace. As the source of the mind remained unpurified, everything was adrift. (Ibid.)

Eventually his tortuous path led him to a mountain retreat where, away from the din and bustle of the world, he could rediscover himself at leisure, a wish long entertained by Teng Huo-ch'ü but never fulfilled.

> Fortunately I was able to return to my mountain home and close my gate to the world. In quietude and calm I silently acquainted myself with my mind. After a long time the mind that had been given to frivolity and boisterousness suddenly fell away; I felt that within me was a righteous thought that invisibly took the reins of my form and spirit. This thought seemed to be both present and absent, but it was deeply penetrating, translucent, boundlessly broad, and completely different from ordinary thoughts. Never separated from my daily

[43] *MJHA*, p. 212.

activities, this thought soon enveloped and contained my whole spirit. I entered into such a calm and ease that my ears and eyes were returned to their proper uses. Heaven and earth became clear and peaceful, where a vast harmony reigned. I seemed to hold the key to every transformation and every regeneration. (Ibid.)

The state of luminosity that Wan describes is probably no different from what Ch'an Buddhist masters refer to as illumination, even though Wan apparently reached it without the catalytic incident that usually immediately precedes the Buddhist experience. He also shares with the perennial seekers the journey figure and the theme of return, with which he appropriately ends his autobiographical sketch. "It was like the return of a wandering son to his homeland, where he finds wonder in every blade of grass and every tree, in every whiff of breeze and every curl of smoke" (ibid.).

Lo Ju-fang (1515–1588) came from the same province as Hu Chih and Wan T'ing-yen, but he belonged to a different group in the Wang school, the T'ai-chou sect. There is no record that he was aware of the spiritual autobiography of Teng Huo-ch'ü or of the writings of another T'ai-chou stalwart, Li Chih, who, however, mentioned him with esteem. Lo was occupied all his life with the quest for enlightenment. Earnest and restless, susceptible to Buddhism and Taoism as well as the allures of various occult persuasions, he often displayed an almost childlike waywardness. Sometimes during his discourse with his disciples he spoke of his endeavors—but not his escapades. This practice of his, reminiscent of the Ch'an sermonizers we have seen in the preceding chapter, was unique among the Confucians. For this reason he deserves mention, even though he fails to demonstrate the complexity that his biographers and critics always attribute to him. The following is the most autobiographical passage among the sayings transcribed by his disciples.

At first I wanted, day and night, to be a good man. To me there were more things in life than mere successes in examinations and the official career. The methods expounded in *Chin-ssu lu* and *Hsing-li ta-ch'üan* I accepted completely, and I practiced them to the point of neglecting food and sleep and forgetting life and death. Then I became ill and had to stop. I turned to the *Ch'uan-hsi lu*, in which the efforts of various Confucians were criticized. I began to search in the books of Lu Chiu-yüan and Yang Chien. What the three authors meant by endeavor [*kung-fu*] frequently puzzled me. I recovered somewhat from the illness but still felt stagnant and uneasy. I was then almost twenty years of age. My father was very much distressed with my plight. From my childhood I was very much loved by my parents, and I loved my parents, brothers, and sisters with an intensity and thoughtfulness that I have never observed in others. Consequently whenever I read discussions of filial piety and fraternity in the *Analects* or *Mencius* I was always moved, sometimes to tears. At that time I took such affections for granted—no more than human nature, nothing to be made much of. I did not expect to find them so labored in the books I would read later. When I attended a conference in the provincial capital and heard my teachers and friends elaborate on filial piety and fraternity I suddenly realized that these two consituted the very path to being a good man. Why had I not taken them seriously instead of running in all directions to the extent of almost forgetting myself? I went back to the *Analects* and read it carefully. Every word and every phrase now appeared to be more valuable than any treasure. I reread the *Mencius*, the *Great Learning*, and the *Mean*; there were no words or phrases in these books that did not reflect or illustrate each other.[44]

In spite of all the appearance of sincerity and spontaneity, the persona in Lo's recorded discourses almost never strays from the straight path of Confucianism. The only hint that in the past he may have been too credulous and too ready for experimentation is the concession that he once ran "in all directions to the extent of almost forgetting [him]self." His close disciple Tsou Yüan-piao (1551–1624) seems to be a little more forthcoming, but he too is eager to stress the return to Confucianism.

When I was young and my spirits were high I wantonly followed false visions and thought that I was enlightened. Little did I know that my impressionistic and impulsive conduct was as far from the Way as earth from heaven. Seven years later, when I was transferred back to the Ministry of Justice, although I had made some gains in my study, I was still quite wild. Fortunately I met Mr. Teng I-tsan on his southern trip. After hearing his sober words I did not dare to remain unruly. Three years later I decided to leave government service, but then I wasted my time for a dozen years. For the next dozen years or so I erred in trying too hard to steer a middle course. I set my goal at inspired knowledge, which I now know is far from true enlightenment. Now with my desk clean, my windows clear, and all things thoroughly examined, I know that enlightenment is nothing other than insight gained from studies. When a man has already risen from his sleep, there is no need of mentioning his awakening; when a man has truly mastered what he has been learning, there is no need to speak of his enlightenment.[45]

[44] *MJHA*, pp. 345–46.
[45] *MJHA*, p. 229.

Although Tsou once studied with Lo Ju-fang, he is listed in the *Ming-ju hsüeh-an* immediately after Hu Chih as a member of the same sect. Presumbly Huang Tsung-hsi believes that Tsou is linked to Hu by philosophical descent. Tsou's link to Kao P'an-lung is more obvious, for they were close political allies in one of the feuds that contributed to the fall of the Ming.

KAO P'AN-LUNG (1562–1626)

The title of Kao's autobiography, *K'un-hsüeh chi*, is exactly the same as Hu Chih's. The course of his life as presented in it is no different in outline from what we have seen in other Neo-Confucian spiritual autobiographies: early resolutions followed by setbacks; inspirations as well as puzzlements from the sayings of earlier Confucian masters; breakthroughs preceded by struggles and impasses; unavoidable errors and fortuitous help from others; and, often as a denouement to the life story, enlightenment or illumination. In one fundamental way, however, Kao differs from all other spiritual autobiographers. While the latter from Teng Huo-ch'ü onward were all members of the Wang Shou-jen school, to whom spiritual experience sometimes bordering on Ch'an Buddhism was a staple in their life story, Kao belonged to the rival Ch'eng-Chu school, where reticence obtained on matters such as enlightenment. That he—alone among the Neo-Confucians outside of the Wang school—should have written anything even resembling a spiritual autobiography testifies to the genre's vogue. In fact, the vogue was such that, as we shall see in the next chapter, a few years after Kao wrote his *K'un-hsüeh chi* a good friend of his, the monk Te-ch'ing, also wrote a spiritual autobiography in a format never before attempted by Buddhists.

Kao's *K'un-hsüeh chi*, much shorter than Hu's, runs to nine pages. About a third of the space is taken up with the most crucial episode of his life, the enlightenment that took place when he was exiled to a remote corner of the south. His spiritual experience is described more fully than that of any other Neo-Confucian. What is more remarkable is that Kao wrote about the exile a second time, using the long-established format of travel literature. In writing about the same journey twice Kao affords us a unique opportunity to note not only the affinity of the two genres—a claim made repeatedly in this chapter—but also the inherent differences. Only by examining the two versions along side of each other can we see the full range of resources that Kao drew from various traditions to make sense out of his double journey.

Kao's exile resulted from the defeat of his faction in the central government in 1593.[46] As punishment he was ordered to take a minor post in Chieh-yang, Kwangtung. Upon leaving the capital he lingered for a while in his hometown and did not depart for the south until the early autumn of 1594. Three months after he completed the long and arduous journey and assumed his new post he was granted a home leave. He was back in his hometown in the early spring of the next year. As his time away from home extended to three seasons, he entitled the account for the trip *San shih chi* (A record of three seasons). As travel literature it seems to have taken its cue from several new developments in the genre. In recording the long philosophical exchange with Neo-Confucians that Kao visited at various stops of his journey he may have had as his model the travel accounts of Lo Hung-hsien mentioned earlier in this chapter. The similarities between Kao's and Lo's pieces even extend to the titles. That Lo labeled each of the three accounts with a particular season—for example, *Hsia yu-chi* (A record of summer travel)—may have influenced Kao's choice of title for his writing. Kao's profound communion with nature, while anticipating the subjectivism of the landscape painters of the next generation, is in line with the style of late Ming travel literature exemplified by writers such as the Yüan brothers. But before we go any further let us hear what Kao the autobiographer says about the background and beginnings of the exile.

> In *kuei-ssu* [1593] I was demoted to a minor position far away from the capital on account of my outspokenness. I thought nothing of it. I lost my equanimity only after I returned to my hometown and noticed how differently I was now treated by some of the people. In the autumn of *chia-wu* [1594] I left for Chieh-yang. When I realized that waging within me there was a war between principle and desire I felt very uneasy. I made a stop in Hangchow and spent several days with Lu Ku-ch'iao and Wu Tzu-wang. One day Ku-ch'iao asked me all of a sudden, "What is the original substance like?" My mind became blank. Even though I replied that "it is without sound or smell," the words were simply a repetition of what I had heard, not from my own understanding. On the eve of my departure several close friends came to bid me farewell by the river. We sat and drank next to the Liu-ho Pagoda under a moon so bright that it seemed to have just been washed. Surrounded by such beautiful landscape and boon companions I had every reason to feel happy, but I was dejected—I

---

[46] For Kao's life and thought see his biography in *DMB*, 1:701–10; Heinrich Busch, *The Tung-lin Academy and Its Political and Philosophical Significance* (Ann Arbor: University Microfilms, 1954); de Bary, *Unfolding*, pp. 180–84; and Rodney Taylor, *The Cultivation of Sagehood as a Religious Goal in Neo-Confucianism: A Study of Selected Writings of Kao P'an-lung (1562–1626)* (Missoula, Mont.: Scholars Press, 1978).

seemed to have been held back by something. I tried to cheer myself but the right spirit never came. Late in the night we parted.[47]

Spiritual autobiography is certainly no place for airing partisan politics or expressing the bitterness of a young official whose promising career has just been interrupted. True to the teachings of Confucianism, Kao sees adversities only as tests of his true worth, opportunities for spiritual progress. He makes no allowances for any feeling of disappointment or dejection but demands almost unreasonably of himself.

> After I boarded the boat a question struck me with great force: Why is it that during the day the scenery and my mood were so much unlike? Deeply and thoroughly I examined myself. I discovered that I did not know anything at all about the Way and that my body and mind had gained nothing. Greatly agitated, I said to myself, "If I do not completely solve this problem during this trip, my life will have been lived in vain!" (*Kao-tzu i-shu*, 3:14b–15a)

This phase of his exile is represented in much greater detail in the *San shih chi*, but he is here just as reticent on politics. Spiritual autobiography seems to demand a severe economy on the facts to be included—there can be detours or impasses, but they must serve as foils to the straight and narrow path from which the seeker strays. Travel literature, however, probably coming from the same matrix as the diary, is the most plastic of all Chinese genres. The *K'un-hsüeh chi* mentions only one stop and two friends for this part of the journey, and they are mentioned to show how badly Kao has stumbled. In contrast the *San shih chi* includes several stops and many visits and reunions, fully illustrating the gregariousness of Ming literati. It is these details that provide us with the clues as to how Kao seeks identity and defines his exile, as well as why he sets so much store on the trip.

As recounted in the *San shih chi*, shortly after Kao left his hometown he received as a farewell gift from a friend a fan with a few lines of Ch'ü Yüan's poetry inscribed on it. This incident reminded Kao that he had the poet's book in his baggage and upon receipt of the fan he took out the volume and reread it. Ch'ü Yüan, as we have noted in a previous chapter, was exalted by the historiographer Liu Chih-chi as the progenitor of autobiography. Exiled by a weak and ignorant king for his outspoken remonstrances, the loyal minister roamed among southern rivers and lakes while dreaming of mythic journeys and a perpetual quest. The invocation of this cultural hero by both Kao and his friend was most appropriate in view of the circumstances of his exile; it even foreshadowed both his

---

[47] *Kao-tzu i-shu* (Written legacy of Master Kao P'an-lung) (1876), 3:14a–b; hereafter referred to as *Kao-tzu i-shu*.

quest and the eventual autobiographical act. That he had taken the book along shows how much he identified himself with his predecessor. The wild fantasies of the poet served not only as an antidote to the austere abstractions of Neo-Confucian philosophy but would inform every mountain and river that Kao was going to see. The rereading of the exiled poet led Kao to mention another hero of his, the Neo-Confucian master Chu Hsi, whose sympathetic commentaries on Ch'ü Yüan Kao praised.

The significance of the second invocation will become clear if we trace the particular route that Kao took to his place of exile. Before the introduction of railroads the easiest and the most usual way to go from Kao's hometown Wu-hsi in the Yangtze Valley to Chieh-yang in northeast Kwangtung would be to sail up the Yangtze into the P'o-yang Lake and then up the Kan River to the Kwangtung border. From there one could take a land or water route to Chieh-yang. The route that Kao chose as delineated in the *San shih chi* was shorter but much more hazardous, traversing the most rugged terrain of Chekiang and Fukien and constantly alternating between rapid and narrow waterways and steep and tortuous mountain paths. Assuming Kao had free choice in the matter—there is every reason to believe so: the political battles of 1593 were much less bloody than subsequent ones and Kao's short exile seemed to be a very relaxed affair—his admiration for Chu Hsi must have contributed to his decision to go by way of Fukien. On his way down he made a stop at Wu-i to pay his homage to the academy founded by Chu Hsi (ibid., 10:30b). On his way back he first went to T'ung-an to visit the shrine for the master (10:44b). Next he spent a whole day at K'ao-t'ing Academy, the last home of Chu Hsi, and was entertained by five descendants of the master (10:46a–b). That night he went back to Wu-i in order to pay one more visit next day to the site made sacred by Chu Hsi (10:46b). Elsewhere in the *San shih chi* the master's name is reverently mentioned several times when philosophical issues are aired. In light of such adulation of Chu Hsi Kao's southern journey is more a pilgrimage than an exile. His enlightenment can then be seen as the ideal destination of every pilgrim, frequently sought but seldom reached.

Going back to Kao's autobiography we last saw him boarding the boat in a desperate mood, determined to break out of the gloom and confusion that he had been thrown into ever since he returned to his hometown from the capital. That he should have expected so much from the trip can be explained, as we have done, by his sense that he was going to the very source of his spiritual and philosophical being. Like every good pilgrim who has to make daily progress over the long and difficult spiritual and geographical terrain, Kao followed a daily program as his boat slowly moved upstream.

Next day I placed a thick mat in the boat and drew up a very strict regimen for myself. I was to practice quiet-sitting for half a day; the other half was to be devoted to reading. During the quiet-sitting, whenever I felt uneasy I would study the methods suggested by Ch'eng I, Ch'eng Hao, and Chu Hsi, practicing one by one items such as being sincere, reverent, and quiescent; observing the emotions of joy, anger, sadness, and happiness before they were aroused; sitting silently and purifying the mind; and comprehending the heavenly principle. I kept on practicing without a moment of cessation, whether I was standing, sitting, eating, or resting. At night I did not untie my clothes. I slept when I was completely exhausted, and I resumed quiet-sitting when I woke up. After I practiced the above-mentioned methods by rotation for a while, I began to feel that, whenever my mind was clear and pure, my spirit could expand and fill up the universe. But this feeling did not last. (Ibid., 3:15a)

It is most fitting that as he was moving in the direction of the land of Chu Hsi he would practice daily the methods suggested by Chu and Chu's own masters, the Ch'eng brothers. What might have been surprising to more orthodox Confucians is the extent of similarity in form between Kao and the Buddhist monks we have met in an earlier chapter. The vow to reach a resolution made just before embarking on a trip, the tenacious hold on a crucial phrase, the necessity of quiet-sitting, the denial of sleep until the point of total exhaustion, and the first but fleeting intimations of the denouement—all staples of Buddhist progress toward illumination—are now repeated, not by a disciple of the Wang school but by a Tung-lin stalwart, defender of the Ch'eng-Chu orthodoxy. Everything was possible in the syncretic climate of late Ming. As we shall see in the next chapter Kao was not without Buddhist friends; even without them Kao might in his unsettled youth have read Tsu-ch'in and other Ch'an autobiographical sermons. There is, however, one crucial element in his spiritual progress that is absent in Buddhist testimonies. He shares his love of nature, as indicated by the next quotation, with travel writers and painters, but not with Buddhist autobiographers, who are doctrinally forbidden to feel attached to things of the senses.

For two months I traveled. Fortunately I was involved in no business but only encountered exquisite landscape. My servant and I became close to each other. At night everything was quiet and peaceful, and I always drank a little. Sometimes the boat stopped at the foot of a green mountain, sometimes it lingered in the shallows where the water had the color of jade. Sometimes I would sit on a big rock and enjoy the sound of the stream, the songs of the birds, the lush trees

and the tall bamboos. They all pleased my mind but my mind did
not attach itself to any aspect of the surroundings. (Ibid., 3:15a–b)

The last sentence of the quotation further betrays Kao's affinity with
Buddhism. Not only the sense of the sentence but the term *ching* (surroundings) used in it show Kao's awareness of the danger of lingering on
the aesthetic level, a danger known to all Buddhists but not to those late
Ming literati who succumbed to wanderlust. Reservations notwithstanding, Kao's communion with nature was a crucially important stage of his
pilgrimage, for it was immediately followed by the episode of enlightenment.

The *San shih chi*, which as travel literature frees Kao from the need to
express any fears of attachment to surroundings, gives a much more detailed account of the events leading up to his enlightenment. We shall
dwell somewhat on the arduousness of the route without which an essential theme of pilgrimage would have been missing.

On the sixth day of the ninth month we arrived in An-sha. After we
had left Yen-p'ing our boat had gone through countless mountains.
As there were hardly any other travelers I felt as if I had gone beyond
the human world. Beyond An-sha the mountains became even more
lofty. On either side of the river the cliffs and precipices were so sheer
and vertical that they seemed to have been cut open with gigantic
swords to let the green stream go through. Sometimes the riverbed
would abruptly rise by more than ten feet, with the cascade dashing
down like a writhing white dragon. There were altogether nine such
cascades, and they were called Nine Dragons. The rapids were less
precipitous than the dragons, and there were eighteen of them.
(Ibid., 10:32b–33a)

The progress of the pilgrim was to be made through the negotiation of
each rapid and the conquest of each dragon. As a premodern Confucian
Kao was not expected to toil literally, but he was as fully exposed to the
hazards of the rapids as his boatman—the small and light boat could accommodate only one passenger—and had to climb up the rocks over
every cascade on his own feet.

Boats would collect below each cascade. When the accumulation
reached a dozen or so, the boatmen would join together and lift up
the boats one by one. They climbed the cliffs like monkeys and
pulled the boats up, one at a time, with long ropes from both banks.
This was why it took so much time to negotiate each dragon. Every
time we arrived at the foot of a cascade I would climb to the top and,
sitting on a huge rock, watch the lifting of the boats. Surrounded by
mountains in all directions and shaded by exuberant foliage, I lis-

tened to the music orchestrated by hundreds of exotic birds. An even greater marvel was the counterpoint between the heigh-hos of the boatmen and the gushing sound of the stream. (Ibid., 10:33a–b)

Kao's immersion in the almost Edenesque wilderness, given such a prominent space in the autobiography, appears here only as a periodic respite, albeit well deserved and important, from the perilous and strenuous movements upstream. These movements, not mentioned at all in the *K'un-hsüeh chi*, are just as important to his spiritual progress as the periodic respites. In the symbolic topography each rapid and cascade is no different from the biblical narrow gate, or the *kuan*, the checkpoint that every Chinese traveler must approach at his peril. Each represents the sort of challenge or ordeal that abounds in quest narratives and fairy tales. To a seeker of truth the graded upward locomotion cannot but remind him of the possibility of a corresponding spiritual kinetics, that in his itinerary each signpost is matched by the successful negotiation of a physical hurdle. In fact sacred sites are frequently located on mountain tops, while Buddhists often represent their processes toward illumination by the traversing of ten realms, each higher than the other. But the marvel of Kao's story lies in the joining of two clusters of archetypal figures: his arduous and relentlessly upward movement is mostly made in water, which only accentuates the elemental perils that accompany each step of his progress. Even the name for the cascades, *lung* (dragon), reverberates with larger and varied significance. As the mythic beast that stirs up storms, it recalls the tempestuous powers that tested Neo-Confucians such as Hu Chih. But the Chinese dragon is also an auspicious figure, promising great changes for the deserving: earlier we have seen Teng Huo-ch'ü alluding to Lung-men (Dragon Gate), the cascade in the Yellow River over which a happy few of the multitudinous leaping fish would be transformed into superior beings. The mythic beast can also stand for obstacles to transformation: in legends all over the world paradise is frequently guarded by dragons, denying easy access to undeserving mortals. That Kao may have felt he was going closer and closer to a wonderland is suggested by a few hints. Earlier he mentioned that he felt he was going beyond the human world. The awesome landscape as well as the almost Edenesque wilderness is reminiscent of the setting in numerous Chinese tales about the fairyland. There were, of course, no literal encounters with immortals in Kao's account of fact, but it is clear that he went through a process of purification, an indispensable accessory, if not the goal, in any pilgrimage. "In the middle of the night when I woke up from a dream the sound of the water became more desolate: its purity penetrated to the marrow of my bones. The mountains and water for several days offered great help to my state of mind" (ibid., 10:33b).

If our reading of Kao's narrative up to this point seems to be too teleological to some readers, their skepticism may be somewhat mitigated by
the following digression that Kao interjects between the passage quoted
above and the episode of his enlightenment. This digression will show
that Kao himself suspects a supernatural design in his adventures, and this
belief informs every turn or twist of his journey with a new meaning. In
the spring of 1592, two years before his exile, Kao went to the capital for
his first official assignment. He had earlier acquired the *chin-shih* degree—
in the parlance of his day, the successful negotiation of the Dragon Gate—
but a death in the family prevented him from seeking office until now.
While waiting for the government decision Kao consulted an oracle and
the oracular verse that he drew by lot said:

> To whom shall you unburden the secret of your life?
> I shall tell you, sir, at the head of the eighteen rapids.
> (Ibid., 10:33b)

It is not surprising that Kao should have found the message incomprehen-
sible. He had asked what his assignment would be, but the answer was
too enigmatic to be of any help. At that time the term "eighteen rapids"
simply made no sense at all. Looking back, he could have found another
clue to his fate. The assignment, contrary to the customary practice,
turned out to be a minor position in the Messenger Office in Peking. The
significance of his unexpected title, *hsing-jen*, literally "traveler," would
become clear once the enigma in the oracle was solved, and the solution
burst on him unexpectedly at one point in his journey when he had to
decide on the route to take for Ch'ao-chou, the major city nearest to his
destination.

> After I set out for Chieh-yang I happened to look at a road map and
> saw that the route to Ch'ao-chou by way of Kiangsi would pass
> through the Eighteen Rapids. I was greatly startled. Through in-
> quiries I discovered an alternate way, which would take me there
> only through Fukien. After I charted the new route to Ch'ao-chou
> via Chang-chou in Fukien I said, playfully, "Now what are the gods
> going to do about it?" (Ibid., 10:33b–34a)

The gods, it turned out, had the last laugh. When Kao reached Ch'ung-
an he discovered that to proceed any further the only practical route was,
after all, the waterway that would eventually traverse the Nine Dragons
and Eighteen Rapids. Bowing to the inevitable, Kao followed the course
that had been predicted in the oracular verse. As to the central message
contained in the verse, the unburdening of the secret, Kao said nothing.
Perhaps it was not necessary for him to refer again to the oracle. Great
things were revealed to him two days after he completed the arduous wa-

ter journey, or rather he, obeying the oracle, would reveal what very few autobiographers would talk about.

Judging by what Kao says later in the *K'un-hsüeh chi* (ibid., 3:16a), he would have been the first to denounce any autobiographer who would dwell on his spiritual experience. For a Confucian of his persuasion enlightenment certainly would not come easily. But, as we have seen earlier, there had been every preparation for and a long sequential process leading to a final breakthrough. Not only was he desperate for a solution, but he was even given supernatural assurance that a solution was predestined. Aside from the eighteen rapids of the oracle, was not the climbing of the awesome cascades, too, something long determined by his stars? Otherwise why did he bear the name *kao p'an lung*, the literal meaning of which was no other than "high, pull oneself upward, dragon"? Whether such questions rose to his consciousness or not, Kao must have felt that a prophecy was about to be fulfilled, and his life would be touched by forces beyond the natural order. If any more propitious condition was still needed when he arrived at T'ing-chou, it was supplied by the location of this border town. T'ing-chou was a watershed: until this point, in all the numerous rivers he always moved against the current, but from now on he was to float downstream. T'ing-chou, moreover, may even have been the highest point that he ever reached in terms of altitude. At any rate even here he would have to make one final ascent, so to speak, before he reached enlightenment.

> We took a land route and stopped at an inn in T'ing-chou. Above the guest rooms there was an attic that commanded a view of the mountains in the front and overlooked a brook in the back. I enjoyed very much going up to the attic. It just happened that I had in my hand a book of the sayings of the Ch'eng brothers. Glancing at the book I came across the saying of Master Ming-tao's that "even amidst one hundred offices and ten thousand affairs, surrounded by one million weapons, one can still find simple delight and drink water with bent elbows.[48] All the myriad of disturbances are in man—there is actually not a thing!"[49] It suddenly occurred to me with great force: "How true it is! There is actually not a thing." The lingering anxiety within me was once and for all completely severed. A burden of several tons seemed to have abruptly fallen off my shoulders. I seemed to have been hit by a flash of lightning, which penetrated and illuminated my entire body. I now merged completely with the great

[48] Alludes to *Analects*, 7:15: "The Master said, 'with coarse rice to eat, with water to drink and my bended arm for a pillow;--I have still joy in the midst of these things. Riches and honors acquired by unrighteousness are to me as a floating cloud" (Legge translation).

[49] For the saying of Ming-tao (Ch'eng Hao) see *Erh-Ch'eng i-shu*, 6:3a.

transformations—there was no longer a gap between man and heaven or interior and exterior. I realized that all universe was my mind, its domain was my body, and its location my heart. Everything was bright and spiritual; in the end there was no way of speaking of direction or position. In the past I always utterly despised some scholars' exaggerated way of discussing enlightenment, but now I felt it was in no way out-of-the-ordinary. I realized that from now on I was in a position to apply my effort. (Ibid., 3:15b–16a)

The intense experience described above does not seem to have differed very much from the illumination or enlightenment that we have seen earlier. Sudden flashes of bright light, the precipitous release from all anxieties, and a sense of total merging with the universe are the characteristics shared by Ch'an Buddhists and Neo-Confucians alike. After long years of tortuous search and exacting regimen there remain two catalytic elements just before the final breakthrough: one last act of physical locomotion, such as the climbing of stairs, the lifting of one's body to the mat on the meditation platform, or in Kao's case the ascent to the attic; and the reading or sudden remembrance of a pertinent saying. There is, however, one fundamental difference between the two groups in their subsequent lives. The Buddhists almost never had anything further to say: presumably reaching illumination was an end in itself, and with the subitists there could not be partial or lesser illuminations, hence no further efforts would make any sense. With the Confucians the quest would terminate only with life. Enlightenment, however great or liberating, only led to new tasks and further endeavors. Kao made this very clear in his closing remark on presumably the most intense experience of his life.

Once he reached enlightenment the exile no longer seemed to have any meaning in his spiritual autobiography, for Kao says nothing more about his banishment except that "in the spring of *i-wei* [1595] I returned from Chieh-yang" (ibid., 3:16a). As for the enlightenment, he makes one oblique reference to it when he discusses the necessity for several decades of patient and silent endeavor if one is to approach sagehood. "My endowment is most deficient and I lack a long period of strict regimen. Even if I come upon some great insight, what use is it? Fortunately ever since my true self was revealed, every time I try to spur myself I am back on the right track" (3:16b). The rest of his autobiography is a record of how he gradually came to understand and absorb the teachings of the Confucian classics. At the end, with great humility, he returns to the theme of *k'un erh hsüeh chih* (striving to learn while beset by difficulties).

Even the sages cannot exhaust what there is between heaven and earth, how much less able are we? How can there be an end to our endeavor? We must be diligent in the study of things, true and proper to others, discreet in speech and ready in action, cautious and industrious until our death. I have striven to learn while beset by difficulties. What little I have accumulated through months and years of painful effort is not enough even to be laughed at by the wise, but it may be of some use to those fellow sufferers who sympathize with me. Recorded in the early spring of *chia-yin* [1614]. (3:17b–18a)

Let us now return to his travel account and see what he says there about the momentous event that took place in the attic above the inn in T'ing-chou. Next to nothing is said: "At noon on the eleventh I arrived in T'ing-chou. There is something about *hsüeh* which is recorded in the *K'un-chih lu*.[50] In the evening I took a stroll" (10:34a). Here Kao is following the long-established practice of dynastic historians in making no more than a bibliographical reference to events which are fully, and justifiably, recorded elsewhere. Implicit in Kao's practice is the belief that spiritual autobiography is a more appropriate place than a travel account to record matters concerning *hsüeh*, spiritual or intellectual endeavor. The *San shih chi* goes on to narrate the rest of his journey to Chieh-yang, his sojourn there, and his return trip. Kao continues to visit scenic spots, shrines of worthies, friends, and fellow Confucians, but absent now is the introspective mode that occasionally intrudes in the early section of the narrative.

From Teng Huo-ch'ü's *Nan-hsün lu* to Kao's twice-told tale, the wheel seems to have completed its circle. If Teng demonstrated, for the first time in the history of Chinese autobiography, the possibilities of casting a life story in the form of a travel account, Kao almost perversely tore the two asunder, depriving his spiritual autobiography of telling details and denying the travel account its climax. Whether Kao was partially responsible or not, after him no more spiritual autobiographies were written by Confucians. Travel literature also returned to its usual style: without the pull of autobiography, it could not sustain the acquired taste for the subjective and introspective. Since we shall dwell on the decline of autobiography in general at the end of this study, it suffices to say that one more spiritual autobiography was written eight years after Kao's, this time by a Buddhist friend of his. This unusual work will be the topic of next chapter.

[50] What Kao meant here is *K'un-hsüeh chi*. The error is understandable since, as we have mentioned in the section on Hu Chih, the terms *k'un-chih* and *k'un-hsüeh* are often juxtaposed in Confucian discourse and the words *lu* and *chi* are synonyms.

SIX

THE SPIRITUAL AUTOBIOGRAPHY
OF TE-CH'ING (1546–1623)

USUALLY considered one of the last great Buddhist masters of the Ming, Te-ch'ing (also known as Han-shan, 1546–1623) in many ways exemplifies the contemporary intellectual climate in general and the style of late Ming Buddhism in particular. He shared with his two equals in critical renown, Chu-hung (also known as Yün-ch'i, 1535–1615) and Chen-k'o (also known as Tzu-po or Ta-kuan, 1544–1604), the adulation of the populace, an easy rapport with the Confucian literati, a profound belief in the syncretism of the Three Teachings, and an insistence on combining the Ch'an regimen with Pure Land practice; but he was more active in worldly affairs than the former and more prolific in exegetical writings than the latter. In fact he wrote commentaries not only on most of the major Buddhist scriptures but also on such Taoist and Confucian texts as the *Tao te ching*, the *Chuang-Tzu*, the *Tso chuan*, and the *Chung-yung* (*Doctrine of the Mean*). His exposition of the *Ta hsüeh* (*Great Learning*) was entirely in line with Neo-Confucian practice, without any explicit reference to his religion. For our purpose, however, the most remarkable thing about him is that less than a year before his death he wrote an account of his long and eventful life.[1]

The format that Te-ch'ing chose for his work is that of a self-written *nien-p'u*, or annalistic autobiography. The *nien-p'u* format, as we have seen, does not seem to be a satisfactory medium for recounting a life with shape or unity. But Te-ch'ing is unique among the annalistic autobiographers: he underwent an essential change, while all the others, in spite of the vicissitudes of the scholar's tenure and the official's career, remained very much the same men from birth to death. It is this change, continuous but nonlinear—the initial crises, the early conditioning, the subsequent reinforcement, the hesitations and temptations, the backslidings, the strenuous efforts, and the ultimate enlightenment—that gives Te-ch'ing's life up to his thirty-first year a meaningful pattern. Making the

---

[1] The text of Te-ch'ing's autobiography used in this study was first published in 1651 with annotations prepared by his disciple Fu-cheng. Page references are to the modern edition, *Tsu-pen Han-shan ta shih nien-p'u su-chu* (Unabridged and annotated annalistic biography of Master Han-shan), ed. Fu-cheng (Soochow: Hung-hua she, 1934); hereafter referred to as *NP*. A slightly variant text is included in Te-ch'ing's collected works, *Han-shan ta-shih meng-yu ch'üan-chi* (Complete works of Master Han-shan), in *HTC*, 127:946–76.

most of the natural drift and purport of his life story, he neither strains
the plausibility of his conversion nor fails to see the significance of even
minor details. When an interesting life is told by a sure-handed master,
even the limitations of the *nien-p'u* format cannot prevent the emergence
of a distinct and coherent narrative, which in this case may be called the
spiritual autobiography of a Buddhist monk.

Te-ch'ing's autobiography begins with the usual account of family and
origin, but he keeps that part to a minimum and proceeds to his first
spiritual crisis, which occurred in his seventh year. One day when he was
out his beloved uncle died and was placed in a bed.

> When I came back from school my mother purposely said to me:
> "Your uncle is asleep. Why don't you go and wake him up?" I tried
> to call him several times. Then my aunt, looking very sad, cried,
> "Alas, he's gone!" Completely puzzled, I asked my mother, "Uncle
> is right here; how can he have gone away?" "Your uncle is dead," my
> mother replied.
>
> Where does a dead man go? I was even more puzzled. Shortly af-
> terwards my aunt gave birth to a boy. My mother went to see her
> and I followed. When I noticed the size of the baby I asked my
> mother, "How did this baby enter into Auntie's belly?" My mother
> patted me and said: "Little fool, how did you get into your mother's
> belly?" I could not answer. The great puzzle of life and death could
> not be understood.[2]

Life and death are the ultimate mysteries with which all religions must
grapple, and it was only fitting that the future Buddhist master should
have been exposed at an early age to the same shattering forces that had
set Prince Siddhartha on his momentous spiritual journey. What is unusual in Te-ch'ing's first crisis is that it was entirely his mother's making.
Not only did she not shield her son, as most post-Freudian mothers
would have done, from traumatic experiences but she actually precipi-
tated him, a mere child of seven, into struggles and puzzles of a sort that
frequently confronted Ch'an disciples. Indeed, the deliberate and decisive
role that the mother played in Te-ch'ing's development clearly emerges
as his childhood and adolescence unfold.

> When I was eight I was boarded with a relative across the river so I
> could attend school. My mother allowed me to come home only
> once a month. One day while on a home visit I clung to my mother
> and refused to go back. She became angry and whipped me. When
> she chased me to the riverbank I refused to board the boat. She was
> so incensed that she grabbed me by the hair and dropped me into the

[2] *NP*, pp. 9–10.

river. She left without looking back. My grandmother happened to
notice my plight and cried for help. After I was rescued she took me
home. My mother said, "What is the use of saving this stupid boy
from drowning!" Relentlessly she again drove me out. Thereupon I
thought that my mother was completely heartless, and from that
time on I was no longer homesick. (*NP*, p. 10)

The mother appears in this episode unreasonably harsh, even by seventeenth-century standards, but Te-ch'ing goes on to relate, apparently
from hearsay, an incident that puts his mother's behavior in a new light:
"My mother often wept by her side of the river. When my grandmother
scolded her, she said, 'I had to wean him of his attachment to me; otherwise he would never be able to study' " (ibid.).

The juxtaposition of the two episodes serves to illustrate the complexity and poignancy of the mother's role in the education of a future Buddhist monk. If the first episode shows the mother as a harsh and resolute
disciplinarian, the second reveals the heartrending inner conflicts that
must have beset her from time to time. The son was deeply loved, as we
shall learn from a subsequent account of his childhood, but he was
weaned of his attachment. This paradoxical relationship might not con-
form to the expectations of modern child psychology, but it provides,
perhaps, a key to the formation of the ideal Buddhist personality—compassion for all beings but attachment to none.

When I was nine I continued my studies in a temple. I heard monks
reciting the Kuan-yin Sutra which promises relief from the sufferings of this world. Greatly pleased, I got the text from a monk, and
memorized it. My mother worshipped Kuan-yin, and I always accompanied her when she burned incense and did obeisances. One
day I told her that Bodhisattva Kuan-yin had a sutra, and she said
that she did not know it. I then recited it for her. She was greatly
pleased and said: "Where did you get it? Your chanting of the sutra
is like that of an old monk." (*NP*, pp. 10–11)

From what we have seen, Te-ch'ing's childhood was no ordinary one,
but there are a number of other reasons that the childhood segment of Te-
ch'ing's autobiography deserves our attention more than any other period. For one thing, no Chinese autobiographer or biographer before Te-
ch'ing ever gave such a detailed treatment of childhood. Another reason
is that every incident in his childhood that he chose to record brought
him one step closer to his eventual conversion. Therefore I shall quote
two more entries from the early section of his autobiography:

When I was ten my mother supervised my studies with extreme
strictness. As I was distressed by it, I asked her, "What is studying

for?" "For becoming an official," she said. "What kind of an official?" "Starting from the bottom, you might get to be the prime minister." "What's after that?" "That would be the end." "It is a pity that after a lifetime of hardship one will come to an end. What's the use of it! I want to be something that will not end." "A stupid boy like you can only be an itinerant monk." "Why should I be an itinerant monk? What's good in it?" "An itinerant monk is a Buddhist disciple who travels all over the world, free and provided for no matter where he goes." "This is exactly what I would like to be." "I am only afraid that you won't have such good fortune." "Why do I need good fortune to be an itinerant monk?" "People often pass the civil service examinations with the highest honors, but there are very few who become great Buddhist masters." "I do have such good fortune, but I am afraid you could not bear to give me up." "If you have such good fortune, I surely can bear to give you up." I silently took mental note of what she said. (*NP*, pp. 11–12)

One day when I was eleven years old I saw several traveling monks approaching our house each carrying a pack, a large ladle, and a rain hat made of bamboo. I asked my mother, "Who are these monks?" She said that they were itinerant monks. I was quite happy to hear this and observed them closely. When the monks entered our compound they took down their packs and leaned them against a tree. Greeting my mother, they asked for alms. My mother seated them and went in to make tea and prepare a vegetable meal. She waited on them with much reverence. When they finished they got up and put on their packs. As they were ready to set off they raised their hands, but my mother backed away from them, saying, "Please don't thank me." The monks left without much ado. I said to my mother: "The monks were rude. They ate and left, without thanking you." My mother replied, "If they thanked me, I would not get the blessing." I said to myself, "This shows why the monk is a superior being." I often thought of it, and soon I decided to become a monk. But at that time I did not know how to go about it. (*NP*, p. 12)

These anecdotes, taken together, constitute an important landmark in the development of Chinese autobiography. When childhood was touched on at all by Te-ch'ing's predecessors, it was usually represented by a few standard topoi such as early signs of precocity or commendable acts of filial piety. Te-ch'ing, on the other hand, was interested in a different order of events—events that were not exemplary or even typical, but were crucial to the destiny of one unique person, even though they might not have appeared noteworthy to other autobiographers. Perhaps the elliptical prose of classical Chinese was suitable for representing the exemplary, but in the context of autobiographical writing a more robust narrative style was necessary. This seems to me the reason why in Te-ch'ing's narration of his childhood there is extensive use of dialogue and a plain language bordering on the vernacular. If each event constitutes a unique and crucial experience, it must be represented with greater particularity than the historiographical convention usually allows. Conversation must not be summarized but transcribed almost verbatim, and the visit of traveling monks must be recorded with visual details. "When the monks entered our compound they took down their packs and leaned them against a tree." The packs have no significance as history, but they endow the scene with an individuality and concreteness found only in vernacular fiction.

Te-ch'ing's reconstruction of his childhood affords us, for the first time in Chinese history, a primary and direct account of the early education of a future Buddhist master—no divine intervention or sudden outburst of faith, but a slow and gradual process of molding and shaping through the determined effort of a pious mother. No childhood experience that Te-ch'ing remembered and chose to record fails to play a part in this particular education. This selective principle, useful as it is in the mode of spiritual autobiography, might be found objectionable by those who insist that childhood should be treated in its own right, not merely as full-time preparation for adult life. Whatever the validity of this objection, we must judge Te-ch'ing's practice in the perspective of the history of human society, mindful of the fact, convincingly established by Philippe Ariès in *Centuries of Childhood*, that the concept of childhood as we know it today is a relatively recent development[3] and noting too, as stated by Paul Delany, that "we know practically nothing about the childhood and adolescence of most Renaissance men, even quite famous ones."[4] In terms of the proportion of his autobiography allotted to childhood, Te-ch'ing stands comparison with even the best autobiographers of the Renaissance. Cellini's fascinating story in the Penguin edition takes up 381 pages, but only four deal with events that had taken place before the dashing sculptor reached the age of fifteen.[5]

The first test of Te-ch'ing's early religious education occurred in his twelfth year, when his father, incredibly and unaccountably kept out of his life story until this time, suggested that a betrothal be made for the son.[6] Te-ch'ing not only rejected the idea but decided to leave home and

[3] Trans. Robert Baldick (New York: Vintage Books, 1962), pp. 128–33.

[4] *British Autobiography in the 17th Century*, p. 14.

[5] *The Autobiography of Benvenuto Cellini*, trans. George Bull (Baltimore: Penguin Books, 1964).

[6] *NP*, p. 13. Although we know more about Te-ch'ing's childhood than that of nearly any Chinese before the seventeenth century, his silences are sometimes more intriguing than

join Abbot Hsi-lin at the Pao-en Monastery. The combined forces of mother and son prevailed over the father's objection, and in 1557 Te-ch'ing was brought to the monastery. The abbot, strange to say, did not admit Te-ch'ing into the order right away, but said: "This child is so exceptional that it would be a pity to let him become an ordinary monk. I shall have him continue his studies with a Confucian teacher and see how he turns out." A visitor at the monastery, Chao Chen-chi, a prominent member of the T'ai-chou sect of Neo-Confucianism, was so impressed by the young Te-ch'ing that he pronounced that the boy would someday be "the teacher of men and heavenly beings." Chao apparently noticed the equivocal position the boy found himself in, for he asked him, "Would you like to be a high official or a Buddha?" "A Buddha," Te-ch'ing replied without hesitation.[7]

Whatever this seemingly commonplace episode meant to Te-ch'ing, its symbolic significance is clear in light of the subsequent course of his life. The exchange between the two epitomizes Te-ch'ing's struggles during the next decade—for a long time, though a monk, he was torn between the contending claims of the Buddhist and Confucian paths. Chao represents the other type of person he might have become—a prominent Confucian scholar-official with more or less Buddhist sympathies—and also the type with whom Te-ch'ing tended to associate in later life.

During the next few years Te-ch'ing seemed to spend most of his time in Confucian studies. He managed to memorize all the Four Books before proceeding to the *Book of Changes*; he also practiced writing classical prose and poetry. Membership in a literary club brought him into close contact with young Confucian candidates, and he won most literary contests. But such a congenial existence did not go on without interruptions. There were several bouts of an unnamed illness and clashes with an inspector of schools. And the real crisis came when he was nineteen. It began with all his close friends in the literary club scoring successes at the local examination, which led him to be tempted to take the examination himself. As he was wavering, Fa-hui (also known as Yün-ku, 1500–1579), a leading monk of the day, happened to visit the monastery. After hearing Te-ch'ing out, Fa-hui vigorously explained to the young man "the glories

---

his revelations. One cannot but wonder, for instance, why he has not said anything about his father until this point. We know from a reference in his collected works (*HTC*, 127:900) that he had a younger brother, but his autobiography mentions no siblings. The omissions suggest that his mother may have played an even greater role in the formation of Te-ch'ing's personality than one would otherwise infer from the autobiography. We do not, however, have sufficient sources to attempt a psychoanalytical interpretation of the various events in Te-ch'ing's life in the way that Erik H. Erikson did for Martin Luther, who died the same year that Te-ch'ing was born.

[7] *NP*, p. 13.

of the contemplative life and the promise of illumination" (*NP*, p. 14) and urged him to read books that contained lives of eminent monks. Apparently the perusal of one of the books tipped the scale: "I went through his box of books and got the *Chung-feng kuang-lu*. Halfway through the book I suddenly became exultant and exclaimed, 'This is what delights my heart!' Thereupon I decided to enter the monastic life and asked the abbot to tonsure me" (ibid.).

Te-ch'ing's succinct account of the crisis, although candid, does not delineate the full complexity of his inner struggles, but fortunately it is possible to obtain further information from his other writings. Leading to the crisis was, of course, the temptation of Confucian officialdom, and the temptation was all the greater to a precocious and self-assured youth from a poor family, especially as the fortunes of Buddhism had reached their lowest point at just about this time. Te-ch'ing was very emphatic about the humble station of the Buddhist clergy in his biography of the Abbot Hsi-lin, who served in the government for many years as a deputy undersecretary in the Bureau of Buddhist Affairs (*Tso chüeh-i*). "The abbot was frequently aware of the contempt that scholar-officials had for the Buddhist clergy. 'When a monk is deficient in education, he invites insults from Confucians and thus brings shame to the church,' he said with a sigh."[8] Furthermore, "earlier most monks were so common and uncouth that they could not utter even a word in the company of the literati. The abbot felt that while the clergy should be concerned with meditation and the teachings of the Buddha, they must also learn from Confucian teachers in order to be able to read and write as well as understand the great principles of loyalty and filial piety."[9] Since Te-ch'ing was the abbot's favorite disciple, perhaps it was inevitable that he would outdo the abbot in his deprecation of loutish clerics as he rose in the esteem of the young Confucian candidates of his region whose camaraderie he enjoyed. In fact, as he revealed in his biography of Fa-hui, it was precisely his contempt for monks that brought him to the verge of defection:

> When I was nineteen I intended to give up the priesthood. When Master Fa-hui heard this he asked me: "Why do you go against your original commitment?" "I am disgusted with the commonness of the monks." "If you don't like the commonness of the monks, why don't you learn to be an eminent monk? The eminent monks in the olden days were not treated as subordinates by the emperors or as sons by their parents. They were even used to the respect shown to gods and Nagas. Just read the *Transmission of the Lamp* or the *Lives of Eminent Monks* and you'll know."

[8] *HTC*, 127:630.
[9] Ibid.

I looked through his bookcase and came across a set of *Chung-feng kuang-lu*. When I showed it to him he said: "Read it carefully and you'll soon know the great worth of being a monk."

Largely owing to his guidance I soon decided to be tonsured.[10]

That the *Chung-feng kuang-lu* should have proved a timely antidote to the young novice's doubts and disillusionment lies precisely in the striking contrast between the exalted career of its author and the sad lot of late Ming Buddhist clerics. If the records of conversations, correspondence, addresses, and self-eulogies of Ming-pen (1263–1323, also known as Chung-feng) failed to demonstrate amply the universal acclaim that the great Ch'an master enjoyed, the three biographies about him included in the collection—two in the form of stupa inscriptions and one commissioned by the emperor—would dispel the youth's last doubt, for they listed all the honors and favors that Ming-pen received from the imperial family and the literati. The king of Korea took a long journey and climbed a high mountain in order to pay personal respects to him; Chao Meng-fu, the great painter and calligrapher, burned incense and did obeisance each time a letter from the master arrived.

Ming-pen, then, represented the embodiment of all the hopes that the young novice had been repeatedly encouraged to entertain ever since his childhood. Considering Te-ch'ing's subsequent career, there is every reason to believe that his emulation of the great Ch'an master continued for a long time: there were the same close association with the Confucian literati, the same adulation from the imperial family, the same balance between preaching and writing, with not all of the latter limited to religious topics. In fact, the name of the great Ch'an master appears once more in the autobiography. When Te-ch'ing visited Peking for the first time in 1574, still a relatively obscure young monk, his arrogance irritated one of the leading scholar-officials of the time. The defense of him by one of the more sympathetic Confucians was that he was no mere monk but would someday prove the equal of Ming-pen.[11] That Te-ch'ing should have remembered this casual remark almost half a century later is one more indication of the indelible place of this model in his consciousness.

But Ming-pen was not the only possible exemplar available: the tradition of the eminent monk who was on easy terms with the literati and enjoyed patronage by the aristocracy was a long and established one, begun in the fourth century. To the demoralized Buddhist clerics of the middle decades of the sixteenth century Ming-pen was obviously the most recent and the most dramatic reassurance that all was not yet lost.

[10] *HTC*, 127:633.
[11] *NP*, p. 27.

But even the Abbot Hsi-lin and Master Fa-hui can be seen as latter-day, if somewhat lesser, lights of the tradition; for, as Te-ch'ing made a point of recalling in his biographies of the two, the former distinguished himself by his eloquence and presence of mind before the emperor[12] and the latter never failed to impress the learned and the powerful among the laity.[13] In their own way, these two elders were also models after whom Te-ch'ing was to pattern himself.

Returning to Te-ch'ing's autobiography, we find him burning all his Confucian literary exercises right after he received the tonsure. Late that year he took his final vows (*chü-chieh*). In the following year, 1565, Master Fa-hui organized a meditation trimester (*Ch'an-ch'i*) at the T'ien-chieh Monastery, which was to last ninety days. Fifty-five prominent monks from various places were invited to participate. Encouraged by Fa-hui, Te-ch'ing enrolled.

> At first, not knowing how to direct my effort, I was very much distressed. I offered incense and asked the master for instruction. He suggested the approach of thorough contemplation of A-mi-t'o-fo [*shen-shih nien-fo*]. Henceforth I concentrated on the contemplation without a moment of interruption or deviation. Three months passed like a dream: I was never aware of the presence of other participants nor did I notice any daily activities. . . . When I completed the trimester and came out, I continued to behave for a long time as if I were still sitting on the meditation seat. Even when I was walking in the marketplace I was not aware of the existence of other people. Everybody was amazed by my behavior. (*NP*, p. 17)

At a time when the Ch'an school was almost completely extinct in the region of the lower Yangtze Valley, Te-ch'ing was fortunate to have received training in sitting meditation. The capacity for deep concentration and control of the senses which he acquired during the trimester was to stand him in good stead ten years later, just before he reached illumination. Another significant aspect of this training is the instruction he received from Fa-hui at the outset—thorough contemplation of A-mi-t'o-fo. This combination of the Ch'an regimen with Pure Land practice was to be one of the tenets of the Buddhist ecumenism that all three of the last great Buddhist masters of the Ming embraced.

The final vows, the meditation training, and even the burning of all his Confucian literary exercises still could not keep him away from Confucian activities for very long. In 1567, when he was twenty-two, the Ministry of Rites ordered his temple to establish a charitable school (*i-hsüeh*)

[12] *HTC*, 127:630.
[13] Ibid., 633.

for the benefit of young monks and acolytes. Te-ch'ing was appointed teacher, and the enrollment was nearly two hundred. Consequently he renewed his acquaintance with the *Tso chuan*, the dynastic histories, and the various philosophers. He continued to teach for the next three years, apparently without any adverse effect on his fundamental Buddhist orientation.[14]

Late in 1571 Te-ch'ing, now twenty-five years old, decided to leave what had become for him a prosaic life of routine and to travel over the vast expanses of central and northern China. Early the following year he arrived in Yang-chou. Illness and a snowstorm stranded him in the city. He discovered that even in such desperate circumstances he was at first not successful in begging for alms.

> I could not bring myself to enter into any dooryard. Examining myself, I suddenly realized that my reluctance was caused by the possession of a little cash on my person. Thereupon I noticed that several Buddhist monks and Taoist priests were shivering in the snow, apparently even less successful than I in getting food. I invited them all to a meal in a restaurant and used up my last penny. The next day when I walked the street again I found myself able to open my mouth and beg loudly for food at people's doorways. (*NP*, p. 22)

Utter poverty and frequent distress were no doubt the usual lot of Buddhist clerics in the Ming, but an eminent monk, even during his apprentice years, had another side to his life. When Te-ch'ing first arrived in Peking, six months after the Yang-chou experience, he still sometimes went hungry, but even then he was received by prominent scholar-officials. Two years later, when he revisited the capital city, he was already in a position to call on all the leading members of the literati and to expect to be treated as an equal. In the exchange of repartee he usually had the upper hand. When Wang Shih-chen (1526–1590), for twenty years the proud arbiter of the literary world, slighted him because of his youth, he returned the insult with even greater arrogance. His behavior amidst the rank and fashion certainly conformed in every way to the long-established tradition of the eminent monk, and that he saw himself in such a role is evidenced by his recording, without any demur, the fact that one leading Confucian compared him to Chih-tun (314–366), while another predicted that he would someday prove the equal of Ming-pen (Chung-feng, Huan-chu) and Tsung-kao (also known as Ta-hui, 1089–1163).[15]

For a monk of Te-ch'ing's disposition, training, and talent, the greatest temptation during his middle years was the easy path of what Hui-chiao,

---

[14] *NP*, p. 21.
[15] *NP*, p. 27.

the author of the *Kao-seng chuan* (Lives of eminent monks), called the famous monk. "If men of real achievement conceal their brilliance, then
they are eminent (*kao*) but not famous (*ming*); when men of slight virtue
happen to be in accord with their times, then they are famous but not
eminent."[16] Perhaps continued residence in the capital city would have
deflected Te-ch'ing from his spiritual goals. Whether or not this was the
reason, early in 1575 he went to Mount Wu-t'ai with his friend, the monk
Fu-teng (also known as Miao-feng, 1540–1613), and settled down in a
secluded spot near the northern summit. "I was surrounded by ten thousand peaks of snow and ice, precisely the sort of place I had always
wanted. Completely gratified, I felt as if I were in paradise. Soon Fu-teng
went to Yen-t'ai and I stayed there alone" (*NP*, p. 33). Now he began his
meditative exercises: "Holding the single thought of A-mi-t'o-fo in my
mind, I refused to speak to any visitors but only stared at them. At last
people to me were just like things, for I got to the point that I no longer
made cognitive distinctions" (ibid.). When spring arrived his meditation
was interrupted.

> The place was very windy; all the myriad holes and fissures whistled
> fiercely whenever the wind blew. Then the ice melted and the tor-
> rents of water dashing against the rocks in the brook sounded like
> thunder. In my quietude all the noises appeared to be even louder
> than they actually were, as if a huge army daily charged by my hut.
> I was quite distressed. When I asked Fu-teng about it he said: "En-
> vironment [*ching*] arises from the mind: it does not come from out-
> side. Have you not heard the ancient saying that if one has been ex-
> posed to the sound of a stream for thirty years without its activating
> the mind, he can bear personal witness to the perfection of Kuan-
> yin?"
> I thereupon chose a narrow wooden bridge over the brook and sat
> or stood on it every day. At first I heard the sound of the water
> clearly. After a while I reached the point where the water would be-
> come audible only when my thought was activated. One day when
> I sat on the bridge I suddenly forgot my own person and the water
> became completely mute. From that time on all sounds were silenced
> and I was no longer disturbed by them. (Ibid.)

The cessation of cognitive and sensory functions, in light of what was
soon to occur, appeared to be no more than a preparation. His simple diet
may have been another preparatory element; his daily ration of one-tenth

---

[16] Quoted in Arthur Wright, "Biography and Hagiography: Hui-chiao's *Lives of Eminent
Monks*," in *Silver Jubilee Volume of the Zinbun Kagaku-Kenkyūsyo* (Kyoto: Kyoto University,
1954), p. 393.

of a pint of rice was supplemented by nothing but bran and wild roots and plants. Before the spring was over he achieved illumination.

> One day after a meal of rice porridge I began circumambulating. All of a sudden I stopped and could not perceive my body or mind; there was only something huge and bright, something perfect, full, and silent like a gigantic round mirror, with mountains, rivers, and the great earth reflected in it. When I awoke I felt very clear. I sought for my body and mind, but they were nowhere to be found. I composed a gāthā:

> > All of a sudden my wild mind stopped:
> > Inside and outside, all the roots and dust are cut across.
> > Turning around I touch and shatter the great empty sky,
> > All the myriad appearances are nipped before they arise.

> From that time on I was clear both internally and externally, and sounds and sights no longer posed obstacles. All the former doubts and confusions were now gone. (*NP*, pp. 33–34)

Although Te-ch'ing was now only thirty years old and his ensuing years were replete with color and drama, as a record of education and spiritual progress the autobiography might as well have ended at this point. The mode of the *nien-p'u* now begins to reclaim its usual place in Chinese autobiography: his account becomes a diary of activities rather than a process with shape and meaning. Consequently I shall not deal here with his later life, interesting as it is, except to summarize it briefly.

The most important event in Te-ch'ing's secular life was his involvement in one of the major political controversies of the Wan-li period. The emperor had three sons, but for many years he refused to designate one as the heir apparent. The empress dowager favored her oldest grandson, and her cause was supported by most of the leading officials. The emperor, however, sided with the son born by the imperial concubine Cheng. Te-ch'ing, as well as his friends Fu-teng and Chen-k'o, was drawn into the controversy because of their close association with the empress dowager, a devout Buddhist. Te-ch'ing was committed to the cause of the eldest prince from the beginning, as he had been commissioned by the empress dowager in 1581, when the emperor was only eighteen years old, to pray for the birth of an heir to the throne. He pointedly mentions in the autobiography that in the fall of the next year "the crown prince was born" (*NP*, p. 48). As the princes grew into adolescence, with the emperor still vacillating, the dispute became increasingly acrimonious: many supporters of the eldest prince, who remonstrated unbendingly with the emperor, were harshly punished. The Cheng faction, seeking to weaken the influence of the empress dowager, decided to undermine her most prominent partisans among the Buddhist clergy. In 1595 Te-ch'ing was arrested and later convicted on a trumped-up charge. Defrocked, he was sent to serve as a common soldier in the garrison army at Lei-chou in the far south. Chen-k'o was more unfortunate. Implicated in the so-called Evil Book (*Yao-shu*) case, one of the many battles over the succession issue, he died in jail.[17]

Te-ch'ing's punishment seems to have solidified his alliance with the leading Neo-Confucians of his day, and the journey south looked more like a triumphant march. The commanders at the garrison were lenient and even respectful to him. In spite of his sentence he was allowed to write, lecture, and travel freely in the south. In 1606 the birth of a son to the oldest prince, who had been formally made crown prince in 1601, occasioned a general amnesty which restored Te-ch'ing to civilian status. However, he continued to live in much the same way as he had during his ten years of exile. In 1622 he wrote his autobiography, and the following year he died—in Ts'ao-ch'i, the Ch'an Buddhists' holiest place, where the Sixth Patriarch Hui-neng preached for several decades.

If we have dwelt so long on Te-ch'ing's life story, it is because his is one of the rare cases where an extraordinary life is matched by an extraordinary autobiography. Why this should have happened is perhaps ultimately unanswerable, but attempts at plausible explanations—by following the clues yielded by his voluminous writings—might further illuminate both the autobiography and its subject, even if in the end we fail to solve the central mystery.

We might begin with the tradition of spiritual autobiography, of which Te-ch'ing was the last exemplar. There is every reason to believe that with his great learning he was familiar with most of the quest narratives and accounts of self-transformation. That he knew of the existence of Ch'an autobiographical sermons and Yüan-miao's autobiographical letter is indicated by his praise of the books in which these texts were collected.[18] He could not have escaped noticing Teng Huo-ch'ü's *Nan-hsün lu*, the notoriety of the man and the book having reached its height during the middle decades of the master's life.[19] If Teng showed him the possibility of writing about one's own search for illumination, his more immediate

[17] For a comprehensive account of the succession controversy, see Ku Ying-t'ai, *Ming-shih chi-shih pen-mo* (Main episodes of Ming history) (Taipei: Shang-wu yin-shu-kuan, 1956), *chuan* 67. As for Te-ch'ing's role and his subsequent activities, see *NP*, pp. 45–103.

[18] *HTC*, 127:597.

[19] There was even an uncanny link between Te-ch'ing and the apostate. As we have seen earlier, when Te-ch'ing first entered a Buddhist monastery he had a memorable exchange with a prominent visitor, Chao Chen-chi, whose prophetic words strengthened the resolve of the young novice. It was the same Chao who had earlier shattered the complacency of Teng Huo-ch'ü and set him in motion.

examples were the Confucian spiritual autobiographers. One of them, Kao P'an-lung, he knew very well. Te-ch'ing was entertained by Kao in 1616.[20] They corresponded and exchanged writings with each other.[21] It is not inconceivable that he had knowledge of Kao's autobiographical essay, which was written in or shortly after 1614. At any rate Te-ch'ing's long and extensive association with the Neo-Confucians must have exposed him to their style of self-examination and their practice of self-revelation. That his affinity with the Confucian world had much to do with his autobiographical act can be seen from his choice of format for the telling of his own life story.

Since the self-written *nien-p'u* or annalistic autobiography was still a relatively unknown genre during Te-ch'ing's lifetime—only some dozen practitioners of the craft were born between 1470 and 1570—there may be some significance in his use of this form. Of all the annalistic autobiographies written before Te-ch'ing, which number not above about a dozen, only two can be assumed with any certainty to have been known to him.[22] One—the very first—was written by Wen T'ien-hsiang, the great Sung loyalist, the other by Yang Chi-sheng (1516-1555), the Ming official who sacrificed his life in a futile attempt to expose the wicked senior grand secretary Yen Sung. No other works seem to have circulated widely in Te-ch'ing's day, while Wen and Yang were adulated by all in the late Ming as paragons of Confucian heroism. Now the significant fact about these two is that each wrote his autobiography in jail, waiting for martyrdom, fully aware that the dominant theme of his life—loyalty—would assure him a place in history. From these facts can we then infer that in Te-ch'ing's case the first inspiration for, if not the beginning of the actual composition of, his autobiography occurred during his imprisonment and that what prompted him to write was his sense of identification with these models of loyalty to the imperial house, for which he, too, suffered cruel persecution?

Te-ch'ing spent eight months in prison. There was much time for soul-searching and self-examination. He was tortured and beaten; his life for quite some time was at the mercy of his tormentors. In the autobiography as well as in other writings, the frequency with which he refers to his role in the service of the heir apparent clearly indicates his awareness of the depth of his commitment and the magnitude of his contribution. He does not fail to mention his friendship or even slight acquaintance with those scholar-officials who also championed the cause of the prince. In his writings he repeatedly compares himself and his friend Master Chen-k'o to

---

[20] *NP*, p. 107.

[21] *HTC*, 127:418.

[22] All information regarding annalistic autobiographies has been obtained from Wang Te-i, *Chung-kuo li-tai ming-jen nien-p'u tsung-mu.*

Ch'eng Ying and Kung-sun Ch'u-chiu, the two loyal vassals of the Spring and Autumn era, whose heroic deeds in saving the Chao orphan have been celebrated at once in popular drama and in the Confucian moral-historiographical tradition, beginning with the *Shih chi*.[23]

In this regard it was perhaps no accident that Te-ch'ing wrote a commentary on the *Tso chuan*, a book in which the ideal of political loyalty reigns supreme. In fact, he mentions pointedly in the autobiography that the piece was inspired by his memory of a discussion of the book with his friend Chen-k'o and that it was written when his freedom of movement was temporarily deprived as a result of his friend's troubles.[24] Left unsaid is the fact that his comrade in the cause of the prince had just died in prison. In the preface to the commentary he gives us another glimpse of his self-image as a Confucian loyalist: "After I was exiled to Lei-yang and sentenced to serve in the army I no longer dared to consider myself a Buddhist monk. Every time I looked back I realized that I had been destined to be a solitary minister and unloved son [*ku-ch'en nieh-tzu*].[25] Consequently I examined my faults and studied the facts pertaining to loyal officials and filial sons" (*HTC*, 127:485).

Te-ch'ing's affinity with the *Tso chuan* holds another key to understanding his autobiographical impulse. For one thing, the *Tso chuan* has always been considered the prototype of annalistic history, which in turn provided the model for the *nien-p'u*. Also, it is the *Tso chuan* which formulated for the first time the concept of Confucian immortality, namely, that one can live forever on the strength of one's virtue, accomplishments, or words.[26] It is the desire for this kind of immortality, in the opinion of the T'ang historiographer Liu Chih-chi, that makes men wish to be the subject of a biography.[27] That Te-ch'ing was not unmoved by such considerations can be seen from an entry in his autobiography. When, early in his exile, he was criticized for printing and circulating one of his exegetical works, he defended his action as follows, "Afraid that I

[23] *HTC*, 127:229, 416, 450, 593. When the house of Chao fell, the heroic pair plotted to save the only male heir from his merciless enemies. By agreement, Kung-sun sacrificed his life so that Ch'eng could escape with the Chao orphan. When Te-ch'ing made the allusion he obviously had in mind the fact that dedication to the cause of the Ming heir apparent, who led a precarious life throughout his father's reign, resulted in Chen-k'o's death and his own exile. For an account of the evolution of the Chao story in Chinese theater and its success in eighteenth-century Europe, see Liu Wu-chi, "The Original Orphan of China," *Comparative Literature* 5, no. 3 (Summer 1953): 193–212.

[24] *NP*, p. 89.

[25] The phrase is from *Mencius*, 7A:18. For a more literal translation see James Legge, trans., *The Chinese Classics* (London: Oxford University Press, 1893), 2:457–58.

[26] Cf. Wing-tsit Chan, *A Source Book in Chinese Philosophy* (Princeton: Princeton University Press, 1963), p. 13.

[27] *Shih-tung*, p. 23.

might die without being known, I expressed myself in words in the hope that I might thus become immortal" (*NP*, p. 75). To write an account of oneself would ensure a double kind of immortality, for in doing so one would not only express oneself in words but also become, so to speak, the subject of a biography.

As a frequent biographer of monks—among his twenty-nine subjects are Chu-hung and Chen-k'o—Te-ch'ing was certainly no stranger to the craft of biographical writing. This fact as well as his own views on Buddhist hagiography may have lain behind his decision to write an autobiography. In his reply to a monk who had asked him to write the biography of a recently deceased abbot, he said: "The format of stupa inscription [*t'a-ming*] being what it is, I shall not be able to include all that I know. I can only enumerate what is appropriate, all other deeds of his perhaps should be recorded in another account" (*HTC*, 127:397). On another occasion he declared that there were only four categories of monks whose biographies could be written: Ch'an masters, founding fathers of schools or sects, theurgists, and eminent monks. "Those who do not belong to any of these categories should not have their biographies written, even if they had other great accomplishments" (*HTC*, 127:476–77). In his youth Te-ch'ing may very well have patterned himself after the model of the eminent monk, but looking back at the age of seventy-six and seeing the whole man, he must have realized that he had gone beyond his early exemplar.

Indeed he was very different from all other monks in that during his middle age he led, at least outwardly, a secular existence for almost twenty years. When he was exiled to an army post in the south in 1595 he was technically a soldier. After he was restored to civilian status in 1606 through a general amnesty he chose, inexplicably, to remain a layman until 1614. According to a commentator on his autobiography, he for many years "went by the name of Ts'ai Te-ch'ing, let his hair grow, sported a long beard and, when he was at ease, wore a Tung-po cap" (*NP*, p. 73). He did return to the priesthood soon after the empress dowager's death, but he never attempted to explain the long delay. Nor did his supporters or critics ever make anything of what must have been extraordinary behavior for a great Buddhist master. To us his two decades of ambiguous identity make his camaraderie with Confucian scholar-officials all the more significant.

In a colophon to a series of poems written in his illness during exile he compared himself with Tsung-kao and Chüeh-fan, the two eminent Sung monks who had been, like him, exiled to a southern garrison.[28] He

_____

[28] Te-ch'ing's sense of affinity with the two Sung masters may have played a minor role in his autobiographical act. Chüeh-fan (1071–1128) included in his collected works a very

conceded that he was not their equal "in the way of Ch'an and the Law of the Buddha" (*HTC*, 127:675); but in loyalty and fortitude he believed that he was more like another exile, the Han hero Su Wu.[29] Once again his self-image as a Confucian hero seems to have overshadowed his Buddhist identity, for Su Wu is another dramatic figure in both Chinese history and folk literature. This being the case, Te-ch'ing could no longer see himself as falling within any of the four categories of monks mentioned above.

Te-ch'ing's identification with heroic figures such as Ch'eng Ying and Su Wu should be seen in conjunction with his frequent exaltation of himself and the people he admired, both lay and Buddhist, in terms of courage and valor. He uses such expressions as *hao-chieh chih-shih* (heroic leader) (*HTC*, 127:474, 617), *t'ieh-han* (man of iron) (ibid., 728, 730), and *ta hsiung-meng chang-fu* (great stalwart of manliness and ferocity) (ibid., 433, 489, 590). This emphasis on heroism is another link between late Ming Buddhists like Te-ch'ing and Chen-k'o and their Neo-Confucian contemporaries, especially those of the T'ai-chou sect.[30] The *hsia* (knight-errantry) ideal is one point at which the more extreme members of the two sides converge—in this regard Chen-k'o is a better representative even than Te-ch'ing. The two masters never failed to act out their self-definitions, nor were they without detractors. A contemporary criticism of Te-ch'ing's public behavior gives us another glimpse of the master cutting a heroic if somewhat unconventional figure as he moved among adoring crowds.

> In every temple, when Te-ch'ing ascends to the great hall to preach and receive homage, he always sits facing south directly before the high altar, the image of the Three-World Buddha having been covered by the monks with large sheets. He is treated there with the deference due to a visiting governor or magistrate. I have my doubts about his behavior. The Ju-lai Buddha is the teacher in the Buddhist school just as Confucius and Mencius are teachers in the Confucian

---

short self-account that touched lightly on his exile and two imprisonments. Tsung-kao was more like Te-ch'ing in his camaraderie with the leading Confucian scholar-officials of his day and in his deep involvement in partisan politics. As we have seen earlier, even when Te-ch'ing was a young monk one of his Confucian admirers already predicted that someday he would prove the equal of the Sung master. Tsung-kao did not write an autobiography, but shortly after his death his disciples wrote a long annalistic biography of him—a very unusual act since the genre, still new, was restricted only to very prominent figures. This fact may have contributed to Te-ch'ing's decision to tell his life story in that format.

[29] For nineteen years Su was held prisoner by the Hsiung-nu, to whom he had been sent as the emperor's emissary. His tormentors, in a futile attempt to obtain his submission, sent him to live in the desolate wilderness near what is now Lake Baikal.

[30] For a cogent discussion of Neo-Confucian heroism and its affinity with Buddhism, see de Bary, *Self and Society*, pp. 169–71 and p. 231, n. 82.

school. If a great Confucian scholar should lecture on the classics, he would never usurp the high seat in the Ta-ch'eng Palace and have the statues of Confucius and other sages to his back. I have asked a friend to caution Te-ch'ing on this, but I doubt if he will listen. Recently I have seen several lesser preachers imitating Te-ch'ing in vainglory. They can be said to be completely uninhibited! I have also seen a calling card of Te-ch'ing's with his name written as large as that of a grand secretary. This is even more astonishing.[31]

Whether these strictures are justified or not, the account certainly lends further support to the suggestion that Te-ch'ing must have seen himself not so much as an eminent monk but as a unique individual of heroic stature untrammeled by clerical inhibitions. To have had such an image of himself and to know only too well the limitations of Buddhist hagiography may have further contributed to his decision to be his own biographer, for he must have realized that no future biographer could possibly understand his unique life story, let alone retell it with all its drama and complexity in an appropriate form.

[31] Shen Te-fu, *Yeh-huo pien* (A collection of unofficial facts) (Fu-li shan-fang edition), 27:22a–b. Against this background, Te-ch'ing's recollection of his meeting with Chao Chen-chi on the day that the future master, a boy of eleven, entered the monastery, takes on a new significance, for Chao, a prominent member of the T'ai-chou school and a grand secretary in 1569, was well known for his daring exploits during the crisis of 1550 when the Mongol invaders were at the gates of Peking (*MJHA*, p. 332). If Chao was the alternative model for Te-ch'ing in his youth, in his old age the great master seems to have succeeded in being at once an illuminated eminent monk and a Confucian grandee.

PART III
THE SELF INVENTED

SEVEN

WANG CHIEH

(1603?–1682?)

In the West the relation between autobiography and fiction has been a complex, rich, and mutually beneficial one. Renaissance prose fiction paved the way for Cellini while Rousseau's *Confessions* appeared only after the autobiographical novel had been the predominant form of French fiction for fifty years. Autobiography in turn has served as the model for many modern novels. The distinction between the two genres is increasingly blurred in the view of modern critics. Typical of this trend is the statement of Renza that "in selecting, ordering, and integrating the writer's lived experiences according to its own teleological demands, the autobiographical narrative is beholden to certain imperatives of imaginative discourse. Autobiography, in short, transforms empirical facts into *artifacts*: it is definable as a form of 'prose fiction.' "[1]

By the time Cellini wrote his exciting story, Chinese autobiography was also becoming susceptible to the allures of imaginative literature. Such a development was in keeping with some of the characteristics of the late Ming intellectual climate. The yearning for immortality, the dissatisfaction with the mundane and the conventional, the vogue for eccentricity and dissent, all noticeable in other fields, manifested themselves in autobiographers' adopting themes and motifs from myths and popular literature. Furthermore, autobiography could find a new ally in vernacular fiction, which had reached full maturity only one generation earlier. The alliance was now possible because the best representatives of the new fiction were, in the words of Andrew Plaks, "literati novels."[2] They were written and read by the same group of people who might try their hands at autobiography. Li Chih, for instance, was at once an autobiographer and a pioneer in developing a critical literature for the great novels. The popularity of this new genre must have shown autobiographers the possibility of breaking away, even if only in a limited and sporadic fashion, from the rigid exigencies of historiography that had prevailed for centuries. In telling their life stories some of them did display a willful embellishment and a sheer inventiveness that seem to disdain credibility. For

[1] Louis A. Renza, "The Veto of Imagination: A Theory of Autobiography," in Olney, ed., *Autobiography*, p. 269.

[2] *The Four Masterworks of the Ming Novel: Ssu ta ch'i-shu* (Princeton: Princeton University Press, 1987), p. 24.

writers such as Tu Wen-huan and Ch'en Chi-ju the aim of the autobio-graphical act was to create a new, fantasized self, with incidents either too trivial or too improbable to be used by historians.

Born in the late sixteenth century on a military post in a border region where his family had for many generations served in the garrison force, Tu Wen-huan (b. 1565?) followed the distinguished martial careers of his father and uncle. He won many battles and served as military governor successively in nearly all border territories. After retirement he ostensibly wrote a short biography of the "untrammeled historian Yüan-ho" who, as revealed near the end of the piece, was none other than the author him-self. It would have been a most interesting document if he had reported his military exploits—no Chinese warrior ever wrote an autobiography before this century. But instead of an eyewitness account of campaigns and battles the narrative was essentially an encomium with many rhetor-ical flourishes but little circumstantial detail about real or plausible events. The persona, so meticulously constructed by the autobiographer, would have been out of place in a dynastic history. "The night when he was conceived his mother saw in her dream a white crane hovering over the courtyard and a white dragon entering into her boudoir. The day he was born she dreamt that a monk in a white robe ascended into the hall while shaking his staff."[3] As in the life of a mythic hero, the emblematic color persists into later life. "Every time he went into battle he would don a brocade armor decorated with white fur and ride a white horse from Ta-yüan [Ferghana]. He moved left and right to give orders, as brave as a tiger. His soldiers gave him the nickname the 'White Tiger' " (*MTW*, p. 123). After his retirement he indulged himself in various Taoist and Bud-dhist pursuits, roaming again on a *white* horse and in an overcoat made of the feathers of *white* cranes.

Another wanderer in old age is Ch'en Chi-ju (1558–1639), a member of the literati known for his versatile artistic talents. His autobiography is in the form of a self-written necrology. Short and sketchy, it ends with a patently fictitious account of the circumstances of his own death, a most extraordinary innovation.

> At such an hour on such a day of such a month, the master died. Shortly before his demise he summoned his children, grandchildren, and friends, saying, "Rather than making sacrifice to me after I die, you had better offer me wine while I am still alive." Thereupon his family and friends formed a line and went forward one by one to present him wine as if they had been participants in a memorial ser-vice. The master drank and ate gleefully. With his chin up, he shouted at the company, "Why don't you show grief and weep?" Thereupon

[3] *MTW*, p. 122.

the whole company burst in tears. Some of them began to sing fu-
nereal songs between rounds of drinking. The sadder the singing,
the more everybody drank; the more everybody drank, the better
the singing. The master was so pleased that he got up and danced.
He pinned flowers to his cap and twisted and clowned like a child.
Nobody was allowed to leave until he was thoroughly drunk. When
the master was finally about to expire he told those who were attending him: "It is always said that dying is accompanied by apparitions. Sometimes the dying one is summoned by messengers riding
on a gold-and-silver floating platform; sometimes a welcome team
descends from the clouds with flying banners and sonorous music. I
am now seeing none of these. If you see anything, it must be an
illusion." When he finished talking he clapped his hands, laughed
loudly, and then expired. At this moment a white rainbow [*hung*]
suddenly rose from the hall and, with its head straight up, it flew
away into the blue sky. Everybody marveled at this occurrence.[4]

It is not always easy to stage-manage one's own death, but an inventive
autobiographer, leaving nothing to chance and allowing no contingen-
cies, can do this to perfection. To face death with cheerful acceptance and
even jocular defiance, to mock superstition and yet end the account with
an ironical nod to the time-honored convention of the free spirit, Ch'en's
imagined death is in perfect accord with the persona—a playful and
unique individual, indifferent to all vanities and desires—that he devoted
his whole life to cultivating.

Both Tu and Ch'en can be said to have thrived in the twilight of the
declining Ming. The diversity and audaciousness of much of late Ming
thinking, sometimes bordering on nihilism, allowed the ego more leeway
than at any time in Chinese history since the Wei-Chin period. The calamity of 1644, however, brought an end to the relative freedom that permitted such movements as the T'ai-chou sect of the Wang school. The
conquest of China by the Manchus and the ensuing establishment of an
authoritarian alien rule dampened spiritual fervor and discouraged unor-
thodox opinions. Yet paradoxically, the next two autobiographies that
we are going to look into, written by Wang Chieh and Mao Ch'i-ling
respectively, grew amid the debris of the fallen dynasty. Each in its own
way carried the range and intensity of self-celebration to new limits, as if
the old order's demise had loosened inhibitions, numbed the sense of propriety, and fostered a new spiritual anarchy in which the self fed on itself
and recognized few restraints. On a scale hitherto inconceivable, Wang
and Mao unabashedly ransacked popular literature for incidents that
could be used either for self-aggrandizement or for self-justification.

[4] *MTW*, pp. 253–54.

Their egomania was of such magnitude that their narratives go on effu-
sively to unprecedented lengths. We shall begin with Wang, the older of
the pair.

Running to nearly ten thousand characters, Wang Chieh's autobiography was not exceeded in length by any other written in the same *tzu-hsü*
style until this century. Even if Wang Chieh had written a much shorter
autobiography the act would have still been quite extraordinary, for outwardly there is hardly anything in his life, by the usual standards of Chinese biography, that is worth recording. I have so far failed to discover
any facts about him outside his autobiography, except a short entry of
four lines in the biography section of the 1880 edition of the local history
of Chia-ting, his native city. From this and his own words it is possible to
reconstruct only a bare outline of his external life. Born early in the seventeenth century, he lived to almost eighty years of age. He took many
civil examinations, but his only success was scored at the local level in
1635. Most of his life was spent as a private secretary (*mu-yu*) to various
officials, one of the very few alternatives open to an aspiring scholar who
failed to obtain a higher degree. His only other semiofficial activity was
his participation in the compiling of the local histories of Honan province
and Chia-ting county.

It is safe to say that Wang Chieh is one of the most obscure among
Chinese autobiographers up to his time. The spiritual climate of the seventeenth century was such that obscurity did not deter, as it would have
in earlier times, at least a handful of humble souls from writing about
themselves. Mindful of their station in life, their brief enterprises were
seldom free from expressions of defiance or self-conscious eccentricity.
The monk Chen-i's autonecrology, as we have seen earlier, is a good example. Wang Chieh, blessed with a sunny temperament and fortified
with an irrepressible egomania, rose above mere defensiveness or apologia. What emerges from the pages of his work is a truly free spirit, a life-
style that is perfectly mirrored by the style of the narrative.

The form that Wang Chieh ostensibly chose for his autobiography, the
tzu-hsü, is the most flexible of all the subgenres. As we have mentioned
in the chapter on authorial self-accounts, it originated from the type of
preface that the author of a book employed to introduce himself to the
reading public, but later on it could be written independently of a book.
Most of the *tzu-hsü* writers followed a more-or-less chronological order,
and in the hands of less enterprising practitioners it could suffer all the
limitations of a typical biography. Wang, however, broke away from historiography by dispensing totally with chronology. Structurally his autobiography is but a succession of episodes and observations, grouped
together on the basis of similarity of subject matter. Every episode is
about, as every observation is on, Wang Chieh himself. No other person

exists unless he serves as a foil to Wang's wisdom or as an accessory to Wang's self-celebration. His children are perceived in his own image: "My four sons have all followed my example well. They too like to read books by the ancients, take part in poetry contests, drink wine, play *wei-ch'i*,[5] dabble in painting and calligraphy, and travel widely."[6]

It is perhaps this uninhibited egotism that led Wang to one of the very few confessions in Chinese autobiography:

> I used to like gambling. Whenever people gathered together for wine and games I always wagered large sums and never failed to win handsomely. I also used to enjoy the company of prostitutes. Even famous beauties never asked me for money; on the contrary they often helped me out with my school expenses. As both types of activities were profitable to me, there were strong reasons for indulging deeply in them. One day I suddenly realized that such reckless and roguish behavior would be frowned upon by people of good taste and that I ought to liberate myself from such wicked pleasures. Once I made the resolution to abstain from them I never relapsed. (*LTW*, 1:33)

Confession of sins, as we shall see in Part IV, was not uncommon in seventeenth century China, but such acts were seldom associated with autobiography. In any case Wang's unburdening of wrongdoings differs from genuine confession in that it was not accompanied by any expression of remorse or sense of guilt. Nor does his seeing the light have much in common with the enlightenment or awakening characteristic of spiritual autobiography. It came without inner struggle. His claim to discipleship with the Neo-Confucian master and Ming loyalist Huang Tao-chou (1585–1646) notwithstanding, in Wang Chieh's self-account the mode of *Bildungsroman*, or a perception of moral progress, never intruded. Consistent with the tone of utter honesty—never explicitly claimed—that fills every page of his work, he attributed his reform to calculation rather than a loftier motive. Still our egotist did not miss an opportunity for self-praise. His lack of contrition is offset by a display of resoluteness, and resoluteness is all the more commendable when the wages of sin are so lucrative. This knack of turning a weakness to his account is shown in many episodes, of which the following is another example:

> An effete scholar of the south, I always depended on boats for travel and was not familiar at all with saddles and reins. One day upon crossing the Yellow River with Censor Li we left our carriage and

---

[5] Known in the West by its Japanese name, *gō*.

[6] *San-nung chui-jen kuang tzu-hsü* (Expanded self-acount of the Useless Man San-nung), *LTW*, 1:34.

mounted horses. The censor suddenly gave my horse a whack and it took off at great speed. I felt as if I had been soaring beyond the clouds: everything became blurred while my ears were bombarded with the sound of furious tidal waves. At first I was frightened; then I felt pleasant; finally I was completely at ease. From that time on whenever I went riding with people my horse always galloped ahead of all others. (Ibid., p. 39)

In Wang's retelling of his triumphs his narrative style departs from traditional historiography as much as do the content and the type of incidents and events that he chooses to include. In general, historical narrative, reinforced by the nature of classical Chinese prose, leans toward diegesis (telling) rather than mimesis (showing)—the *Shih chi* is the most notable exception and for that Ssu-ma Ch'ien has often been criticized, while fiction, especially vernacular fiction, shifts the balance. In Wang's narrative the proportion between the diegetic and the mimetic varies, with the latter favored in accordance with the magnitude of his success. He is not very specific in reporting his victory over vice, but his horsemanship is described in a much more mimetic manner. The episode that is apparently his favorite is the one in which his celerity at literary composition scored him another triumph.

In the year *keng-tzu* [1660] I participated in the work of revising the local history of Honan. On the day of the Spring Festival Governor Chia invited all of the local history staff to a drinking party. Conversation drifted to the relative strengths and weaknesses of Chu-ko Liang and Wang Meng, and opinions differed. It just happened that Magistrate Yu of Hsiang-ch'eng had presented the governor with three hundred bottles of Hsiang wine, and they were all brought in and lined against the stairs in front of the great hall. My colleagues were just about to open them when the governor with a smile said: "May I ask that all you gentlemen each write an essay comparing Chu-ko and Wang Meng? The one who writes the best essay will take all the wine; there is no need to divide the bottles." Hearing this my colleagues all returned to the tables, mustering their courage and collecting their thoughts. I smoothed the paper as my pen moved along, writing without stop and making no corrections. In no time at all I finished. The governor asked me to read it aloud. Clearly and metallically my voice carried to the end of the hall, and the governor himself uttered praises while beating music to the rhythm of the prose. All my colleagues dropped their pens and sighed deeply; some even tore up their compositions. I bowed to the governor before I left the hall, walking slowly behind the four sergeants who were carrying the bottles of wine I had just won. (Ibid., p. 65)

Wang Chieh's almost compulsive recitation of his feats should be
viewed against the background of a frustrated and uncompleted life, a life
of setbacks and adversities. His hometown Chia-ting put up a heroic resistance to the invading Manchu army, and when the city was captured in
1645 almost every citizen was put to the sword. He barely survived the
holocaust, but his books—the most cherished of all his possessions, already decimated by fire in 1632—were looted. Later in the year he had
another close brush with the horrors of war. As soon as the Ch'ing authorities reopened the civil examinations he took them again, and again
he failed. In 1657 he was implicated in a major criminal case involving
hundreds of civil candidates; many of the codefendants were executed.
He was acquitted—yet not before he lost all of his reassembled and much
smaller library to the court officials. But in the depth of his heart the
greatest of all his misfortunes must have been his repeated failures at the
examinations. Until this century nearly all educated Chinese youth had
no aim in life other than advancing through the official ranks: literary or
other accomplishments were considered secondary. For Wang Chieh the
humiliation of failure was hardly softened by time, for he spent the rest of
his working life as a *mu-yu*, a private secretary to magistrates or governors, a position with no official status and little recognition, so close to
the seat of power but forever barred from a share of the fame or glory.
His disappointments were all the greater because his hopes were higher
and he held out longer than most candidates:

> I no longer believe in astrologers. In my day none were as famous as
> Li Hsü-chung and T'ang Chü, and both of them predicted, from the
> configuration of the stars under which I was born, that I would even-
> tually rise to the highest position. Furthermore, I was to reach the
> cabinet rank between the ages thirty and forty. Many, having heard
> this, congratulated me, and at first I enjoyed their congratulations.
> But nothing has turned out as predicted. Now that I am past seventy,
> I no longer harbor delusions of worldly success. The long dream has
> been shattered. Even if I still wanted to believe the predictions, how
> could I manage to do so? (Ibid., p. 51)

The poignancy of disillusionment notwithstanding, Wang Chieh nowhere else indulged in self-pity or despair. Self-vindication may well be
a component in his egotism, but his preoccupation with the self is more
complex than a mere defense. It permeates every page of his autobiography and spills over even to the minutest details of his life. It is of such a
magnitude and intensity that it endows his narrative and personality with
a unity otherwise hardly discernible. Without it all the anecdotes could
not be told with such a refreshing exuberance, a total lack of self-consciousness, and a marvelous sense of aliveness. But Wang's preoccupation

with the self goes beyond the enumeration of events and situations. He takes a keen and exhaustive interest not only in what the self has done but what the self is in all its phenomenological richness. Now he dispenses with any narrative structure but proceeds to paint a self-portrait—a man who travels all over China, befriending innkeepers and coachmen, and is not above letting the boat float aimlessly in the river; who grows flowers and plays *wei-ch'i*; who loves tea as much as wine; who indulges in magic tricks and amateur theatricals; who collects antiques but often loses them; who loves mountains and lakes; who enjoys the company of monks and singing girls; who composes music and writes poetry.

The irrepressible outpouring of the myriad facets and characteristics of the self even includes what must appear to others totally insignificant. Perhaps it is the mark of the supreme egotist to insist on recording such trivia as that he did not take baths at all when he was young, but now in his old age he takes them daily; that he likes vinegar, and no food is palatable without it; that he was nearsighted when young, but now he writes with a fine hand even under a lamp. But Wang Chieh is still not content: to insure that nothing of his unique self is left unnoticed he includes a meticulous and classified list of his likes and dislikes:

> In certain ways I am different from other people. I like the sounds of bubbling springs, orchestras, children reciting books, boatmen swinging oars at midnight.
>
> I dislike the sounds of crows, mounted escorts of noblemen shouting for the clearance of the road, merchants using the abacus, women cursing, men sighing, blind women singing tales to the accompaniment of a balloon guitar, and the scraping of the bottom of a pot.
>
> I like the moon late at night, the snow scene at dawn, flowers at noon, women lightly made up, the glow of inebriation at a plain meal.
>
> I dislike withered flowers and shriveled willows, the fawning mien of a sycophant, the false countenance of the high and mighty. (Ibid., p. 52)

Contrary to what Wang believes, his likes and dislikes do not seem to differ very much from other Chinese literati of the seventeenth century, nor is making such a list a great innovation. What is remarkable is Wang's insistence that he be accorded a uniqueness that probably existed only on account of his egocentricity, a significance not recognized by the world. It is the first time that a Chinese of obscure station in life had the audacity to demand full hearing for what he is, not for his exemplary conduct or his role in the making of history. But significance on a human scale still cannot gratify the insatiable celebrant of the self; a tale of wonder filled with magical resonance must be pressed into service:

As my companions and I were walking under a cliff I saw in the hollow just below us a tiger with a white forehead sitting by the brook. Seeing us, it started to flex its claws and raise its tail, obviously getting ready to spring at us. My companions all fell to the ground trembling. I saluted the tiger with my hands clasped in each other and said: "Prince of the Mountain, Prince of the Mountain, I have long heard of your fame. Today I finally have the good fortune to meet your august person. Please do not obstruct my way. What I carry with me is no more than an insignificant pen, but I shall wield it to compose a long poem in your honor."

The tiger nodded his head thrice. With a loud roar he leaped into the woods and disappeared. That night my companions and I stayed in the hut of a woodcutter. I sat up under a lamp and in a great haste wrote a long regulated poem with five words to each line, using altogether sixty rhymes. At the crack of dawn I went back to the place where I had seen the tiger. There I burned the paper on which my poem was written and prayed to the spirit of the tiger: "Allow me to say a word to you. As I have not broken my promise, can you, through your great spiritual powers, show me a sign of your acknowledgment?"

That night I dreamt that a man with a tiger head came to thank me. He brought along a piece of deer meat and a jug of wine. Just as we were enjoying ourselves greatly I was awakened by the servant and lost the visitor. (Ibid., p. 37)

The tiger story takes its cue from the long-held Chinese belief that animals would respond to written incantations. The belief, probably derived from the prehistoric practice of magic and symbolic action, sometimes prompted upright magistrates to rely on their pens rather than bows and arrows to relieve the distressed citizenry of man-eating beasts. The well-known ninth-century writer Han Yü drove the crocodiles away from his county by addressing to them an intimidating proclamation, while a more recent magistrate, Hsüeh Ching-chih (1435–1508), who was also a revered Neo-Confucian philosopher, placed a written curse on a tiger who was terrorizing a mountainous section of Ying-chou. Within ten days the beast was found dead.[7] The tiger has haunted the Chinese imagination from pre-Confucian times to the day of Chairman Mao, who remembered the fictional Wu Sung who killed the menacing animal with his bare fists. It was at once a symbol of death—to early Confucians the only greater evil was tyranny—and a means for a legendary hero to test his mettle. Measuring up to the challenge from the primordial forest, Wang Chieh triumphs again. The pen once more serves him well; even

[7] *MJHA*, p. 52.

the most ferocious of beasts was persuaded to behave with Confucian bonhomie. If he is fated never to join the ranks of magistrates, his pen— so we are led to believe—is just as efficacious as that of the most renowned of them.

Wang Chieh's autobiography records only one recurring dream, and that involves a magic pen. The pen was bestowed on him by an angel, then taken back and smashed because of his misusing it, then given back to him again. The dream of the magic pen is one of the standard topoi in Chinese literary mythology, but for Wang's life the pen is the most appropriate emblem. It is the pen that failed him repeatedly in the civil examinations. It is also the pen that not only eked out a living for him as a *mu-yu*, the scribe who often wrote better bureaucratic prose than his employer the magistrate, but vindicated him, in his reconstructed life story, again and again in contests and during crises. Now, close to eighty, he wielded his pen again to vindicate himself—not before his contemporaries but for subsequent generations. It was a magic pen indeed, but the greatest wonder that it performed was not the taming of a wild beast but the redemption of a life, the invention of a self.

EIGHT

MAO CH'I-LING

(1623–1716)

LIKE Wang Chieh, Mao Ch'i-ling was vain and boastful. But unlike Wang, he excelled in the examinations and established himself as one of the leading scholars of early Ch'ing. He knew most of his peers but feuded with almost all over interpretations of the classics and other scholarly matters. A man of vast and varied talents, he produced a prodigious quantity of scholarship while dabbling in playwriting, poetry, music, and calligraphy. He was as well known as Wang Chieh was obscure. As an adherent of the Wang Shou-jen school of Neo-Confucianism he carried to new heights the individualistic and iconoclastic tendencies that characterized much of late Ming thinking. Chu Hsi was the target of his bitter attacks while the entire Sung Neo-Confucian tradition was dismissed by him with cavalier abandon. His most audacious act was the publication in his old age of the *Ssu-shu kai-ts'o* (The Four Books corrected), which consists of 451 long and scathing entries on what he considered as errors in Chu Hsi's collected commentaries on the cannonical classics. More than an arrogant display of his erudition or a series of outbursts of ill-temper, the book, by its very title and its irreverent treatment of some of Confucius's disciples, borders on sacrilege. When such a willful and conceited man chose to write an autobiography, he cannot be expected to have respected convention or observed propriety.

Several other factors seem to have inclined Mao to an imaginative recounting of his life. As a scholar and compiler, he was not always scrupulous with regard to the integrity of the text. His critics often accused him of unjustified interpolations and even outrageous alterations. They might have doubted that such a fanciful man could have recorded his own life with probity. As an accomplished poet and dramatist with the sharp eye of a painter and an enlivened sense of history, he probably could not have resisted having his life story imitate art, recreating memorable scenes and tableaux with himself holding center stage. The shape of his life during the middle years may have also contributed to the imaginative turn of his memory. For more than a decade he wandered under different aliases over several provinces of east China, a fugitive from the law. To assume a persona or to strike a pose is of course very common with Chinese writers of the self, but none had to change his identity so frequently or over such a long duration. Mao's plight was further complicated by his frequent recognition by friends or acquaintances, so there was a constant shifting back and forth between his true self and one of his assumed identities. Perhaps in the end Mao, accustomed to the practice of inventing selves, took to invention not of necessity but by artistic choice.

Both Wang Chieh and Mao are survivors of great calamities. When the Manchu army invaded his region Mao took part in a hopeless armed resistance that cost the lives of many of his relatives and friends. A monk's disguise saved him from the avenging victors, and nimble feet on several occasions kept him barely beyond the reach of his mortal enemies. In 1657 his life was again in danger. His acerbic pen had often incurred enmities, but this time a trumped-up charge of a capital crime kept him on the run for more than ten years. It may have been the consciousness of survival against great odds that gave both Wang Chieh and Mao their exuberant self-satisfaction. Survival may have also contributed, more for Mao than for Wang, a sense of providential design, a fatalistic pattern out of the intractable and the precarious—a novelistic plot rather than the fortuity of haphazard existence.

Like the autobiography of Ch'en Chi-ju that we have seen earlier in chapter 7, Mao's is also under the rubric of a self-written necrology. Running to over seven thousand characters, Mao's is much longer—in fact much longer than any other specimen of this subgenre that I have seen. Not only in sheer length but in nearly all other aspects Mao's self-account departs from the usual format of autonecrology. He is no more restrained by the formal conventions of his genre than by the canons of narrative economy that obtained among earlier autobiographers.

Mao's autobiography begins with a dream that his mother had on the eve of his birth. She dreamt that a foreign monk came into the chamber and hung on the wall a monk's certificate on which there was a drawing of five dragons linked in a circle. As the narrative points out, the significance of the certificate became clear to the mother twenty-two years later, when she realized that the monkish disguise saved her son from certain death. Although Mao does not specify what the dragon prefigures, it is obvious that this symbol of elusiveness and swift transformations was quite appropriate for the decade of constant motion and frequent changes of disguise. The mythic creature also possesses other attributes that Mao shares—vigor, expansiveness, creative powers. The dragon and the tiger are usually thought of as the two most potent of all beasts—the pair are frequently juxtaposed in rhetorical contrasts or decorative designs—which enjoy supremacy each in its own exclusive domain: seas and rivers and the sky for the former, hills and mountains for the latter. It is fitting then that our self-admiring autobiographers should invoke them: the taming of the Prince of the Mountain marks the high point of Wang Chieh's own magic powers while the dragon appears as one of the birth signs in Mao's life story. As the dragon had long since been the emblem of the imperial family, Mao was for once prudent in not disclosing the meaning of the five linking beasts.

Very early in the narrative is another story that combines a dramatic scene with a sign of fate. In 1646 Mao briefly joined his relative, the earl of Pao-ting, in a battle against the invading Manchus. When he realized the hopelessness of the cause, he abandoned the earl and found refuge in the cellar of a Buddhist temple. What others may have condemned as cowardly decampment is softened by his pen into a poetic submission to the inexorable will of Heaven, with all the ambience of a historical romance.

> One night during the Ch'ing-ming Festival the earl of Pao-ting sent his retainers to bring me to his camp in the hills. When it began to rain we had our tents moved into a grove of figwort trees, which were blooming with white flowers. The earl's astrologer and I sat tensely in a tent. The rain stopped, the stars appeared, and we got out and looked in all directions. With a bitter sigh the stargazer exclaimed, "All is lost!" Returning to the tent we put out the candles and wept.[1]

Another trait which Mao shares with Wang Chieh but hardly with any previous autobiographers is the frequent use of anecdotes, dramatically presented with all the trappings of popular literature, to show the self in a favorable light. As we have noticed in discussing Wang Chieh's style, such episodes are narrated with greater use of mimesis than diegesis. The actions as well as their attendant circumstances tend to be described with much specificity. Historians may mention how dynastic changes touch on individual lives, but in their pages such incidents as figwort trees blooming with white flowers and stalwarts weeping with candles put out would be out of place. Mao's chance encounter with a former maidservant is another anecdote treated in a fictional way. One of the most poignant figures in Chinese literature is the woman, once an attractive attendant in a noble or even the imperial household, now living in obscure poverty, a survivor of calamitous upheavals. Poets and painters lament her fate, which reflects the transitoriness of both beauty and worldly glories. Whether recording a real encounter or inventing a scene with great appeal to traditional Chinese literary sensibilities, Mao situates himself inside a perfect tableau. One day during his decade of wanderings he came upon a cluster of shacks by the side of a river.

> There was a store with a signboard on which the name Li was written in red. There steamed dumplings were sold to travelers. Next door to the store a woman was selling beverages in a tent. As she

[1] Mao Ch'i-ling, *Mao Hsi-ho hsien-sheng ch'üan-chi* (Complete works of Master Mao Ch'i-ling) (1761), 35:11:2b–3a; hereafter referred to as Mao.

kept on staring at me I went over and asked her about it. It turned
out that she had been a maidservant in the household of the late earl
of Pao-ting. When the earl's forces dispersed she drifted to this place
and for quite a few years she had eked out a living like this. I sat
down in the tent and reminisced with her about the earl's family.
Both of us wept. When I was set to leave I took off the wool coat I
was wearing and gave it to her. (Mao, 35:11:8a–b)

Much is left unsaid in the account. Was Mao's sadness in any way tinged
by a sense of guilt over his desertion of the earl's cause and his survival
while so many died fighting for the fallen dynasty? Was his parting gift—
at great cost to the fugitive that he was, often in desperate straits himself—prompted by his compassion for a fellow survivor, or was it a symbolic act of expiation?

Mao's long march differs from the journeys we have discussed in the
chapter on Confucian spiritual autobiographies in that Mao moved from
place to place not to seek truth or salvation but to elude his enemies. Such
movements were dictated by shifting circumstances: the availability of
refuge, the location of friendly stopovers, the intelligence with regard to
the plans of the pursuers. Luck and aimlessness may also play a part. Accounts of such adventures even without embellishments or deliberate re-
arrangement tend to model themselves more readily on imaginative literature than on historiography. For Mao, moreover, the flow of events in
his narration cannot be permitted to be random or even entirely motivated by naturalistic factors. Ever expansive and fanciful, he sees the
course of his peregrinations as shaped by his own sagacity in conjunction
with forces of an occult order. Indeed the very beginning of his long journey
set the tone for the rest of the adventures. "When I was leaving my
second elder brother Yü-san escorted me to the gate and wept. He then
said to me: 'When ancient men of virtue found themselves in sorrows and
troubles they always kept counsel with the *Book of Changes*. Do you know
how to proceed?' I knelt before him and received instructions" (ibid.,
11:5a).

The *Book of Changes* indeed served him in good stead. By acting upon
his own correct interpretations of the messages received from the book
he came through unscathed during the most perilous period of his exile.
On one occasion he heeded the signal of danger the book issued and left
his place of hiding just before the arrival of his pursuers. Again it was
through the suggestion of the book that he made contact with a trust-
worthy friend who in turn passed him on to another haven, where he was
treated as the guest of honor. Basking under the benign sun of friendliness
and security, he lowered his guard and indulged his literary talent.

Chang Hung-lieh, a compiler in the Han-lin Academy, and his father, who used to hold a high position in the Ministry of Personnel,

were the proud owners of a garden by the East Lake. On the night of the Autumn Festival they gave a party in their garden. Draperies and lanterns dotted the water pavilions and terraced levees. Singing girls, an orchestra, and a theatrical troupe provided various entertainments. Invited were the entire local literati who, numbering several scores, gathered in the garden to drink, compose poetry, or simply amuse themselves. After several rounds of drinks and against the distant orchestral music and singing, I beat the plate and gave free rein to my intoxicated imagination, thus composing a poem on the sky river which ran to almost a hundred lines. When day arrived the poem had already been copied and circulated throughout the city. (11:5b–6a)

The episode resembles the essay contest that Wang Chieh won so handily. Celerity in literary composition is something on which both our autobiographers pride themselves, although Mao, whose renown as a leading man of letters was beyond doubt, is less obsessive about flaunting the powers of his pen. In fact on this occasion his pen again was, so to speak, a two-edged sword: as the story of his versification in the celebrated garden became more widely known, his cover was blown. Heeding again the warning of the *Book of Changes*, Mao suddenly abandoned the congenial haven and returned to the road.

Mao's account of his peregrinations is closer to the Western genre of the picaresque than any Chinese autobiography written before modern times. There is the same rapid change of fortunes, the same constant movement, the same outwitting of the enemies, the same frequent disguises and small victories. The picaresque, however, has to give way to spiritual autobiography in the end, for Mao was, after all, a Neo-Confucian, an heir, at least in his own eyes, to the Wang Shou-jen School of the Mind. For such a man a long journey that lasted more than a decade cannot remain merely a series of narrow escapes and perpetual search for temporary havens. The journey will become a progress and kinetic energy must serve teleology. But Mao, vain and inventive, could not content himself with the plain narration that served Hu Chih and other Neo-Confucians so well. His is the story of enlightenment retold by a fictionist.

To begin with, Mao could hardly have chosen a better locale for what we may call his conversion. Lofty mountains, as we have seen in the case of Te-ch'ing, Teng Huo-ch'ü, and others, are conducive to illumination or other forms of awakenings. Strenuous upward movement for seekers of truth such as Kao P'an-lung suggests the accompanying spiritual or moral progress. The Sung mountain, which Mao visited twice, has the additional distinction of being one of the five sacred mountains of China—the appellation dating back at least to the first century. The first visit, which took place early in his exile, was inconclusive. On his way to the top he climbed a few heights but, overcome by a sense of malaise and despair, failed to reach the summit. He went back a second time when once more his poetry—this time a song on willow flowers composed on the White Cloud Tower in Yü-chou—had attracted attention and forced him into hiding again. A Taoist priest provided him refuge in a mud hovel. In the middle of the night he got up and began to review his past life. He found the canonical classics and dynastic histories which he had studied since his childhood all obscure and distant, affording him no succor in his hour of need.

> Furthermore, I realized that I had accomplished nothing. I had nei-ther the hope of a meritorious career nor the comfort of cultivated virtue. Nor had I progressed in learning. I wept and dozed off. Sud-denly someone said to me, "Why don't you go to the south side of the mountain and seek an answer to your problem?" I replied by saying "yes." But when I raised my head and looked around, I did not see any person. That night I took my leave of the Taoist priest and went to the Shao-lin Temple, where I found lodging in the monks' dormitory. A month later I happened to pass by the temple market. I noticed standing next to the bookseller a monk wearing a tall bamboo hat. The monk suddenly picked up a copy of the *Great Learning* and told me to buy it. I asked him, "What is so unusual about the book that you should tell me to buy?" He replied: "Is there such a thing as a usual book? If you cannot read even usual books, what have you to do with unusual books?" Startled by what he said, I suddenly remembered the words I heard in the middle of the night a month ago. In a state of agitation I followed him to his lodging south of the Sung-yang Academy. (11:6b–7a)

The monk turned out to be a layman in disguise. As he revealed to Mao, he was originally a native of Liao-tung. The lone survivor of a massacre which took the life of every member of his clan, he had been a wanderer for more than thirty years. In his youth he studied under Ho Ling-t'ai, the grandson of Ho Ch'in.[2] From his teacher he received the ancient text of the *Ta hsüeh* (*Great Learning*) which, Ho asserted, contained the true essence of Confucianism but had been lost to the Confucians for more than eight hundred years. Now the stranger in monk's disguise offered to pass on to Mao the teachings he had received, and for three days Mao listened to his instructions. This legendary encounter with the stranger

---

[2] A prominent Neo-Confucian, Ho Ch'in (1437–1511) had a wide following in his native province, which bordered on Jurchen territory. His writings were included in the lists of books for destruction issued by the Ch'ing court in the late eighteenth century.

marked a turning point not only in Mao's career as a scholar but also in his life as a fugitive.

> When I studied the *Great Learning* during my childhood I depended on the text altered by Chu Hsi. As a result I mistakenly considered the investigation of things and the exhaustive study of Principle [*li*] as the primary task of the correct way. The final goal I took to be the examination of texts and documents and detailed study of things and events. When I met anyone from the School of the Mind I always showered my disdain on him. Only now did I know how to comprehend all learning within my personal illumination. As there was now a solid foundation within me, there were few mishaps or gaps without. Since then I have remained imperturbable whatever the dangers and difficulties that I have had to go through. (11:8a)

In achieving a drastic breakthrough and gaining an inner peace that could meet any test of adversity, as well as in his being helped by a sagacious teacher and a canonical text, his experience basically conforms to the tradition of Neo-Confucian spiritual progress. The sense of utter despair and desolation that seized him during the night in the mud hovel is reminiscent of the dark night of the soul that often precedes the great upward leap in the life of mystics and seekers. His narration, however, is interspersed with motifs and elements that had seldom found favor with autobiographers before his time but were always stock-in-trade with storytellers. The invisible voice in the night, the prophetic admonition, the recovery of the lost sacred text, and the personal transmission of the secret message all tend to strain credulity and provoke critics. Even Ch'an Buddhist monks when bearing witness to their own path toward illumination were extremely scrupulous in excluding any incidents that require the reader's willing suspension of disbelief. Mao was apparently under no such restraint. The chain of circumstances that led him to the fateful meeting with the stranger is plausible only in a tale of the miraculous. The fortuitous helper, not an infrequent figure in *Bildungsroman* or fairy tale, is here shrouded in an especially tantalizing mystery: he was ostensibly a man who—for reasons to which Mao gave only the vaguest hint—chose to remain incognito, yet his disguise was outlandishly conspicuous. His message, for which he so adroitly sought out Mao, took three days to impart, yet Mao fails to report it except very briefly, revealing none of the importance that the autobiographer imputed to it, first by dramatizing the circumstances attendant to its delivery, then by asserting how it changed his subsequent modus vivendi in adversity.

There is nevertheless a poetic justice to the construction of the episode. It is most fitting that our disheartened fugitive should have been given aid and comfort by a fellow sufferer who had been thrown onto the road by calamities far greater and whose exile was much longer and more distant from home. If a monk's disguise saved Mao from the Manchu invaders, it was under the same disguise that the stranger first had escaped with his life and now came to transmit the teaching. Once his mission was accomplished, the nameless teacher faded again into darkness, seemingly without regret, for both in the Ch'an Buddhist and Neo-Confucian traditions there is hardly any task more important than the transmission from person to person of a rediscovered message so as to save it from oblivion. As is true with a great deal of historical romance and tales of wonder, such a crucial episode is prefigured—in Mao's case on the very first page of his autobiography. Mao the fantast is also a fatalist. Just before his birth his mother was visited by a monk in her dream, as we have noted above. The visitor's being a foreigner and holding a monk's certificate anticipate the salient features of the son's savior: a native from the distant border territory of Liao-tung, the outlandish hat, and the monk's disguise. The crucial text of the *Ta hsüeh* (*Great Learning*) as well as the motif of oral transmission was similarly foreshadowed. Not only was the *Ta hsüeh* the very first book that Mao ever studied; it also was, so to speak, emblematic of the bond between Mao and his mother—the father is mentioned only very briefly near the end of the autobiography.

> When I was five years of age I expressed a wish to begin reading books. As no tutor was available, my mother recited, and I repeated after her, the *Great Learning*. After I succeeded in committing the text to memory, I asked her what the corresponding characters were. My mother bought a popular edition of the book and told me to read the text by myself, using my memorized version as the guide. After two readings there was no character that I could not recognize. (11:1a)

Comparing the episode of his conversion with what Mao allowed to have taken place at his birth and during his childhood, it is possible to read the former as an reenactment of the later. In a sense after the dark night of the soul Mao was reborn and reeducated, a new man with an "older" version of the *Ta hsüeh* (*Great Learning*), a true adult—for whom the *Ta hsüeh* was originally meant in the Confucian curriculum—without fear or perplexities.

Although Mao's exile was to last another four years, he does not seem to have had any more setbacks or narrow escapes. Another indication of his progress is that, in contrast to his earlier reliance on oracles, he never again consulted the *Book of Changes*. With his plight eased, the picaresque structure soon comes to an end. So does the mode of spiritual autobiography, except for a short incident during which his conversion to the Wang school was confirmed.

Around 1667, through the intervention of friends in power, Mao was cleared of all charges. To signal his full support of the new regime and thus to gain a measure of protection from his numerous enemies, an academic degree in Mao's name was purchased from the government. This was not his first act of accommodation, for as early as 1651 he had already made his peace with the Manchu conquerors by registering for the official examinations. That Mao, brought up on Neo-Confucian morality which places loyalty above everything, could not but feel uneasiness over these two questionable acts is shown by the way he presents them. In neither case did he himself make the move: it was always friends who took the initiative by approaching the authorities on his behalf; whether he himself was a party to the plan he does not reveal. What he makes abundantly clear is that in both cases he had no choice other than acquiescence if he was to escape from the murderous wrath of his enemies. A sense of guilt may have lain behind the very last episode of wonder in the autobiography, which marks the end of the picaresque phase. This follows abruptly, immediately after the purchase of the academic degree.

> One night when I was in Nanking I dreamt that a man clad in black came to me with silver chains in his hand. He said to me, "It is time to go!" A prominent-looking person halted him, saying: "This man has suffered enough. As my lifework is not yet finished, let him stay so he can finish it." The man in black replied: "I shall do so, but how am I going to discharge my order? I must take something in his stead." After a little while I saw him put the chains around the neck of a green parrot and take it with him. As they were leaving the parrot turned back and wept. Someone pointed at it and said to me, "That is your soul!" Right after that I became gravely ill. (11:9b–10a)

The dream, a fitting last act to a drama of adventures, is so rich in allusive and symbolic meaning that a full analysis of its complex texture would take us too far afield. Just a few points will suffice. Was his nemesis, who finally caught up with him even when he was no longer a fugitive from mundane authorities, an image of his sense of guilt over his double betrayal, both as a former member of the resistance and as an academic candidate who always took pride in his celerity at writing occasional pieces and could easily have won at any fair and open competition? That he had deserved punishment was conceded even by his defender who said that "this man has suffered enough." Who was, then, the personage who interceded with the angel of death? It was perhaps only his sense of modesty, so seldom exercised in the telling of his long life story, that prevented Mao from naming him. There is, however, sufficient hint and circumstantial evidence to identify him with none other than Confucius. First of all only a man of great stature could alter the course of fate. Earlier in the narrative Mao asserts that on the sacred Mount Sung he received the true version of Confucianism that had been lost for eight hundred years. Since he was the sole chosen one—the mystery of the attendant circumstances only enhances his uniqueness—there was every reason for the great Sage to desire his survival so that the sacred but secret teaching could be passed on. The invocation—implicit, to be sure—of Confucius is in line with Mao's exalted self-esteem, not even slightly dented by adversity, and his sense of mission, but it may also underline the magnitude of his guilt, so great that it could only be redeemed by his completion of the unfinished work of the great Sage.

Although Mao's life was spared for a good cause, he did not escape from punishments. We have noticed that he lost one of his souls—he probably believed with most Chinese of his time that each normal human being was in possession of three *hun*—during the dream and suffered a grave illness afterwards. He was further incapacitated in that after the dream he could no longer perform the mnemonic feats of his youth. Is the forgetfulness a hint of his amnesia about his past, his turning his back, for the last time, on the fallen dynasty? The memory loss was inconsequential in the light of his subsequent career—none of his creative powers was impaired, and the only examination he was to take and pass was the special examination of 1679 which, too exalted to be a test of memory, was in any case designed to win over the remnants of Ming loyalists. Therefore his afflictions may have a deeper meaning. Likewise, does the loss of one of his souls suggest a loss of integrity, a permanent impairment of his moral mind?

Whatever the symbolic meaning of the dream and its aftermath, Mao chooses to move on rapidly to his new life. The next incident has to do with his preparation, in 1678, for the special examination in which he greatly distinguished himself the following year. There is a yawning gap of ten years, about which Mao says nothing. Probably we should not read too much significance into this lacuna, for in the second half of his autobiography—the dream episode marks exactly the midpoint of Mao's narrative in terms of space—there is no longer a keen interest in events and incidents. The end of Mao's exile also marks an end to the kinetic energy of the picaresque or the teleological motion of the *Bildungsroman*. Nor do supernatural elements have a place in the recording of successful official and scholarly activities. Similarly, mimesis gives way to diegesis in the style of narration. Two themes now predominate: the glorification of the emperor, who bestowed on Mao various favors, and the boastful listing of his ancestors and his own talents. Between the panegyrics, however, there are occasionally somber notes, expressions of regret or even guilt, that culminate in the closing section of the autobiography.

Audiences with emperors had occasionally been recorded in Chinese memoirs, but such meetings were usually narrated in a succinct and formal manner. Only a vain and obsequious courtier in retirement like Mao would note in such detail his last meeting, brief and inconsequential by any standard, with his emperor; but this is the only incident in the last half of the autobiography that affords an opportunity for the storyteller to elaborate: diegesis simply will not do, and even the most ordinary exchange must be reproduced verbatim. In 1689, when Mao had already been gone from the court for three years, the emperor took one of his southern tours and on his return trip passed through Mao's hometown.

> I accompanied the imperial retinue beyond the Wang-ching Gate. His majesty reined in his horse when he saw me. He called me by my name and inquired after my health. I said, "I have not recovered." "Why didn't you seek treatment?" he asked. "I was treated, but it did not help," I replied. "What is wrong with you?" he then asked. "I am suffering from paralysis in both legs," I said.
>
> The emperor asked me more questions, but I could not make them out because I was hard of hearing. So I touched the ground with my head and said: "The petty ailments of your humble servant do not deserve the solicitude of your majesty. Nor does your servant dare to claim any more imperial grace." The emperor wished me well and left.[3]

Mao's sycophancy toward the emperor contrasts with his exaggerated amour propre as well as his uneasiness, increasingly explicit as his narrative approaches its end, over serving the new dynasty. To sing his own praises, he no longer depends on the art of the raconteur, which has served the other egomaniac, Wang Chieh, so well, but largely resorts to diegetic exposition. His most fulsomely laudatory self-appraisal he attributes to someone else.

> My teacher, Chancellor Li of Ho-fei, once said: "In three ways Mao is insurpassable. First, he never carries a book with him: when he travels, there is not even a sheet of paper in his luggage. But when he wields his pen words gush out torrentially as if there were a million volumes within him. Second, he had to go into hiding in his youth, and in his prime he was constantly on the move; as a result he has frequently suffered from attacks of fright. But even during a relapse if there is someone at his door begging for an occasional com-

[3] 11:13b. Many others wrote about their meetings with the peripatetic K'ang-hsi emperor. When he visited the Confucian shrine at the Sage's birthplace during 1681–1682, K'ung Shang-jen, a sixty-fourth generation descendant of Confucius, served as a guide. For a complete translation of K'ung's memoir of the emperor's visit see Richard E. Strassberg, *The World of K'ung Shang-jen: A Man of Letters in Early Ch'ing China* (New York: Columbia University Press, 1983), pp. 75–116.

position he simply slaps his chest and belly several times and then
finishes the piece in a few minutes. He immediately hands over the
draft to the supplicant, yet there is never an error. Third, he is extremely thorough and exact in his learning: from the canonical classics, philosophers, and other major texts to ritual and musicology as
well as even the most trivial matters he knows all the fundamentals
and all the ramifications. Whenever he discourses on scholarship he
can always render Han or Sung experts totally speechless and sub-
missive. As for his achievements in Confucian philosophy I cannot
even begin to measure them. Once I compared his poetry with Tu
Fu's and his prose with Han Yü's and found that he stood comparison. . . . Tu Fu is inferior to him in prose and Han Yü inferior in
poetry. Neither of the two had the talent to excel in both arts."
(11:18b–19b)

It is doubtful that such a preposterously inflated self-regard was ever
matched outside of an insane asylum.

Such vainglory may very well be a necessary antidote to a gnawing
sense of guilt that manifests itself more and more. Following the extraordinary self-praise abruptly comes self-stricture. He feels great agony in
his heart when he compares himself with two ancient writers, Lu Chi and
Yü Hsin, who survived the destruction of the old order and flourished
under new dynasties. "Even they lamented their fate and grieved over
their degradation. How much more must I, who in youth held high standards in loyalty and integrity and in my prime wished to achieve by
words or deeds. Their florid compositions are a minor matter, not worth
comparison. But I have neither established myself as a virtuous man nor
have I completed my studies" (11:19b). The choice of parallel lives is very
revealing. The salient feature that Mao and the two ancients share is their
switch of dynastic allegiances. Lu Chi (261–303) came from one of the
leading families of the kingdom of Wu. After Wu fell he retired to his
hometown for a few years, but eventually went north to the capital of the
conquerors where he had a brilliant literary and political career. Yü Hsin
(513–581) first distinguished himself in the Liang court, but on an em-
bassy to the north was kept against his will by the non-Chinese potentate.
Although he thrived in Ch'ang-an as a highly respected courtier, his writings abound in longings for the south and sorrows over his captivity.
While ostensibly Mao contrasts their successes under new masters with
his own deficiencies, there are enough hints in his wording as well as the
evocation of the two names to suggest that he also regrets his collaboration. The regret becomes more explicit when he goes on to lament his
failure to fulfil his promise to his late brother—the one who instructed
him on the *Book of Changes* just before he fled home—and pointedly adds

that "after the Ming fell my brother threw himself into the river by the Confucian temple, but rescuers brought him back to life; he never again took part in the government examinations" (11:19b). The example of the brother, who never wavered in his stubborn loyalty to the fallen dynasty and whom Mao greatly admired, must have been a painful reminder and constant reproach. Mao then proceeds to denigrate his own writings, urging his friends and presumably his heirs to save only one tenth of the some four hundred volumes, but none of his poetry.[4] Only his writings on the canonical Confucian classics must be completely preserved, because they are—the dream is borne out—"the results of applying myself to what had been passed down from a thousand sages" (11:20a). Concluding his autobiography, Mao launches into bitter self-reproach.

> As it was morally dubious for me to serve the court, I failed to make any real contribution. My abilities were held in vain. I was fortunate enough to have met with a sagely and perspicacious emperor, but I was not employed in a substantial way. As a result my empty words served no purpose. My heart is anguished. When I die I shall not be capped; no shoes shall be worn. Do not have me bathed or my clothes changed, nor shall mourners be admitted. (11:20a–b)

The self-abasement at the end contrasts starkly with earlier effusive exercises in self-exaltation. The posthumous penance that he wishes to inflict on his own person is not merely a rhetorical gesture, for this practice, though uncommon, was not unknown in Chinese wills or testaments. The poet Wu Wei-yeh (1609–1672), another former Ming loyalist whose turnabout earned him the chancellorship of the National University, left similar instructions on his deathbed. Wu's anguish may have been a little less unbearable than Mao's, for he had long before his death unequivocally poured out his guilt in his poetry. Mao's emotions are more complex. He is too vain to admit his fundamental error in his early writings; too enamored of imperial favors not to flaunt them, and in doing so only adds to his sense of regret. He prides himself on being the prime heir to Confucian learning, but he is too clear-eyed not to see that by his time loyalty had been firmly established as the first virtue in the code of Confucian conduct. Earlier in his autobiography he had been shielded from self-scrutiny by the momentum of a raconteur's imagination. But now, nearing the end of both his life and the life story, this fatal knowledge can no longer be staved off. Not a man of half measures, he carries his self-abasement to the very end of his autonecrology, the *ming* (inscription) section. In contrast to the conventional tone of resignation and even peace

---

[4] His instructions were not followed.

with which autonecrologists usually pronounce the final word on their lives, Mao's verse suggests only an unquiet grave:

> When he was young he did not die in battle;
> In his prime he did not die on the execution ground or on the road.
> Blatantly he showed his face to the world;
> Blushingly he advanced in the imperial court.
> Although he was fortunate to have survived into retirement,
> His life was lived in vain.

(11:20b)

NINE

WANG SHIH-MIN

(1592–1680):

ARTIST AS

MODEL CITIZEN

BY ANY standard other than that of consummate contrast, the autobiography of Wang Shih-min does not belong in this section. His is a sober, plain, and systematic account of the life of a model citizen—filial son, dutiful official, philanthropic and self-effacing member of the gentry, diligent scholar with innocuous interests and impeccable tastes. His mannerly account is totally devoid of any supernatural omens or dramatic incidents; it is a model autobiography in that it is carefully constructed with a clear design—first a summary of his life history and then a balanced self-portrait.[1] He is included in this section precisely because he is in every way the diametric opposite of fictionists and fantasts. To place the perfect foil to Wang Chieh and Mao Ch'i-ling in this section is to give us some idea of the wide range of different styles of self-presentation from which a seventeenth-century autobiographer could choose. The last reason is that Wang, the paragon of common sense and good taste, had as an aunt the notorious Wang Tao-chen, whose short but miracle-ridden life contributed to the spiritual climate of the following century in which our fictionists of the self thrived, even if her example did not inspire this or that detail of their fantasies.

The Wang family was one of the wealthiest and most prominent in the lower Yangtze Valley. The autobiographer's grandfather Wang Hsi-chüeh, a grand secretary from 1585 to 1594, was widely respected for his uprightness and literary accomplishments. Wang Shih-min's own grandson also rose to the same lofty position in the early eighteenth century. The most unusual member of the family was the aunt we have just mentioned. The second daughter of Wang Hsi-chüeh, Wang Tao-chen (1558–1580) conjured a life for herself that even the wildest imaginings of Wang Chieh or Mao Ch'i-ling could not match. She was the greatest inventor of the self in an age of growing individualism and experimentation. A year after the death of her fiancé in 1574 the young girl led her family to

[1] Wang's autobiography (*MTW*, pp. 41–46) is in the form of a self-account (*tzu-shu*). For a complete translation of Wang's autobiography see appendix C.

believe that she was in possession of supernatural powers. She could travel afar in spirit, confer with various immortals and deities whom she received in her chambers, and go without food for long periods. A wide following gathered around her and she preached to huge crowds. Many prominent members of the scholar-official class as well as her own father became her disciples. The spectacle of her death-transfiguration, which she first predicted and then stage-managed, attracted a multitude of some one hundred thousand. Several years after her ascension to immortality there were reports of her reappearance in several different places. Charges of imposture were made and there was a hint of scandal. From the beginning the cult was not without its detractors; her father and other prominent disciples were censured by officials for their seemingly improper conduct.[2] As the notoriety persisted to the time when Wang Shih-min was growing up, it is quite understandable that he avoids in the account of his life anything that even borders on the occult or eccentric. His birth was not heralded by auguries, nor were his peaceful slumbers ever disturbed by strange dreams. His aunt was, so to speak, his negative model.

The first third of the autobiography is devoted to his official career, a proportion unjustified in terms of the insignificance of his positions and activities, at least to the modern reader. The imbalance would appear all the greater in light of his fame as a painter and calligrapher. But who can quarrel with an autobiographer about the way he sees himself? He entered civil bureaucracy in 1614 as an assistant director in the Office of Imperial Seals. The post, high for a youth of twenty-two, was obtained not through the normal avenue of passing successive examinatons but as a special imperial favor on account of his grandfather's lofty official rank. This special avenue, although well-established and frequently used, would lead only to sinecures without real power. That Wang Shih-min shunned the rough and tumble of the open contests in the examination halls—the vagaries of which Wang Chieh learned to his great grief—and contented himself with such limited prospects is the first indication of a cautious and self-effacing stance that colors the entire self-account. Perhaps Wang Shih-min's real love, even in his youth, was art; and a sinecure that provoked little envy and entailed few risks would provide the best possible refuge for an unambitious scion of a great family who wanted to practice painting and calligraphy. This is not, however, the reason that Wang himself gives: he is apologetic about the choice and enumerates the series of events and circumstances that led, or compelled, him to accept the sinecure.

> When I was eighteen my father died. Thereupon I began to spit blood, and for more than a year I was on the verge of death. My

---

[2] See Wang Tao-chen's biography in *DMB*, 2:1425–27.

grandfather died when I was nineteen. Several calamities were visited
upon me within two years, and I was left not only forlorn but in
mortal peril. All the burdens of the household fell on my shoulders,
for I was the only man left in the family. I had to manage all the
internal affairs as well as to deal with the outside world. Furthermore, the snobbery of the world was such that the family could be
saved from tumbling down further only by some member's acquisition of rank and office. It just happened that in recognition of my
grandfather's service to the country I was offered the post of an assistant director in the Office of Imperial Seals. I thereupon registered
my name and signified my acceptance of the offer.[3]

That his work was often routine and prosaic Wang Shih-min acknowledged again and again,[4] but he nevertheless gave a lengthy account of his
conscientious execution of his duties. For all his protestations of humility
and inadequacy, in his account he always—without the blatancy of Wang
Chieh or Mao Ch'i-ling—presented himself in the best possible light. He
never accepted monetary gifts, wasted government funds, or absented
himself from court sessions or state sacrifices at inconvenient hours or in
bad weather. Whenever the court had to send an imperial emissary to a
feudal prince on a ceremonial occasion he always volunteered. On such
onerous and sometimes hazardous missions he never harassed local officials or indulged in extravagances.

In contrast with other autobiographies we have seen in this section,
here the picaresque mode never intrudes even briefly, notwithstanding all
the long journeys that Wang had taken into some of the most exotic corners of China—he was on the road for more than half of his official tenure
of twenty-four years. Nor do any of his putative adventures—presumably even his official status could not shield him completely from contin-
gencies—find their way into his pages. There are absolutely no recorded
conversations, anecdotes, scenes, or tableaux. If he was ever awed by the
lofty mountains or responded to the allures of nature, if his travels in any
way inspired or shaped his art—he was, after all, one of the greatest landscape painters of his generation—he chooses not to mention it. To the
end of his austere autobiography he never wavers in his resolute resistance
to imaginative literature. He is no less oblivious to the possibilities of
spiritual autobiography: whatever the vicissitudes of life he does not seek

[3] *MTW*, p. 42.

[4] The work of the Office of Imperial Seals was largely ceremonial and procedural. For
instance, each imperial edict had to be stamped with a particular imperial seal chosen in
accordance with the nature and occasion of the edict—there were altogether twenty-four
different seals. The office also manufactured and issued seals, stamps, emblems, and tallies
to various civilian and military officers.

any deeper meanings, nor do fortuitous insights ever come his way. The concluding section on his official career is a fair example of his style: a careful balance between self-regard and humility, an avoidance of circumstantial specificity, a preference for telling (diegesis) rather than showing (mimesis)—even in relating what must have been the gravest crises in his career.

> There were altogether scores of colleagues who served with me at one time or another. During the early years of the T'ien-ch'i reign [1621–1628] many of the talented were brought into the government: offices were filled to capacity with men of renown and experience who had won public acclaim. As an uncouth novice I presumed to rub shoulders with distinguished elders who, fortunately, did not shunt me aside but favored me with an occasional word of undeserved approbation. The only unpleasantness occurred during the routine merit evaluations of k'uei-hai [1623] and hsin-ssu [1641]. On the former occasion the man in power bore an old grudge against my forebears, while on the latter difficulties arose when the wicked desired to expel those who did not belong to their clique. I was subjected to much scrutiny and faultfinding, but in the end nothing at all was found that could be used against me. (MTW, p. 42)

Wang Shih-min's official career came to an end with the change of dynasties. True to the ideal of the loyal Confucian official, he stayed in his hometown and never served the new regime. The life of a Ming loyalist was not without its hazards, even if he refrained from participation in the resistance movement. He had to steer a narrow course in a perilous sea. The new government, busy consolidating its conquest, did not consistently harass those who refused to collaborate. But to survive unmolested, all Ming loyalists, especially those whose families had been prominent in the old regime, had to be on their best behavior.[5] And on his best behavior Wang was. "I am especially attentive to the matter of taxes. I always try to pay the taxes early; my books are always in order. Even in my straitened old age I would sell property or pawn possessions in order to meet my obligations. Sometimes I might be a little later than I prefer, but I am seldom in arrears" (MTW, p. 43).

How to manage a limited accommodation with government officials

---

[5] The transition from Ming to Ch'ing in general and Ming loyalism in particular have received much scholarly attention in recent years. A small but interesting strain in the larger fabric is the ambiguous relation between the conquerors and the loyalists. I believe it was almost like a subtle game played with unwritten but definite rules. The loyalists of course did not collaborate, but they all "cooperated" with the authorities in various ways—for the aims of the two sides sometimes coincided and limited accommodations worked to the interests of both. Wang Shih-min's testimony can be read as a case in point.

without either giving offense or compromising one's integrity was a test to which Ming loyalists, especially those in whom the authorities for one reason or another liked to see a change of allegiance, were constantly subjected. By paying his taxes scrupulously Wang denied his potential tormentors the most convenient pretext and his tempters a powerful means. The temptations were always there, but he makes it clear that he will not cooperate in a process that would erode away his resolution.

> I have always considered it improper for me to intervene with government officials on behalf of a supplicant. Therefore I have never written as much as a short note to a government agency with a view to influence an official decision. Sometimes a family friend or an old acquaintance who is in a position of power may hint at a willingness to gratify my wishes, but I still set firm limits of propriety and never ask even for a small favor. (*MTW*, pp. 43–44)

Indeed there are firm limits to his accommodation, beyond which he will not step. In a summary of his life near the end of the autobiography he stresses once again his perpetually striving to be blameless: "Throughout my life I . . . have behaved as if I could never be sufficiently discreet, respectful, and yielding." But he hastens to add, with a vehemence seldom seen elsewhere in his narrative, that "if one places survival above honor and shamefully seeks safety at any cost, his would be merely the cautious conduct of women and children, nothing to be proud of" (ibid., p. 46).

That he always strives to be a model citizen and exemplary Confucian extends to every aspect of life. He holds a tight rein over his retainers, succors the indigent and supports the needy, takes into his household all poor relatives, and performs faithfully and meticulously all rites and rituals that are the responsibility of the only heir of an ancient family. In his relation to his community he bends over backwards to be above reproach:

> It is my nature to be intolerant of incivility. I myself am always ruled by modesty and self-effacement. I constantly repeat to myself the ancient exhortation to respect one's own community, which I maintain without deviation. I treat with sincerity and respect all relatives and acquaintances in my hometown irrespective of their station in life. Even youths who are many years my junior I befriend as equals without standing on ceremony, as if for fear of being rejected by them on account of my senility. Those who make improper requests I always forgive.
>
> I am not acquisitive or greedy. Things that do not belong to me I never take, not even one thread of silk or one grain of rice. In recent years I have been under great pressure from tax collectors and mon-

eylenders. On several occasions I was forced to part with some of my properties. The buyers, fully aware of my pressing need for cash, tried their best to take advantage of my difficulties. I knew their perfidy but I did not wrangle with them. For I have always believed, during the last several decades, that I would let others take advantage of me rather than that I should take advantage of them and that I would rather suffer losses than pocket improper gains. I swore that I would never deviate from this practice. Everybody in my hometown can testify to this. (Ibid., p. 44)

If Wang Shih-min from time to time sounds like Dr. Primrose, his self-satisfaction is never lightened by the authorial irony of a Goldsmith. For all his avowals of inadequacy and obtuseness, he never admits to one real flaw. The only instance of excess in a life of moderation is his love of gardens—understandable in a painter—which brought him almost to the brink of bankruptcy.

Having been amply provided for by my forefathers, I am ignorant of anything to do with livelihood: I do not even know how to use a scale or handle an abacus. Yet I was fatally addicted to gardens. Wherever I lived I set up rock arrangements and planted trees so as to express my sentiments and amuse my eyes. During the prime of my life I was bent on constructing and planting in heroic proportions. Once I gave in to my extravagant fancy I no longer thought about the consequences.

I started two gardens—the east and the south—simultaneously. For each I planted several acres of red Lo-chiao peonies. I had dikes built, slopes enlarged, hilltops erected, and ridges raised. When trees and vines were fully grown both gardens gained great renown. However, I gradually found it hard to make both ends meet as my charity work, building expenditures, and other expenses got out-of-hand. In time I was further burdened with several mishaps. The costly weddings of my sons and daughters never seemed to end while tax collectors and moneylenders became more and more importunate. With the last drop of blood squeezed out of my estate, there was left only an empty shell. I had no alternative but to surrender some of my property.

The south garden was pawned to monks and nuns, who proceeded to break up the ground. My thousand flowering plum trees and the thick cassia bushes that circumscribed the land were all cut down and sold as firewood. The east garden was daily trampled underfoot by yokels and swains to the extent that ornamental rocks were toppled and hilly paths eroded away. The place is now hardly recognizable. As I was no longer capable of looking after it, I divided it up among

my sons and let each of them take care of his share. But all my sons
are too destitute to do any repairs. The garden is daily approaching
a wasteland. The sight is so painful that nowadays I visit it but once
or twice a year.

   About a dozen miles to the northwest of the town there was a piece
of wetland some twenty acres in size. A meandering stream, a clear
pond, willows on the banks, a rush-covered isle—a place of simple
and quiet beauty. I wished to build a cottage there to while away my
old age. But enfettered by worldly cares and ties I was never free to
do anything about it. Nowadays every time I pass by the place on
my way to the city I notice that things there are quite different from
what they once were. My wish will never be gratified. I am now
resigned to spending my remaining days in sorrow and poverty.
(Ibid., pp. 45–46)

Today Wang Shih-min is remembered as a great painter, one of the
"Four Wangs" of the seventeenth century. Even during his lifetime his
achievements in painting and calligraphy were already well known. Living in one of the major art centers—they were all near each other—where
practitioners and collectors had congregated for centuries, he knew and
exchanged frequent visits with most of the prominent painters of his day.
All biographical facts point to the central place of art in his life, especially
during the long years—1644 to his death in 1680—of his self-chosen retirement from officialdom. How does he, then, see himself as an artist?
What is the place of art in the first autobiography ever written by a Chinese painter? It might be instructive to compare him with Benvenuto Cellini, the artist and autobiographer. If Chiang-nan during the Ming and
early Ch'ing had much in common with northern Italy during the Renaissance, Wang Shih-min and Cellini could not be more unlike. Flaunting
his genius and living by his wits, the blusterous Florentine is very conscious of being an artist. His self-identity, reinforced by the Renaissance
ethos of manhood, freed him from all restraints and fueled his adventures. On the other hand, our mannerly scholar-official, careworn all his
life and burdened with a strong Confucian ethic, hews a narrow path of
rectitude. Not to seek new glories but to preserve the family legacy, he
relegates his artistic activities to an insignificant place in his life story, a
section on friendship and interests. After listing his friends, describing his
timid attempts at versification, dismissing games such as chess, and lamenting the meager results of his reading, he gives the briefest mention
to his painting.

   As for painting, it is my addiction. Whenever I see a genuine work
   by an ancient master I always try to add it to my collection without
   regard for the price. Often I practice my brush by imitating the fa-

mous masters of the Sung and Yüan. But because of lack of leisure time I have not been able to do my utmost and study thoroughly. Time passes fleetingly and now I realize that I have accomplished nothing. I still remember that every time Mr. Tung Ch'i-ch'ang, vice-minister of rites, saw my painting he never failed to praise or inscribe on it his observations. One time he commented, "Exquisitely green and loftily luxuriant, your works have overtaken the ancients." This of course proceeded from the excessive kindness of a family friend who bent his judgment in offering encouragement to a youth. I knew that if I examined myself I would discover that the compliment was undeserved. (Ibid., p. 45)

The concept of the artist as we know it today is of course a product of the post-Renaissance West, with Cellini supplying much of its source. Needless to say, such a concept would have been unthinkable to Wang Shih-min. To live for one's art and by one's art—to see oneself primarily as an artist—is something Chinese literati-painters, of whom Wang is a fair example, could not have understood. Even Wang's mentor Tung Ch'i-ch'ang (1555–1636), a more self-conscious theorist and practitioner of art than any of his generation, spent many years in government and rose to high positions. To write an autobiography Wang must have relied on models, just as he depended on past exemplars for his painting. The dynastic histories, the most likely source for his autobiographical inspiration, made no provision for painters or calligraphers. Unless an artist distinguished himself in officialdom or in one of few other categories, he would be excluded by the rigid and narrow taxonomy consistently observed by historians. Even Huang Kung-wang, often considered the greatest landscape painter of the Yüan and the master whom Wang Shih-min studied and imitated more than others, did not merit so much as a mention in the *Yüan shih* (Dynastic history of the Yüan). Included in its biographical section was Chao Meng-fu, whose artistic fame rivaled Huang's and to whom Tung Ch'i-ch'ang often compared himself. In Chao, Wang Shih-min must have found an almost perfect exemplar, in life as well as in art. They were alike in their noble birth, versatility, emphasis on refinement, and painstaking rectitude in everyday conduct. Both of them thrived as artists under an alien dynasty. Wang admired Chao very much, even though Chao submitted to the alien conquerors and had a distinguished career in their government. In fact, it was because of that career that he was included in the *Yüan shih*, and not because of his fame as an artist. His achievement as a painter was dismissed by the biographers with one sentence, "He was especially fine in painting landscape, trees and rocks, flowers and bamboos, as well as human figures and horses." Even such a brief statement must have looked like overpraise to his biographers, for they hastened to add, quoting a commentator, that "Chao Meng-fu's real genius was overshadowed by his reputation as a calligrapher and painter. People who knew his calligraphy and painting failed to know his literary achievements; people who knew his literary achievements failed to know his expertise in governmental affairs."[6] As if to forestall the imbalance that his own reputation might also suffer, in the sequence of his narration Wang Shih-min not only placed his official career first and his artistic next to his literary activities but, following the format of the dynastic histories, gave ten times as much space to his inconsequential tenure in the bureaucracy than to his art.

Cellini of course followed an entirely different narrative tradition. To see the context of his autobiography, which was dictated in 1558, we need to note two cognates of his: Vasari's biographies of Italian painters (1550) and La vida de Lazarillo de Tormes (1554). To say that the two immediately preceded him does not mean that he was influenced directly by either. I have no knowledge that he had read Vasari's book, even though he was briefly mentioned in it; as for the Spanish novel, there is no reason to believe that he was aware of it. But his work shared the episodic and colloquial fluency of the one and the picaresque structure of the other. Each of the three was the initiator of a different genre, but all of them were very much the children of the middle decades of the sixteenth century.

The brash and headstrong Cellini never tired of boasting of his originality: he did not believe in copying others. In contrast Wang Shih-min, for all his refinement and exquisite skills, broke no new ground and created no new style. He sincerely admired and imitated the Sung and Yüan masters. With them, as with all seventeenth-century literati painters, landscape was the preferred subject. Wang's autobiography is in a sense not unlike his landscape paintings in somber monochrome, with their carefully balanced deployment of constituent parts, their clearly drawn trees and rocks juxtaposed with mist-shrouded obscurities, their elegiac evocation of autumnal resignation. There would be no unruly brushstrokes or inelegant composition: everything had to be contained within the canons well established by the masters of what Wang and his mentors conceived to be the exemplary era of "antiquity."

[6] Yüan shih, Po-na ed., 172:9b–10a.

TEN

SELF-PORTRAITISTS

WANG SHIH-MIN'S preoccupation with official career was shared by the vast majority of Chinese autobiographers. Their number is much greater than the present study indicates, for I have ignored almost all works that are no more than res gestae or detailed curricula vitae. Still, that the proliferation of even this type of writing did not begin in China until after the middle of the sixteenth century is suggestive. It supports the idea, implicit in previous chapters, that there was a golden age of Chinese autobiography which ran roughly from 1566 when Teng Huo-ch'ü completed his *Nan-hsün lu* to the death of Wang Shih-min in 1680. All the autobiographers we have met from chapter 5 onward flourished between those two dates. During that period the surge of autobiographical expression also manifested itself in genres not readily recognizable as self-literature. This complex topic, however, requires a separate study.[1] Here we shall limit ourselves to just one facet, the conjunction of painting and autobiography.

CHANG HAN (1511–1593)

We shall begin with a digression. The *pi-chi* (miscellaneous notes) is a large and almost amorphous genre of Chinese writing which has flourished for more than a thousand years. Going often under other names such as *sui-pi*, *tsa-chi*, and *pi-t'an*, it is a convenient repository of random reading notes, anecdotes, or observations, sometimes grouped together under specific headings, sometimes totally without any scheme or structure. The writers in this vast genre seldom report on their own lives, not even in the prefaces. The first to do so was Chang Han who in 1593 completed his *Sung-ch'uang meng-yü* (Dreams behind the pine window). Neither by its title nor its organization is the book distinguishable from thousands of other *pi-chi*, but the author is so often the subject that the *Sung-ch'uang meng-yü* is no longer a mere collection of miscellaneous notes but a memoir. Chang had a distinguished official career, rising to minister of personnel in 1573. This fact is the central theme of his book, and two chapters are explicitly devoted to it. There is, however, very little reflection or introspection, even though one chapter is ostensibly entitled "Tzu-hsing chi" (Record of self-examination).

[1] I have touched on this topic in "Varieties of the Chinese Self," pp. 107–31.

A man of letters, Chang Han was also known for his painting and calligraphy. The only thing remarkable about Chang's art is that he—a minister of personnel under a painter's frock—is known to have done a series of self-portraits to illustrate the course of his rise in officialdom.[2] While literary sources yield several earlier cases of men of letters and artists trying their hand at painting themselves, Chang Han appears to have been the first to draw *a series of* self-portraits. The merging of autobiography with portraiture was certainly an innovation. Moreover, to see the self in sequential stages of development was something new, a perception that Chang shared with his contemporaries who wrote spiritual autobiographies, even though they had little else in common.

In the West the repeated attempts by Dürer and Rembrandt to capture their essential selves have often been cited as exemplifying Renaissance individualism and self-conciousness. Critics have even found "a close correlation between the development of self-portraiture and autobiography in the various European countries."[3] Whether a similar case can be made for China will remain undecidable until art historians begin to show greater interest in this topic. In the meantime we can make a beginning by noting that while earlier prominent portraitists almost never overcame their inhibitions to the extent of using themselves as subjects, Ch'en Hung-shou (1598–1652), the greatest figure painting master who lived during what may be called the golden age of Chinese autobiography, was at his most expressive and free when he painted self-portraits. Interesting as he is, we shall not proceed any further because he, unlike the next two artists discussed in this chapter, did not merge self-portraiture with autobiography. His two extant self-portraits were not meant to be items in a sequence.

WAN SHOU-CH'I (1603–1652)

Flourishing during exactly the same decades as Ch'en Hung-shou, Wan Shou-ch'i, a man of letters renowned also for his talents in painting and calligraphy, was born into a prominent family. Well-known as a leader in the resistance movement against the Manchu conquerors, he participated in 1645 in a short-lived uprising. The following year he took Buddhist vows, the same choice made by Ch'en Hung-shou at about the same time. There is no way of knowing whether he did so out of conviction or simply, like many other Ming loyalists, to fend off persecution or to avoid collaboration with the new regime. In any case he is not known to

---

[2] For this and other facts of his life see his biography in *DMB*, 1:72–74.

[3] Delany, *British Autobiography in the 17th Century*, p. 12. "The first substantial English autobiography and the first self-portrait by a native Englishman were produced within a year of each other, so far as we can tell" (pp. 12–13).

have adopted the ordinary details of the Buddhist way of life except the wearing of a monk's cap and the occasional use of a Buddhist name. His ambiguous identity may have contributed to his painting a series of portraits of himself in different costumes and roles. None of these paintings, to my knowledge, has survived, but we have a good idea of what six of them must have been like from an item in his collected literary works. Entitled *Tzu-chih* (Notes on myself), the piece begins very much like an autobiography: "Wan Shou-ch'i had an alternate name [*tzu*] of Chieh-jo. Another alternate name was Nei-ching. He was also known to the world as Nien-shao. His native place was Nan-ch'ang of Kiangsi. His great-grandfather, a physician, traveled from Hu-Kuang to Hsü-chou, and the family settled down there. He loved to read and was good at both the *k'ai* and *li* styles of calligraphy."[4] But the narrative soon becomes a series of six notes, each apparently written to accompany a particular self-portrait and to explain how the painting represents a crucial point in his life. The first note is on his being tested as a young candidate for the highest degree by the emperor personally; the last one explains why he chose the contemplative life of Buddhism. The two events to which the two notes refer are the appropriate beginning and end of a loyalist's life. The fourth, an account of his unsuccessful resistance activities, ends as follows: "During the eighth month our forces collapsed and I was taken prisoner. As I refused to submit, I was about to be killed. But someone secretly intervened on my behalf. After some two months of imprisonment I was released. I returned to the north of the river. [This is why] I have painted myself sailing over a lake in the fourth painting."[5] In all likelihood each of the notes was inscribed on the portrait with which it was associated, for they differ very little in style or format from the colophons that frequently fill up the empty spaces in Ming and Ch'ing paintings. In any case Wan's use of autobiography as a kind of running commentary on a series of self-portraits was very much an innovation.

In addition to the six that Wan mentioned in his essay, he is known to have painted a few other self-portraits. Nevertheless, it cannot be said that he, a man highly esteemed by his contemporaries for his virtues, was self-obsessed. Like his contemporary Wang Shih-min, he was an innovator with respect to the broad and varied art of self-expression. The two loyalist painters felt the urge—widespread during their century—to delineate their exemplary lives, but neither went to excess. Inventors or fictionists they were not.

⁴ *Shih-hsi ts'ao-t'ang wen-chi* (Collected writings of Wan Shou-ch'i), vol. 2 of *Ming-chi san hsiao-lien chi* (Collected works of three Ming scholars) (1919), 3:3b.
⁵ Ibid., 3:4a.

Shih-lien (1633–1702?)

The next self-portraitist was very different. All the traits that we have found earlier in fantasts such as Wang Chieh and Mao Ch'i-ling are magnified almost beyond belief in the Buddhist monk Shih-lien (also known as Ta-shan). Appearing in Kuang-chou around 1670 from complete obscurity, he eked out a living by selling his portraits of Kuan-yin, the Goddess of Mercy. His artistic and literary skills, his wit and imaginativeness as well as his claim—discredited later by his detractors—to have been designated by the long-dead eminent master Chüeh-lang (d. 1648) as his heir impressed members of the local literati, who took him in as one of their own. With their help and the connivance of local officials who appreciated generous gifts of fine furniture and porcelain, all designed by him and manufactured under his supervision, he took possession of the Ch'ang-shou Temple, which he completely remade by renovating the buildings, replanting the gardens, and adding streams and ponds. His exquisite taste and great ingenuity were praised even by his critics. The temple became one of the main attractions of the city and gained a place in the guidebooks. An eloquent preacher and witty raconteur, he gathered a large following. As his fame reached afar, he was invited in 1695 by King Ming of Annam for a state visit. On his return he wrote a book about the trip. In contrast to nearly all previous Chinese travelers' accounts of foreign lands, Shih-lien's first-person narrative contains a minimum of ethnology or folklore but concentrates on his own activities. He reports how the king and all his court received a Buddhist vow from him on their knees; how during his sea voyage when his ship was caught in a raging storm his order to the Dragon King brought an instant and total calm. In his account he performed more miracles than Wang Chieh and received greater adulation than Mao Ch'i-ling.[6] His triumphs at home and abroad only further infuriated his enemies, whose number grew as he embarked on more adventures and plunged into fresh polemics. When a new surveillance commissioner (*an-ch'a shih*) arrived in Kuang-chou in 1702, the monk's enemies brought charges against him. Shih-lien was accused of breaking every vow of the priesthood, making false pretensions to imperial patronage, swindling the ignorant with his fraudulent claim of rainmaking powers, smuggling luxury goods from Vietnam, buying boys and girls and selling them to theatrical troupes, and numerous other crimes. Convicted and sentenced to be exiled to a northern city, Shih-lien died on the road.[7]

[6] See Ch'en Ching-ho, *Shih-ch'i shih-chi Kuang-nan chih hsin shih-liao* (New historical sources of seventeenth-century Annam) (Taipei: Chung-hua ts'ung-shu wei-yüan-hui, 1960).

[7] This account of Shih-lien's life is based on the following sources: Ch'en Ching-ho, *Shih-*

Charges of imposture aside, Shih-lien must have had at least a measure of genuine talent, for among those who corresponded and exchanged poems with him were Wu Wei-yeh and Wang Shih-chen (1634–1711), the two foremost arbiters of literature of the time, whose high standards were never challenged. Even his critics conceded his ability in drawing, but very few of his paintings are extant. For us, the most important thing is that woodblock prints of his thirty-four self-portraits have survived. They are found as frontispieces in a collection of his poetry, *Li-liu t'ang chi* (Collected works from the Li-liu Studio).[8]

As indicated by the captions on the prints, each of the pictures was meant to depict the great master in one of his many and varied roles and capacities. The first picture is certainly true to its caption, *Dispatching the Demon*. We see a faceless youth with his head slightly bowed sitting on a rush prayer mat, and standing in front of and smiling at him is a young woman with the beauty and beguiling posture often found in contemporary illustrated popular literature. The absence of facial features no doubt represents a renunciation of the senses, a total refusal to lend his ears to or cast his eyes on his nearly irresistible temptress. The irony in the contrast between the sternly ascetic youth at the beginning of the series and the discredited master at the end of his life is all the greater if his detractors can be believed. One of the charges lodged against him was that in order to ingratiate himself with the powerful he presented them with paintings of amorous scenes drawn with his superb skill.

In the second picture, titled *Traveling as an Itinerant Monk*, is a youth with a sweet and innocent face in a monk's habit. There are the usual trappings—the prayer beads, the big straw hat, the staff—but not the tonsured head. Throughout all the portraits the vain master always wears his hair long, while others who are identifiably members of the Buddhist clergy are all bereft of hair. The discrepancy is nowhere more striking than in the tenth print, *Expounding the Law*, where the benevolent-looking master, now sporting a mustache, sits on a rock with bamboo plants at his back and receives homage from three ancient but cleanly shaven and tonsured monks.[9]

---

ch'i shih-chi, pp. 1–33; Hsieh Kuo-chen, *Ming-Ch'ing pi-chi t'an-ts'ung* (Shanghai: Chung-hua shu-chü, 1962), pp. 65–68.

[8] Banned by the Manchu government, very few copies of this book survived. The text I use contains no information about the publication date or publisher.

[9] Along the left border near the bottom of this print there is a note that the wood was "respectfully cut by disciple Chu Kuei." The leading woodcut artist of his time, Chu enjoyed imperial patronage. That his name should have been associated in such a way with Shih-lien's self-glorification is another measure of the monk's standing in his heyday. For a brief evaluation of Chu's art see A-ying [Ch'ien Hsin-ts'un], *Chung-kuo lien-huan-t'u-hua shih-hua* (A history of Chinese illustrations in narrative sequence) (Peking: Chung-kuo ku-tien i-shu ch'u-pan-she, 1957), pp. 18–19.

Shih-lien is portrayed one more time as a juvenile in the third print, *Carrying Firewood.*[10] Our master begins to sport a mustache in the fourth print, *Reading.* As the portraits have more to do with his roles and poses than with specific episodes in his life, there is no strict chronological order to the sequence. However, beginning with the thirteenth, *Visiting Kindred Spirits,* he is never without a goatee or wrinkles around the eyes. A slightly receding hairline is another concession to the passage of time.

In contrast to the autobiographers we have met in Part II of this study, Shih-lien hardly says anything about his apprenticeship. There is no earnest seeking for truth and illumination. The sixth print, *Silently Communing,* shows the musing young master sitting on the ground with his head bent slightly forward and one leg outstretched. In his relaxed posture there is no sign of the burning urgency or desperate struggle that characterized the sitting-in-meditation of earlier Ch'an masters. If he ever benefited from a teacher, as he apparently did in the next picture, *Meeting a Miraculous Stranger,* his representation of this episode has much more in common with popular literature than with spiritual autobiography. For once humble and deferential, Shih-lien listens attentively to a gesticulating elder with bushy eyebrows and a long beard who, extremely ancient both in his mien and costume and carrying an elaborately decorated staff, is clearly a figure of great power and authority. What the august stranger has to impart cannot be easily indicated pictorially, but that the message is of great import can be further seen in the posture of the disciple who, with his back reverentially bent and his head at an obsequious angle, clings most eagerly to the elder. Represented with great vividness here— there is absolutely none of the stiffness and formality that often characterize Chinese self-portraiture—the tableau is a familiar one in Chinese literature. It is also reminiscent of an archetypal theme, the conferring of charisma. The fortuitous encounter with an awe-inspiring elder occurred often in the early life of a legendary hero, and the secret word imparted to the lucky youth would utterly transform him, marking the turning point in his career. We have seen how another fantast, Mao Ch'i-ling, received the long lost secret of true Confucianism from a mysterious stranger. Although Shih-lien always maintained that he was the principal heir to Master Chüeh-lang, as a fictionist he could not content himself with an oral transmission in the plain and austere Ch'an tradition or a personal illumination that did not lend itself readily to a picturesque externalization. He was after stranger gods and more prodigious powers. Judging by the next two prints, *Stargazing* and *Casting Hexagrams,* we can see that Shih-lien is now indeed practicing occult arts, presumably thanks

[10] This particular form of physical labor is one of the standard topoi in the life of an improvished but genteel student who ekes out a living in an altogether respectable way.

to his initiation by the stranger in the immediately preceding print. We can also conclude that the august imparter of the secret code was none other than Fu Hsi, the legendary figure of high antiquity believed by many to be the earliest practitioner of divination. He was often revered as the progenitor of the Confucian Way for having provided the source for the *Book of Changes*.[11] Having received the transmission of truth from the primordial sage, Shih-lien was now, at least in his own eyes, the first among the latter-day Confucians.

The most audacious of his claims to supernatural powers is represented in the twenty-second print, *Rainmaking*. It is a claim that perhaps even our brash master cannot substantiate with ease, for here he resorts to indirection, the only time he ever does so. On the other hand, it may have been merely for effect or to add an element of mystery that he absents himself from the picture. Instead, we are shown a well landscaped temple behind a wall. On the wall next to the gate there is a big poster proclaiming Abbot Shih Will Sell Rain. A few chatting and pointing potential customers or curious onlookers in the foreground complete the only "self-portrait" in which Shih-lien makes no appearance.

Adeptness in occult arts is only one of the many facets of the self that Shih-lien is eager to portray. The total effect points to a unique individual exemplifying the life-styles of both the literati and of the free spirits who are above ordinary rules and natural laws. His versatility is shown in no. 11, *Composing Poetry*; no. 14, *Painting*; no. 15, *Playing the Flute*; no. 29, *Writing Commentaries*; no. 32, *Making Furniture*. In *A Gathering of Friends* (no. 19) he enjoys the company of the most exalted of the Confucians, while in *Roaming* (no. 12) he assumes the persona of a Taoist immortal who, armed with a long sword but otherwise unencumbered, looks completely at ease with motion and space. His rising above all the formalities and ordinary concerns—he is never once seen performing the mundane duties of the Buddhist abbot presiding over a fashionable temple—is further expressed in two actions characteristic of Chinese hermits: fishing (no. 17) and whistling loudly (no. 34). Like another egotist Wang Chieh, whom we have seen earlier, Shih-lien is so obsessed with exhibiting every detail of himself that he even includes such scenes as his feeding a horse (no. 21) and being sick in bed (no. 25).

In content and style the prints frequently resemble the illustrations found in seventeenth-century popular literature. Indeed Shih-lien's life has almost every element of a tale of wonder, a story of striking contrasts and tantalizing complexities.[12] His spectacular rise and sudden downfall

---

[11] Cf. Joseph Alan Adler, "Divination and Philosophy: Chu Hsi's Understanding of the *I-ching*" (Ph.D. dissertation, University of California, Santa Barbara, 1984), pp. 79ff.

[12] It has been suggested that P'u Sung-ling (1640–1716) may have based one of his short

illuminate his times probably better than any plot from seventeenth-century drama or fiction. During the time of dynastic transition a clever adventurer from humble origins but with obvious talents could readily find acceptance in high places. But even earlier—during the latter part of the preceding century—Ming Neo-Confucians, especially those of the T'ai-chou sect of the Wang school, were well known for their susceptibility to prophets of dubious probity. It was also an age when the Chinese imagination demanded more fantasy and novelty than ever before. Other fictionists of the self may have had to exercise a measure of caution—both Wang Chieh and Mao Ch'i-ling were survivors of great calamities. Shih-lien, having neither ties to the old regime nor obligations to a family, recognized no limits to his grandiosity and inventiveness. His only match in automythopoeia was the young woman Wang Tao-chen—Wang Shih-min's aunt—who had achieved self-transfiguration half a century before he was born. As a daughter of a good family Wang had only a narrow field of operation, however wild her flights of fancy may have been; but her fantasies seem to have been acted out on a much wider stage by the untrammeled and self-made Shih-lien.[13] Wang departed from this world too early to cause serious legal problems to her illustrious family; Shih-lien in blazoning his connections and powers seems to have flirted with danger. His enemies, in bringing him down, needed not much more than to cite his own words.

Shih-lien's fall marked the closing of an era. Although the collection of his writings that contained his self-portraits was not formally included in the official list of proscribed books until 1788, his ruination in 1702 signified clearly that the Ch'ing government, having now consolidated its conquest, would suffer no more departures from normal behavior. Fantasts and adventurers may not have become totally extinct in the new era, but they wrote or painted at their own peril.

stories partially on the life of Shih-lien. See Hsieh Kuo-chen, *Ming-Ch'ing pi-chi t'an-ts'ung*, p. 66.

[13] There is no record that Shih-lien and Wang Tao-chen's nephew ever knew each other, even though they shared at least one acquaintance in the person of Wu Wei-yeh, the chancellor of the National University.

PART IV
THE SELF EXAMINED

THE TWO major groups of Chinese self-literature we have dwelt upon, spiritual and fictional autobiographies, have one thing in common: an affirmation of the self. The tortuous quest in the first and the exuberant display in the second were both predicated on a fundamental optimism. If the autobiographer finds fault with his life at this or that point, he is usually sustained by hope. There may be occasions for despair, but never harsh self-stricture. The only exception is Mao Ch'i-ling's autonecrology, but even his does not acquire a somber tone until late in the narrative. The ending, however, shows us another side of the Chinese view of the self that we have not touched upon.

What I would call the golden age of Chinese autobiography—roughly from 1566 when Teng Huo-ch'ü completed his *Nan-hsün lu* to the death of Wang Shih-min in 1680—also witnessed a deep awareness of the human proclivity to evil, an urgent need to counter this proclivity, a readiness for self-disclosure, and a deep anguish over one's own wrongdoings, all to an extent and with an intensity never known before in Chinese history. The category of writings that shows us this side of the age is a diverse lot. For lack of a better name I shall call these penitential texts. Some are entitled *tzu-sung* (self-indictment) or *tzu-tse* (self-reproach). Others may take the form of an appeal to a divinity begging for forgiveness, a covenant with Heaven promising reform, a manual for a confession ritual, or simply a short memoir reporting the author's misdeeds with an expression of remorse. None of the texts belongs to any major genre of traditional Chinese literature, nor have they been considered a part of formal philosophical discourse. But when they recur with any frequency during a relatively short period, they probably reflect a changing attitude or a new mood in the moral climate. For this reason, and for the contrast they present to the major autobiographies and the light they shed on the views of the self during this pivotal age in Chinese history, they deserve a place in the present study, even though some of them can hardly be called autobiographies.

What emerges from even a casual perusal of these texts is a greater recognition of individual responsibility than ever before and a new moral agency that approaches what in the West would be called the sense of guilt. To see clearly why this is so—and to understand further the golden age of Chinese autobiography—we need a backward glance at the practice of confession in recorded history. Much of the next section will be a digression from our main concern, but a brief history of the Chinese confessional will provide the background necessary for an appropriate appreciation of the texts under discussion. The confessional plays as fundamental a role in chapter 12 as historiography does in the earlier chapters. Furthermore, in China as in the West, written confessions were preceded by oral confessions, and the two forms tended to interact with each other.

ELEVEN

TAOIST AND BUDDHIST
CONFESSIONALS

ALTHOUGH self-examination and mending of errors were important elements in classical Confucianism, no formal procedure or ritual was de-
vised that would enable sinners to make a clean breast of their misdeeds
and prepare themselves for a fresh start. Nor did early writers dwell on
their own transgressions. For the earliest recorded practice of confession
we have to turn to the quasi-Taoist secret societies that led large-scale
peasant uprisings during the reign (A.D. 168–188) of the Emperor Ling of
the Later Han. A common practice in several of these secret societies was
faith healing, and a component in the healing process was the confessions
of sins by the patient. From the *Hou-Han shu* (Dynastic history of the
Later Han) we have the following account: "Chang Chüeh of Chu-lu
styled himself the Great Sage and Good Teacher. He followed the way of
Huang-ti and Lao-tzu, collecting around himself a number of disciples.
They were taught by him to practice healing. The patients were asked to
kneel, make obeisance, and confess their offenses. This procedure, together with Chang's spells, holy water, and incantations, cured a great
number of the sick."[1] From the *Tien-lüeh* (An outline of institutions),[2]
quoted in P'ei Sung-chih's commentary to the biography of Chang Lu in
the *San-kuo chih* (Dynastic history of the Three Kingdoms), comes the
following:

> Chang Hsiu's method was similar to Chang Chüeh's, except that he
> had silent chambers provided for the sick in which they would reflect
> on their transgressions. . . . He appointed "demon deputies" who
> appealed to the gods through prayers on behalf of the sick. For each
> patient the demon deputy would write down his name and his con-
> fession. Three copies of the document were made: one was to be
> placed on a mountain peak for presentation to Heaven, one was to
> be buried underground, and one sunk into water. These were called
> the dispatches to the Three Offices.[3]

[1] *Hou-Han shu*, Po-na ed., 71:1a–b.
[2] This third-century work is no longer extant.
[3] *San-kuo chih*, Po-na ed., *Wei chih* (Dynastic history of the Wei), 8.23b.

One detail in the above account is of great significance for our purpose: the confessions were transcribed and written versions presented to the divinities. The quick transition from oral performance to the production of written texts seems to have foreshadowed what was to become standard practice in China.

A more moralistic interpretation of the faith healing associated with the peasant uprisings occurs in the *Shen-hsien chuan* (Biographies of immortals):

> Chang Tao-ling wished to govern the people by inculcating a strong moral sense in them rather than by applying punishments. Therefore he stipulated that anyone suffering from disease should confess all the misdeeds he had committed since birth. Chang would then write down the confession and have the patient sign a covenant with the Divine Intelligence (*shen ming*) swearing that he, on pain of death, would never violate the laws again. The document was to be cast into the river. From that time on whenever anyone became sick he would confess. Not only would he get well but he would also be so shamed that he would not dare to offend again. Moreover, his fear of Heaven and Earth would make him mend his ways.[4]

All historical accounts of the faith healing practiced by the secret societies are tantalizingly brief but, sketchy as they are, they suggest that the peasants' leaders may have anticipated some of the findings of modern psychology. The public unburdening of guilt could reintegrate the sick person into his community, while the cathartic effects of the confession, the relief of tension and anxiety, could cure most psychosomatic diseases. The physically reinvigorated and spiritually cleansed peasant, now bound to his leader by shame, gratitude, and awe, would be completely at his beck and call. It is not surprising that these sectarian uprisings spread swiftly throughout most of China and nearly brought down the dynasty.

The peasant rebellion was eventually put down; the last leader, the grandson of the legendary Chang Tao-ling, surrendered to the government in A.D. 215. But the religious Taoism that had been used by the rebels continued to flourish. In the fourth century, a sect by the name of T'ien-shih Tao was embraced by many noble families in the lower Yangtze Valley. Faith healing combined with confession of sins seems to have reappeared in a new form, as evidenced by the following episode. When Wang Hsien-chih, a member of the most prominent Eastern Chin family, was stricken with illness, his relatives, who were believers in the T'ien-shih Tao, decided to present a written appeal on his behalf to the

---

[4] Quoted in Sun K'o-k'uan, *Yüan-tai tao-chiao chih fa-chan* (The development of Taoism during the Yüan) (Taichung: Tung-hai ta-hsüeh, 1968), p. 11.

Taoist Supreme Being. He was asked to reveal his wrongdoings. Wang replied that he was not aware of any except a divorce suit he had won over the Ch'ih family.[5]

Faith healing, or to use a broader term, symbolic therapy, has continued to play a role in Chinese medicine down to the present day, but after the sixth century confession of sins seems to have almost completely disappeared from the Taoist liturgy of healing. The only case that I have found so far involves Chao P'u, a tenth-century prime minister. According to one version of the account, Chao, alerted by a Taoist medium that victims of his official misdeeds had lodged complaints against him in the netherworld, wrote a confession and submitted it to the divinities by means of a burning ritual.[6] Another version, found in Chao's biography in the official dynastic history, does not mention a confession but has the additional element of sickness. Chao, gravely ill, sent a representative to pray for his recovery at a Taoist temple but the mission failed because, as the divine message indicated, the grievances against the autocratic official were too serious.[7] When combined, the two versions seem to contain all the familiar elements of the Taoist healing procedure that obtained several centuries earlier. As religious Taoism evolved from its early days of peasant rebellions, an elaborate liturgy gradually came into being. Confession also played a part in some of the services and rites unconcerned with healing. We shall not, however, take up this topic until we have dealt with Buddhist confession, in view of the unceasing interchange between the two religions.

Confession as a regular feature of religious life has a long history in India going back to Vedic times. With the Buddhists the rite of confession, called *uposatha* in Sanskrit, was as ancient as the first establishment of monastic orders. As stipulated by the monastic rules, twice a month, on the days of the new moon and full moon, monks met for *uposatha*, which was preceded by fasting and sacrifices. During the rite the sections of the monastic code were read to the assembly. At the end of each section there was an interrogatory portion, during recitation of which a guilty monk would confess his offenses.[8]

It is impossible to determine when the *uposatha* was first brought to China. Since the performance of the rite required the assembly of a min-

---

[5] Liu I-ch'ing, *Shih-shuo hsin-yü* (A new account of tales of the world) SPPY, 1A:10a. Other references to confession in connection with faith healing are scattered in the *Tao-tsang*, the vast Taoist canon. For details see my article "Self-Examination and Confession of Sins in Traditional China," *Harvard Journal of Asiatic Studies* 39, no. 1 (June 1979): 8–9.

[6] Li Yu, *Sung-ch'ao shih-shih* (Facts of the Sung Dynasty) TSCC, 7:115–21.

[7] *Sung shih* (Dynastic history of the Sung) Po-na ed., 256:9a–b.

[8] Sukumar Dutt, *Early Buddhist Monachism* (New York: E. P. Dutton, 1924), pp. 100–104.

imum number of ordained monks, it is unlikely that the *uposatha* could have been enacted in a city without a sizable quota of foreign monks in the early days before the ordination of Chinese monks became feasible. Moreover, as early translators of Buddhist sutras were primarily interested in doctrine, the texts dealing with monastic rules were ignored. Before the middle of the third century, when the Indian monk Dharmakala undertook the translation of monastic rule books in Loyang, the Chinese could not have known the *uposatha* except through oral transmission, for which historical evidence is meager. Nevertheless, we can be certain that after the eminent monk Tao-an (312–385) placed his authority behind the *uposatha*, the rite was observed by all Chinese monastic organizations.[9]

Prince Ching-ling (461–495), patron of Buddhism and man of letters, introduced the rite of *uposatha* to the patrician laity.[10] There is no record of how detailed the self-disclosures of the lay penitents were during this rite. However, a collection of ceremonial texts associated with penitential services attended by emperors and courtiers during the sixth century has fortunately been preserved in a Buddhist anthology.[11] With one exception, all these texts are ornately rhetorical in style but silent on personal misdeeds. The exception is the piece written by Shen Yüeh (441–513), historian and courtier.

Shen begins with a salutation to the "various Buddhas and all saints." He goes on to concede that he must have committed countless sins in all his former lives, but he has no way of remembering them. As for this life he admits: "Even when I was a child I was given to gluttony. My voraciousness knew no compassion, nor did my appetite understand retribution. In my mind I consigned all scaly, furry, and feathery creatures to the kitchen, excluding them from my sympathy on account of their not being human. From morning to night and from season to season I devoured them, never satisfied with a vegetable meal."[12] He acknowledges other offenses in less vivid language: in his childhood he wantonly killed birds and beasts; each summer he destroyed thousand of flies and mosquitoes; in hunting and fishing he killed more living beings; he allowed his underlings to loot farms and orchards so that he could have a share of the spoils; his love of rare books led him to acquire two hundred volumes by unlawful means; in his youth he indulged in many amorous escapades with both girls and boys; he was frequently given to buffooneries and angry outbursts. He ends the list of offenses with the following resolution: "In the presence of the Buddhas of the Ten Directions and Three Worlds, before

    [9] Hui-chiao, *Kao-seng chuan* (Lives of eminent monks) 2 vols. (Nanking, 1884; reprint, Taipei: T'ai-wan yin-ching-ch'u 1958), 1:9 and 20.

    [10] *Kuang hung-ming chi* (Expanded collection on the propagation of light), comp. Tao-hsüan, SPPY, 36:1a.

    [11] Ibid., 36:2a–12a.

    [12] Ibid., 36:3b.

this assembly of monks and laity, I take an oath to subjugate myself. I reproach myself and deeply repent my past transgressions. Examining all my bad habits, I clean and wash my present mind. I shall entrust my destiny to the Great Buddha."[13]

After Shen Yüeh, the Chinese Buddhist laity continued to write penitential texts, but all were vague and abstract in dealing with personal misdeeds. Nor did subsequent Buddhist penitential services require each individual participant to reveal his own wrongdoings, either orally or in writing. This was also true in other lands where Buddhism took root. As stated by Heinrich Dumoulin: "In Mahayana Buddhism there has evolved a great number of rites of repentance, varying according to the school and the preferred sutras, but in the main quite similar to one another. None includes a detailed confession of transgressions committed. The repentance expressed refers primarily to the general sinful condition of man."[14]

Against this background, Shen Yüeh's confession stands out as a unique landmark in the history of Buddhism, having neither predecessor nor imitator until the sixteenth century. Indeed Shen Yüeh and his Buddhist associates introduced into the practice of confession two features that had no precedent in Indian Buddhism. These two features, the participation of the laity and the writing of depositions to be presented to the divine order, were, as the reader will recall, the foundation of Taoist healing from as early as the second century.[15] The T'ien-shih sect of religious Taoism was still very much in vogue during Shen Yüeh's time; Shen Yüeh himself, although he was a Buddhist convert, turned to a Taoist priest for succor shortly before his death, when he felt overwhelmed by a guilty conscience.[16] In view of these circumstances and the well-known fact that Chinese Buddhists and Taoists have continuously borrowed copiously and unscrupulously from each other, one may attribute the innovations made by Shen and his group to direct Taoist influence.

The spread of Buddhism in China during the early days was much facilitated by the wondrous skills and magical powers displayed by proselytizing monks. Healing was one of the devices that drew crowds and won converts. Confession of sins by the afflicted, however, does not seem to have been a regular element in the Buddhist practice of healing. The

---

[13] Ibid., 36:4a.

[14] *Christianity Meets Buddhism*, trans. John C. Maraldo (La Salle, Ill.: Open Court Publishing Co., 1974), p. 123.

[15] For the nonparticipation of the Indian laity see Sukumar Dutt, *Buddhist Monks and Monasteries of India* (London: George Allen and Unwin, 1962), p. 105. As for the absence of written confessions in Indian Buddhism, I have no support for my conjecture other than a concurred opinion conveyed to me by Prof. Alex Wayman during a conversation in September 1977.

[16] *Liang shu* (Dynastic history of the Liang) Po-na ed., 13:20a–b.

only clear-cut case that I have found is supposed to have taken place in 560. Hui-k'o, the Second Ch'an Patriarch, was visited one day by a lay Buddhist: "Without announcing his name, the visitor made obeisances to the master and said: 'I am suffering from rheumatism. Please repent my sins for me.' The master replied, 'Tell me your sins, and I shall repent them for you.' After pondering for a long time, the lay Buddhist said: 'I looked for my sins, but could not find any.' "[17] The brevity of this episode belies its significance. The exchange between Hui-k'o and his visitor, obviously a summarized version rather than a verbatim transcription, suggests that both were acquainted with a healing rite in which a patient whose affliction could not be attributed to a specific wrongdoing was required to disclose all his sins to a confessor who would expiate them and effect a cure for the penitent. Such a rite resembles Taoist faith healing rather than the Buddhist *uposatha*. The episode is quite in keeping with the state of Buddhism in northern China during the sixth century, where belief in magic was quite widespread and enthusiasm for Taoist ideas and practices resulted in massive forgery of sutras. The Ch'an school, however, soon took a new orientation. None of the subsequent patriarchs established his fame as a healer of physical afflictions, nor was the problem of guilt and sin a concern in its teachings.

If the Buddhists were inclined to borrow from the Taoists, the Taoists for their part never hesitated to return the compliment, especially in matters of liturgy. Perhaps as a response to the Buddhist *uposatha*, toward the end of the sixth century the Taoists included confession in some of their rites other than healing. The *Sui shu*, the dynastic history completed in 656, has the following description of the Taoist Chieh-chai, the rite of purification:

> The altar is divided into three sections whose boundaries are made of ropes tied to sticks standing upright. Each section has its own entrance and images. The penitents are admitted to a section in a small group forming a single line. With their hands tied behind their backs, they proceed one by one to the front of the images and confess their sins to the gods. The rite goes on day and night without stop for seven or fourteen days.[18]

The rites of purification had a long history in China extending back far before the rise of religious Taoism. But the inclusion of confession does not seem to antedate the above instance.[19] Another reference to Taoist

[17] *Ching-te ch'uan-teng lu* (Transmission of the lamp), comp. Tao-yüan (Taipei: Chen-shan-mei ch'u-pan-she, 1968), 3:50.

[18] *Sui shu* (Dynastic history of the Sui) Po-na ed., 35:27b.

[19] Derk Bodde in his *Festivals in Classical China* (Princeton: Princeton University Press,

ritual confession is found in the *Ta-T'ang liu tien*, the book on T'ang institutions and codes written toward the middle of the eighth century. The section on Taoist liturgy mentions a set of three services called the San-yüan. "The Shang-yüan, the service for the Office of Heaven, falls on the fifteenth day of the first month; the Chung-yüan, the service for the Office of Earth, falls on the fifteenth of the seventh month; the Hsia-yüan, the service for the Office of Water, falls on the fifteenth day of the tenth month. All services are for the priests to confess and repent their offenses and sins."[20] The Three Offices of Heaven, Earth, and Water recall the healing rite of the Later Han rebels, but the San-yüan services, at least in their later versions, do not seem to have had much to do with healing. Preserved in the *Tao-tsang* (Taoist canon) are liturgical texts associated with the San-yüan services of a later period, perhaps as late as the eleventh century. Like all other Taoist penitential rites described in the *Tao-tsang*, the *San-yüan* services do not require the confession of specific personal transgressions: the worshiper only acknowledges the general guilt of mankind and repents all possible sins of this and all former lives.[21]

The formalization of penitential liturgy and the generalization of sin afforded each believer a ritual redemption without the necessity of avowing his specific sinful acts. The immensity of the crimes accumulated over myriad past incarnations by all mankind, when acknowledged or contemplated by the worshiper, would by comparison invariably dwarf whatever sense of guilt he might feel over the transgressions he may have committed as an individual in this life. The urge to unburden oneself of real or imagined wrongdoings before the divine order or the community, never strong in a Confucian society, now seemed to disappear almost completely with the increasing institutionalization of Taoism.[22]

1975) has a chapter (pp.273–88) on the "lustration festival." He describes various practices and rites of purification in ancient China, but mentions no confession of sins.

[20] *Ta-T'ang liu tien* (The six codes of the great T'ang) (Taipei: Wen-hai ch'u-pan-she, 1962), 4:42b.

[21] For the similarities between Buddhist and Taoist penitential texts see my article, "Self-Examination," pp. 14–15.

[22] During the past two decades much has been written on Chinese popular religion in general and Taoism in particular, with emphasis on the late traditional and contemporary periods. None of the writings that I have consulted mentions the practice of confession, except for a brief reference in Kristofer M. Schipper, "The Written Memorial in Taoist Ceremonies," *Religion and Ritual in Chinese Society*, ed. Arthur P. Wolf (Stanford: Stanford University Press, 1974), pp. 309–24. "During certain rituals the head priest performs a silent meditation while the reading goes on. His meditation takes the form of a confession of sins, directed to the patriarchs of the Taoist church, notably the original Heavenly Master" (p. 321). Schipper did not further characterize the confession; perhaps nothing much can be known about it if nothing is vocalized. My conjecture is that the above-mentioned confession does not deal with the specific sins of any participant in the ritual but only acknowledges the general sinful state of mankind.

TWELVE

CONSCIENCE AND CONFUCIANS

THE Confucians, as we have noted before, did not have a liturgy of confession. Perhaps revealing one's own sins in public ran against the grain of a culture molded by classical Confucianism, which put so much emphasis upon propriety and discretion. Those who were most prone to self-examination were precisely those who were expected to be paragons of virtue, exemplars for the masses. A sage-king in the Confucian mold might occasionally take personal responsibility for the calamities visited on or the transgressions perpetrated by his subjects, but he would never have understood Cromwell's passionate self-mortification, his branding himself the worst sinner of the realm. The emperors from time to time issued edicts of self-condemnation (*tsui-chi*), but there was never any disclosure of serious offenses or offenses that were not public knowledge. Autobiographers of humbler station were equally reticent about their wrongdoings. Only one autobiographer before the sixteenth century violated this taboo. Ssu-ma Hsiang-ju (d. 118 B.C.), as we have noticed in chapter 3, mentioned, apparently in an unrepentant manner, one disreputable episode in his life. His temerity was doubly penalized: his autobiography did not survive, and he was denounced by the great T'ang historiographer Liu Chih-chi. Through his authority as the foremost Chinese historiographer of his day Liu seems to have shut the door to any further public confessions. The door remained closed for many centuries.

But even before the interdict handed down by Liu there had not been any sign that *written* confession would flourish, the early emergence of oral confession notwithstanding. The formulaic generalities of liturgy were not conducive to a deeply felt sense of individual guilt, nor would the decorous reticence of Confucian behavior encourage a public expression of it. Great changes, however, occurred in the late Ming. Among the forces that contributed to the new moral culture and spiritual climate the most powerful were the teachings of Wang Shou-jen. It was he who postulated the self-sufficiency of every moral being, the promise of radical transformation for any mortal who would faithfully follow his own inner light. He took the term *liang-chih* (innate knowledge) from *Mencius* but endowed it with almost magic powers. It was a very heady potion for some of the adherents of the Wang school. The belief in innate knowledge as the unerring guide inherent in everyone freed the bold from all restraints and gave the restless an impetus to embark on experiments and adventures. When Teng Huo-ch'ü heard the message he could no longer stay at home; Hu Chih and others of the second and later generations discovered that there was a long and tortuous journey from the initial promise to the promised land. If Wang Shou-jen was the single most important force behind Confucian spiritual autobiographies, his influence was no less strong in the reemergence and proliferation of what may be called penitential literature.

After Wang had reached enlightenment in the wilderness, the great master never once displayed doubt or uneasiness, much less remorse or repentance. Some of his disciples and followers, however, would eventually lose confidence in themselves. They discovered that innate knowledge could not always be relied upon. They recoiled from their own excesses and those of their associates. Early optimism turned bitter and they bitterly turned against themselves. It was Wang Chi (1498–1583), probably the disciple whom Wang Shou-jen trusted the most, who led the way. The year 1570, in which he prepared a bill of particulars against himself, represents a turning point in Chinese moral culture, for to find a precedent for Wang Chi's extraordinary act we have to go back one millenium to Shen Yüeh, and even his penitential text was far less specific and vehement than Wang's.

Wang Chi's Self-Indictment

Wang Chi's philosophy was characterized by a strong streak of subjectivism and an excessive reliance on *liang-chih* (innate knowledge). To him

> *Liang-chih* is the mind that knows right from wrong. The crux of the matter lies entirely in the occasion when any idea occurs. If one is at peace with the idea, then the idea is morally right; if one is uneasy with the idea, then it is morally wrong. If one is at peace with the idea, then one should carry it out even if the whole world should disapprove of it. If one is uneasy with the idea, then one should not carry it out even if it should lead to great benefits. Only if one acts in this way can he be considered to have actually applied his innate knowledge, to have achieved self-satisfaction, and to have transcended the conventional and ordinary.[1]

Many of Wang Chi's contemporaries considered that discarding all traditional rules and regulations in favor of one's innate knowledge as the only arbiter of one's actions could lead to perilous excesses. Indeed Wang

---

[1] Wang Chi, *Wang Lung-ch'i ch'üan-chi* (Complete works of Wang Chi) (1882 ed.; reprint, Taipei: Hua-wen shu-chü, 1970), 15:32b–33a; hereafter referred to as *Wang Lung-ch'i ch'üan-chi*. The term *liang-chih* (innate knowledge) comes originally from *Mencius*, 7A:15: "The ability possessed by men without having been acquired by learning is innate ability, and the knowledge possessed by them without deliberation is innate knowledge" (Legge translation).

Chi was frequently misunderstood and had his share of detractors. But the courage born of his strong conviction and the faith he had in innate knowledge were sufficient to steel him against any criticism for almost all his long life. However, he lost his composure, perhaps for the first time, when an unprecedented calamity befell him in 1570 at the age of seventy-two. A fire started in the quarters of his daughter-in-law and spread to the whole family compound. Most of the buildings and all his own belongings were destroyed. Shaken by the calamity into an uncharacteristic state of doubt and humility, Wang wrote an essay entitled *tzu-sung* (Self-indictment).

He begins by describing the fire, lamenting the reduction to ashes of the collection of "imperial appointments, ancestral shrines, books, paintings, maps, and calligraphic samples of my late teacher." Recalling his last fifty years of devotion to the Confucian endeavor—the cultivation of his person and imitation of the sages, the gathering of friends and students in the propagation of Wang Shou-jen's teachings—and acknowledging the approbation of his peers, he asks himself:

> Can I be really bright and clear, externally as well as internally, even down to the bone and marrow, like the sun fresh from a bath in the Hsien Pond, totally without the dark clouds of worldliness or other misty impurities? In a large assembly and among the mass of people, I appear to be amiable and faultless enough; but in private can I really be strict with myself and commit nothing dishonorable in the eyes of the supernatural beings? (*Wang Lung-ch'i ch'üan-chi*, 15:17b)

Then he launches into a bill of particulars:

> I seem to love all people, but I may be too indiscriminate. I seem to be much concerned with the affairs of the world, but I may be too pedantic in my approach. Sometimes I give full rein to my passions in dealing with people, yet I take it as being consistent in my likes and dislikes. Sometimes I form partisan alliances and attack outsiders, which I justify by pretending to be impartial. When I do someone a favor and continue to remember it, I err in exaggeration. When I fail to repay favors done me by others, I am ungrateful. My integrity is compromised when I let calculations guide my actions. If I take my conjecture as true understanding, then my judgment suffers. (Ibid., 15:17a–b)

His self-stricture, growing in harshness, culminates in the final disclosure: "What is worst of all is that my evil thoughts and desires to deceive Heaven and humanity grow in secrecy and emerge from time to time. Only my concern for reputation has held them in check. All these, witnessed by gods and spirits, bring about retribution" (Ibid., 15:17b).

What is most remarkable is his awareness of the complexity of human motives, the disparities between appearances and inner workings. He does not simply list his faults but seeks the truth even behind what may have seemed to be his good points. Indeed he seems to have rejected the primacy of innate knowledge and repudiated his past when he goes on to say: "I used to be so self-confident that even if the whole world had condemned my position I would not have changed. Nothing could have swayed my mind. Now I realize that the difference between the fearless independence of a gentleman and the impudence of a mean person is very slight. It all depends on the subtle motive behind every thought" (Ibid.)

If *liang-chih*, as defined by the Wang school, is the mind that knows right from wrong, then it is puzzling that Wang Chi fails to indicate what role *liang-chih* has played in his arrival at his present state of awareness. Does his *liang-chih* protest at all when his "evil thoughts and desires to deceive Heaven and humanity grow in secrecy and emerge from time to time"? Is it his *liang-chih* that has responded to the calamity and prompted his self-scrutiny? Wang Chi's failure to involve *liang-chih* in his self-stricture leads us to assume that while *liang-chih* may point out the right course of action, it does not judge, as conscience does, deeds already perpetrated. This difference between *liang-chih* and conscience as the term is understood in the West is borne out in all the subsequent penitential texts.

Within a few years of Wang-Chi's unprecedented self-indictment there appeared another penitential text written by the monk Chu-hung (1535–1615). Entitled *Tzu-tse* (Self-Reproach), it narrates in a straightforward manner all his wrongdoings:

> In my youth, before I took orders, I did not know the Three Treasures, nor did I believe in retribution. It goes without saying that I committed various evils with my body, speech, and thought. After taking orders, although I have been vigilant in the larger matters concerning body, I have overlooked some small points. As for speech I have erred even more. I indulge so much in desultory discourse on worldly issues that I absent myself from correct thinking. I speculate out of ignorance and end in deviating from the holy scripture. I give free rein to my tongue and offend the leaders of the day. I am wantonly critical and reproachful, humiliating the young and the lowly. In this way countless evils have been caused by speech. As for thought, my errors are even greater. Greed, desire, anger, envy, foolishness, and obsession come and go at random. Sometimes they seem to disappear but actually they are always present. Sometimes I am carried away by the moment and forget to hold them in check; at other times the more I try to control them, the stronger they grow. In this way countless evils have been caused by my body, speech, and thought. Thus I realize that I am just an enfettered ordinary person, far removed from the Way. How am I going to fulfill the wise orders

of the Buddha, enlighten the students in their perplexities, repay the boundless kindness of my parents, or rescue sentient beings from the Sea of Sorrows? Consequently day and night I am plagued by shame, anxiety, and fear: I travel, dwell, sit, and sleep as if I were always in thorns and brambles. Therefore how can I dare to drift and idle? It is hoped that everybody will believe in my sincerity, sympathize with me, and point out my errors. Let us admonish and guide each other, so that our endeavor may succeed and the declining world be saved from the fall. This is the wish I hold most dearly, and I can never rest until it is fulfilled. I am not someone who dares to say that having perceived completely the Way he no longer depends on his teachers and friends for anything.[2]

One of the three great masters of Ming Buddhism, Chu-hung has been credited with the revival of the *uposatha* as part of the Buddhist monastic life,[3] but this piece is closer to Wang Chi's *Tzu-sung* (Self-Indictment) than to any of the Buddhist penitential texts. Although he judges his behavior against a Buddhist norm, the selection of a secular format, the absence of any invocation of Buddhist divinities, and the appeal to other mortals—friends—for mutual support all point to the blurring of religious differences in the late Ming. Like Wang Chi, Chu-hung does not name a mental faculty that points out the wrongs he has committed and admonishes and chastises him, a faculty that in the West would be called "conscience." On the other hand, when he said that "day and night I am plagued by shame, anxiety, and fear: I travel, dwell, sit, and sleep as if I were always in thorns and brambles," could it be that, unbeknownst to himself, he was describing precisely the workings of a stern conscience?

Like Chu-hung, Chang Lü-hsiang (1611–1674) also entitles his essay *Tzu-tse* (Self-Reproach). According to the notes supplied by the author himself, the piece was written in response to some unnamed event.

> You are shameless and unkind; you are impudent and unrighteous. Above, you have incurred the anger of Heaven and Earth, and the punishment has not been limited to yourself. Below, you have lost the confidence of your family and clan, and frequently you are brought into unreasonable disputes. Alas! Why can't you understand?
>
> When I see how wrong and wicked I am, I wish to die. But when I realize that there is none to whom I could entrust the ancestral sacrifices, I dare not forsake life. It is difficult either to live or to die.

---

[2] *Tzu-tse* (Self-Reproach), in *Yun-ch'i ta-shih i-kao* (Written legacy of Master Chu-hung), vol. 31 of *Yun-ch'i fa-hui* (Collected works of Chu-hung) (Nanking: Chin-ling k'o-ching-ch'u, 1897), 3:86a–87a.

[3] See Chün-fang Yü, *The Renewal of Buddhism in China: Chu-hung and the late Ming Synthesis* (New York: Columbia University Press, 1981), pp. 199–202.

The only way is to discipline myself strictly and harshly, moving in the direction of goodness and distancing myself from guilt. Every day I shall be more careful than the day before. I hope in my old age I shall have completely redeemed myself.[4]

The unnamed event, judging from the above, must have been a family dispute possibly combined with or resulting in a personal misfortune. It is surprising that Chang, well known for his Neo-Confucian work, his moral integrity, and his unflinching loyalty to the fallen Ming, should have been so harsh in judging himself. What interests us most in his essay is the use of the second-person singular in the first paragraph. It is obvious that the grammatical subject stands for Chang himself while the words of reproof are uttered by the self and addressed to the self. Again *liang-chih* or the mind plays no explicit role here. In the West conscience is frequently described as the ethical voice of the individual—the "voice of conscience" being a common metaphor. In the hour of Chang's moral crisis there is apparently no need of an additional agency: we might say that for Chang *self* is *conscience*.

In 1669, three years after he wrote *Tzu-tse* (Self-Reproach), Chang composed a treatise on self-compounds, in which he further demonstrated that the self can be an active and sufficient agent, enabling every individual to lead a moral life without reference to *liang-chih*, conscience, divinity, or even Confucian scriptural authority. He began the treatise by listing a hundred compounds, each of which is formed by a verb prefixed by the character *tzu* (self). The first forty-six compounds fall into twenty-three pairs of opposites; for instance, self-succeeding and self-defeating, self-respecting and self-debasing. The next twenty all have a negative meaning in compounds such as self-abandoning, self-justifying, self-indulging, and self-injuring. These are followed by eight compounds that suggest introspection, penitence, and rehabilitation: self-mirroring, self-reflecting, self-blaming, self-criticizing, self-cleansing, self-healing, self-renewing, and self-lifting. The next group continues the upward movement, with self-understanding as the connecting element. The affirmative sequence goes on as follows: self-acting, self-encouraging, self-searching, self-cultivating, self-governing, self-manifesting, self-achieving, self-appointing, self-establishing, self-valuing, self-cherishing, self-fulfilling, self-guiding, self-examining, self-restraining, self-anguishing, self-alerting, self-strengthening, self-restoring, and self-being. The list ends with a category of qualities that suggests a vigorous, autonomous individual with a will free and strong: self-mastering, self-loving, self-directing, self-deciding, and self-choosing.[5]

---

[4] *Yang-yüan hsien-sheng ch'üan-chi* (Complete works of Master Chang Lü-hsiang) (Nanking: Chiang-su shu-chu, 1872), 23:5a.

[5] Ibid., 20:28a–30a.

The list clearly expresses, simply by the grouping and ordering of the compounds, the progression that Chang envisioned for a moral being, but he appended to the list an exposition of the implications. "All men are born of Heaven in the identical way. Yet they differ in intelligence and character. Who causes it? It is each man himself who causes it. This is why there are differences in rank and position, diversities in accomplishment and fortune." He cites all the negative compounds as results of the willful choice of evil. After explaining the process of self-redemption, the treatise concludes on an optimistic note.

> Everything depends on the self-acting of each individual. When his will to self-acting is strong, he is capable of self-mastering. This will lead to his self-loving. When his heart of self-love is firm, he is capable of self-direction. He will then know what the gains should be and what the losses should be. He will know what to take and what to forgo; he will know how to decide and how to choose.[6]

Other writers of penitential texts frequently concluded their essays with hope, but none wrote about redemption with as much conviction as Chang did in his treatise. Nor had the problem of free will, never explicitly formulated in Chinese philosophy, been confronted in such a forthright manner. Indeed Chang's serene certitude recalls an earlier age when the robust optimism of classical Confucianism had not yet been eroded.[7]

THE SELF ON TRIAL: LIU TSUNG-CHOU'S IMAGINARY TRIBUNAL

During the Ming, the concern for moral improvement through self-rectification was not limited to the scholar-official class. Didactic tracts writ-

---

[6] Ibid., 20:29a–30a. Vytautas Kavolis in his illuminating article, "On the Self-Person Differentiation," in *Designs of Selfhood*, ed. Vytautas Kavolis (Cranbury, N.J.: Associated University Press, 1984), maintains that seventeenth-century England was by far the most productive period for the coinage of self- compounds. "The peak of productivity in the seventeenth century suggests an increased preoccupation with the problem of the self and its relations with its semantic environment" (p. 136). It is not at present feasible to determine how many among Chang's one hundred compounds were coined in his day; however, the very fact that a collection of such magnitude should have been made in 1669 but not earlier is another measure of the change in Chinese moral culture that took place during the hundred years after Wang Chi wrote his *Self-Indictment*. For a comprehensive and cogent account of the intellectual and spiritual background of seventeenth-century China in general and the Ming experience of the self in particular, see Wm. Theodore de Bary, "Individualism and Humanitarianism in Late Ming Thought," in *Self and Society*, pp. 145–248, as well as his introduction to the same book, pp. 1–28.

[7] Chang's short essay can also be read as the most concise statement of the kind of "Neo-Confucian ethic" to which scholars in recent years have attributed the economic successes of the newly industrialized countries in East Asia.

ten in plain language, embodying the syncretic belief in retribution and aiming at all walks of life, known collectively as the *shan-shu* (morality books), circulated widely throughout China. The most popular subgroup of the *shan-shu* was the *Kung-kuo ko*, or *Ledgers of Merits and Demerits*. In such books good and bad deeds are each assigned a number of positive or negative points. The reader is instructed to enter into the ledger at the end of each day his good and bad deeds with their numerical values. Offsetting positive points against negative points he would arrive at his moral balance for the day, just as a storekeeper does with his account book.[8]

During the Ming many members of the scholar-official class kept moral ledgers, while others rejected the practice on the ground that it was too utilitarian, calculating, and mechanical. Liu Tsung-chou (1578–1645), the great Neo-Confucian renowned for his loyalty to the fallen Ming, was an especially severe critic of this type of moral bookkeeping. However, his book, the *Jen-p'u* (A manual for men), is essentially a specimen of the genre he rejected. One section of the book, entitled "Sung-kuo fa" (A method for the prosecution of bad deeds), is worthy of detailed analysis. Since Liu believed that good deeds should be performed for their own sake rather than to offset bad deeds, it became necessary to find a way to purge the bad deeds one had already committed. His "Method" serves this purpose by combining confession with a dramatization of self-castigation.

The "Method" begins like a confessional in a religious setting, somewhat reminiscent of the Taoist purification rite mentioned earlier, yet characteristically ambiguous about any actual divine presence in a Confucian ritual. "I put a bowl of water and a stick of burning incense on a clean table. In front of it I place a rush mat. After dawn, I sit on the mat facing the table in the lotus position, erect and reverent. I hold back my breath and assume a serious mien, as if there were a majestic and awesome presence to whom I confess my misdeeds without concealment."[9] The solitary ritual then turns into an imitation of a trial with the self playing alternately the role of accuser and defendant:

---

[8] For a study of the subject see Sakai Tadao, *Chūgoku zensho no kenkyū* (A study of Chinese morality books) (Tokyo: Kōbundō, 1960), pp. 356–98. It is a curious coincidence that Puritans in seventeenth-century England also engaged in activities which may be described as moral bookkeeping. For instance, as quoted in George A. Starr, *Defoe and Spiritual Autobiography* (Princeton: Princeton University Press, 1965), p. 11, Thomas Gouge proclaimed in 1679: "As he is the best Tradesman that every day in the Evening taketh an account of his worldly losses and gains; so he is the best Christian that every day in the Evening taketh an account of his spiritual losses and gains whether he go forward in the ways of Godliness." Starr cites other examples and discusses their implications on pp. 9–13.

[9] *Jen-p'u* (Taipei: Shang-wu yin-shu-kuan, 1968), p. 11; hereafter referred to as *Jen-p'u*.

I proceed to accuse myself, saying: "You certainly have the appearance of a human being. But once you have stumbled, you act like a
beast. Degradation after degradation, you never stop." I reply, "Yes!
Yes!" I then imagine that the above accusations are repeated by ten
voices, while ten eyes and ten fingers are staring and pointing at me.
I again reply, "Yes! Yes!" At this moment my heart throbs. Bitter
sweat begins to flow, my face flushes, as if my body were being tortured in a court of law. Thereupon I leap up and shout, "I am guilty!"
I then accuse myself further, "You are making an insincere confession!" To that I reply, "No! No!" (*Jen-p'u*, p. 11)

To a student of the history of conscience in the West, Liu's psychodrama must have a familiar ring. The representation of moral self-scrutiny as a judiciary process has a long tradition that began with Greek and
Roman writers, was strengthened by Judeo-Christian religion, and continues down to this day, if no longer as literal truth, at least as a powerful
metaphor. But in the West the self is divided into two components during
the trial, with conscience as the accuser and the soul as the accused. For
instance, Philo in *On the Decalogue* (87) states that "For every soul has for
its birth-fellow and house-mate a monitor whose way is to admit nothing
that calls for censure, whose nature is ever to hate evil and love virtue,
who is its accuser and its judge in one."[10] To Polybius there is "no witness
so fearful nor accuser so terrible as the conscience which dwells in the
soul of every man."[11] Relying on both classical and biblical sources, the
Reformation theologian John Calvin makes the judiciary theme even
more explicit. To him conscience serves as "an additional witness" for
men, which "permits them not to conceal their sins, or to elude accusa-
tion at the tribunal of the supreme Judge. . . ." Furthermore conscience,
"which places man before the Divine tribunal, is appointed, as it were, to
watch over man, to observe and examine all his secrets, and nothing may
remain enveloped in darkness. Hence the old proverb, Conscience is as a
thousand witnesses."[12] With Liu, however, just as in all the penitential
texts discussed in this study, the self is not divided into conscience and
soul but plays the twin roles alternately. Allowing for this difference,
Liu's psychodrama corresponds point for point with the Western theme
of the soul on trial. The tortures inflicted on Liu with their resultant man-
ifestations of agony have a counterpart in the so-called pangs of con-

---

[10] Quoted in *The Interpreter's Dictionary of the Bible*, ed. George Arthur Buttrick et al., 12
vols. (New York: Abingdon Press, 1962), 1:673.

[11] Ibid.

[12] *Institutes of the Christian Religion*, trans. John Allen, 6th American ed., 2 vols. (Philadelphia: Westminister Press, 1936), 2:91. I wish to thank Irene Bloom for calling my attention
to this reference.

science or fire of remorse; the accusing voices, angry stares, and pointing fingers that confront Liu, although a classical Confucian allusion,[13] recall the Western proverb quoted by John Calvin.

One fundamental difference between Chinese and Western moral discourse is the latter's richness in personification and allegory. For this reason, conscience has amassed such a wealth of associations that no Chinese concept could possibly match it. *Liang-chih* has been likened to a scale or a compass, but it has never acted as a judge, a critic, or a tormentor. When translators around the turn of the century were seeking a word to render "conscience" into Chinese, they settled on another Mencian term, *liang-hsin*, rather than *liang-chih*. Today *liang-hsin* does reproach or punish, but in spite of ample Westernization it still cannot turn bad or become sick. The lack of a name should not deny Chinese self-examiners the equivalent of a conscience, if we agree with Austin Warren that "self-castigation, repentance, the determination to lead a new life which must be bound up with true penitence, are the chief functions of conscience."[14]

WEI HSI, THE GUILTY CONFUCIAN

The need to bare one's soul, first seen in Wang Chi when he wrote his self-indictment in 1570, culminated with Wei Hsi (1624–1681) about a century later. A native of Ning-tu in mountainous east Kiangsi, Wei Hsi and his two brothers were well known for their literary and practical talents. When chaos spread to east Kiangsi after the fall of the Ming dynasty, the Weis moved to a secluded area high in the mountains where they, assisted by other kindred spirits from their county, built a fortified colony and subsisted on farming and hunting. At night Neo-Confucian and literary studies were resumed. The security of the place and the literary fame of the group, as well as their discreet resistance activities, soon attracted a large following. In the neighboring county, Nan-feng, another group of Neo-Confucian scholars was formed at about the same time. Both groups remained loyal to the fallen dynasty. In their philosophical outlook the members of the Ning-tu group were sympathetic to the Wang Shou-jen school, while those of the Nan-feng group eventually returned to the Ch'eng-Chu persuasion. But philosophical differences never interfered with the strong alliance and easy camaraderie between the two groups. Wei Hsi traveled a great deal all his life, partly on behalf of the resistance movement and partly because of his own propensities.

When Wei Hsi reached the age of twenty-nine, he was still without a

[13] The *Great Learning*, 6:3: "When ten eyes are staring and ten hands are pointing [at you], how stern [the judgment] is!"

[14] *The New England Conscience* (Ann Arbor: University of Michigan Press, 1966), pp. 13–14.

son, a serious plight in traditional China. His own father and his teacher Yang Wen-ts'ai had had the same difficulties, but by pleading to the God of the Dipper each had subsequently been blessed with three sons. His distress and the knowledge of the apparently proven remedy induced him to write the following memorial addressed to the same god:

God, you are immense in your kindness to men and unfathomable in your miraculous ways. You act as the pivot of the meridian, and in bestowing light on the earth you are mankind's exemplar. Respectfully I make my obeisance and fearfully I express my repentance. I am a mere student, having lived half my life amid old books. At fifteen I married my wife with whom I have been living happily. Without a son at thirty, I have failed to please my parents. In the past when the country was strong and prosperous, I used to hope for the honors that children would bring to the family; now that mourning and disorders alternate with each other, I find it easy to hurry through a life span. Nevertheless I am aware that to have a son is to defeat death and that to be without posterity is the gravest sin against one's parents. Perhaps the punishment has been handed down from Heaven, but the guilt was entirely my own making. Recollecting past wrongdoings further aggravates my present sorrows. My mind always notices my erratic propensities, but my actions constantly bring new grief. Carried away by my righteous indignation, I frequently behave recklessly and in the end cause unintended harm. Giving free rein to my desires and indulging my passions, my wicked thoughts often pervert my virtue. On every occasion I am prompted by selfishness, seeking my own gain without considering injuries done to others. Now and then I do some small charity or help others in an inconsequential way. Although I act without thought of seeking divine blessings, afterwards I always expect repayment. The heavenly principle within me cannot overcome the rampancy of my selfish desires; my intention to do good is never as firm as my love of repute. In attending to my parents I am especially remiss. With indolent limbs I never exert myself in waiting on them; by failing to cultivate social virtues I wilfully disobey their orders. Their son has failed them, but they long for grandsons. I feel their disappointments and dread to be alone and childless. Therefore I shall imitate the good and mend my ways, never again wallowing in self-despair. To bring about good fortune and to fend off disaster, I shall daily strengthen my cultivation and self-examination. Although everything is predestined, great good deeds can still alter the course of events. Even guilty men can please the gods with the slightest sign of sincerity. I respectfully plead to the Supreme Being to extend his kindness to living beings, and beg the Mysterious Heaven to open the gate of repentance. Please bestow on me new blessings and forgive my former transgressions. Do not let me cause further decline in my family as an unworthy son, nor disappoint my parents in their longing for grandchildren and honorable descendants.[15]

With the growth of syncretism and the popularity of many Taoist practices and beliefs among numerous otherwise quite-strict Confucians, this appeal to the God of the Dipper cannot be regarded as extraordinary. Both Wei's father and teacher were certainly Confucians, yet when they were desperate for sons, they felt no qualms about trying a Taoist remedy. As we have mentioned earlier, the long tradition of the Taoist confessional has unfortunately left no written transcriptions. Wei's memorial may well have the distinction of being the earliest extant specimen of the Taoist confession. Another unusual circumstance was the inclusion of this piece in the collected works of a prominent Confucian, for even Wei himself felt somewhat uneasy about the whole thing. He mentions in a postscript written in 1663 that even when he was going through the ritual he was "two-minded" about it, reverent to the divinity but sceptical about the efficacy of the undertaking. The only reason that he included the article in the collection is that "the words of self-indictment are quite appropriate" (*Wei Shu-tzu wen-chi*, 6:2738). Whether he is overconscientious or not, the piece accords with the state of fear, anxiety, and remorse that recurs in his writings. His recorded dreams betray a deep-seated anxiety that must have plagued him constantly. When he was forty-three years old, he still dreamt of his childhood teacher, Yang Wen-ts'ai. In a letter to the two sons of his late teacher he reports that

I dreamt that I was in bed when my late teacher called me to get up. He pointed out for me six or seven of my misdeeds, all involving basic human relations. His reproach touched my deep-seated maladies. Criticizing my luxury in daily living, his countenance was kinder but his words harsher than in the old days. When I woke up I was moved to tears by my gratitude to him. He and I were as close as father and son. Even now every morning I bow reverently to his memory, which remains vivid and real to me. My teacher's love for me was such that, as evidenced by the dream, it bridges that gap between the world of the dead and the world of the living. (Ibid., 2:837)

[15] *Wei Shu-tzu wen-chi* (Collected writings of Wei Hsi) 7 vols. (late 17th-century ed.; reprint, Taipei: Shang-wu yin-shu-kuan, 1973), 6:2735–37; hereafter referred to as *Wei Shu-tzu wen-chi*.

From the dream it is clear that Wei never concealed anything from his strict but beloved teacher. At his teacher's knee he may even have acquired the habit of reporting truthfully every dream, for in writing about his dreams Wei is unprecedentedly candid. The confessions written in China up to this time never disclose any specific sinful act with particularities such as time, place, or accomplices. The lack of specificity in self-disclosure was of course universal: in the West the admission of particular deeds of which the author is really ashamed began only with the Puritans. Saint Augustine was the sole exception. Saint Theresa, in spite of lengthy examinations of the self, is vague when she writes about her sins.

The dreams Wei had during his travels in 1675 were more frightful; the worst and most revealing one he dreamt while lodging in a Buddhist temple on the tenth day of the ninth month:

> I dreamt that I was sharing a bed with the abbot and the receptionist. The three of us spent the whole night talking about intimate and lewd matters. At dawn the receptionist got up, but suddenly he bent over, clutching the bedding and screaming with pain. His eyes froze into a fixed state, very much like those of a dead goat. Instantly his body became dead stiff. Startled, I ran into the hall, where a milling mob was loudly discussing the incident. What I could make out was that the monk was struck by the Divine Judge (Ling-kuan) who was going to cut him open and pluck out his heart. Suddenly the Divine Judge appeared, carrying in his hand entrails dripping with blood. He threw them on the ground and ordered that they be eaten by dogs. Then he nodded to me and motioned for me to come forward. He pointed to his heart and said to me: "This is something no man likes to lose. You'd better behave yourself." Although he spoke mildly, his meaning was quite menacing. I was very frightened for I thought he must have known what I had discussed with the monks during the night. The mob again became clamorous. They began to denounce the dead monk, saying, "He used to injure people in another temple; this time he came here to do more harm." A coffin was carried in but the mob could not fit the dead monk into it now that his legs were firmly bent. When I saw his blood-smeared clothes I ran into the kitchen, wishing to find water to wash my face. Suddenly I came upon Uncle Tu-fei, my father's cousin. As I put down the water basin in order to make obeisance to him I woke up. (Ibid., 6:2818–19)

On one level this dream can be read as a typical *shan-shu* story, a cautionary tale embellished by the vivid imagination of a literary man. A Freudian, however, would detect significance in the gory detail, the macabre sequence, and above all in the gnawing realization on the part of the dreamer that even though he was not yet punished, he could never escape the deepening implication, the envelopment of guilt. A most revealing detail is his running to the kitchen to wash after witnessing the blood-smeared body of the lesser monk, even though physically he himself was not soiled. The urgent search for water is a symbolic representation of the need to expurgate the inner stain. We have in this dream almost every symptom of Freudian guilt: shame over wrongdoings of a sexual nature, anxiety about possible discovery, and fear of the punishment of mutilation. The unexpected encounter with a clan elder near the end of the dream echoes the earlier confrontation with the punitive Divine Judge, for both can be seen as the same superego under different guises. In fact, reproach by a father figure who returns from the world of the dead is a recurring theme in Wei's dreams. In addition to his teacher, his father is another disturber of his peaceful slumbers. The following account, written by Wei when he was forty-nine years old, indicates that the father of his dreams must have been a Freudian father par excellence.

> In my childhood I was frequently sick. On the days of ancestral sacrifices I often got up late, which repeatedly angered my father. Sometimes his anger was so great that for days he remained implacable. He passed away nineteen years ago. During the first ten years after his death I dreamt of him two or three times a month. From the eleventh year up to this day I have dreamt of him four or five times a year. But I have been unfilial. Deeply engrossed in my bad habits, I have not been able to prevent my kind father from worrying about me in the other world. He has had ample cause for anger and little for rejoicing. (Ibid., 4:1637)

Shame naturally accompanies a man when he reviews his own wrongdoings. It is also natural that his sense of shame will incline him toward concealment, omission, or rationalization. In this regard guilt will, under certain moral climates and in some situations, counteract shame, for guilt compels self-disclosure as an act of expiation. Self-disclosure may bring shame to the sinner, but it palliates or even absolves one from guilt. Humiliation resulting from self-abasement in public is a part of the expiation of sins. This is why in faith healing, from the peasant uprisings in the Later Han to Alcoholics Anonymous of modern-day America, confession plays a crucial role. One might even say that in all writers of self-stricture guilt prevails over shame, and the more specific the revelation, the greater the feeling of guilt. Wei Hsi cannot even comment on his dreams without revealing more of his guilty self. "Even now I shiver when I recall the chilling experience. All my life I have never actually committed any debauchery, but the thought of it arose whenever there was a possible occasion. Fortunately, circumstances were never such that perpetration was possible. But frequently I indulged in lewd imagination. Bad deeds were about to bear fruit when gods sent down timely warnings" (ibid., 6:2819). Then he goes on to report a friend's dream. The dream itself is as bizarre as his own, but in reporting the circumstances attendant on his hearing of it he confesses yet another specific sinful act of his own:

> In the *jen-tzu* year [1672] I visited Soochow. One day early in the morning Tseng T'ing-wen sent a messenger to summon me. When I arrived at his door he came out to welcome me. Looking puzzled, he said: "I had a strange dream. I dreamt that you and my younger brother Ch'ing-li were together copulating with a sow. Then I heard someone remarking that the late Mr. Wei—your worthy father—was respected by gods and spirits on account of his never having committed debauchery. When I woke up I wondered if it could be that you had recently misbehaved." When I heard this I began to sweat. At that time Ch'ing-li was keeping company with a prostitute. I frequently flirted with her and strongly desired her. Although I knew that it could not be done, still I was unable to put the thought out of my mind. But the matter was not known to T'ing-wen. I am now writing this down both as a warning to myself and as an instruction to the younger generation of my family. They must realize that the way of divine perspicuity is never afar. (Ibid., 6:2819–20)

Seventeenth-century Neo-Confucians seem to have had much in common with their Puritan contemporaries: both groups, among other things, were given to harsh self-examination and were deeply concerned with spiritual progress. Earlier we observed the curious coincidence that both groups were frequently engaged in a practice that may be called moral bookkeeping. A detailed comparison, however, would take us too far afield.[16] I shall limit myself to citing one dream of an American contemporary of Wei Hsi's to show that Confucian and Puritan alike were tempted by lust, viewed the frailty of their own flesh with utter disgust, and, above all, perhaps in each case an innovation against their own culture's convention of discretion, felt the same urge to confess in writing in spite of shame. The guilt-ridden Massachusetts clergyman Wigglesworth (1631–1705), like Wei Hsi, was plagued all his life by ill health, troubled by bad relations with his father, and haunted by indelicate dreams, as revealed in his diary. He recorded on February 17, 1653: "The last night a filthy dream and so pollution escaped me in my sleep for which I desire

---

[16] In his book, *The Religion of China: Confucianism and Taoism*, trans. Hans H. Gerth (New York: MacMillan, 1964), Max Weber made sustained attempts to compare Confucianism and Puritanism but his total lack of access to Neo-Confucian spiritual autobiography and penitential literature led him to questionable conclusions.

to hang down my head with shame and beseech the Lord not to make me possess the sin of my youth and give me into the hands of my abomination."[17]

SHAME OR GUILT

There are plenty of additional penitential materials pertaining to the late Ming and early Ch'ing, but a full discussion of these texts, interesting as they are, would take us further away from the main concern of this book. A brief summary will suffice.

Hai Jui (1513–1587) seems to have anticipated Liu Tsung-chou's imaginary tribunal by acting as his own judge. He summoned his own spirit (*shen*) before him and examined it for all possible failings. The spirit then swore humbly to reform.[18] Yüan Chung-tao (1570–1624) wrote a treatise on the discipline of the mind, which includes long sections on his transgressions. As a Buddhist-Confucian he is reminiscent of Shen Yüeh, but his revelations are more detailed and his remorse more intense. Li Yung (1627–1705) addressed a curious document to his students. Entitled *Yü t'ien yüeh* (A covenant with Heaven), the document begins as a self-stricture very reminiscent of Liu Tsung-chou's "Sung-kuo fa" (A method for the prosecution of bad deeds). It then exhorts the students to examine themselves every day in a ritualistic setting and to call on Heaven to be a witness to their moral endeavor.[19] Similar to other penitential texts where self-reproach is the main theme, the document is suffused with a sense of anguish and urgency.

Concurrent with the repentant mood was a pessimistic assessment of human nature, another departure from classical Confucianism. At the beginning of his *Jen-p'u* (A manual for men), Liu Tsung-chou lists five basic steps for achieving humanity (*cheng-jen*). He then states with undisguised pessimism that "before a student has gone through the five steps his whole person is covered with sins (*tsui-kuo*). Even after he has gone through them he is still covered all over with sins."[20] On another occasion he admonishes his students by saying: "Since we are all deeply engrossed in our habits, everything we do is evil, not just a fault. Students should concentrate on the problem of ridding themselves of evils. This is not yet the time to talk about correcting faults."[21] This sense of all-pervading sin

---

[17] *The Diary of Michael Wigglesworth, 1653–1675*, ed. Edmund Morgan (New York: Harper & Row, 1965), p. 5.

[18] *Hai Jui chi* (Collected works of Hai Jui) (Peking: Chung-hua shu-chü, 1962), pp. 1–2.

[19] *Erh-ch'ü chi* (Collected works of Li Yung) (Taipei: Shang-wu yin-shu kuan, 1973), 19:13a–b.

[20] *Jen-p'u*, p. 6.

[21] *MJHA*, p. 689.

and personal responsibility is echoed by Lü K'un (1536–1618), who in his autonecrology proclaims: "My mind is responsible for all the sins (*tsui-kuo*) of my person; my limbs and organs are guiltless. My person is responsible for all the sins in the universe; heaven and earth and the myriad things are guiltless."[22]

To realize that such somberness and anguish is a new development in the history of Chinese moral culture we need only examine the records before 1570. Except for Shen Yüeh's ceremonial text there is hardly any writing surviving from that long era that may be considered as self-stricture. The sole piece bearing the name of *tzu-sung* (self-indictment) exists only to prove our point: it is written with no expression of remorse or resolution to reform. The author, Liu Shu, an eleventh-century historian, simply gives a list of twenty faults and twenty-eight defects, none of them very serious. I shall quote just the first five from each category.

> FAULTS: Impatient and irritable, I frequently lose my temper over small matters. Upright and high-minded, in my moral indignation I ignore consequences. Attached to the ancient and contemptuous of the modern, I run against the times. Suspicious and indecisive, I labor much to no avail. Having a high opinion of myself, I measure my peers to see if they are more than my match.

> DEFECTS: My language is broad but my aim is small. I love to offer advice and pontificate. I am loquacious and indiscriminate. I try to be cautious but inadvertently reveal secrets. I respect style and integrity but am narrow and petty.[23]

This list is followed by a concluding remark: "It is not that I don't regret after the fact, but the next day I err again. I blame and ridicule myself, but why I behave as I do, I do not understand."[24] His good-natured toleration of himself, his sunny resignation to more erring, his refusal to delve into motives and responsibilities, and above all, his reticence on

---

[22] *Lü K'un che-hsüeh hsüan-chi* (Selected philosophical works of Lü K'un), ed. Hou Wai-lu (Peking: Chung-hua shu-chü, 1962), p. 84. Although avowals of specific offenses are not found in the kind of autobiography that we have seen in the first three sections of this study, one author, Chang Tai (1597–1684?), expresses remorse for his "crimes" in his self-written preface to a collection of essays. After giving a list of contrasts between his former extravagances and present destitution he goes on to say: "My crimes are seen in the retributions that have been visited on me. . . . How am I going to bear the thought? I decide to write down things of the past whenever I recall them, and then I bring them before the Buddha and repent them one by one." *T'ao-an meng-i* (T'ao-an's remembrances of dreams) (Taipei: T'ai-wan k'ai-ming shu-chü, 1972), p. 1. His promise notwithstanding, the essays reveal no deeds of his own that can be considered as crimes. For a complete translation of the preface see Owen, *Remembrances*, pp. 134–35.

[23] *LTW*, 2:523–24.

[24] Ibid., 2:524.

serious offenses contrast with the conscience-stricken writers previously discussed.

The same fundamental optimism and sobriety seem to hold sway among the Sung Neo-Confucian philosophers. I have not been able to locate any sign of anguish or remorse expressed by the masters over their own misdeeds, even though self-examination has always been a basic tenet of Confucianism. So far I have found only two general statements on self-reproach made by Sung philosophers. Ch'eng I says: "To blame and reproach one's self is something that cannot be dispensed with. But it should not be carried on too long, causing lingering remorse in one's heart."[25] Chu Hsi is quoted as follows: "If tonight someone feels ashamed and remorseful about something and next day succeeds in giving it up completely, then it is all right. If he cannot but relapse, then what use is it to feel ashamed and remorseful?"[26] A guilty conscience is something the two masters would not have approved of.

The anguish over personal wrongdoings, the acceptance of individual responsibility, the pessimistic view of man, and the insistence on self-disclosure and repentance that we have sketched represent one strain, though perhaps a minor one, in the complex fabric of the intellectual and spiritual history of the late Ming and early Ch'ing. As we have shown, however, this strain is a new development and one that defines a basic difference between Sung and Ming Neo-Confucianism. Many factors contributed to the formation of such a somber mood. The Buddhist view of human existence, the syncretic emphasis on sin and punishment, the reality of social and economic disintegration, corrupt administrations under some of the worst emperors, the decline in moral behavior of the gentry and literati, and the brutal persecution and martyrdom of Neo-Confucian officials all played a part. One manifestation of this strain, I believe, is a sense of guilt.

In his stimulating pioneer work on guilt and sin in traditional China, Wolfram Eberhard has suggested that "the upper class of a society typically attempts or propagates socialization of the masses by a system based upon guilt, while relying upon shame as the socializing factor for themselves. In other words, perhaps Confucianism, as the ideology of China's elite of the traditional period, was built upon the principle of shame."[27] Eberhard's suggestion may very well be true for China up to the late sixteenth century; after 1570 guilt, at least for a significant number of Neo-

---

[25] Quoted in Chang Wei-hsin, Pien-chi ming-yen (Well-known sayings on self-admonition) (1591 ed.; National Library of Peiping microfilm), 24:33a.

[26] Ibid., 24:33b.

[27] Guilt and Sin in Traditional China (Berkeley and Los Angeles: University of California Press, 1967), p. 122. Other social scientists, unaware of the penitential literature cited in this chapter, have tended to overemphasize the role of shame in Chinese moral culture.

Confucians, seems to have played a more important role than shame. For it is guilt, as I have suggested above, that compels individuals to disclose their wrongdoings, while the predominance of shame would lead to reticence and even concealment. On the other hand, Professor Eberhard's dichotomy may remain valid if we argue that by the seventeenth century Chinese society was already sufficiently egalitarian for a blurring of class differentiation in moral culture.

As THE seventeenth century was approaching its end, peace was once again established in China, the pattern of dynastic stability following decades of upheaval having reasserted itself. The last hope of Ming loyalists died with the fall of Taiwan in 1683. Manchu rule, now fully consolidated, was efficient and vigilant. There was little tolerance of the sort of reckless behavior and bold experimentation that had thrived under the disintegrating Ming. Censorship and literary inquisition were carried out on a scale unsurpassed until recently. The Wang Shou-jen school, which could claim most of the autobiographers during the genre's golden age, was now out of favor. It had more than its share of martyrs who died for the cause of the Ming and loyalists who never succumbed to the blandishments of the new regime, but very few collaborators. Although there was no lack of soul-searching in the aftermath of the catastrophe, the survivors were more concerned with the fundamental causes of the dynastic fall than with their own participation or responsibilities. Scholars in the next and subsequent generations turned away from ontological questions to matters of philology and textual criticism. If there was still any secret longing for the blooming of a hundred flowers that had been nourished by the rank but fertile late Ming soil, the elevation of Chu Hsi to the Confucian pantheon by an imperial edict in 1712 signified to all that the court would not suffer any dissension from orthodoxy. Gone were the spiritual fervor and restlessness, the earnest belief in self-transformation, and the burning urgency in the search for ultimate truth. To a combination of all of these factors we must attribute the cessation of the kind of autobiographical writing that has been the main concern of this book.[1]

In terms of quantity Chinese autobiography did not decline after 1680, but thrived. The subgenre that flourished in the eighteenth century and later was the annalistic autobiography that seldom differed in style or format from its model, the annalistic biography. It was best suited for the charting of an official career, the recording of activities least likely to arouse the suspicions of the court. Autobiographies were once again self-written biographies. Historiography now resumed its supremacy. If au-

---

[1] The K'ang-hsi emperor, whose reign (1661–1722) witnessed the changes we have just discussed, was himself, ironically, the most autobiographical of all Chinese monarchs up to his time. He never wrote a formal autobiography, but he wrote so unabashedly and voluminously about himself that a modern historian was able to construct a long memoir for him, a first-person narrative based entirely on his own words. See Jonathan Spence, *Emperor of China: Self-Portrait of K'ang-hsi* (New York: Alfred A. Knopf, 1974).

tobiographies are, or should be, in the representative words of a recent critic, "private, meditative, nostalgic, and seemingly informal, preoccupied more often than not with the personal life, and imbued with sentiment and a kind of wistfulness,"[2] then hardly anything I have examined that was written in China between 1680 and 1900, with only one exception, would pass the test. But what an exception!

During those two long centuries there may have been voices crying in the wilderness, but they are lost to us if the voices were not recorded or the records were not preserved. Fate permitted the survival of only one autobiography that preserves an individual voice and affords us a glimpse of a private world. Written by Shen Fu (b. 1763), a hapless and obscure figure, the manuscript of the *Fu-sheng liu-chi* was not discovered and printed until this century.[3] The discovery could not have come at a more propitious time, for the Chinese reading public had then just acquired a taste for the autobiographical form through translations of Western works as well as a new appreciation of types of traditional sensibilities rediscovered in the aftermath of the May Fourth movement. Shen Fu's long-lost work rapidly became the most widely read as well as the most frequently translated Chinese autobiography. It has even been made into a film—a dubious distinction shared by no other premodern Chinese autobiography. It is at once an important link between traditional and modern Chinese autobiography and a touchstone for the universality of the genre. The description of autobiography quoted in the preceding paragraph seems to fit Shen Fu's story point by point, even more than any of its Western counterparts, although the modern critic, judging by the tone and content of his article, could not have had the Chinese work in mind when he made the above formulation. Clearly this delightful masterpiece deserves a critical evaluation on a scale well beyond the scope of the present study.[4] To account for the wide appeal of Shen Fu's life story, to do

[2] Paul Jay, "What's the Use? Critical Theory and the Study of Autobiography," *Biography* 10, no. 1 (Winter 1987): 51. In China this kind of autobiographical sensibility, no longer welcome in self-written biography, found its fullest expression in the great eighteenth-century novel, *The Dream of the Red Chamber*.

[3] The book has been translated several times into European languages. The most readable among them are: Shen Fu, *Six Records of a Floating Life*, trans. Leonard Pratt and Chian Su-hui (London: Penguin Books, 1983) and Shen Fu, *Six récits au fils inconstant de jours*, trans. Pierre Ryckmans (Brussels: Larcier, 1966).

[4] Three recent representatives of what seems to be a rapidly growing critical literature on Shen Fu are: Owen, *Remembrances*, pp. 100–113; Han-liang Chang, "The Anonymous Autobiographer: Roland Barthes/Shen Fu," *The Chinese Text: Studies in Comparative Literature*, ed. Ying-hsiung Chou (Hong Kong: Chinese University Press, 1986), pp. 61–73; and Jonathan Hall, "Heroic Repression: Narrative and Aesthetics in Shen Fu's *Six Records of a Floating Life*," *Comparative Criticism* 9 (1987): 155–72.

justice to its complex fortunes in the twentieth century, a full-fledged evaluation of it may need to provide a detailed comparison between Chinese and Western autobiographical traditions, something I have hitherto attempted only in passing. Limitations of space dictate that such a comparison must await a future occasion.

APPENDIX A

T'ung Yang-shan Hsüeh-yen ho-shang i ssu shu
(A letter to Master Hsüeh-yen [Tsu-ch'in]
of Yang-shan expressing doubts about
succeeding him) by Yüan-miao (1238–1295)

LAST TIME I was in a quandary I made a thorough confession before you, my master. Now that I am in doubt again, I cannot help but retell the story from the beginning. I left home at fifteen and became a monk at sixteen. I studied the T'ien-t'ai teachings at eighteen, and at twenty I changed my affiliation and entered into the Ching-tz'u Temple, where I set myself a three-year limit in studying Ch'an. I asked instructions from Master Tuan-ch'iao, who ordered me to dwell on the *kung-an* [Ch'an paradox] "where one came from to life and where one goes in death." My thinking was thus divided into two threads and my mind was no longer in unity. Furthermore, I never clearly understood Master Tuan-ch'iao's instruction on how to proceed. More than a year I remained in this stalemate; every day I felt like a traveler who had lost his way. Since I had set a three-year limit for myself, I was greatly troubled. One day Brother Ching from T'ai-chou said to me: "Master Hsüeh-yen [Tsu-ch'in] often asked about your progress. Why don't you go over there?" Delighted, I came to you.

Carrying incense I arrived at the Pei-chien Pagoda in the hope of asking you, my master, for instruction. Right after I lit the incense and paid my homage you drove me out with heavy blows. With the door slammed behind me, I wept all the way back to the dormitory. Next morning after breakfast I went to see you again. This time you allowed me to approach you. You asked me about my previous work and I made a complete and detailed report. You were kind enough to eradicate all the defects I had accumulated and ordered me to concentrate on the word "nothingness," taking a fresh start in my work. I felt like one who had acquired a lamp in the darkness or one released from being hung. Only now did I understand how to apply myself.

You further ordered me to report to you daily so you could see how I proceeded each day. You said: "It should be like a man going on a journey: every day he must register some progress. You must not remain in the same spot day after day." Daily as soon as I arrived in your presence you would ask me my accomplishment for the previous day. Later, as I was able to report satisfactorily, you ceased to ask about my progress.

Instead, as soon as I entered, you asked: "Who told you to drag in this dead corpse?" Before you even finished you drove me out with hard blows. Every day you asked the same thing and hit me the same way. As I was getting desperate, I began to feel that I was on the verge of getting somewhere. But just then you were invited to go to Nan-ming. At your departure you told me, "After I settle down I shall send for you." But nothing came of it.

Finally I decided to join you on my own, but I first had to go to my secular parents for a supply of travel clothing. I went with brother Tse of Ch'ang-chou. Little did I expect that my parents would take away our luggage and monks' certificates, thinking that we were too young and too inexperienced to travel on our own. It was already early in the second month, too late to obtain residence in another temple. We could do nothing other than take what was left of our belongings and return to Ching-shan.

We arrived around the middle of the second month. During the night of the sixteenth of the next month, in my dream I remembered the question once asked by Master Tuan-ch'iao in his room, "If all the dharmas return to unity, then where does unity return to?" From that time on I was again in doubt. I was so confused that I lost my sense of direction and did not remember to eat or sleep. On the sixth day, late in the morning, I was walking in the corridor when I saw the monks leaving the meditation hall. Without knowing what I was doing I joined them, and we went to the Three Pagoda Pavilion for a recitation of sutras. All of a sudden I saw on the wall a portrait of Master Wu-tsu Yen and noticed the last two lines of the eulogy inscribed on the painting:

> After one hundred years or thirty-six thousand days,
> No matter what happens—there is still this man![1]

Instantly I solved the puzzle that you, my revered master, confronted me with before you left, the puzzle about the dead corpse that I was dragging with me. I was so stunned and overwhelmed by the sudden illumination that I fainted. When I came to I felt as if a load of one hundred and twenty pounds had been lifted from my shoulders. This happened on the twenty-second day of the third month in the year *hsin-yu* [1261], an anniversary of Master Shao-lin's death. I was just twenty-four and I thought that I had arrived at my goal within the time limit I had set for myself. I thereupon wanted to visit you at Nan-ming and see if you would verify my

[1] The text of the eulogy, written by Fa-yen (also known as Wu-tzu, d. 1104) himself, is in *T*, 47:666b. For a translation of the text as well as a discussion of the genre of *tzu-tsan* (self-eulogy) see my paper "Self-Eulogy: An Autobiographical Mode in Traditional Chinese Literature," presented before the University Seminar on Traditional China, Columbia University, November 20, 1973.

success. But as summer was near I could not leave. I was not able to visit you and be shown my inadequacies until the end of the summer. Although I was toughened by your instructions and reached the stage where I could no longer be easily overwhelmed by Ch'an paradoxes, my mind still became muddled every time I tried to say something. I was still not free enough to progress in daily applications—I felt as if I had been burdened with debts. I had thought that I would stay there to wait on you till the end of my life, but I had to take reluctant leave of you when my companion brother Tse had to depart for another temple.

In the year of *i-ch'ou* [1265] when you, my master, presided over a service at the T'ien-ning Temple, I was again able to attend to you. You once asked me, "During the day when you are surrounded by all affairs, can you be the master of yourself?" I said, "Yes." You then asked: "How about during a dream?" Again I replied affirmatively. You finally asked, "When you are in a deep sleep, dreamless, thoughtless, seeing and hearing nothing, where is the master?" Now I had nothing to say, nothing to go on. At this point you instructed me: "From today on I do not want you to emulate the Buddha or study the Law. Nor do I want you to try to exhaust all ancient or modern teachings. You just eat when you are hungry, sleep when you are tired. As soon as you wake up, muster all your strength and ask yourself: 'Where did the master of my self settle itself down during my sleep?' " Although I believed everything you said and tried to follow your instruction, my obtuse nature did not lead me to a solution. Therefore I went to Lung-hsü. I swore that I would persevere until I came to a full understanding, even if the price I paid were that I became an imbecile for the rest of my life.

I struggled for five years. Then one night I stayed in a temple dormitory. As I was dwelling on this puzzle a roommate's pillow fell on the floor and made a loud noise. My doubts were instantly smashed and I felt as if I had leaped out of a snare. When I recalled the disputes and paradoxes of the patriarchs which had troubled me as well as the differences and predestined affinities between the ancient and the modern, I felt as if I had met the Great Sage at Ssu-chou or like a traveler returning to his homeland from afar.[2] I was nevertheless still the same man of former

---

[2] The legend of the Great Sage who subdued a water demon and saved the city of Ssu-chou from flooding has often been made use of by playwrights, with the earliest dramatization going back at least to the middle of the thirteenth century. Here Yüan-miao apparently compares his own achievement of peace and serenity to the restoration of order in that ancient city. On the other hand, the reference to the Great Sage of Ssu-chou may also indicate Yüan-miao's solution of a Ch'an paradox based on the enigmatic name and origin of a Central Asian Buddhist monk who settled down in Ssu-chou during the T'ang. For a summary of the disputes arising from this thorny enigma see Ch'en Yüan, *Chung-kuo fo-chiao shih-chi kai-lun* (A bibliographical guide to Chinese Buddhism) (Peking: Chung-hua shu-chü, 1962), pp. 133–34.

times without any change from his former ways. From that time on the state has been stabilized, the country secured, and the whole world is at peace. I have continuously held my thought on inaction and retained my equilibrium with regard to all ten directions. Everything that I have submitted above is completely true. It is my humble wish that you, my respected master, would extend me the kindness of giving this letter a close reading. (*HTC*, 122:678–80)

K'un-hsüeh chi (A record of
learning through difficulties)
by Hu Chih (1517–1585)

As a child I was rather ignorant. From time to time I heard my father discussing Confucian studies with others, but I did not know how to participate. At seventeen I boarded at the county school in town where I led an untrammeled and pleasure-seeking life. In the winter my father died and I became even more self-indulgent. But I was rather impressed with romantic figures in history and loved to discourse on great personalities such as K'ung Jung, Kuo Chen, Li Po, Su Shih, and Wen T'ien-hsiang. In my dreams I met with Kuo and Li. I was very fond of rhetorical and florid writings. The poetry and prose of Li and Ho were the rage of the day and I tried to imitate them.[1]

I was short-tempered, full of desires, constantly agitated, and lacking in self-control. I wrote an essay on the investigation of things to refute the theory of Wang Shou-jen.[2] When I was nineteen I became good friends with a classmate by the name of Ou-yang Wen-ch'ao. From time to time I became aware of my wrongdoings and made resolutions to pursue Confucian studies in earnest. I invited Wen-ch'ao to join me in the new regimen. We tried our best for a month or two, but as we did not know how to go about it, we soon lapsed into our old ways.

In the *jen-yin* year of the Chia-ching reign [1542] I turned twenty-six and bought a house below the White Crane Monastery. It happened that Master Ou-yang Te came to town from his country residence.[3] He met with his old friends and gave public lectures. Every member of the local literati went to the meetings, but I refused to go. A few days later Wen-ch'ao said to me, "Couldn't you at least pay him a courtesy call?" Thereupon I went with Wen-ch'ao to call on him at the P'u-chüeh Temple. As soon as Mr. Ou-yang saw me he addressed me by my old name, I-chü, and said, "Why did it take you so long to come?" Then he asked my age. When I answered, he said, "On the basis of your age you should take

---

[1] For Li Meng-yang (1472–1529) and Ho Ching-ming (1483–1521) see their entries in *DMB*.

[2] Wang Shou-jen (1472–1529) was the founder of the Wang school of Neo-Confucianism. See *DMB*, 2:1408–16.

[3] Ou-yang Te (1496–1554), Wang Shou-jen's disciple and onetime minister of rites, belonged to the same clan as Hu's good friend, Ou-yang Wen-ch'ao.

your seat next to Mr. So-and-so." Impressed by his simplicity in word and manner, as well as his freedom from the current fashion, I was completely won over by him. He proceeded to expound on the saying, "It is only the virtuous man who can love [or who can hate] others."[4] He said:

> Only the virtuous man has the mind of great empathy. So when he sees others doing good, he feels as though he himself were doing it, but without loving them deliberately. Therefore he can love others. When he sees others doing evil, he suffers as though he himself were involved, yet without hating them deliberately. Therefore he can hate others. Nowadays people love and hate others deliberately, therefore they are entangled in love and hate. It may not be said that they can love or hate others.

As I had always suffered from an intense hatred for evil, I was quite shaken by his words, as if they had been designed for me.

A day or two later I called on him again at his residence. For over a month I waited on him daily at the Hai-chih Temple. In the meantime I was quite worried about my habit of self-indulgence which, I was afraid, would not permit me to enter into the Confucian Way. One day Mr. Ou-yang told me how to set my aim, saying, " 'To illustrate illustrious virtue throughout the kingdom' should be that at which we set our aim. The effort to reach it consists in extending our innate knowledge." He further said, "If our aim is set genuinely, then our innate knowledge will naturally suffer no impediments." His words were in perfect accord with my own thinking.

One day I heard him chanting a line from Chu Hsi's poetry, "In the boatman's song there is the mind that has come down from an eternity."[5] Suddenly everything became clear to me, and I felt that my bad habits could be eradicated. For the first time my mind was truly set on higher goals. However, during the next spring, because of the pressures of the preliminary examination, my will wavered although my good intentions remained.

In the autumn I passed the provincial examination. Returning home, I visited Mr. Ou-yang, but soon I had to depart for the metropolitan examination in the capital. Mr. Ou-yang had high hopes for me, and I was quite confident. The next year, *chia-ch'en* [1544], I failed the metropolitan examination in the capital. On the way back I had some trouble with a

---

[4] *Analects*, 4:3.

[5] The poem can be found in Chu Hsi, *Hui-an hsien-sheng Chu Wen-kung wen-chi* (Collected writings of Master Chu Hsi) SPTK 9:6b: "Above Wu-ch'ü the mountains are high and clouds deep. / Lingering mist and rain darken the forest below. / In the forest there is a visitor nobody knows; / In the boatman's song there is the mind that has come down from an eternity."

companion. After my return I saw Mr. Ou-yang again, but every time I embarked on the right way, I soon fell. I remained anxious, unresigned to my plight. In the autumn of the *i-ssu* year [1545] I was fully occupied with the mourning for my grandmother, since I was the oldest male descendant alive. The next year I returned to study at Lung-chou together with Ou-yang Wen-ch'ao and Lo P'eng. But I amused myself by taking up exchange of poems with Mr. K'ang Shu, the county magistrate. As a result, my endeavor to study became slackened.

In the *ting-wei* year [1547] I was enmeshed in a lawsuit over the choice of a place for my grandmother's burial. When Mr. Ou-yang went north to assume office as vice-minister of rites I accompanied him to the provincial capital. On my return I resolved the litigation. I realized that my efforts in learning were ineffective and regretted the passage of time. My main defects were love of florid composition, anger, and desires. All three were deeply entrenched within me. From time to time I succeeded in overcoming them, but the victory never lasted. I was already over thirty, yet I remained unsettled in my aim. What more could I say about my sins?

In the winter the idea of leaving all the mundane involvements and indulging in distant travels suddenly occurred to me. I told my friend Wang T'o about it. He said, "To travel to distant places in not as good as to strive in learning." Then he took me to visit Mr. Lo Hung-hsien.[6] After I had stayed at Stone Lotus Grotto and listened daily to Mr. Lo's words for a month, I was moved to acknowledge him formally as my teacher. At first he did not care too much for the theory of innate knowledge; yet he did not turn his back completely on the teachings of Wang Shou-jen. He instructed us students solely on quietude and desirelessness. Although I was not in full accord with his teachings, as I listened daily to his exhortations on desirelessness, I became more accustomed to his method and practiced it each day with greater earnestness. In the end I came to understand the meaning of scrupulousness in personal conduct.

In the spring of the year *wu-chen* [1548] I visited Shao-chou. The prefect Ch'en Ta-lun invited me to teach at the Ming-ching Academy, which he had established for the benefit of the bright youths of the six counties under his jurisdiction. Before I arrived he had appointed another teacher, a member of the local gentry by the name of Teng Lu, who came to live in the academy to keep company with the students. The prefect had been a student of Wang Shou-jen, but subsequently he had concentrated on Taoist teachings.

In my youth I suffered from a lung disease. I spit blood and my heart

---

[6] Lo (1504–1564) was another prominent member of the Wang school. See *DMB*, 1:980–84.

pounded at night, and consequently I slept poorly. I tried to cure it by taking up a Taoist regimen with the prefect, but it was not effective. Then I inquired into the Ch'an [Buddhist] school from Teng who, although once a student of Confucian teachers such as Wei Chiao and Ou-yang Te, now devoted himself solely to Ch'an. He told me, "Your disease is a form of inflammation and should be treated by Ch'an." Henceforth every day after class he and I got together and practiced quiet-sitting, sometimes on the bed, sometimes on a mat on the floor. We often sat until late in the night. After a brief sleep we would resume sitting when the cock crowed. The endeavor was directed chiefly at the calming of the mind and the ceasing of random thoughts. The goal was the perceiving of one's true nature.

Accustomed to a life of galloping activities, I could not but begin to see strange apparitions day and night after having practiced sitting for a month or two. Mr. Teng said: "This is the realm of Mara as described by Buddhists and Taoists. The anger, desires, greed, vanity, and various thoughts and anxieties of your past have transformed themselves into these sights. This is what is meant in the *Book of Changes* when it speaks of 'the wandering souls bringing about change.'[7] Do not be startled by them. They will disappear of their own accord when your endeavor has reached a certain stage." Just as he said, in four or five months, the strange sights gradually went away. At the end of the sixth month they disappeared altogether.

One day my mind was suddenly opened and illuminated. It was completely free of extraneous thoughts. I saw into heaven, earth, and the myriad things: They are all the substance of my mind. With a deep sigh I said, "Now I know that heaven, earth, and the myriad things are not external to me!" From that time on I could confront all circumstances without anxiety as if I could cope with everything. My health improved greatly, and I began to recover from the disease of inflammation that had troubled me for more than ten years. I could also sleep at night.

Greatly delighted, I told Teng about it. He said, "Your true nature has been revealed." After some time I got to the point that even when I slept I retained my awareness: I noticed every step and every utterance made by people while I was asleep. Teng explained this phenomenon as a case of gradual "penetration to the course of day and night,"[8] saying, "Keep it up and you will be able to transcend life and death." I asked him what he meant by "transcend life and death." He replied, "If you do not transcend life and death, your former diseases will not be eradicated." Every day I felt I gained a new insight. We visited Ts'ao Ch'i and paid our respects to

[7] *Chou I cheng-i*, 7:6a.
[8] Ibid., 7:6b.

the stupa of the Sixth Patriarch.[9] There I had an unsual dream that led me to the idea of leaving the secular world.

In the autumn Mr. Ch'ien Te-hung[10] came to Shao-chou. Prefect Ch'en invited him to stay in the academy. I was overjoyed and asked for his instructions. However, I realized that Mr. Ch'ien had traveled far away from home when he was not yet quite out of mourning for his parent. Moreover, I noticed that he rode in a carriage that had blue curtains and a black panoply, with outriders to clear the way for him.[11] I said to myself, "Although I am a student of otherworldly matters, I still do not think what he is doing is right."

Soon winter came to an end. As I was making plans for returning home, anxious thoughts began to arise. Consequently I lost my initial illumination. All of a sudden I had a sensation of dullness and stagnation, the cause of which I could not determine, try as I might. Although my perceptions seemed to remain as before, the true substance of my mind was darkened and obstructed, and I felt quite uneasy. I told Mr. Ch'ien my plight and asked him about it. He made an elaborate explanation, but it failed to satisfy me. One day I went sight-seeing to Chiu-ch'eng Terrace with several members of the literati. Just as I stood up and stretched myself after having sat down for some time, the insight suddenly came back to me that heaven, earth, and the myriad things are truly not external to me. I verified this insight against what various Confucian masters—Tzu Ssu seeing the Way above and below,[12] Mencius finding all things already complete in the self,[13] Ch'eng Hao forming one body with all things,[14] Lu Chiu-yüan believing the universe to be his mind[15] —and they were in perfect accord. I examined my previous understanding and everything became clear and coherent once more. Therefore I said to myself: "Fortunately I have reduced my former hindrances. This is the time to finish all the entanglements. How can I enmesh myself once more in the affairs of the world, seek after worm-eaten crumbs, only to submerge my true substance?"

After I returned home I realized that my father's remains were only shallowly interred while a propitious permanent site for burial was yet to be found. This distressed me. I was further upset by the poor treatment

---

[9] Hui-neng (638-713), the great Ch'an Buddhist master.

[10] One of the chief disciples of Wang Shou-jen. *DMB*, s.v. "Ch'ien Te-hung."

[11] White is the Chinese color for mourning. A strict observation of all elaborate rules of mourning was expected of prominent Confucians.

[12] Alludes to *Mean*, 12:3. Tzu Ssu, the grandson of Confucius, is traditionally believed to be the author of this Confucian classic.

[13] Alludes to *Mencius*, 7A:4.

[14] Alludes to *Erh-Ch'eng i-shu*, 2A:3a.

[15] Alludes to *Hsiang-shan ch'üan-chi* 22:5a.

my old mother received in the household. In my heart there was often much discontent, yet I knew no solution. At this time I vaguely saw the differences in aims and principles between Confucianism and Buddhism, but I could not yet reach any decision.

During the year *chi-yu* [1549] I stayed in my hometown. I formed a literary club with people of the county such as Tseng Ch'ien, Lo Ch'ao, Hsiao Lung-yu, Wang Yu-hsün, and my old friend Ou-yang Wen-ch'ao. Their company was very inspiring. In the winter I went to the capital to take part in the metropolitan examination. On the same boat was Wan Chu, the uncle of Wang Yu-hsün and an instructor at the county school. From dawn to night we did nothing but discuss learning. As we were sailing in the P'eng-li Lake a tempest raged during the night. Unable to reach a harbor, the ship was rocked several times to the verge of capsizing. Most people on the boat wailed until dawn, while I alone ordered wine and proceeded to drink to my heart's content. After singing a few tunes loudly I fell into a deep slumber. I did not awake until daybreak when the wind abated. Some of my companions criticized me for having no feelings, but it did not matter to me.

After I failed the examination I stayed in the house of Mr. Ou-yang Te during the early part of *keng-wu* [1550]. One day I reported the tempest incident to him and asked for his comment. Mr. Ou-yang remarked: "What you did was of course not ordinary. But to accord with the substance of humaneness it was not." I asked him what one should have done to accord with the substance of humaneness. He replied, "If one's mind remains undisturbed when confronted with a crisis, yet one is able to devise plans for succoring others—then and only then is one in accord with humaneness." Although I acceded to him, I was unable to search deeply into his meaning. In midsummer Mr. Li Ch'un-fang invited me to his home in Hsing-hua to tutor his sons. As a result I came to know exhaustively the teachings of Wang Ken. Wang was truly a heroic figure of his time, but his disciples had lost the genuine principles in the transmission of his teaching. They tended to be self-indulgent and arrogant. As a result scholars of Hsing-hua had little faith in Confucian studies. After a while when they became fully acquainted with my behavior they came to me with their questions and we established a study group. Toward the end of the winter I embarked on my homeward journey from I-chen. For three days we saw pirates, but fortunately each time a favorable wind took our ship out of their reach. Some of my shipmates wept. I alone remained undisturbed because I calculated that if worse came to worse I would simply give the boarding pirates all my money—I saw no other reason for worry.

In the year *hsin-hai* [1551] I returned with my family to the old homestead at Ts'ang-chou in I-ho district. As I studied by myself without companions, my efforts were somewhat slackened. Next year I worked as a tutor in Ch'ien-nan. There I relapsed so much into my old ways that I almost foundered. In the winter I went with Ou-yang Shao-ch'ing, the second son of Mr. Ou-yang Te, to take part in the metropolitan examination. Tseng Ssu-chien, who was invited by Shao-ch'ing to tutor his sons, was also on the same ship. Although the three of us often discussed learning and encouraged each other, my self-indulgence did not abate.

I failed the *k'uei-ch'ou* [1553] metropolitan examination. At first I planned to apply for a teaching position with the state school system. When the time for interviews came I changed my mind and refused to go. My friends Chou Hsien-i, Tseng Ssu-chien, and Ou-yang Shao-ch'ing all urged me to take the interview. Ssu-chien went so far as to start pounding the desk. He said to me angrily: "Your mother is old. If you do not earn some salary and take care of her while she is still alive, you are unfilial!" Reluctantly I went to the interview and obtained a teaching position at Chü-jung. After I took the post I still entertained hopes of an eventual success at the metropolitan examination, but every day I was fully occupied with teaching. I knew that my otherworldly studies were not something I could discuss with people; moreover, because of my self-conceit I was not on good terms with my superiors or my students. Often I blamed myself. Finally I said to myself, "Could it be that what I learned through illumination was not sufficient?" In the second month of *chia-yin* [1554] I received the news of Mr. Ou-yang's death. I set up a memorial tablet for him and wept bitterly before it. When I thought that my teacher was now far away and I had not accomplished anything in learning, I began to reproach myself for the wasted years. I felt a bitter remorse over my having failed both my teacher and myself.

Sometime later I had the occasion to compose an essay entitled "Extending with Learning and Restraining with Propriety."[16] I put down my pen and many thoughts came to my mind. In the teachings transmitted from Confucius to his disciple Yen Hui nothing is more cogent than what is summarized in the title of the essay. Only things that proceed from it can be considered as belonging to the School of the Sages; whatever does not proceed from it must not be in the school. I thereupon reflected on it again and again and searched for its meaning with an open mind. I dared not follow recent scholars, nor dared I advance my own opinions. After much endeavor I still could not compel myself to accept what earlier Confucians had thought on this matter. I had four reservations. Recent

[16] Alludes to *Analects*, 6:25: "The Superior Man, extensively studying all learning, and keeping himself under the restraint of the rules of propriety, may thus likewise not overstep what is right." (Legge translation). The idea is repeated in 9:10 and 12:15.

Confucians I could not accept completely either. There were three reservations. . . .[17]

From that time on none of my endeavors seemed to be in vain. My handling of daily affairs also seemed to have improved, and my relations with the above and the below looked somewhat better. Only now did I understand completely the idea of the substance of humaneness expounded by Mr. Ou-yang Te.

I went to Nanking to visit friends, among whom were Ho Ch'ien and T'an Lun. Mr. T'ang Shun-chih was kind enough to visit me at my residence, and I went with him to call on Mr. Chao Chen-chi. I noticed that that there was a diversity of opinions among the leaders regarding the nature of extensive learning. Although I did not dare to dispute them, I gained a great deal in self-confidence.

Two years later, in *ping-ch'en* [1556], I passed the metropolitan examination. For the first time I was in a position to befriend all the leading scholars within the Four Seas. In my discussions and deliberations with them, I remained convinced that one cannot depart from the heavenly standard nor can one speak of it in terms of the inward, outward, earlier, or later. If one grasps this then that which stood right above Yen Yüan will stand right above him. If anyone does not understand this yet asserts himself to be in the mainstream of the Confucian school, I am afraid he is caught up in cross purposes. Later when I returned home I asked Mr. Lo Hung-hsien for his opinion about my views. At first he was afraid that I might have sought after impressions and conjectures. He challenged me by asking: "Now you see things everywhere, can you say that you see the heavenly standard everywhere?" I did not dare to go into details with him. Several years later, in the year *jen-hsü* [1562], I was in Hupeh when I received a letter from him in which he said: "I have absolutely no doubt about your theory on extending with learning and restraining with propriety. Could it be that Confucian learning is about to be revived?" Later when I returned home again I went for a second time to ask Mr. Lo's opinion. He said, "The important thing is to have both eyes and feet." He was afraid that I might set my sights too high for my weak feet.

After I retired from my post in Szechwan I returned home. Three years later I was appointed superintendent of education in Hupeh. Later on I was transferred, first to eastern Kwangtung, then to western Kwangtung. After twenty years of government service I suddenly realize that I am old. Yet I am ashamed that I have not truly returned to the Way of the sages. Could it be that I have finally been undone by my weak feet? This year, *k'uei-yu* [1573], I have again submitted my resignation. Now I am more

[17] The discursive section (pp. 223–24) is omitted from this otherwise complete translation.

apprehensive and perplexed than ever before, for I think there has been none, from ancient times to this day, who is as much beset by difficulties as I am. I say to myself: " 'Once the knowledge is acquired it comes to the same thing. . . . Once the achievement is made, it comes to the same thing.'[18] If this is true, then when will it be my turn?" I hereby record my struggles for the purpose of admonishing myself. (*MJHA*, pp. 221–24)

---

[18] Alludes to *Mean*, 20:9: "Some are born with the knowledge; some gain it by study; and some acquire the knowledge after undergoing difficulties. But once the knowledge is acquired, it comes to the same thing. Some practice it under easy circumstances; some with quickness; and some by strenuous effort. But once the achievement is made, it comes to the same thing."

The *Tzu-shu* (Self-Account) by
Wang Shih-min (1592–1680)

An Outline of My Official Career

AT FIRST I was named Tsan-yü. When I was four years old I was given to my grandfather's younger brother Hsüeh-hsien to be adopted as his grandson. During that year my second older brother Chi-yu died of measles, and my oldest brother Ming-yu passed away when I reached fourteen. I was then restored to my grandfather's branch of the family and given my present name. I began to sleep in my grandfather's room when I was a young boy: when he went to his country estate I always accompanied him. Only when I married at seventeen did I move out of his room.

When I was eighteen my father died. Thereupon I began to spit blood, and for more than a year I was on the verge of death. My grandfather died when I was nineteen. Several calamities were visited upon me within two years, and I was left not only forlorn but in mortal peril. All the burdens of the household fell on my shoulders, for I was the only man left in the family. I had to manage all the internal affairs as well as to deal with the outside world. Furthermore, the snobbery of the world was such that the family could be saved from tumbling down further only by some member's acquisition of rank and office. It just happened that in recognition of my grandfather's service to the country I was offered the post of an assistant director in the Office of Imperial Seals. I thereupon registered my name and signified my acceptance of the offer.

Having completed the burial of my grandfather in the year of *kuei-ch'ou* [1613], I went to the capital the following spring to assume office. As we were in constant attendance on the emperor, we were housed in the imperial compound and enjoyed great pomp and honor. Our duties were uncomplicated: making summaries of memorials; applying imperial seals on the edicts and rescripts; issuing seals to the circuit censors, ivory tablets to civil and military officers, and brass tallies to inspectors and guard officers.

Day and night I discharged my duties with caution and diligence, never taking liberties on account of the lack of power or substance of the office. Nor did I ever absent myself from morning court meetings or state sacrifices, going out and coming home under the stars and braving winter cold and summer rain. To ward off the ridicule that I occupied an idle sinecure, I frequently volunteered for missions that involved long and difficult travel. As a result I traversed almost half of the realm, from the northern and southern capitals to provinces such as Ch'i, Yü, Ch'u, Min, and Chiang-yu.

Every time I embarked on a journey I always admonished my servants, saying: "This trip lasting several thousand miles will incur great expenses to the government. Without spending a penny, I am enjoying a nice tour and getting to visit my hometown. This is already far too much. How could I allow additional troubles to the local officials?" Everywhere I insisted on economy and simplicity in the care of myself and my retinue; and as we passed through towns and villages my men were under strict orders not to make noise or cause disturbances. On every mission as soon as the official business was completed I left the next day without lingering, lest the local burdens be increased. Even post functionaries and clerks at fief chancelleries were impressed: they remarked that they had never seen such behavior before. I refused all gifts from the local officials that I encountered on my missions. Four times I visited feudal princes by imperial order—to assist at a succession ceremony, to inquire after a prince's health, to make sacrifice at a memorial service, and to participate in a burial ceremony. When gifts came from a principality I only accepted books or stone rubbings: cash I always firmly declined. In this regard my behavior sometimes differed from that of my colleagues, but that never deterred me.

During the years *jen-shen* and *kuei-yu* [1632–1633] of the Ch'ung-chen reign the emperor repeatedly ordered all officials to show consideration for the post service. Imperial commissioners who had failed to return to the capital before their commission expired would be denied the continued use of their post privileges. During that time I went as an imperial emissary to inquire after the health of Prince Chou; on my way back I made a stop at my hometown. I fell sick on my way north the next year. After I reported my condition to the emperor an edict came down granting me leave to seek a cure at intermediate points on the journey. Consequently I overstayed my commission. Upon recovery I traveled back to the capital at my own expense. When I returned my travel tally to the Bureau of Equipment with a full report, everybody there laughed at my obtuseness. Even the bureau director was politely derisive. But I only knew how to obey the law.

By the usual practice, assistant directors of the seals office appointed on the basis of hereditary privileges were to be promoted two grades only after the completion of nine years of satisfactory service. But almost every contemporary of mine took advantage of the special favors customarily granted by newly enthroned emperors: they thus rose several grades within just a few years. I alone did not benefit from such occasions be-

cause I was often away from the court on missions. Even routine pro-
motions I failed to receive: I did not rise to the directorship of the Office
of Imperial Seals until *chia-tzu* [1624]. In *ting-mao* [1627] my mother, Lady
Ting, died just after I came back from a mission to Fukien to deliver an
imperial edict. I observed mourning for more than two years before I
returned to office. In *ping-tzu* [1636] I was promoted to vice-minister,
Court of Imperial Sacrifices, while still directing the seals office. In *chi-
mao* [1639] I was sent to Min to officiate at the naming of the heir apparent
to the feudal prince. The journey to Min, which was situated in the extreme south of Ch'u, was long and arduous. Suffering from the scorch-
ingly hot weather and attacked by both malaria and dysentery, I was a
mere bag of bones when I began the journey north. I managed to get as
far as my hometown; next spring I sent my commission to the court with
a request for a sick leave. The emperor not only granted my wish but
promised me a reappointment upon recovery. I had not expected that
such unusual imperial benevolence should be bestowed on an inconsequential functionary, and my awe and respect became even greater when
I recalled my limitations.

In the early summer of *chia-shen* [1644], when I was still in my hometown on sick leave, suddenly the news came that the emperor had passed
away. My grief was such that I did not expect to live. Soon a new government was established in the southern capital and I was reappointed to my
old office. Fully conscious of the importance of timely withdrawal from
official life, I declined the appointment on account of bad health. The
next spring as a result of the special recommendation memorialized by
the grand secretaries, the reappointment was issued again. Just as I was
about to submit another earnest declination, all of a sudden the hills tum-
bled and the valleys reared.[1]

From the beginning of my government service to the day I took a leave
of absence I was in office for altogether twenty-four years. More than half
of the time I was on the road: I was actually in the capital for no more
than some ten years. There were in all scores of colleagues who served
with me at one time or another. During the early years of the T'ien-ch'i
reign [1621–1628] many of the talented were brought into the government: offices were filled to capacity with men of renown and experience
who had won public acclaim. As an uncouth novice I presumed to rub
shoulders with distinguished elders who, fortunately, did not shunt me
aside but favored me with an occasional word of undeserved approbation.
The only unpleasantness occurred during the routine merit evaluations of
k'uei-hai [1623] and *hsin-ssu* [1641]. On the former occasion the man in

---

[1] A euphemism for the fall of Nanking to the invading Manchu army. A discreet Ming
loyalist, Wang never served the new dynasty.

power bore an old grudge against my forebears, while on the latter diffi-culties arose when the wicked desired to expel those who did not belong to their clique. I was subjected to much scrutiny and faultfinding, but in the end nothing at all was found that could be used against me.

My Life in Retirement

From the time that I began to wait on my grandfather as a child I often heard him remarking that a scholar-official out of office and residing in his hometown should consider as his primary duties the early payment of taxes and the diligent performance of good deeds. I made a mental note of this saying and never forgot it day or night. When I became the sole head of the household I decided to emulate Huang Chien-chi in his prac-tice of *p'ing-t'iao*: in the early summer of every year when the price of grain was at its highest I would sell mine cheaply to aid the poor. I have never tired of distributing clothes during winter, food during a famine, or medicine and coffins to the indigent. Whenever a stranded traveler comes to ask for assistance I always give him the necessary fare, without inquiring into the veracity of his claim. I am especially attentive to the matter of taxes. I always try to pay the taxes early; my books are always in order. Even in my straitened old age I would sell property or pawn possessions in order to meet my obligations. Sometimes I might be a little later than I prefer, but I am seldom in arrears.

I have always considered it improper for me to intervene with govern-ment officials on behalf of a supplicant. Therefore I have never written as much as a short note to a government agency with a view to influence an official decision. Sometimes a family friend or an old acquaintance who is in a position of power may hint at a willingness to gratify my wishes, but I still set firm limits of propriety and never ask even for a small favor.

I control my servants most sternly. At times my retainers amount to several hundred, but none dares to interfere with any business outside of my household or engage in fights. If the word gets to me that a retainer of mine has violated the rules I have laid down, he will receive a sound whipping without my first inquiring into the exact circumstance of his offense. Consequently peace and quiet reign in my compound and no fracas ever comes within my earshot.

It is my nature to be intolerant of incivility. I myself am always ruled by modesty and self-effacement. I constantly repeat to myself the ancient exhortation to respect one's own community, which I maintain without deviation. I treat with sincerity and respect all relatives and acquaintances in my hometown irrespective of their station in life. Even youths who are many years my junior I befriend as equals without standing on ceremony, as if for fear of being rejected by them on account of my senility. Those who make improper requests I always forgive.

I am not acquisitive or greedy. Things that do not belong to me I never take, not even one thread of silk or one grain of rice. In recent years I have been under great pressure from tax collectors and moneylenders. On several occasions I was forced to part with some of my properties. The buyers, fully aware of my pressing need for cash, tried their best to take advantage of my difficulties. I knew their perfidy but I did not wrangle with them. For I have always believed, during the last several decades, that I would let others take advantage of me rather than that I should take advantage of them and that I would rather suffer losses than pocket improper gains. I swore that I would never deviate from this practice. Everybody in my hometown can testify to this.

My Filial Acts

I recall that when my grandfather retired to the hometown as a former premier, my father, having passed the highest civil examinations, cut short his career and returned home to attend him. Both earned great glory and admiration, even from the far corners of the realm. As a child I observed personally their exemplary conduct, the praise of which I heard everywhere.

However, as soon as I came of age several calamities befell my family, and our household was almost desolated. Although overwhelmed with grief, I mustered all my strength and forced myself to perform all the necessary tasks. For my grandfather I petitioned the throne for an official encomium. A posthumous title with full honors was bestowed on him. For both my father and grandfather I begged prominent writers to immortalize them through literary means. Some of the compositions thus obtained were inscribed on their tombstones while others were buried with their coffins. I edited and then published the copies of their memorials to the throne as well as their complete literary works. Special shrines were built for them and the family temple was augmented. All together seven burial sites were auspiciously chosen as the permanent resting places for my grandparents, parents, stepmothers, and my eldest brother. For each I sought from famous writers suitable tomb inscriptions and necrologies so as to perpetuate their memories. In my supervision of the funerals and the burials no effort or expense was spared in the hope that there would be no regrets in the future. During mourning for my mother I always wept whenever she was mentioned, and for three years I never donned any garment not made of hemp.

My eldest brother—three years older than I—and I were deeply affectionate to each other. Since his death he has always remained in my memory. I always weep at sacrifices to him. According to the rites, bachelors could not have sons adopted posthumously. However, I thought that the rites originated in what was right, so I prepared a statement and delivered it to the family temple, thereby making my third son Chuan the heir to my deceased brother, who would thus always enjoy sacrifices and libations.

My widowed aunt from Wu-chiang and my widowed elder sister from K'un-shan were both aged and destitute, so I built houses for them in my family compound, thus enabling them to spend their last years in peace and comfort. To see them to the end as sincerity and faith would dictate, I took care of the burial at their deaths. On the occasions of marriage, birth, or death among my relatives I always send gifts and offer generous financial assistance. Over the years I have spent a great deal of money in this regard.

My Friends and Preferences

I am by nature straightforward and unreserved. Although I do not meddle in matters outside of my household, I always express my opinion squarely and impartially. When I harbor any grievance, it is like holding pebbles in my mouth: the discomfort does not go away until I spit everything out. Yet after the act I forget everything; nothing remains with me overnight. In any gathering, no matter how large, if I see someone open and bright I immediately approach him, hold his hand, and pour out my heart to him. Those who are fierce or devious I avoid as if they might soil me.

Since my return to my hometown I have not associated much with people; most of the days I close the gate and pass the time quietly. My doorsteps have never been darkened by those who indulge themselves in licentiousness, music, drinking, or gambling. My father's friends such as Messrs. Ch'en Chi-ju, Lou Tzu-jou, and T'ang Shu-ta I always waited on as my uncles: to the end of their days I never dared to slacken in my respectful attendance. Among my own friends Chang Hsiu-yu, who had shared a desk with me in school, remained poor and proud. Sympathetic to his plight, I had an old house repaired for his shelter, regularly succored him with food and clothing, and saw to it that he had no want. After I buried him with proper ceremony I have never ceased to support his widow and orphans. Time only increased my attentiveness to them. Whenever I hear of a knowledgeable and learned man, whether he lives in my county or just outside of it, I call on him and serve him humbly in order to benefit from his erudition. In my later years I became close friends with Wu Mei-ts'un,[2] the chancellor of the National University. Although our affinity is based on a similarity in taste, my fondness for him can also be attributed to my admiration for his prose and poetry. Everytime he finishes a piece I always copy it with my own hand.

From time to time I dabble in versification, but I am too ashamed of my deficiency to show my product to people. As I am inept, I know nothing about chess or other parlor games. When I was young I prepared myself for the civil examinations, but I had to stop on account of illness. After I entered into government service I did not have time to continue with my studies.. Only late in life when I retired did I have much leisure to read widely. In my declining years my eyes became weak, but I stay on the porch making the most of the sunlight, never without a book in hand. Yet the senile mind is obtuse: everything that passes the eye passes into forgetfulness: to my mortification nothing is retained.

As for painting, it is my addiction. Whenever I see a genuine work by an ancient master I always try to add it to my collection without regard for the price. Often I practice my brush by imitating the famous masters of the Sung and Yüan. But because of lack of leisure time I have not been able to do my utmost and study thoroughly. Time passes fleetingly and now I realize that I have accomplished nothing. I still remember that every time Mr. Tung, vice-minister of rites,[3] saw my painting he never failed to praise or inscribe on it his observations. One time he commented, "Exquisitely green and loftily luxuriant, your works have overtaken the ancients." This of course proceeded from the excessive kindness of a family friend who bent his judgment in offering encouragement to a youth. I knew that if I examined myself I would discover that the compliment was undeserved.

As for calligraphy, I have studied the regular and running scripts of Ch'u Sui-liang.[4] But as I am weak my wrist is totally lacking in power. My handwriting sometimes looks like a twisted earthworm, sometimes like the smudges left by a crow who has stumbled into an ink bowl. Therefore I seldom have the courage to face brush and paper. Only in the pa-fen style I have learned something from the ancients. When I am in an expansive mood I can turn out large characters several feet in size, which are widely admired for their expressive power. But it is still no more than a case of the one-eyed man being king in the country of the blind. In my own mind nothing much can be said of it.

As for Buddhism, I have always been a believer; I am particularly interested in the Ch'an school. Whenever I hear of an eminent monk trav-

---

[2] His formal name was Wu Wei-yeh (1609–1672).

[3] Tung Ch'i-ch'ang (1555–1636), a prominent painter and man of letters.

[4] Ch'u (596–658) was one of the great T'ang calligraphers.

eling to my region I never fail to don a humble dress and go to visit him. Although I have received a great deal of instruction, I have not gained even the slightest insight or enlightenment: due to my poor endowment and strong delusions, every time a religious intention rose, it was always diverted by some worldly concern. I am afraid I shall have spent my life in frivolities and willful submersion.

How I Began in Wealth and Ended in Poverty

Having been amply provided for by my forefathers, I am ignorant of anything to do with a livelihood: I do not even know how to use a scale or handle an abacus. Yet I was fatally addicted to gardens. Wherever I lived I set up rock arrangements and planted trees so as to express my sentiments and amuse my eyes. During the prime of my life I was bent on constructing and planting in heroic proportions. Once I gave in to my extravagant fancy I no longer thought about the consequences.

I started two gardens—the east and the south—simultaneously. For each I planted several acres of red Lo-chiao peonies. I had dikes built, slopes enlarged, hilltops erected, and ridges raised. When trees and vines were fully grown both gardens gained great renown. However, I gradually found it hard to make both ends meet as my charity work, building expenditures, and other expenses got out-of-hand. In time I was further burdened with several mishaps. The costly weddings of my sons and daughters never seemed to end while tax collectors and moneylenders became more and more importunate. With the last drop of blood squeezed out of my estate, there was left only an empty shell. I had no alternative but to surrender some of my property.

The south garden was pawned to monks and nuns, who proceeded to break up the ground. My thousand flowering plum trees and the thick cassia bushes that circumscribed the land were all cut down and sold as firewood. The east garden was daily trampled underfoot by yokels and swains to the extent that ornamental rocks were toppled and hilly paths eroded away. The place is now hardly recognizable. As I was no longer capable of looking after it, I divided it up among my sons and let each of them take care of his share. But all my sons are too destitute to do any repairs. The garden is daily approaching a wasteland. The sight is so painful that nowadays I visit it but once or twice a year.

About a dozen miles to the northwest of the town there was a piece of wetland some twenty acres in size. A meandering stream, a clear pond, willows on the banks, a rush-covered isle—a place of simple and quiet beauty. I wished to build a cottage there to while away my old age. But enfettered by worldly cares and ties I was never free to do anything about it. Nowadays every time I pass by the place on my way to the city I notice that things there are quite different from what they once were. My wish will never be gratified. I am now resigned to spending my remaining days in sorrow and poverty.

Conclusion

In my youth I made a solemn resolution to uphold myself, discarding completely all the luxuries and frivolities that often corrupted young members of prominent families, thus extricating myself from the pervading worldliness and decadence. Alas, little did I expect that a prominent family would frequently incur resentment and that a brotherless man would stumble easily. I wasted months and years in timidity and vigilance, while my means were exhausted in meeting social obligations. Therefore I failed to match the glories of my forefathers by mastering one canonical classic, nor did I achieve fame and excel among my contemporaries through the practice of one art.

Now the setting sun approaches the hills, and the traveler is near the end of the road. I have not, like Hsiang P'ing,[5] gained the freedom to roam the world, nor can I be certain that I may be granted a few more years to live—the same wish that Confucius had.[6] I gathered all my sons and exhorted them to maintain a fraternal solidarity, lest they be vanquished one by one. It was difficult not to grieve at the death of my wife. Sorrows congest deeply in my chest, but to few of my numerous friends could I unburden myself, nor can I talk plainly with many of my relatives.

However, when I look back, I have never in all my life trangressed Confucian morality. From childhood to youth I was day and night in the company of my grandfather, so I witnessed the way he comported himself. Surrounded by his friends or family, he would sit in front of the stove, trimming the wick of the candle while discussing the classics and calligraphy, going over some historical facts, or lamenting current affairs. There was never a word about advancement, fame, or business. What I constantly saw and heard permeated my heart and mind. Consequently throughout my life I have always found serenity in being generous and loyal, have judged myself sternly in terms of purity and integrity, and have behaved as if I could never be sufficiently discreet, respectful, and yielding. Only by having done all the above did I escape the faults of superficiality and grossness. But if one places survival above honor and

---

[5] I.e., Hsiang Tzu-p'ing, also known as Hsiang Chang, a first-century hermit. After his sons and daughters were married he took to the road and never went back home.

[6] Alludes to *Analects*, 7:16.

shamefully seeks safety at any cost, his would be merely the cautious conduct of women and children, nothing to be proud of.

I have just made a summary of my life to be kept in the family temple,
whereby my descendants in future generations will be acquainted with an
outline of my life history. Through the document they will trace everything back to the family instructions of my father and grandfather. They
must strive to emulate former ways and do nothing to diminish the fame
of the family. Perhaps someday they will restore the glory of the family
by having several members simultaneously serving the government in
high offices. (*MTW*, pp. 42–46)

GLOSSARY OF IMPORTANT
CHINESE NAMES AND TERMS

(Names and book titles already entered in the Bibliography are not repeated in the following list.)

ai-ming 愛名
ai-se 愛色
ai-shen 愛身
ai-ts'ai 愛財
A-mi-t'o-fo 阿彌陀佛
an-ch'a shih 按察使
Chan-kuo ts'e 戰國策
Ch'an-ch'i 禪期
Chang 漳
Chang Chüeh 張角
Chang Hsiu 張脩
Chang Hung-lieh 張鴻烈
Chang Kun 章袞
Chang Tao-ling 張道陵
Chang Wen-ch'eng 張文成
Ch'ang-p'ing 昌平
Ch'ang-shou 長壽
Chao 趙
Chao Chen-chi (Ta-chou)
　趙貞吉大洲
Chao Meng-fu 趙孟頫
Chao Ming-ch'eng 趙明誠
Chao P'u 趙普
Ch'ao-yang 潮陽
Chen-k'o (Tzu-po, Ta-kuan)
　真可紫柏達觀
Ch'en Chia-mo 陳嘉謀
Ch'en Hung-shou 陳洪綬
Ch'en Ta-lun 陳大論
Cheng 鄭
Cheng Hsüan 鄭玄
cheng-jen 証仁
Cheng Man 鄭鄤
Ch'eng-Chu 程朱
Ch'eng Ying 程嬰
chi 記
Chi-tsu 雞足
chi-wen 祭文

chia-p'u 家譜
Chia-ting 嘉定
Chieh-chai 潔齋
Chieh-yang 揭陽
Chien-niang 監娘
Ch'ien Ch'ien-i 錢謙益
Ch'ien Lou 黔婁
Ch'ien Te-hung 錢德洪
chih 誌
Chih-tun 支遁
Ch'ih 郗
chin-shih 進士
Chin-ssu lu 近思錄
ching 境
Ching-ling 竟陵
Ching-tz'u 淨慈
Ch'ing-ming 清明
Cho 卓
Cho Tso-chü 卓左車
Cho-wu 卓吾
Chu-ko Liang 諸葛亮
Chu Kuei 朱圭
chu-p'u 竹譜
Ch'u-chou 處州
Ch'u-k'ung 楚倥
Ch'u Sui-liang 褚遂良
chü-chieh 具戒
chü-shih 居士
ch'ü 曲
Ch'ü Yüan 屈原
chuan 傳
Ch'uan-hsi lu 傳習錄
chüan 卷
Ch'üan 泉
chuang 狀
Chuang-tzu 莊子
Chüeh-fan 覺範
Chüeh-lang 覺浪

Ch'un ch'iu 春秋
Chung-feng kuang-lu 中峯廣錄
Chung-yüan 中元
Chung-yung 中庸
Ch'ung-an 崇安
Fa-hui (Yün-ku) 法會雲谷
Fang Chen-ju 方震孺
Fang-shan 方山
Feng Ching-t'ung 馮敬通
Feng-niang 奉娘
Feng Yen 馮衍
Fu Hsi 伏羲
Fu Hsüan 傅玄
Fu-sheng liu-chi 浮生六記
Fu-teng (Miao-feng) 福登妙峯
Han shu 漢書
Han Yü 韓愈
Hang Shih-chün 杭世駿
hao 號
hao-chieh chih-shih 豪傑之士
Ho Ch'in 賀欽
Ho Ching-ming 何景明
Ho Ling-t'ai 賀凌臺
Hsi-lin 西林
hsia 俠
Hsia yu-chi 夏遊記
Hsia-yüan 下元
Hsiao T'ung 蕭統
hsien 覞
hsing 形
hsing-jen 行人
Hsing-li ta-ch'üan 性理大全
hsiu 修
Hsiu 修
Hsiung-nu 匈奴
hsü (account) 叙
hsü (preface, postface) 序
Hsü Chien 徐堅
hsü-chuan 序傳
Hsü Hung-tsu (Hsia-k'o) 徐宏祖霞客
Hsü Wei 徐渭
hsüeh 學
Hsüeh Ching-chih 薛敬之
hsüeh-p'u 學譜
Hsüeh-yen 雪巖
Hsün-tzu 荀子
Hu T'ien-feng 胡天鳳

Hua-yen ching 華嚴經
Huan-niang 環娘
Huang-an 黃安
Huang Chien-chi 黃兼濟
Huang-fu Mi 皇甫謐
Huang Ju-heng 黃汝亨
Huang Kung-wang 黃公望
Huang Tao-chou 黃道周
Huang-ti 黃帝
Hui-k'o 慧可
Hui-kuan 慧觀
Hui-neng 慧能
hun 魂
hung 虹
i-ch'ou 乙丑
i-hsüeh 義學
Jen An 任安
jen-hsü 壬戌
jo-ku 若谷
k'ai 楷
K'ang-hsi 康熙
kao 高
Kao-feng 高峯
Kao-shih chuan 高士傳
K'ao-t'ing 考亭
keng-hsü 庚戌
Keng Ting-li 耿定理
Ko T'ien Shih 葛天氏
ku-ch'en nieh-tzu 孤臣孽子
Ku K'ai-chih 顧愷之
Ku Ying-t'ai 谷應泰
kuan 關
Kuan-yin 觀音
Kuang-chou 廣州
k'uang-chih 壙誌
kuei-hai 癸亥
K'un-chih chi 困知記
K'un-chih lu 困知錄
k'un erh hsüeh chih 因而學之
k'un-hsüeh 困學
kung-an 公案
Kung-ch'eng 共城
kung-fu 功夫
Kung-kuo ko 功過格
Kung-sun Ch'u-chiu 公孫杵臼
k'ung 孔
k'ung 空

K'ung Jo-ku 孔若谷
K'ung Jung 孔融
K'ung-k'eng 空坑
K'ung Shang-jen 孔尚任
Kuo Chen 郭振
kuo-kuan 過關
Lao Tzu (book) 老子
Lao Tzu (person) 老子
lei 誄
Lei-chou 雷州
li (calligraphy style) 隸
li (principle) 理
li (unit of distance) 里
Li Ch'un-fang 李春芳
Li Ling 李陵
Li Meng-yang 李夢陽
Li Po 李白
Li sao 離騷
Liang 梁
liang-chih 良知
liang-hsin 良心
Liao-tung 遼東
Lin-chi 臨濟
Lin-ch'iung 臨邛
Ling-kuan 靈官
Ling-yin 靈隱
Liu-niang 柳娘
Liu Tsung-yüan 柳宗元
Lo Ch'in-shun 羅欽順
Lo Hung-hsien 羅洪先
Lo Ju-fang 羅汝芳
Loyang 洛陽
lu 錄
Lu Chi 陸機
Lu Chiu-yüan (Hsiang-shan)
　陸九淵象山
Lu Chung 陸終
Lu Ku-ch'iao 陸古樵
Lu Kuei-meng 陸龜蒙
Lu Yü 陸羽
Lü Tuan 呂端
lun 論
lun-hui 輪迴
lung 龍
Lung-hsi 隴西
Lung-men 龍門
Ma Jung 馬融

Miao-feng (Chih-shan) 妙峯之善
ming (name) 名
ming (inscription) 銘
Ming-ching 明經
Ming-pen (Chung-feng, Huan-chu)
　明本中峯幻住
Ming-shih chi-shih pen-mo 明史記
　事本末
Ming-tao 明道
mu chih ming 墓誌銘
mu-yu 幕友
nan-hsün 南詢
Nan-shih 南史
Nei-chiang 內江
nien 年
nien-p'u 年譜
Ou-yang Te 歐陽德
Ou-yang Wen-ch'ao 歐陽文朝
Pa-pa 八八
Pan Ku 班固
Pao-p'u tzu 抱朴子
Pao-ting 保定
pei 碑
P'ei Sung-chih 裴松之
P'eng-li 彭蠡
pi-chi 筆記
pi-t'an 筆談
Po-lo 博羅
pu shuo p'o 不說破
p'u 譜
P'u Sung-ling 蒲松齡
san-kuan 三關
San-yüan 三元
shan-shu 善書
Shan-ts'ai 善財
Shang shu 尚書
Shang-yü 上虞
Shang-yüan 上元
Shao-hsing 紹興
Shao-lin 少林
shen 神
Shen Fu 沈復
Shen-hsien chuan 神仙傳
shen ming 神明
shen-shih nien-fo 審實念佛
Shen Yüeh 沈約
sheng-hsüeh 聖學

Sheng-hsüeh ch'ih-chin san-kuan
　聖學吃緊三關
shih (history) 史
shih (poetry) 詩
Shih chi 史記
Shih-fan (Wu-chun) 師範無準
Shih-t'ien (Fa-hsün) 石田法薫
Shou-niang 壽娘
shou-ts'ang-chih 壽藏誌
Shuang-lin 雙林
shui-mu 水母
Ssu-chou 泗州
Ssu-ma Hsiang-ju 司馬相如
Ssu-shu kai-ts'o 四書改錯
Su Shih 蘇軾
Su Wu 蘇武
sui-pi 隨筆
Sung 宋
"Sung-kuo fa" 訟過法
Sung-yüan (Ch'ung-yüeh) 松源崇嶽
Ta-chou 大州
ta hsiung-meng chang-fu 大雄猛丈夫
Ta hsüeh 大學
Ta-shan 大汕
t'a-ming 塔銘
T'ai-chou 泰州
T'ai-ho 泰和
T'an Lun 譚綸
T'ang Hsien-tsu 湯顯祖
T'ang Shun-chih 唐順之
tao 道
Tao-an 道安
Tao te ching 道德經
T'ao Mei 陶梅
Teng I-tsan 鄧以贊
Teng Lu 鄧魯
T'ieh-chüeh-yüan 鐵橛遠
t'ieh-han 鐵漢
T'ieh-shan Ai (Ch'iung) 鐵山璦瓊
Tien-lüeh 典論
T'ien-mu (Wen-li) 天目文禮
T'ien-ning 天寧
T'ien-shih Tao 天師道
T'ien-t'ai 天臺
ting 定
Ting-niang 定娘
T'ing-chou 汀州

tsa-chi 雜記
tsan 贊
Tsan-yü 贊虞
Ts'ao Ch'i 曹溪
Ts'ao-tung 曹洞
Tseng 曾
Tseng Tzu 曾子
Tso chuan 左傳
Tso chüeh-i 左覺義
tso kung-fu 做功夫
Tsou Yüan-piao 鄒元標
tsui-chi 罪己
tsui-kuo 罪過
Tsung-kao (Ta-hui P'u-chüeh) 宗杲
　大慧普覺
Tu Fu 杜甫
Tuan-ch'iao 斷橋
Tung Ch'i-ch'ang 董其昌
Tung-fang Shuo 東方朔
Tung-lin 東林
Tung yu-chi 冬遊記
T'ung-an 同安
tzu (name) 字
tzu (auto or self-) 自
tzu (word) 字
tzu-chi 自記
Tzu-chih 自志
"Tzu-hsing chi" 自省記
tzu-hsü (self-account) 自敘
tzu-hsü (self-written preface or
　postface) 自序
tzu-hsü nien-p'u 自敘年譜
tzu-shu 自述
Tzu Ssu 子思
tzu-sung 自訟
tzu-tse 自責
tz'u 詞
wan-ko-shih 挽歌詩
Wan-li 萬曆
Wan T'ing-yen 萬廷言
Wang Chi-chung (Ssu-jen) 王季重
　思任
Wang Hsi-chüeh 王羲之
Wang Hsien-chih 王獻之
Wang Ken 王艮
Wang Meng 王猛
Wang Shih-chen (1526–1590) 王世貞

Wang Shih-chen (1634–1711) 王士禎
Wang Shou-jen (Yang-ming) 王守
   仁陽明
Wang Tao-chen 王燾貞
wei-ch'i 圍棋
Wei-Chin 魏晉
Wei Chung-hsien 魏忠賢
Wei Ta-chung 魏大中
Wei-tse (T'ien-ju) 惟則天如
wen 文
Wen-fu 文賦
Wen hsüan 文選
wu (illumination) 悟
wu (nothingness) 無
Wu Huai Shih 無懷氏
Wu-i 武夷
wu-men-kuan 無門關
Wu Sung 武松
Wu-t'ai 五臺
Wu Tzu-wang 吳子往
Wu Wei-yeh 吳偉業

Wu-wen (Ssu-ts'ung) 無聞思聰
Yai-shan 厓山
Yang Chi-sheng 楊繼盛
Yang Chien 楊簡
Yang Hsiung 楊雄
Yang Wen-ts'ai 楊文彩
Yao 猺
Yao-shu 妖書
Yen Sung 嚴嵩
ying 影
yu-chi 遊記
Yu-hsien k'u 遊仙窟
Yu-Huang-ch'i chi 遊黃溪記
Yü Hsin 庾信
Yü-men-kuan 玉門關
Yü-san 與三
Yü Ta-fu 郁達夫
Yü t'ien yüeh 籲天約
Yüan Chung-tao 袁中道
Yüan Tsung-tao 袁宗道
Yün-ch'i 雲棲

A List of Chinese Autobiographical Writings

Whenever possible, I base my translations on the texts included in the following four accessible anthologies: Kuo Teng-feng 郭登峯, ed., *Li-tai tzu-hsü-chuan wen-ch'ao* 歷代自叙傳文鈔 (Anthology of autobiographies) 2 vols. (Taipei: Shang-wu yin-shu-kuan, 1965); Huang Tsung-hsi 黃宗羲, *Ming-ju hsüeh-an* 明儒學案 (Philosophical records of Ming Confucians) (Taipei: Shih-chieh shu-chü, 1965); Tu Lien-che 杜聯喆, ed., *Ming-jen tzu-chuan wen-ch'ao* 明人自傳文鈔 (Anthology of Ming autobiographies) (Taipei: I-wen yin-shu-kuan, 1977); Tu Mu 都穆, ed., *Wu-hsia chung-mu i-wen* 吳下冢墓遺文 (Necrologies recovered from the Wu area) (Taipei: T'ai-wan shu-chü, 1969).

Chang Han 張瀚 (1511–1593). *Sung-ch'uang meng-yü* 松窗夢語 (Dreams behind the pine window). Shanghai: Shang-hai ku-chi ch'u-pan-she, 1986.

Chang Lü-hsiang 張履祥 (1611–1674). *Tzu-tse* 自責 (Self-Reproach). In *Yang-yüan hsien-sheng ch'üan-chi* 楊園先生全集 (Complete works of Master Chang Lü-hsiang), 23 : 5a. Nanking: Chiang-su shu-chü, 1872.

Chang Tai 張岱 (1597–1684?). *Tzu-hsü* 自序 (Self-written preface). In *T'ao-an meng-i* 陶庵夢憶 (T'ao-an's remembrances of dreams). Taipei: T'ai-wan k'ai-ming shu-chü, 1972, pp. 1–2.

Ch'ao-hung 超弘 (b. 1605). *T'a-ming* 塔銘 (Stupa inscription). In *Sou-sung chi* 瘦松集 (Works collected under a lean pine), pp. 440–41. Taipei: Hsin-wen-feng ch'u-pan kung-ssu, 1975.

Chen-i 真一 (d. 1629?). *Tzu-chih t'a-ming* 自製塔銘 (Self-made stupa inscription). In *MTW*, pp. 386–87.

Ch'en Chi-ju 陳繼儒 (1558–1639). *K'ung-ch'ing hsien-sheng mu-chih-ming* 空清先生墓誌銘 (The tomb notice and inscription of Master K'ung-ch'ing). In *MTW*, pp. 252–54.

Ch'eng Hsiang 程珦 (1006–1090). *Tzu-tso mu-chih* 自作墓誌 (Self-written tomb notice and inscription). In *LTW*, 2 : 345.

Ch'ien Shih-yang 錢世揚 (1554–1610). *Ch'i-jen chuan* 畸人傳 (Biography of an odd person). In *MTW*, pp. 349–52.

Ching-lung 景隆 (1393–1466?). *K'ung-ku Lung ch'an-shih Ching-lung tzu-chih t'a-ming* 空谷隆禪師景隆自製塔銘 (Self-made stupa inscription of Ch'an master K'ung-ku Ching-lung). In *MTW*, pp. 392–93.

Chu-hung 袾宏 (1535–1615). *Tzu-tse* 自責 (Self-Reproach). In *Yün-ch'i ta-shih i-kao* 雲棲大師遺稿 (Written legacy of Master Chu-hung), 3 : 86a–87a. Vol. 31 of *Yün-ch'i fa-hui* 雲棲法彙 (Collected works of Chu-hung). Nanking: Chin-ling k'o-ching-ch'u, 1897.

Chu Yüan-chang 朱元璋 (1327–1398). *Huang-ling pei* 皇陵碑 (Imperial epitaph). In *MTW*, pp. 67–69.

Feng Tao 馮道 (882–954). *Ch'ang-lo Lao tzu-hsü* 長樂老自叙 (Self-Account of the Old Man of Perpetual Happiness). In *LTW*, 1:11–16.

Hsü Jih-chiu 徐日久 (1574–1631). *Chen-shuai hsien-sheng hsüeh-p'u* 真率先生學譜 (Master Hsü Jih-chiu's record of education). National Library of Peiping microfilm.

Hu Chih 胡直 (1517–1585). *K'un-hsüeh chi* 困學記 (A record of learning through difficulties). In *MJHA*, pp. 221–24.

Huang Hsing-tseng 黃省曾 (1490–1540). *Lin-chung tzu-chuan* 臨終自傳 (Death-bed autobiography). In *MTW*, pp. 290–93.

Kao P'an-lung 高攀龍 (1562–1626). *K'un-hsüeh chi* 困學記 (A record of learning through difficulties). In *Kao-tzu i-shu* 高子遺書 (Written legacy of Master Kao P'an-lung), 3:13a–18a. 1876.

———. *San shih chi* 三時記 (A record of three seasons). In *Kao-tzu i-shu*, 10:25b–48a.

Ko Hung 葛洪 (250?–330?). *Tzu-hsü* 自叙 (Self-written postface). In *LTW*, 1:157–73.

Ku Te-hui 顧德輝 (1310–1369). *Chin-su tao-jen Ku-chün mu-chih* 金粟道人顧君墓志 (Tomb notice of Mr. Ku, also known as Chin-su, a man of the Way). In *WHCMIW*, pp. 69–72.

Li Chih 李贄 (1527–1602). *Cho-wu lun-lüeh* 卓吾論略 (Brief comment on Cho-wu). In *MTW*, pp. 118–21.

Li Ch'ing-chao 李清照 (1084–1151?). *Chin shih lu hou-hsü* 金石錄後序 (Postface to A *Record of Stone and Metal Inscriptions*). In *LTW*, 1:191–98.

Li Hsing-chih 李行之 (d. 581?). *Tzu-wei mu-chih-ming* 自為墓誌銘 (Self-written tomb notice and inscription). In *LTW*, 2:335.

Liu Chih-chi 劉知幾 (661–721). *Tzu-hsü* 自叙 (Self-Account). In *Shih-t'ung t'ung-shih* 史通通釋 (*Universals in History* with collected annotations), edited by P'u Ch'i-lung 浦起龍, pp. 138–41. Taipei: Shih-chieh shu-chü, 1962.

Liu Chün 劉峻 (463–522). *Tzu-hsü* 自序 (Self-Account). In *LTW*, 1:7–8.

Liu Hsüan 劉炫 (544?–611?). *Tzu-tsan* 自贊 (Self-Eulogy). In *LTW*, 2:532–34.

Liu Hsün 劉壎 (1240–1319). *Tzu-chih* 自志 (Self-Notice). In *Shui-yun-ts'un kao* 水雲村稿 (Manuscript from the Shui-yun Village), 8:11a–12b. SKCSCP, fourth series.

Liu Jo-yü 劉若愚 (1584–1642?). *Lei-ch'en tzu-hsü* 纍臣自叙 (Self-Account of an incarcerated vassal). In *Ming-kung shih* 明宮史 (History of the Ming palace), 8:1a–5b. Kuo-hsüeh fu-lun she, 1910.

Liu Shu 劉恕 (1030?–1076?). *Tzu-sung* 自訟 (Self-Indictment). In *LTW*, 2:523–24.

Liu Ta-hsia 劉大夏 (1437–1516). *Shou-ts'ang-chi* 壽藏記 (Sepulcher note). In *MTW*, pp. 331–32.

Mao Ch'i-ling 毛奇齡 (1623–1716). *Tzu-wei mu-chih-ming* 自為墓誌銘 (Self-written tomb notice and inscription). In *Mao Hsi-ho hsien-sheng ch'üan-chi* 毛西河先生全集 (Complete works of Master Mao Ch'i-ling), 35:11:1a–20b. 1761.

Meng-shan I 蒙山異 (1231–?). *Meng-shan I ch'an-shih shih-chung* 蒙山異禪師

示衆 (A sermon of the Ch'an master Meng-shan I). In *CKTC*, pp. 13–16.

Ou-yang Hsiu 歐陽修 (1107–1072). *Liu-i chü-shih chuan* 六一居士傳 (The biography of the Retired Gentleman Six-One). In *LTW*, 2:279–82.

Po Chü-i 白居易 (772–864). *Tsui-yin hsien-sheng chuan* 醉吟先生傳 (Biography of Master Singing When Intoxicated). In *LTW*, 2:256–59.

Shao Yung 邵雍 (1011–1077). *Wu-ming chün chuan* 無名君傳 (Biography of Mr. Nameless). In *LTW*, 2:283–85.

Ssu-ma Ch'ien 司馬遷 (145?–90? B.C.). *T'ai-shih Kung tzu-hsü* 太史公自序 (Postface by the Grand Historian). In *LTW*, 1:102–35.

Sun Ai 孫艾 (b. 1452). *Hsi-ch'uan chü-shih tzu-wei sheng-chih* 西川居士自為生誌 (Self-written tomb notice of the retired gentleman Hsi-ch'uan). In *MTW*, pp. 178–79.

Sung Wu 宋无 (b. 1260). *Wu I-shih Sung Wu tzu-chih* 吳逸士宋无自誌 (Self-Notice of Sung Wu, a hermit of Wu). In *WHCMIW*, pp. 34–39.

T'ao Ch'ien 陶潛 (365–427). *Wu-liu hsien-sheng chuan* 五柳先生傳 (Biography of Master Five Willows). In *LTW*, 2:247–48.

Te-ch'ing 德清 (1546–1623). *Tsu-pen Han-shan ta shih nien-p'u su-chu* 足本憨山大師年譜疏注 (Unabridged and annotated annalistic biography of Master han-shan). Edited by Fu-cheng 福徵. Soochow: Hung-hua she, 1934.

Teng Huo-ch'ü 鄧豁渠 (1498–1570?). *Nan-hsün lu* 南詢錄 (The record of a quest in the south). Ca. 1599.

Ts'ao P'ei 曹丕 (187–226). *Tien-lun tzu-hsü* 典論自叙 (Self-written preface to *Model Discussions*). In *LTW*, 1:153–57.

Tsu-ch'in 祖欽 (1216–1287). *P'u-shuo* 普說 (A sermon). In *Hsüeh-yen ho-shang yü-lu* 雪巖和尚語錄 (The sayings of Master Tsu-ch'ing). In *HTC*, 122:512–15.

Tu Wen-huan 杜文煥 (b. 1565?). *Yüan-ho i-shih chuan* 元鶴逸史傳 (Biography of the untrammeled historian Yüan-ho). In *MTW*, pp. 122–25.

Wang Chi 王畿 (1498–1583). *Tzu-sung* 自訟 (Self-Indictment). In *Wang Lung-ch'i ch'üan-chi* 王龍溪全集 (Complete works of Wang Chi), 15:16b–21a. 1882 ed. Reprint. Taipei: Hua-wen shu-chü, 1970.

Wang Chieh 汪价 (1603?–1682?). *San-nung chui-jen kuang tzu-hsü* 三儂贅人廣自序 (Expanded self-account of the Useless Man San-nung). In *LTW*, 1:32–67.

Wang Ch'ung 王充 (A.D. 27–97?). *Tzu-chi* 自紀 (Self-Record). In *LTW*, 1:136–51.

Wang Shih-min 王時敏 (1592–1680). *Tzu-shu* 自述 (Self-Account). In *MTW*, pp. 41–46.

Wang Ssu-jen 王思任 (1575–1646). "Wang Chi-chung tzu-hsü nien-p'u" 王季重自叙年譜 (The annalistic autobiography of Wang Ssu-jen). Manuscript. Peking University Library.

Wang Yü 王鬱 (1204–1234). *Wang tzu hsiao-chuan* 王子小傳 (An informal biography of the philosopher Wang). In *LTW*, 2:289–92.

Wen-pao (13th century) 文寶. *Hsiao-ts'an* 小參 (A sermon). In *Fang-shan Wen-pao Ch'an-shih yü-lu* 方山文寶禪師語錄 (The sayings of Ch'an master Wen-pao). In *HTC*, 122:453–56.

Wen T'ien-hsiang 文天祥 (1236–1283). *Chi-nien lu* 紀年錄 (Record of the years). In *Wen-shan hsien-sheng ch'üan-chi* 文山先生全集 (Complete works of Master Wen T'ien-hsiang). SPTK, 17:1a–41a.

Wu Yü-pi 吳與弼 (1392–1469). Diary selections. In *MJHA*, pp. 3–7.

Yang Hsün-chi 楊循吉 (1458–1546). *Tzu-chuan sheng-k'uang pei* 自撰生壙碑 (Self-prepared epitaph). In *MTW*, pp. 306–9.

Yüan-miao 原妙 (1238–1295). *T'ung Yang-shan Hsüeh-yen ho-shang i ssu shu* 通仰山雪巖和尚疑嗣書 (A letter to Master Hsüeh-yen [Tsu-ch'in] of Yang-shan expressing doubts about succeeding him). In *Kao-feng Yüan-miao Ch'an-shih yü-lu* 高峯原妙禪師語錄 (The sayings of Ch'an master Yüan-miao). In *HTC*, 122:678–80.

Yüan Ts'an 袁粲 (?–477). *Miao-te hsien-sheng chuan* 妙德先生傳 (Biography of Master Subtle Virtue). In *LTW*, 2:248–50.

PRIMARY AND SECONDARY WORKS IN
CHINESE AND JAPANESE

Ch'an-kuan ts'e-chin 禪關策進 (Cantering through Ch'an passes). Compiled by Chu-hung 袾宏. Hong Kong: Hsiang-kang fo-ching liu-t'ung ch'u, 1965.

Chang Hsüeh-ch'eng 章學誠. *Chang-shih i-shu* 章氏遺書 (Written legacy of Mr. Chang). 2 vols. Shanghai: Shang-wu yin-shu-kuan, 1930.

———. *Wen-shih t'ung-i* 文史通義 (General principles of literature and history). Taipei: Shih-chieh shu-chü, 1968.

Chang Wei-hsin 張維新. *Pien-chi ming-yen* 砭己名言 (Well-known sayings on self-admonition). 1591 ed. National Library of Peiping microfilm.

Chao Chen-chi 趙貞吉. *Chao Wen-su kung wen-chi* 趙文肅公文集 (Collected writings of Chao Chen-chi). Fukien, 1586.

Ch'en Ching-ho 陳荊和. *Shih-ch'i shih-chi Kuang-nan chih hsin shih-liao* 十七世紀廣南之新史料 (New historical sources of seventeenth-century Annam). Taipei: Chung-hua ts'ung-shu wei-yüan-hui, 1960.

Ch'en Yüan 陳垣. *Chung-kuo fo-chiao shih-chi kai-lun* 中國佛教史籍概論 (A bibliographical guide to Chinese Buddhism). Peking: Chung-hua shu-chü, 1962.

Ch'eng Hao 程顥, and Ch'eng I 程頤. *Erh-Ch'eng ch'üan-shu* 二程全書 (Complete works of the two Ch'engs). SPPY ed.

———. *Erh-Ch'eng i-shu* 二程遺書 (Written legacy of the two Ch'engs). In *Erh-Ch'eng ch'üan-shu*.

Ching-te ch'uan-teng lu 景德傳燈錄 (Transmission of the lamp). Compiled by Tao-yüan 道原. Taipei: Chen-shan-mei ch'u-pan-she, 1968.

Chou I cheng-i 周易正義 (Correct meaning of the *Book of Changes*). SPPY ed.

Chou Ju-teng 周汝登. *Tung-Yüeh cheng-hsüeh lu* 東越證學錄 (Testimonials to learning in East Yüeh). 1595 ed. Reprint. 2 vols. Taipei: Wen-hai ch'u-pan-she, 1970.

Chu Hsi 朱熹. *Chu-tzu yü-lei* 朱子語類 (Classified conversations of Master Chu Hsi). 1473 ed. Reprint. Taipei: Cheng-chung shu-chü, 1972.

———. *Hui-an hsien-sheng Chu Wen-kung wen-chi* 晦庵先生朱文公文集 (Collected writings of Master Chu Hsi). SPTK ed.

Hai Jui 海瑞 *Hai Jui chi* 海瑞集 (Collected works of Hai Jui). Peking: Chung-hua shu-chü, 1962.

Hou-Han shu 後漢書 (Dynastic history of the later Han). Po-na ed.

Hsieh Kuo-chen 謝國楨. *Ming-Ch'ing pi-chi t'an-ts'ung* 明清筆記談叢 (Studies of Ming-Ch'ing miscellaneous notes). Shanghai: Chung-hua shu-chü, 1962.

Hsin T'ang shu 新唐書 (New dynastic history of the T'ang). Po-na ed.

Hsüan-tsang 玄奘. *Ta-T'ang hsi-yü chi* 大唐西域記 (T'ang records of the western regions). In *T*, 51:868c–947c.

Huang Tsung-hsi 黃宗羲, ed. *Ming-ju hsüeh-an* 明儒學案 (Philosophical records of Ming Confucians). Taipei: Shih-chieh shu-chü, 1965.

Hui-chiao 慧皎. *Kao-seng chuan* 高僧傳 (Lives of eminent monks). Nanking, 1884. Reprint. 2 vols. Taipei: T'ai-wan yin-ching-ch'u, 1958.

Hui-li 慧立, and Yen-ts'ung 彥悰. *Ta-tz'u-en ssu san-tsang fa-shih chuan* 大慈恩寺三藏法師傳 (Biography of Master Hsüan-tsang of the Ta-tz'u-en Temple). In *T*, 50:221b–80a.

Keng Ting-hsiang 耿定向. *Li-chung san i-jen chuan* 里中三異人傳 (Biographies of the three eccentrics who once resided in my neighborhood). In *Keng T'ien-t'ai hsien-sheng wen-chi* 耿天台先生文集 (Collected works of Master Keng Ting-hsiang). 1598. Reprint. 4 vols. Taipei: Wen-hai ch'u-pan-she, 1970.

Kuang hung-ming chi 廣弘明集 (Expanded collection on the propagation of light). Compiled by Tao-hsüan 道宣. SPPY ed.

Kuo Teng-feng 郭登峯, ed. *Li-tai tzu-hsü-chuan wen-ch'ao* 歷代自敘傳文鈔 (Anthology of autobiographies). 2 vols. Taipei: Shang-wu yin-shu-kuan, 1965.

Li Chih 李贄. *Hsü Fen shu* 續焚書 (Sequel to *A Book to Be Burned*). Peking: Chung-hua shu-chü, 1961.

Li Yu 李攸. *Sung-ch'ao shih-shih* 宋朝事實 (Facts of the Sung dynasty). TSCC ed.

Li Yung 李顒. *Erh-ch'ü chi* 二曲集 (Collected works of Li Yung). Taipei: Shang-wu yin-shu kuan, 1973.

Liang shu 梁書 (Dynastic history of the Liang). Po-na ed.

Liu Hsiang 劉向. *Lieh nü chuan* 列女傳 (Biographies of women). SPPY ed.

Liu I-ch'ing 劉義慶. *Shih-shuo hsin-yü* 世說新語 (A new account of tales of the world). SPPY ed.

Liu Tsung-chou 劉宗周. *Jen-p'u* 人譜 (A manual for men). Taipei: Shang-wu yin-shu-kuan, 1968.

Lu Chiu-yüan 陸九淵. *Hsiang-shan ch'üan-chi* 象山全集 (Complete works of Lu Chiu-yüan). SPPY ed.

Lu Shih-i 陸世儀. *Lu Fu-t'ing Ssu-pien-lu chi-yao* 陸桴亭思辨錄輯要 (The essentials of Lu Shih-i's *Records of Deliberations*). Edited by Chang Po-hsing 張伯行. 2 vols. TSCC ed.

Lü K'un 呂坤. *Lü K'un che-hsüeh hsüan-chi* 呂坤哲學選集 (Selected philosophical works of Lü K'un). Edited by Hou Wai-lu 侯外廬. Peking: Chung-hua shu-chü, 1962.

Ming shih 明史 (Dynastic history of the Ming). Peking: Chung-hua shu-chü, 1974.

Sakai Tadao 酒井忠夫. *Chūgoku zensho no kenkyū* 中國善書の研究 (A study of Chinese morality books). Tokyo Kōbundō, 1960.

San-kuo chih 三國志 (Dynastic history of the Three Kingdoms). Po-na ed.

Shen Te-fu 沈德符. *Yeh-huo pien* 野獲編 (A collection of unofficial facts). Fu-li shan-fang edition.

Shih-lien 石濂. *Li-liu t'ang chi* 離六堂集 (Collected works from the Li-liu Studio). Late 17th century.

Sui shu 隋書 (Dynastic history of the Sui). Po-na ed.

Sun K'o-k'uan 孫克寬. *Yüan-tai tao-chiao chih fa-chan* 元代道教之發展 (The development of Taoism during the Yüan). Taichung: Tung-hai ta-hsüeh, 1968.

Sung shih 宋史 (Dynastic history of the Sung). Po-na ed.

Ta-T'ang liu tien 大唐六典 (The six codes of the great T'ang). Taipei: Wen-hai ch'u-pan-she, 1962.

Taishō Shinshū Dai-zōkyō 大正新脩大藏經 (Taisho edition of the Buddhist canon]. 85 vols. Tokyo, 1914-22.

T'ang Yung-t'ung 湯用彤. *Han Wei Liang-chin Nan-pei-ch'ao fo-chiao shih* 漢魏兩晉南北朝佛教史 (A history of Buddhism during the Han, Wei, two Chins, Northern and Southern Dynasties). 2 vols. Peking: Chung-hua shu-chü, 1963.

T'ao Ch'ien 陶潛. *Ching-chieh hsien-sheng chi* 靖節先生集 (Works of Master T'ao Ch'ien). SPPY ed.

T'ao Hung-ching 陶宏景. *Chen Kao* 真誥 (True commandments). TSCC ed.

Tao-tsang 道藏 (Taoist canon). 110 vols. Shanghai: Shang-wu yin-shu-kuan, 1924-26.

Te-ch'ing 德清. *Han-shan ta-shih meng-yu ch'üan-chi* 憨山大師夢遊全集 (Complete works of Master Han-shan). In *HTC*, 127:946-76.

Tu Lien-che 杜聯喆, ed. *Ming-jen tzu-chuan wen-ch'ao* 明人自傳文鈔 (Anthology of Ming autobiographies). Taipei: I-wen yin-shu-kuan, 1977.

Tu Mu 都穆, ed. *Wu-hsia chung-mu i-wen* 吳下冢墓遺文 (Necrologies recovered from the Wu area). Taipei: T'ai-wan shu-chü, 1969.

Wan Shou-ch'i 萬壽祺. *Shih-hsi ts'ao-t'ang wen-chi* 隰西草堂文集 (Collected writings of Wan Shou-ch'i). Vol. 2 of *Ming-chi san hsiao-lien chi* 明季三孝廉集 (Collected works of three Ming scholars). 1919.

Wang Ch'ung 王充. *Lun-heng chi-chieh* 論衡集解 (*Balanced Discussions* with collected commentaries). Edited by Liu P'an-sui 劉盼遂. 2 vols. Taipei: Shih-chieh shu-chü, 1962.

Wang Shou-jen 王守仁. *Wang Yang-ming ch'üan-shu* 王陽明全書 (Complete works of Wang Shou-jen). 4 vols. Taipei: Cheng-chung shu-chü, 1955.

Wang Te-i 王德毅. *Chung-kuo li-tai ming-jen nien-p'u tsung-mu* 中國歷代名人年譜總目 (A comprehensive catalogue of annalistic biographies of eminent Chinese). Taipei: Hua-shih ch'u-pan-she, 1979.

Wei Hsi 魏禧. *Wei Shu-tzu wen-chi* 魏叔子文集 (Collected writings of Wei Hsi). Late 17th century ed. Reprint. 7 vols. Taipei: Shang-wu yin-shu-kuan, 1973.

Yüan Hung-tao 袁宏道. *Yüan Hung-tao chi ch'ien-chiao* 袁宏道集箋校 (Collected writings of Yüan Hung-tao with bibliographical notes). Edited by Ch'ien Po-ch'eng 錢伯城. 3 vols. Shanghai: Shang-hai ku-chi ch'u-pan-she, 1981.

Yüan shih 元史 (Dynastic history of the Yüan). Po-na ed.

WORKS IN WESTERN LANGUAGES CONSULTED OR CITED IN THE TEXT

Ariès, Philippe. *Centuries of Childhood.* Translated by Robert Baldick. New York: Vintage Books, 1962.

Barkin, Kenneth D. "Autobiography and History." *Societas* 6, no. 2 (Spring 1976): 83–108.

Bauer, Wolfgang. "Icherleben und Autobiographie im älteren China." *Heidelberger Jahrbücher* 8 (1964): 12–40.

Billeter, Jean-François. *Li Zhi, philosophe maudit (1527–1602): Contribution à une sociologie du mandarinat chinois de la fin des Ming.* Geneva: Librairie Droz, 1979.

Bloom, Irene. *Knowledge Painfully Acquired: The "K'un-chih chi" by Lo Ch'in-shun.* New York: Columbia University Press, 1987.

Bunyan, John. *The Pilgrim's Progress.* Edited by Roger Sharrock. New York: Penguin Books, 1981.

Cahill, James. *The Compelling Image: Nature and Style in Seventeenth-Century Chinese Painting.* Cambridge: Harvard University Press, 1982.

Calvin, John. *Institutes of the Christian Religion.* Translated by John Allen. 6th American ed. 2 vols. Philadelphia: Westminister Press, 1936.

Cellini, Benvenuto. *The Autobiography of Benvenuto Cellini.* Translated by George Bull. Baltimore: Penguin Books, 1964.

Chan-kuo ts'e. Translated by J. I. Crump, Jr. Oxford: Oxford University Press, 1970.

Chan, Wing-tsit. *A Source Book in Chinese Philosophy.* Princeton: Princeton University Press, 1963.

Chang, Han-liang. "The Anonymous Autobiographer: Roland Barthes/Shen Fu." In *The Chinese Text: Studies in Comparative Literature,* edited by Ying-hsiung Chou, pp. 61–73. Hong Kong: Chinese University Press, 1986.

de Bary, Wm. Theodore. "Individualism and Humanitarianism in Late Ming Thought." In *Self and Society in Ming Thought,* edited by Wm. Theodore de Bary, pp. 145–247. New York: Columbia University Press, 1970.

———. "Neo-Confucian Cultivation and the Seventeenth-Century 'Enlightenment.'" In *The Unfolding of Neo-Confucianism,* edited by Wm. Theodore de Bary, pp. 141–216. New York: Columbia University Press, 1975.

Delany, Paul. *British Autobiography in the 17th Century.* New York: Columbia University Press, 1969.

de Man, Paul. "Autobiography as De-facement." *MLN* 94 (December 1979): 919–30.

Dumoulin, Heinrich. *Christianity Meets Buddhism.* Translated by John C. Maraldo. La Salle, Ill.: Open Court Publishing Co., 1974.

Dutt, Sukumar. *Early Buddhist Monachism.* New York: E. P. Dutton, 1924.

Eakin, Paul John. *Fictions in Autobiography: Studies in the Art of Self-Invention.* Princeton: Princeton University Press, 1985.

Eberhard, Wolfram. *Guilt and Sin in Traditional China.* Berkeley and Los Angeles: University of California Press, 1967.

Fleishman, Avrom. *Figures of Autobiography: The Language of Self-Writing.* Berkeley and Los Angeles: University of California Press, 1983.

Goodrich, L. Carrington, and Fang Chao-ying, eds. *Dictionary of Ming Biography.* 2 vols. New York: Columbia University Press, 1975.

Hall, Jonathan. "Heroic Repression: Narrative and Aesthetics in Shen Fu's *Six Records of a Floating Life.*" *Comparative Criticism* 9 (1987): 155–72.

Hanan, Patrick. *The Chinese Vernacular Story.* Cambridge: Harvard University Press, 1981.

Hightower, James R. "The *Wen Hsüan* and Genre Theory." *Harvard Journal of Asiatic Studies* 20 (1957): 512–33.

Hui-neng. *The Platform Sutra of the Sixth Patriarch.* Translated by Philip B. Yampolsky. New York: Columbia University Press, 1967.

The Interpreter's Dictionary of the Bible. Edited by George Arthur Buttrick et al. 12 vols. New York: Abingdon Press, 1951–57.

Jay, Paul. "What's the Use? Critical Theory and the Study of Autobiography." *Biography* 10, no. 1 (Winter 1987): 39–53.

Kavolis, Vytautas. "On the Self-Person Differentiation." In *Designs of Selfhood,* edited by Vytautas Kavolis, pp. 132–53. Rutherford, N.J.: Fairleigh Dickinson University Press, 1984.

Legge, James, trans. *Confucian Analects.* In *The Chinese Classics,* vol. 1. Oxford: Clarendon Press, 1893.

———. *The Works of Mencius.* Vol. 2 of *The Chinese Classics.* Oxford: Clarendon Press, 1893.

Lejune, Philippe. *L'autobiographie en France.* Paris: Librairie Armand Colin, 1971.

Lodge, David. *Language of Fiction: Essays in Criticism and Verbal Analysis of the English Novel.* New York: Columbia University Press, 1966.

Misch, Georg. *A History of Autobiography in Antiquity.* Translated by E. W. Dickes. 2 vols. Cambridge: Harvard University Press, 1951.

Olney, James, ed. *Autobiography: Essays Theoretical and Critical.* Princeton: Princeton University Press, 1980.

———. *Metaphors of Self: The Meaning of Autobiography.* Princeton: Princeton University Press, 1973.

Owen, Stephen. *Remembrances: The Experience of the Past in Classical Chinese Literature.* Cambridge: Harvard University Press, 1986.

Plaks, Andrew H., ed. *Chinese Narratives: Critical and Theoretical Essays.* Princeton: Princeton University Press, 1977.

———. *The Four Masterworks of the Ming Novel: Ssu ta ch'i-shu.* Princeton: Princeton University Press, 1987.

Pope Costa, Randolph D. "La autobiografía española hasta Torres Villarroel." Ph.D. dissertation, Columbia University, 1973.

Renza, Louis A. "The Veto of Imagination: A Theory of Autobiography." In *Autobiography: Essays Theoretical and Critical,* edited by James Olney, pp. 268–95. Princeton: Princeton University Press, 1980.

Scholes, Robert, and Kellogg, Robert. *The Nature of Narrative.* New York: Oxford University Press, 1966.

Spacks, Patricia Meyer. *Imagining a Self: Autobiography and Novel in Eighteenth-Century England.* Cambridge: Harvard University Press, 1976.

Starobinski, Jean. "The Style of Autobiography." In *Autobiography: Essays Theoretical and Critical,* edited by James Olney, pp. 73–83. Princeton: Princeton University Press, 1980.

Starr, George A. *Defoe and Spiritual Autobiography.* Princeton: Princeton University Press, 1965.

Sturrock, John. "The New Model Autobiographer." *New Literary History* 9, no. 1 (Autumn 1977): 51–64.

Taylor, Rodney. *The Cultivation of Sagehood as a Religious Goal in Neo-Confucianism: A Study of Selected Writings of Kao P'an-lung (1562–1626).* Missoula, Mont.: Scholars Press, 1978.

———. "Journey into Self: The Autobiographical Reflections of Hu Chih." *History of Religions* 21, no. 4 (May 1982): 321–38.

Warren, Austin. *The New England Conscience.* Ann Arbor: University of Michigan Press, 1966.

Watson, Burton, *Ssu-ma Ch'ien: Grand Historian of China.* New York: Columbia University Press, 1958.

———, trans. *Basic Writings of Mo Tzu, Hsün Tzu, and Han Fei Tzu.* New York: Columbia University Press, 1967.

Watt, Ian. *The Rise of the Novel.* Berkeley and Los Angeles: University of California Press, 1967.

Weintraub, Karl Joachim. "Autobiography and Historical Consciousness." *Critical Inquiry* 1, no. 4 (June 1975): 821–48.

———. *The Value of the Individual: Self and Circumstance in Autobiography.* Chicago: University of Chicago Press, 1978.

Wigglesworth, Michael. *The Diary of Michael Wigglesworth, 1653–1675.* Edited by Edmund Morgan. New York: Harper & Row, 1965.

Wright, Arthur. "Biography and Hagiography: Hui-chiao's *Lives of Eminent Monks.*" In *Silver Jubilee Volume of the Zinbun Kagaku-Kenkyūsyo,* pp. 383–432. Kyoto: Kyoto University, 1954.

Wu, Pei-yi. "Education of Children during the Sung." In *Neo-Confucian Education: The Formative Stage,* edited by Wm. Theodore de Bary and John Chaffee, pp. 307–24. Berkeley: University of California Press, 1988.

———. Review of *Li Zhi, philosophe maudit (1527–1602): Contribution à une sociologie du mandarinat chinois de la fin des Ming,* By Jean-François Billeter. *Harvard Journal of Asiatic Studies* 41, no. 1 (June 1981): 304–17.

———. "Self-Eulogy: An Autobiographical Mode in Traditional Chinese Literature." Unpublished paper, University Seminar on Traditional China, Columbia University, November 20, 1973.

———. "Self-Examination and Confession of Sins in Traditional China." *Harvard Journal of Asiatic Studies* 39, no. 1 (June 1979): 5–38.

———. "The Spiritual Autobiography of Te-ch'ing." In *The Unfolding of Neo-Confucianism,* edited by Wm. Theodore de Bary. New York: Columbia University Press, 1975.

Wu, Pei-yi. "Varieties of the Chinese Self." In *Designs of Selfhood*, edited by Vytautas Kavolis. Rutherford, N.J.: Fairleigh Dickinson University Press, 1984.

Yü, Chün-fang. *The Renewal of Buddhism in China: Chu-hung and the Late Ming Synthesis.* New York: Columbia University Press, 1981.

INDEX